The Two Romanticisms, and Other Essays

The Two Romanticisms, and Other Essays

Mystery and Interpretation in Romantic Literature

William Christie

SYDNEY UNIVERSITY PRESS

First published by Sydney University Press
© William Christie 2016
© Sydney University Press 2016

Reproduction and Communication for other purposes
Except as permitted under the Act, no part of this edition may be reproduced, stored in a retrieval system, or communicated in any form or by any means without prior written permission. All requests for reproduction or communication should be made to Sydney University Press at the address below:

Sydney University Press
Fisher Library F03
University of Sydney NSW 2006
AUSTRALIA
Email: sup.info@sydney.edu.au
sydney.edu.au/sup

National Library of Australia Cataloguing-in-Publication Data

Creator:	Christie, William, 1952– author.
Title:	The two romanticisms, and other essays : mystery and interpretation in romantic literature / William Christie.
ISBN:	9781743324646 (paperback)
	9781743324653 (ebook: epub)
	9781743324660 (ebook: mobipocket)
Notes:	Includes bibliographical references and index.
Subjects:	Romanticism--Great Britain.
	English literature--19th century--History and criticism.
Dewey Number:	820.9007

Cover image: J.M.W. Turner, *The Red Rigi* 1842, watercolour, wash and gouache with some scratching out, 30.5 x 45.8 cm (sheet), *Wilton 1525*, National Gallery of Victoria, Melbourne Felton Bequest, 1947 (1704-4).
Cover design by Miguel Yamin

For Angie Dunstan,
with gratitude and affection

Contents

Acknowledgements	ix
Preface	xi
Chronology of the Romantic Period	xvii

1	Coleridge, Austen, and the Two Romanticisms	1
2	Wordsworth and the Language of Nature	27
3	Crossing Over: Samuel Taylor Coleridge and the Conversation Poems	51
4	'The burden of the mystery': William Wordsworth's 'Tintern Abbey'	77
5	The Search for Meaning in *The Rime of the Ancient Mariner*	107
6	Interpreting the Politics of *Pride and Prejudice*	133
7	'Such is modern fame': The Byronic Hero from *Childe Harold* to *Don Juan*	165
8	Amelioration and Madness in Percy Bysshe Shelley's 'Julian and Maddalo'	203

9 Mary Shelley's *Frankenstein*: A Critical and Cultural Heritage 231

10 Questing and Questioning in the 'Ode on a Grecian Urn' 269

Epilogue: The Romantic Imagination 289

Further Reading 307

Index 312

Acknowledgements

Versions of a number of these essays have previously appeared in print. I'd like to thank David Kelly, editor of *Sydney Studies in English*, for permission to revise and republish 'The Act of Love in Coleridge's Conversation Poems', 'Wordsworth's *Tintern Abbey*: Inspiration or Aspiration?', '"Impassioned Clay": Reading the Grecian Urn', and 'The Critical Metamorphoses of Mary Shelley's *Frankenstein*', and Taylor & Francis, the publishers of *Nineteenth-Century Contexts* (http://tandfonline.com), for permission to revise and republish 'Pride, Politics, and Prejudice'.

Preface

This book comprises a collection of critical essays on Romanticism and on select British Romantic texts. The essays began their lives as lectures to university undergraduates and to senior secondary school students and their teachers. Along with Romanticists and other scholars interested in the period, these are the audiences I have in mind as readers. Each chapter deals with a different canonical poem or novel: Samuel Taylor Coleridge's 'This Lime-Tree Bower My Prison', 'Frost at Midnight', and *Rime of the Ancient Mariner*; Jane Austen's *Northanger Abbey* and *Pride and Prejudice*; William Wordsworth's Preface to *Lyrical Ballads* and 'Lines written a few miles above Tintern Abbey'; Lord Byron's *Childe Harold's Pilgrimage*, Turkish Tales, and *Don Juan*; Percy Bysshe Shelley's 'Julian and Maddalo'; Mary Shelley's *Frankenstein*; John Keats's 'Ode on a Grecian Urn'. The collection is designed to help undergraduates, teachers, and senior school students to an understanding of the concept of Romanticism and of the poems and novels that appear most frequently on curricula of Romantic studies. Individual chapters offer self-contained readings of their texts and topics, but will be found to be related to the other chapters in the collection in their argumentative preoccupations. Of these preoccupations, two stand out: one is with the crucial 'uncertainties, Mysteries, doubts' of the Romantic text (to use Keats's formulation of 'Negative Capability'[1]), so that even a High Romantic text like Wordsworth's 'Lines written a few miles above Tintern Abbey' can be seen as more exploration than discovery, more aspiration than inspiration, more desire than affirmation. The other preoccupation, obviously related to the first, is with interpretation—with the way the Romantic text, as well as being the object of critical interpretation, can itself be seen as a dramatic acting out of the uncertain process of interpretation.

Of all the historical periods currently discussed and taught at school and university, only the Romantic period takes its name from a cultural and literary category, making it more engaging and challenging for students, but at the same time making it more confusing, exposed as students and scholars are to a variety of possible instantiations and definitions. The question of what Romanticism is, therefore, has to take priority in any book dedicated to a selection of literature from the period—hence my title and first chapter, distinguishing between the 'Romantic' as we (broadly) use the term, and the 'romantic' as it was used by writers and commentators during the period itself: the two romanticisms. This basic distinction helps to organise the texts chosen for discussion and to make important critical discriminations between them and their authors, not least between those traditionally considered Romantic and those (like Jane Austen) traditionally considered anti-Romantic. The basic argument of Chapter 1 is that not only are there these two different meanings of the term 'romanticism' that need to be distinguished, but that Romanticism is itself a conflicted category and Romantic literature characterised by uncertainty, division, and self-division. I use 'Kubla Khan' and *The Rime of the Ancient Mariner* by Samuel Taylor Coleridge to illustrate the difference between the two romanticisms (they are both) and Jane Austen's *Northanger Abbey* to show that texts cannot easily be categorised as either Romantic or anti-Romantic.

---

1 *'Negative Capability,* that is when a man is capable of being in uncertainties, Mysteries, doubts, without any irritable reaching out after fact & reason', in a letter to his brothers George and Tom Keats, 27 (?) December 1817, *The Letters of John Keats, 1814–1821*, ed. Hyder E. Rollins, in 2 vols (Cambridge, Mass.: Harvard University Press, 1958), 1:193.

Preface

If students and general readers know nothing else, they know that William Wordsworth was a Nature poet and that nature was a powerful and characteristically Romantic interest and exaltation. Chapter 2 looks closely at what Wordsworth meant by a poetry of 'low and rustic life' designed to embody 'the beautiful and permanent forms of Nature'. Focusing on his manifesto, the Preface to *Lyrical Ballads*, and ranging widely through Wordsworth's early poetry, the chapter is designed as an introduction to the intellectual history of the period by examining the politics and metaphysics of Wordsworth's formal and stylistic choices.

Chapter 3 looks at the formal and biographical rationale for Coleridge's influential conversation poems (not least influential on Wordsworth's 'Lines written a few miles above Tintern Abbey'), and at the way the poet's choices are re-enacted in, and variously inform, the poems themselves. After characterising the conversation poems as a group as a reaction against the priorities and orientation implicit in inherited practices and an inherited rhetoric, the chapter concentrates on 'This Lime-Tree Bower My Prison' and 'Frost at Midnight'. I use the rhetorical figure of chiasmus—crossing over—to express and explain the multi-layered transformations sought and celebrated in the poems.

Chapter 4 on 'The burden of the mystery' takes up from where the Wordsworthian affirmation of nature in Chapter 1 leaves off. In his famous 'Lines written a few miles above Tintern Abbey', Wordsworth celebrates nature as 'the nurse, / The guide, the guardian of my heart, and soul / Of all my moral being'. Why, then, did Keats find Wordsworth's great paean to nature and its role in the poet's own salvation to be 'explorative of those dark passages' of human life? What dark passages? This chapter looks closely at the poem known to literary history as 'Tintern Abbey' to reveal the confusion and self-doubt behind its magniloquent affirmations. Far from guaranteeing, the poem yearns for a fundamental continuity and community of consciousness that can survive the depredations and dislocations that it anticipates. When all is said, 'the burthen of the mystery' of human life remains.

The basic premise of most of my readings is that what is true of all literature is especially true of Romantic literature—which is that it can be seen to reflect upon its own mode of existence, its own function, and its own interpretation. Time and again, Romantic poetry makes poetry itself—or the mind in the act of creative discrimination—its subject matter as well as its means. Beyond being the *object* of interpretative exploration, the Romantic poem can be read as a *model* for the kind of interpretative activity that goes on in the process of understanding and of reading, and in the conversation of the classroom. I ask the reader to think of poems as lessons on the drama and dangers of interpretation. This is spectacularly so of Coleridge's classic tale of 'mystery and imagination', *The Rime of the Ancient Mariner*, which Chapter 5 argues challenges our interpretative ingenuity precisely because the whole question of interpretation becomes central to the poem itself.

It is no longer possible to discuss Jane Austen's writing independently of the urgent political issues that occupied her more historically minded contemporaries, or to suggest that it was her indifference to issues of politics and history that enabled her to shape her exquisite, self-contained comedies of manners. On the contrary, Austen's apparent indifference is now recognised as artistic indirection, and her novels read as articulate forms of an acute historical awareness. In their concern with authority in the face of new philosophies that brought all in doubt, and with the relationship between the individual and society, Austen's fictions have taken their place alongside the more overtly political forms that have entered the Romantic canon. The identification of manners in Austen's novels with morals and with culture—with what we would call 'ideology'—charges everything in the text with significance. Having said that, however, it has to be acknowledged that Austen's own position on some of the urgent questions of authority debated by her contemporaries remains unclear. In Chapter 6, I explore the divided political allegiance of *Pride and Prejudice* by isolating and examining its two, discrepant perspectives or positions—one progressive, the other conservative—and I ask, among other things, how persuasive they are and whether their political implications are in co-operation or conflict with each other in the novel.

In *Childe Harold's Pilgrimage*, Lord Byron sketched the lineaments of a character his contemporaries were quick to identify with the poet himself, a character which would mesmerise Europe for decades and which has gone down in literary history as the Byronic hero. Chapter 7 offers an anatomy of this hero and his appeal before turning to *Don Juan*, in which Byron at last found the appropriate form and voice in which to express his perverse and often pessimistic vision of 'the world exactly as it goes'. Instead of brooding, as he had in the earlier works, over the frustration and futility of existence—over the cruelties of fate and the self-sabotaging tendencies of humanity—Byron in *Don Juan* wallows in them, recommending an approach to life and ideas that is sceptical and self-sceptical, mocking and self-mocking. Yet in spite of the 'sad truth' that 'turns what was once romantic to burlesque', Byron is reluctant to let go of his idealism and betrays the ambivalent yearning at the heart of the mock-heroic, thus confirming the aphorism of W. B. Yeats that poets make poetry out of the argument with themselves.

This is certainly the case with Percy Bysshe Shelley's self-projection as the character Julian in his 'Julian and Maddalo'. By figuring himself as Julian, Shelley is able to dramatise and analyse his own political and philosophical position—to isolate and exaggerate, among other things, its inconsistencies and his own hypocrisies. But poets also make poetry out of arguments with others, and 'Julian and Maddalo' represents Shelley's most direct contribution to an intense conversation with Byron, who figures in the poem as Count Maddalo. What was at issue, I argue in Chapter 8, was nothing less than Shelley's preoccupation with the role of poetry in the amelioration of society. He asks what, if anything, poetry has to contribute to the way we understand and shape our own lives and the lives of other suffering human beings.

Like Coleridge's Mariner, who erupts into *Frankenstein* as occasionally and inevitably as the Monster erupts into Victor Frankenstein's life, Mary Shelley's famous novel and myth pass from land to land, addressing themselves with strangely adaptable powers of speech to an audience arguably larger and more diverse than that of any other work of literature in English. In Chapter 9 I am concerned with the extent and variety of the academic attention *Frankenstein* has received—with its 'critical metamorphoses'. Designed to introduce readers to the many ways in which the novel has been interpreted, the chapter also asks questions about how faithful these many interpretations aspire to be, and what this famous 'interpretability' has to say about the novel itself.

All of these themes and preoccupations come together in the poetry of John Keats, which shares with just about every other Romantic poem a concern with the poetic or creative consciousness—that is, with questions of meaning and value, and with the mind's role in the shaping and valorisation of the world. As with all our major lyrics, this involves an unending dialogue of the mind with tradition and with itself. In 'Ode on a Grecian Urn' we have an ostensibly single-minded (or single-voiced) Romantic lyric that on closer inspection can be seen to be 'in uncertainties, Mysteries, doubts', as the histrionic speaker of the poem irritably reaches out after fact and reason in ways that expose the quest for meaning as frustrated, potentially even futile. Like 'Lines written a few miles above Tintern Abbey', *The Rime of the Ancient Mariner*, *Don Juan*, 'Julian and Maddalo', *Frankenstein*, and the novels of Jane Austen, the 'Ode on a Grecian Urn' dramatises the doubtful vacillation and questioning that is the act or process of interpretation. In doing so, I argue in Chapter 10, it anticipates and to some extent pre-empts the reader's own struggle to make sense of the experience the poem conveys and raises a set of fascinating questions about the mode of existence of a work of art.

Finally, by way of an epilogue, I offer a brief history of a potent idea especially associated with the Romantic poets—the imagination—in order to help orient readers in a complex and contested area and to give them a sense of what was at stake. Readers will find a succinct historical timeline at the opening of the book, to allow them to see how the authors and texts discussed relate to one another. At the end of the volume are suggestions for further reading, including general studies of Romantic literature worth consulting alongside the selection of primary and secondary texts specific to each chapter.

Chronology of the Romantic Period

1757	William Blake born
	Edmund Burke, *A Philosophical Enquiry into the Origin of Our Ideas of the Sublime and the Beautiful*
1759	Mary Wollstonecraft born
1770	**William Wordsworth born**
	Ludwig van Beethoven born
	Capt. James Cook lands on the east coast of Australia
1771	Walter Scott born
1772	**Samuel Taylor Coleridge born**
1774	Robert Southey born
1775	Charles Lamb born
	Jane Austen born

1776   American Declaration of Independence

1778   William Hazlitt born

1781   Coleridge's father dies
        Immanuel Kant, *Critique of Pure Reason*

1782   Coleridge goes to school at Christ's Hospital

1785   Thomas De Quincey born

1788   **George Gordon (later Lord) Byron born**
        Capt. Arthur Phillip establishes the penal colony of New South Wales

1789   The fall of the Bastille initiates the French Revolution
        William Blake, *Songs of Innocence*

1790   Edmund Burke, *Reflections on the Revolution in France*

1791   Thomas Paine, *Rights of Man*

1792   **Percy Bysshe Shelley born**
        Mary Wollstonecraft, *A Vindication of the Rights of Woman*

1793   Louis XVI of France executed
        War declared on England and Holland by France
        William Godwin, *Political Justice*
        William Blake, *Marriage of Heaven and Hell*
        Marie Antoinette executed

Chronology of the Romantic Period

1794   Robespierre executed

State trials for treason of Thomas Hardy, John Horne Tooke, and John Thelwall, who are acquitted

William Blake, *Songs of Experience*

1795   **John Keats born**

'Gagging Acts' introduced to prevent 'seditious' gathering and writing

1796   England threatened with invasion

1797   **Mary Shelley born**

Mary Wollstonecraft dies

1798   Irish uprising

Napoleon invades Egypt

Nelson wins the Battle of the Nile

Wordsworth and Coleridge, *Lyrical Ballads*, including 'Lines written a few miles above Tintern Abbey' and *The Rime of the Ancyent Marinere*

1799   Napoleon becomes First Consul of France

Combination Acts introduced to prohibit trade unions

1800   Highland clearances

Union of Great Britain and Ireland

1801   Prime Minister William Pitt resigns

Henry Addington's ministry begins

Napoleon signs Concordat with the Pope

1802   Peace of Amiens with the French

1802 Napoleon becomes Consul for life
Edinburgh Review founded
William Cobbett's *Weekly Political Register* launched
French army invades Switzerland

1803 Britain declares war on France

1804 Napoleon proclaimed Emperor for life
Code Napoléon
Spain declares war on Britain
Pitt's second ministry

1805 Napoleon declared King of Italy
Nelson's victory at the Battle of Trafalgar
Wordsworth, *The Prelude*

1806 William Pitt dies
'Ministry of all the Talents' formed under Lord Grenville
Charles James Fox dies

1807 Portland ministry
Abolition of the slave trade
War on the Spanish peninsula begins

1808 Convention of Cintra signed
Napoleon invades Spain

1809 *Quarterly Review* founded
Spencer Perceval forms ministry

Chronology of the Romantic Period

1810   Napoleon annexes Holland
        George III goes mad

1811   Prince of Wales declared Regent
        Luddite uprisings begin
        Austen, Sense and Sensibility

1812   **Byron, Childe Harold's Pilgrimage (Cantos I and II)**
        Byron, *The Giaour* and *The Bride of Abydos*
        Prime Minister Perceval shot
        United States declares war on Britain over trade restrictions
        Napoleon invades Russia

1813   Austria declares war on Napoleon
        Southey becomes Poet Laureate
        Austen, Pride and Prejudice
        Leigh Hunt imprisoned for libel
        Wellington's peninsular campaign successful

1814   Allies invade France
        Treaty with Austria, Prussia, and Russia against Napoleon
        Napoleon defeated and exiled to Elba
        George Stephenson constructs steam locomotive
        Wordsworth, *The Excursion*
        Austen, *Mansfield Park*
        Walter Scott, *Waverley*
        Byron, *The Corsair*
        Congress of Vienna
        America and Britain at peace

1815   Napoleon escapes from Elba
        The Battle of Waterloo
        Napoleon imprisoned on St Helena
        Economic depression in Britain
        Scott, *Guy Mannering*
        Austen, *Emma*

1816   **Coleridge, *Christabel; Kubla Khan, a Vision; the Pains of Sleep***
        Byron, *Childe Harold's Pilgrimage* (Canto III)
        Percy Bysshe Shelley, *Alastor ... and Other Poems*
        Byron goes into exile
        Roman Catholic relief rejected in Lords again
        Cobbett, *Political Register*
        Scott, *The Antiquary*
        Spa Fields riot

1817   *Blackwood's Edinburgh Magazine* ('Maga') founded
        Coleridge, *Biographia Literaria* and *Sybilline Leaves*
        Keats, *Poems*
        Byron, *Manfred*
        Scott, *Rob Roy*
        Roman Catholic relief rejected in Lords again
        Jane Austen dies

1818   Agitation and vote (rejected) for reform of the electoral system
        Emily Brontë born
        Byron, *Childe Harold's Pilgrimage* (Canto IV)
        Mary Shelley, *Frankenstein*

Chronology of the Romantic Period

1818   Scott, *Heart of Midlothian*
       Austen, *Persuasion* and *Northanger Abbey*

1819   **Byron, *Don Juan* (–1824)**
       The Peterloo Massacre
       Percy Bysshe Shelley composes 'Julian and Maddalo'
       Scott, *Ivanhoe* and *The Bride of Lammermoor*

1820   George III dies; accession of George IV
       Cato Street conspiracy
       Revolution in Spain and Portugal
       Trial of Queen Caroline
       Keats, *Lamia and Other Poems*, including 'Ode on a Grecian Urn'
       Percy Bysshe Shelley, *The Cenci* and *Prometheus Unbound*
       John Clare, *Poems Descriptive of Rural Life*
       Wordsworth, *The River Duddon* sonnets

1821   **Keats dies in Rome**
       Percy Bysshe Shelly, *Adonais*
       Napoleon dies
       Greek War of Liberation begins

1822   **Percy Bysshe Shelley drowns off the coast of Italy**
       Lord Castlereagh, Secretary of State for Foreign Affairs, suicides
       Protestants and Catholics clash in Ireland

1823   War between France and Spain

1824   **Byron dies at Missolonghi in Greece**

1825   Stockton and Darlington railway completed

1826   First crossing of the Atlantic under steam

1828   Repeal of Test and Corporation Acts

1829   Third Catholic Relief Bill passed in Lords

1830   George IV dies; accession of William IV

1831   Charles Darwin's Pacific voyages

1832   Reform Bill finally passes through both houses of Parliament
        Sir Walter Scott dies

1834   Slavery abolished in the British Empire
        Coleridge dies
        Charles Lamb dies

1837   William IV dies; accession of Queen Victoria

1847   Emily Brontë, *Wuthering Heights*

1850   **Wordsworth dies**

1
Coleridge, Austen, and the Two Romanticisms

[W]e should learn to use the word 'Romanticism' in the plural. This, of course, is already the practice of the more cautious and observant literary historians, in so far as they recognise that the 'Romanticism' of one country may have little in common with that of another, and at all events ought to be defined in distinctive terms. But the discrimination of Romanticisms which I have in mind is not solely or chiefly a division upon lines of nationality or language. What is needed is that any study of the subject should begin with a recognition of a *prima facie* plurality of Romanticisms, of possibly quite distinct thought-complexes, a number of which may appear in one country. There is no hope of clear thinking on the part of the student of modern literature, if—as, alas! has been repeatedly done by eminent writers—he vaguely hypostasizes the term, and starts with the presumption that 'Romanticism' is the heaven-appointed designation of some single entity, or type of entities, to be found in nature.[1]

Thus Arthur O. Lovejoy, in an article which, though written as long ago as 1924, has operated as the conscience of Romantic studies ever since,

---

1 Arthur O. Lovejoy, 'On the Discrimination of Romanticisms' (1924), reprinted in his *Essays in the History of Ideas* (Westport, Conn.: Greenwood Press, 1978), 228–53 (235).

and is still cited or quoted as a warning against the sin of oversimplifying when dealing with ideas in literary history—as I am quoting it now. What I have to offer, however, would hardly have satisfied Lovejoy, for whom the meanings of the word 'Romanticism' in current usage in the 1920s were so many and so various, and at times so mutually incompatible, as effectively to render it meaningless. I, too, want to use the term in the plural, but I am only interested in two Romanticisms, two uses of the epithet 'romantic', which I can distinguish easily enough in print by leaving one in lower case—'romantic'—while capitalising the other (as Lovejoy does): 'Romantic'.

Small 'r' romantic

What I mean by small 'r' romantic is what the period itself meant when it used the term: exotic, remote in time or place, strange, fabulous, extravagant, improbable, unrealistic—a meaning or meanings never far away from our own usage today. Movements, motifs, or styles subsequently identified as small 'r' romantic all make their (re)appearance in the eighteenth century and will be exploited by major Romantic poets in a variety of expressive ways: the Gothic; graveyard poetry; Bardism and Druidism and Celtism; Medievalism; Orientalism. What William Beckford's Orientalist *Vathek*, Ann Radcliffe's Gothic novels, and Sir Walter Scott's verse tales of knights, goblins, and fair damsels (not to mention his "Celtified pageantry")[2] all have in common is that they are all *romantic*, actively dislocating and alienating in their settings and landscapes, and conjuring either with patently fantastic incidents and characters or with what Freud has taught us to call the *unheimlich* or uncanny: the familiar turned unfamiliar, strange.

The word 'romantic' (or 'romantick') as it was used in the late eighteenth and early nineteenth centuries still foregrounded its etymological derivation from the Medieval poetic *romance*, chivalric tales of adventure and love featuring heroic knights and virtuous maidens overcoming often thinly disguised allegorical obstacles in their quest for the

---

2 John Gibson Lockhart, *Memoirs of the Life of Sir Walter Scott*, second edition, in 10 vols (London: Cadell, 1839), 7:50.

ideal. Depending on your point of view—or, as I will suggest later of Jane Austen, depending on your temperament – a romance was either a fabulous narrative in verse or prose taking place in exotic settings and marked by extraordinary subject matter, improbable events, and larger-than-life characters, or it was an unrealistic narrative in verse or prose taking place in unlikely settings and marked by extravagant subject matter, silly events, and stereotypical characters. Dr Johnson made his own position on the issue clear in his famous *Dictionary* when he defined 'Romantick' as 'Resembling the tales or romances; wild, improbable; false; fanciful; full of wild scenery'.

Wilfully strange and deliberately estranging, Samuel Taylor Coleridge's 'Kubla Khan', *The Rime of the Ancient Mariner*, and 'Christabel' are archetypal romantic poems in the sense that Coleridge's contemporaries used the word—bizarre and otherworldly, 'supernatural'. 'Kubla Khan' and *Christabel* remained in manuscript for nearly twenty years, until they were finally published at the behest of Lord Byron in 1816, but *The Rime of the Ancient Mariner*—or, more accurately, *The Rime of the Ancyent Marinere*—made its first appearance not long after its composition as the lead poem in Coleridge and William Wordsworth's celebrated joint publication, *Lyrical Ballads, with a Few Other Poems* (1798):

> During the first year that Mr Wordsworth and I were neighbours, our conversations turned frequently on the two cardinal points of poetry: the power of exciting the sympathy of the reader by a faithful adherence to the truth of nature, and the power of giving the interest of novelty by the modifying colours of the imagination. The sudden charm which accidents of light and shade, which moonlight or sunset diffused over a known or familiar landscape, appeared to represent the practicability of combining both. These are the poetry of nature.
>
> The thought suggested itself (to which of us I do not recollect) that a species of poems might be composed of two sorts. In the one, the incidents and agents were to be (in part at least) supernatural—... For the second class, subjects were to be chosen from ordinary life ... In this idea originated the plan of the *Lyrical Ballads*, in which it was agreed that my endeavours were to be directed to

persons and characters supernatural, or at least romantic; yet so far as to transfer from our inward nature a human interest and semblance of truth sufficient to procure for these shadows of imagination that willing suspension of disbelief for the moment, which constitutes poetic faith.[3]

'Persons or characters supernatural', note, '*or at least romantic*'. The phenomenology of reading the romantic that Coleridge outlines here—the 'willing suspension of disbelief'—is one that criticism has subsequently adopted to characterise the act of reading literature generally, but Coleridge's surely faithful account of how we voluntarily collaborate with the fantastic, imaginatively accommodating the improbable, was especially designed to explain and justify his own poetic experiments with the fantastic and the improbable. Coleridge's contribution to *Lyrical Ballads* was to be romantic. Wordsworth's was not.

That some such explanation as Coleridge offers here in the *Biographia* was required at the time *The Rime of the Ancient Mariner* was published becomes immediately apparent when we look at its reception. For Coleridge's brother-in-law, Robert Southey, writing in the *Critical Review*, and for the reviewer in the *Analytical Review*, it could not possibly be English: the former thought it a 'Dutch attempt at German sublimity' and the latter that it had 'the extravagance of a mad german poet'.[4] The reaction of Charles Burney, the musicologist and father of the novelist Fanny Burney, was typical:

> The author's first piece, the 'Rime of the ancyent Marinere', in imitation of the *style* as well as the spirit of our elder poets, is the strangest story of a cock and a bull that we ever saw on paper: yet, though it seems a rhapsody of unintelligible wildness and incoherence, (of which we do not perceive the drift, unless the joke lies in depriving

---

3 *Biographia Literaria*, The Collected Works of Samuel Taylor Coleridge, 7, ed. James Engell and W. Jackson Bate, in 2 vols (Princeton, N. J.: Princeton University Press, 1983), 2:5–6.
4 Robert Southey, review of *Lyrical Ballads* in the *Critical Review* 24 (October 1798), and Anon., *Analytical Review* 28 (December 1798), reprinted in *Coleridge: The Critical Heritage*, ed. J. R. de J. Jackson (London: Routledge & Kegan Paul), 55–7 (56) and 51–2 (52).

1 Coleridge, Austen, and the Two Romanticisms

the wedding guest of his share of the feast) there are in it poetical touches of an exquisite kind.[5]

The suggestion that the existential 'joke' of the poem lies in alienating the wedding guest from the symbolic society and harmony of the wedding seems to me inspired, but if we look at the points Burney makes they all concern what I am calling the romantic elements of the poem, which come with its self-conscious literary heritage. As Burney himself points out, the poem was written 'in imitation of the *style* as well as the spirit of our elder poets'.

This was especially true of the first version of the poem, in which an antiquarian impulse is unmistakable, from the *Ancyent Marinere* of its title to numerous other examples of pseudo-Medieval orthography: 'sate' (for 'sat'); 'Minstralsy' (for 'Minstrelsy'); 'cauld' (for 'cold'); 'Emerauld' (for 'emerald'); 'ne' (for 'nor'); and so on. 'This 1798 version tries to adhere so closely with the conventions of ancient balladry', writes Jerome McGann, 'that the work sometime approaches pastiche'.[6] Many of these deliberate archaisms would be altered for the next edition of the poem in 1800, but the same antiquarian impulse can still be detected in later versions in occasional locutions used by Coleridge to ape Medieval poetry: 'quoth he', 'I wist', 'eftsoons'. *The Rime of the Ancient Mariner* was fashioned to look old, remote and Medieval, and not just in these odd phrases, but also and more importantly in its imaginative seascape, a projection of the Mariner's outdated superstition and religiosity. Coleridge was capitalising on a taste for antiquarianism, using it to ask questions about ways of seeing and understanding that we will look at more closely in Chapter 5.

---

5 Charles Burney, review of *Lyrical Ballads* in the *Monthly Review* 29 (June 1799), in *Coleridge: The Critical Heritage*, ed. Jackson, 55–7 (56).
6 Jerome McGann, 'The Meaning of the Ancient Mariner', *Critical Enquiry*, 8:1 (Autumn 1981), 35–67 (39–40).

Capital 'r' Romantic

From images and incidents drawn from ancient and exotic travel literature, *The Rime of the Ancient Mariner* slides effortlessly into the bizarre and threatening world of nightmare, creating an allegory of mental and spiritual alienation and isolation. In doing so, however, Coleridge, like the Mariner and his companions, has crossed the line. (Coleridge was especially fond of the rhetorical and imagistic strategy of crossing over, as we will see in Chapter 4.) We are in another world, where the capital 'r' Romantic has supervened upon the small 'r' romantic, as infection supervenes upon a wound. What we mean by capital 'r' Romantic when we apply the term to the period, and to the literature of the period, alludes to no one particular idea, belief, or style—indeed, if we confine ourselves to the major poets, from Blake and Wordsworth to Keats and Clare, it is hard to imagine more philosophical and stylistic variety emerging from so comparatively brief a period (1790–1830). Instead, 'Romantic' refers to a set of preoccupations revolving around the co-ordinates of Nature, on the one hand, and, on the other, the interactive Mind and Self. Even here, the different terms meant different things, and bore different valences, for each of the major writers. (Blake, for example, protested that Wordsworth's 'Nature' gave him a bowel complaint that nearly killed him,[7] yet we think of Wordsworthian nature as a powerful and characteristically Romantic phenomenon that has informed our cultural sensibilities.)

Differences aside, the Romantics were preoccupied with the idea of a vitally creative human imagination in collaborative relation to a sublime and/or beautiful natural world—a natural world that was at once independent of humanity (with what Coleridge conceded was 'a Life of it's own'[8]), and yet at the same time part of humanity's physical and figurative universe—as *symbolic* in the sense that Coleridge

---

[7] To Henry Crabb Robinson—as quoted in the entry under 'Wordsworth' in S. Foster Damon, *A Blake Dictionary: The Ideas and Symbols of William Blake* (London: Thames & Hudson, 1973), 451.
[8] *The Collected Letters of Samuel Taylor Coleridge*, ed. Earl Leslie Griggs, 6 vols (Oxford: Oxford University Press, 1956–1971), 2:864.

1 Coleridge, Austen, and the Two Romanticisms

made famous: 'It always partakes of the Reality which it renders intelligible'.[9] Preoccupied with the mind and with its intermediary and creative capacities, the Romantics were also preoccupied with the idea of genius; with the self-authenticating power of feeling, and of the passions; with *desire* in all its creative and destructive consequences; with self-consciousness and the individual ego; as well as with the possibility of transcendence. To explore as well as express these preoccupations, Romantic poets often adapted and internalised the 'concepts, schemes, and values' of traditional religion and inherited mythology, reformulating them 'within the prevailing two-term system of subject and object, ego and non-ego, the human mind or consciousness and its transactions with nature',[10] impelled by a self-declared need to evolve alternative mythologies to figure a new mental terrain:

> All strength, all terror, single or in bands,
> That ever was put forth by personal forms—
> Jehovah, with his thunder, and the quire
> Of shouting angels and the empyreal throne—
> I pass them unalarmed. The darkest Pit
> Of the profoundest Hell, chaos, night
> Nor aught of [blinder] vacancy scooped out
> By help of dreams can breed such fear and awe
> As fall upon us often when we look
> Into our minds, into the mind of Man,
> My haunt and the main region of my song.
> (Wordsworth, *Home at Grasmere*, ll. 980–90)[11]

---

9 *Lay Sermons*, The Collected Works of Samuel Taylor Coleridge, 6, ed. R. J. White (Princeton, N. J.: Princeton University Press, 1972), 30.
10 M. H. Abrams, *Natural Supernaturalism: Tradition and Revolution in Romantic Literature* (London: Oxford University Press, 1971), 13.
11 Unless otherwise stated, the text for all quotations from Wordsworth's poetry is *The Poems of William Wordsworth: Collected Reading Texts from the Cornell Wordsworth*, 3 vols, ed. Jared Curtis (Penrith: Humanities-Ebooks, LLP, 2009).

These are the kinds of preoccupations and propensities to which we refer whenever we use the term 'Romantic'. As we shall see in the chapters that follow, they were never the naive affirmations they are sometimes mistaken to be—particularly by later writers and critics determined to define and exalt their own ideas and values in contradistinction to those of the Romantics. On the contrary, throughout the period, not only were the ideas and images of individual Romantic writers under constant interrogation by other writers of the period, they were under constant self-interrogation by the writers themselves.

Evidence of these preoccupations and propensities justifies our calling a patently romantic poem like *The Rime of the Ancient Mariner* a Romantic one as well. First and foremost, that is, *The Rime* is fascinated by the 'Mind of Man' in its negotiations with the natural world, by mental powers and mental states and their transformative potential. On our journey through the strange seas of the Ancient Mariner's historically superannuated imagination, we explore ways of seeing, understanding, and feeling in a universe—a *nature*—whose constitution and rationale remain (to quote Charles Burney) 'a rhapsody of unintelligible wildness and incoherence'.

The realm of the ideal

What the romantic and the Romantic have in common is their negotiation of the realm of the ethical and metaphysical ideal. Many, but by no means all Romantic poems are also romantic. John Keats's 'La Belle Dame Sans Merci' is an obvious example, using the remoteness and strangeness of the Medieval dream vision to question the reliability of erotic and artistic vision. But 'Ode to a Nightingale' and the 'Ode on a Grecian Urn' are not romantic, any more than Coleridge's conversation poems ('The Eolian Harp', 'The Nightingale', 'This Lime-Tree Bower My Prison', 'Frost at Midnight'). Their world is the one familiar to the poets' readers in their daily lives, even if this familiar world sometimes teeters on the brink of transformation or transcendence.

It cannot be stressed enough, however, that the Romantic period did not see itself as Romantic. That came later, although because of the continued currency of the word 'romantic' it is hard to say

1 Coleridge, Austen, and the Two Romanticisms

exactly when. No earlier than 1830, certainly, and the word did not assume its current literary-philosophical charge until the 1860s.[12] By the time Henry Beers published his *A History of English Romanticism in the Eighteenth Century* in 1899, cultural commentary had adopted the idea that 'Romantic' connoted a complex of thought and feeling of revolutionary significance. Only after it had passed, then, did the historical period in the English-speaking world between the French Revolution in 1789 and the Great Reform Act in 1832 acquire the name of the Romantic period. Since then, and only since then, has the assumption prevailed that Romanticism is something shared by writers of the period that can be critically identified and characterised in this way.

There was at the time, admittedly, in some writers at least, an acute self-consciousness about the violence and collective aspirations of the period, one that would feed into its later characterisation and valorisation. 'The world-inverting events of the later eighteenth century', writes Fiona Stafford, 'from the American Declaration of Independence in 1776 to the Battle of Waterloo in 1815 combined to ensure a general awareness of living in unprecedented times':

> In between came war between Britain and America, the Storming of the Bastille, the execution of the French King and Queen, the outbreak of war with Revolutionary France, the rising of the United Irishmen, Napoleon's rise to power in France and conquest over much of Europe, the Act of Union between Britain and Ireland, the Abolition of the Slave Trade, the assassination of the British Prime Minister, and the Regency crisis, which followed the declaration of George III's insanity. This was a period in which extraordinary public events were taking place with bewildering rapidity and the state and fate of Europe seemed perpetually in flux.[13]

---

12   Aidan Day, *Romanticism*, New Critical Idiom Series (New York and London: Routledge, 1996), 87–89.
13   Fiona Stafford, *Reading Romantic Poetry* (Malden and Oxford: Wiley-Blackwell, 2012), 27–28.

With the French revolutionary wars spreading across Europe and into Africa and the Middle East and impacting at every level on the trade and labour markets, and with the expansion of the media throughout the eighteenth century giving literate citizens unprecedented global access, the sensational social and political events of the period pressed upon the physical lives and consciousnesses of rich and poor alike.

Some critics who, with Lovejoy, have abandoned as reductive the idea of a Romantic movement with a single, coherent set of ideas or attributes have sought the answer instead in a 'spirit of the age' that takes its cue from the French Revolution. 'It looks to me as if I were in a great crisis', declared the conservative political theorist Edmund Burke, 'the French revolution is the most astonishing that has ever happened in the world'.[14] So for the younger, radical Percy Bysshe Shelley, writing to Lord Byron nearly thirty years after the event, the French Revolution remained 'the master theme of the epoch in which we live'.[15] If Alexis de Tocqueville is right, and the French Revolution 'created the politics of the *impossible*, turned madness into a theory, and built audacity into a cult',[16] the literature of the period was hardly likely to remain unaffected, and the Revolution and revolutionary social phenomena are generally acknowledged to have given a self-conscious sense of urgency and portentousness not just to social and political activity of the period, but also—indeed, especially—to its acts of imagination. 'The Literature of England', Shelley wrote in his 'Defence of Poetry' (1821), 'has arisen as it were from a new birth'; 'our own will be a memorable age in intellectual achievements', he continued, establishing at the outset an essentially historical reading of Romanticism that saw it in intimate, if sometimes vexed relationship with contemporary political and social revolutions:

---

14   Edmund Burke, *Reflections on the Revolution in France: A Critical Edition*, ed. J. C. D. Clark (Stanford: Stanford University Press, 2001), 154.
15   *The Letters of Percy Bysshe Shelley*, ed. Frederick L. Jones, 2 vols (Oxford: Clarendon, 1964), 1:362.
16   As quoted in R.R. Palmer, *The Age of Democratic Revolution*, 2. *The Struggle* (Princeton, N. J.: Princeton University Press, 1964), 130.

1 Coleridge, Austen, and the Two Romanticisms

It is impossible to read the compositions of the most celebrated writers of the present day without being startled with the electric life which burns within their words. They measure the circumference and sound the depths of human nature with a comprehensive and all-penetrating spirit, and they are themselves perhaps the most sincerely astonished at its manifestations; for it is less their spirit than the spirit of the age.[17]

It is, however, a long way from acknowledging the period to have been unique to settling upon a fixed set of assumptions and formal characteristics at once shared by, and exclusive to, all writers between 1789 and 1832. The writers themselves—and, perhaps more to the point, the literary critics of the period—identified instead distinct and rival schools among their contemporaries. Francis Jeffrey, writing in the influential periodical the *Edinburgh Review*, criticised Wordsworth and Coleridge (and Robert Southey) as 'a *sect* of poets', one that he would go on to call 'the lakers' or 'Lake poets'.[18] Later, in the 1820s, the radical-turned-conservative Southey vilified a 'Satanic school' that included the largely unread Shelley, along with Lord Byron at its head, and *Blackwood's Edinburgh Magazine* and the *Quarterly Review* attacked the presumption of what they called the 'Cockney school', including John Keats with the poet, editor, and journalist Leigh Hunt and essayist William Hazlitt. William Blake, on the other hand, was neither read nor heard of by the vast majority of his literate contemporaries. Only later, and in hindsight, would Blake and Wordsworth and Coleridge and Byron and Shelley and Keats become the Romantic poets. For many, that act of identification in itself remains formally and ideologically dubious, lending support to Lovejoy's thesis that a single ideational entity called Romanticism is an illusion.

---

17 Percy Bysshe Shelley, 'A Defence of Poetry', in *Shelley's Poetry and Prose*, 2nd edition, ed. Donald H. Reiman and Neil Fraistat (New York: W. W. Norton, 2002), 535.
18 See William Christie, *The Edinburgh Review in the Literary Culture of Romantic Britain: Mammoth and Megalonyx* (London: Pickering & Chatto, 2009), 65, 201, n.31.

Still, there were preoccupations and priorities of the kind I have mentioned that were new to the period and common to all these poets—not the same attitudes and ideas, by any means, but the same preoccupations with mind and nature, identity and relationship, blindness and insight. But what about all the *other* individuals writing and publishing between 1789 and 1832? Are they, too, Romantic writers by virtue of their historical coincidence? What of Jane Austen, an almost exact contemporary of Wordsworth and Scott and Coleridge?

If the audacity of the French Revolution and its Napoleonic sequel left its mark on the age, so too did the conflicts they embodied and initiated. It was not just carnage that the French left in their wake, in other words, it was also deep, argumentative, and sometimes even violent divisions within the cultures with which they came into conflict. As it happens, this is true not just of the different, bickering 'schools' of writers, with their different political and cultural affiliations, it is also true of individual writers and individual poems or novels, involved as they are in ideological and formal debate with and among themselves (what I earlier called self-interrogation). The so-called 'idealism' of Romantic literature is, as Jerome McGann reminds us, a case in point:

> In a Romantic poem the realm of the ideal is always observed as precarious—liable to vanish or move beyond one's reach at any time. Central Romantic poems like 'Ode to a Nightingale' or 'La Belle Dame Sans Merci' typify this situation in the Romantic poem, which characteristically haunts, as Geoffrey Hartman has observed, borderlands and liminal territories. These are Romantic places because they locate areas of contradiction, conflict, and problematic alternatives. In short, Romantic poems take up transcendent and ideal subjects because these subjects occupy areas of critical uncertainty. The aim of the Romantic poem—especially in its early or 'High Romantic' phases—is to rediscover the ground of stability in these situations. Later Romantic poems will often adopt a different procedure and attack the early Romantic terms of solution with the merciless critical razors of their despair.[19]

---

19 Jerome McGann, *The Romantic Ideology: A Critical Investigation* (Chicago and London: Chicago University Press, 1983), 72–73.

1 Coleridge, Austen, and the Two Romanticisms

'Characteristic of romantic discourse', writes Paul Hamilton, 'self-critique is just the fashion in which it struggles with itself, is about itself, beside itself even'.[20] Self-critique. What that means for our purposes is that Romantic literature is also at the same time anti-Romantic literature, distrustful of its own assertions about transcendence and imagination: 'Fled is that music. Do I wake or sleep?' To enter the world of the Romantic lyric is to enter a world of 'critical uncertainty'. As we shall see, this is no less true of 'Lines written a few miles above Tintern Abbey', in which Wordsworth discovers a rapt, prophetic voice commensurate with an exalted relationship with nature, than it is of the more openly questioning, even querulous, 'Ode on a Grecian Urn'. 'My body with my soul is ever querulous', writes the anonymous author of the Medieval morality play *Mankind*, and so it was for the Romantics.

Northanger Abbey

Often during the Romantic period, however, the critique of both romanticisms—of the romantic exotic and the Romantic visionary—is turned outwards, and expressed either as formal renunciation (Wordsworth, 'Elegiac Stanzas Suggested by a Picture of Peele Castle in a Storm'), as nightmare (Mary Shelley, *Frankenstein*), or in the form of parody or satire. This last is the case with Jane Austen's *Northanger Abbey*. With Austen, no less than with Coleridge, we need to distinguish between the two romanticisms overlapping during the period (though only the one, small 'r' romanticism, was part of their everyday and their critical vocabulary). It may seem perverse to anyone used to applying the word 'romantic' exclusively to narrative forms in which a love story predominates to hear Austen described as an anti-romantic writer, but in spite of the central emotional attachments troubled and resolved in novels that climax with more or less satisfactory marriages, Austen was nonetheless anti-romantic. She was also, at times, an anti-Romantic writer—bearing in mind, of course, that all the major poets could be anti-Romantic, questioning

---

20 Paul Hamilton, *Metaromanticism: Aesthetics, Literature, Theory* (Chicago and London: Chicago University Press, 2003), 2.

their own and their peers' cherished assumptions and priorities. Unlike the poets, however, Austen addressed these issues from the outside, from the vantage point of the familiar novel, whose very form, as she was personally responsible for developing it, resisted many of the pieties of the poets.

To call Austen anti-romantic is to characterise what she was doing both generically and temperamentally, as well as to position her *vis-à-vis* the poets of her own period. Perhaps I can do this most effectively by comparing two passages—two versions of pastoral, if you like—published within a year of each other. The first is from Coleridge:

> In Xanadu did Kubla Khan
> A stately pleasure-dome decree:
> Where Alph, the sacred river, ran
> Through caverns measureless to man
> Down to a sunless sea.
> So twice five miles of fertile ground
> With walls and towers were girdled round:
> And there were gardens bright with sinuous rills,
> Where blossomed many an incense-bearing tree;
> And here were forests ancient as the hills,
> Enfolding sunny spots of greenery.
>
> But oh! that deep romantic chasm which slanted
> Down the green hill athwart a cedarn cover!
> A savage place! as holy and enchanted
> As e'er beneath a waning moon was haunted
> By woman wailing for her demon-lover!
> And from this chasm, with ceaseless turmoil seething,
> As if this earth in fast thick pants were breathing,
> A mighty fountain momently was forced:
> Amid whose swift half-intermitted burst
> Huge fragments vaulted like rebounding hail,
> Or chaffy grain beneath the thresher's flail:
> And 'mid these dancing rocks at once and ever
> It flung up momently the sacred river.
> Five miles meandering with a mazy motion

1 Coleridge, Austen, and the Two Romanticisms

    Through wood and dale the sacred river ran,
    Then reached the caverns measureless to man,
    And sank in tumult to a lifeless ocean.
                        ('Kubla Khan', ll. 1–28)[21]

The second is from Austen's *Emma*:

> It was hot; and after walking some time over the gardens in a scattered, dispersed way, scarcely any three together, they insensibly followed one another to the delicious shade of a broad short avenue of limes, which stretching beyond the gardens at an equal distance from the river, seemed the finish of the pleasure grounds.—It led to nothing; nothing but a view at the end over a low stone wall with high pillars ... it was in itself a charming walk, and the view which closed it extremely pretty.—The considerable slope, at nearly the foot of which the Abbey stood, gradually acquired a steeper form beyond its grounds; and at half a mile distant was a bank of considerable abruptness and grandeur, well clothed with wood;—and at the bottom of this bank, favourably placed and sheltered, rose the Abbey-Mill Farm, with the meadows in front, and the river making a close and handsome curve around it.
>
>   It was a sweet view—sweet to the eye and the mind. English verdure, English culture, English comfort, seen under a sun bright, without being oppressive.[22]

The similarities and differences between these two literary landscapes say it all. The two are worlds apart, while being strikingly similar in their topography—so similar, it is tempting to think that Austen is revising, domesticating, 'englishing' (as they used to say of translating other languages into English) Coleridge's exotic oriental

---

21 Unless otherwise stated, the text for all quotations from Coleridge's poetry is the *Poetical Works*, The Collected Works of Samuel Taylor Coleridge, 16, volume 1, parts 1 and 2, ed. J. J. C. Mays (Princeton, N. J.: Princeton University Press, 2001).
22 Jane Austen, *Emma*, The Cambridge Edition of the Works of Jane Austen, ed. Richard Cronin and Dorothy Macmillan (Cambridge: Cambridge University Press, 2005), 390–1.

landscape. It is extremely unlikely that Austen had heard—or even heard of—Coleridge's brilliant 'fragment', composed in 1797 or 1798 and not published until 1816, the year after *Emma*. It is an intensely nationalistic moment in which the author comes as close as she ever does to exoticising and mythologising England, rather as Blake is celebrated for doing in his epigraph to *Milton*, known to us as the hymn 'Jerusalem' ('And did those feet in ancient time'). Except that Austen's ideologically suggestive passage remains invested in the here and now, self-consciously present and at home—homely or *heimlich*, that is, and the opposite of the romantic uncanny.

Under the combined influence of a variety of genres—journalism, history, personal diaries and familiar letters, for example, as well as drama and satire—romance in the eighteenth century metamorphosed into the novel as we think of it,[23] and the novel as we think of it is indebted to the evolution of domestic realism and Jane Austen's renunciation of the romantic. Walter Scott recognised this in a famous review of *Emma* in the *Quarterly Review* of 1815:

> In its first appearance, the novel was the legitimate child of the romance; and though the manners and general turn of the composition were altered so as to suit modern times, the author remained fettered by many peculiarities derived from the original style of romantic fiction.

The early novelist, continued Scott, was 'expected to tread pretty much in the limits between the concentric circles of probability and possibility', and his or her characters possessed minds 'purified by a sensibility which often verged on extravagance'. Since the turn of the nineteenth century, however, 'a style of novel has arisen' of which Austen is preeminent, argues Scott, a style which achieves its effects by 'neither alarming our credulity nor amusing our imagination by wild variety of incident, or by those pictures of romantic affection and sensibility'.[24] 'That young lady

---

23 See Michael McKeon, *The Origins of the English Novel* (Baltimore: Johns Hopkins University Press, 1987) and J. Paul Hunter, *Before Novels: The Cultural Contexts of Eighteenth-Century English Fiction* (New York: W. W. Norton, 1990).
24 Ioan Williams (ed.), *Sir Walter Scott on Novelists and Fiction* (London: Routledge and Kegan Paul, 1968), 227-30.

1 Coleridge, Austen, and the Two Romanticisms

had a talent for describing the involvements and feelings and characters of ordinary life which is to me the most wonderful I ever met with', Scott would confide in his journal in March 1826.[25] By that time, *Northanger Abbey* was in print (1818), and its opening would have confirmed everything Scott had said of its author's anti-romanticism:

> No one who had ever seen Catherine Morland in her infancy, would have supposed her born to be an heroine. Her situation in life, the character of her father and mother, her own person and disposition, were all equally against her. Her father was a clergyman, without being neglected, or poor, and a very respectable man, though his name was Richard,—and he had never been handsome. He had a considerable independence, besides two good livings—and he was not in the least addicted to locking up his daughters. Her mother was a woman of useful plain sense, with a good temper, and, what is more remarkable, with a good constitution. She had three sons before Catherine was born; and instead of dying in bringing the latter into the world, as any body might expect, she still lived on—lived to have six children more—to see them growing up around her, and to enjoy excellent health herself. A family of ten children will be always called a fine family, where there are heads and arms and legs enough for the number; but the Morlands had little other right to the word, for they were in general very plain, and Catherine, for many years of her life, as plain as any. She had a thin awkward figure, a sallow skin without colour, dark lank hair, and strong features;—so much for her person;—and not less unpropitious for heroism seemed her mind. She was fond of all boys' plays, and greatly preferred cricket not merely to dolls, but to the more heroic enjoyments of infancy, nursing a dormouse, feeding a canary-bird, or watering a rose-bush.[26]

---

25 W. E. K. Anderson (ed.), *The Journal of Sir Walter Scott* (Oxford: Clarendon, 1972), 114.
26 Jane Austen, *Northanger Abbey*, The Cambridge Edition of the Works of Jane Austen, ed. Barbara M. Benedict and Deirdre Le Faye (Cambridge: Cambridge University Press, 2006), 5–6.

What is 'remarkable' about the Morland family is precisely their being so unremarkable, making no sensational or exotic claim upon our overeager sympathies. Austen pillories the stereotypes of gender here, no less than the stereotypes of romance itself, suggesting a direct link between them that makes women the victims of society's and their own infantilising romanticisation.

Northanger Abbey is about the way in which reality, or the perception of reality, can become distorted, either by individuals themselves—by their vanity, for example, or their ignorance—or by any of the arbitrary codes or conventions evolved by society, including (indeed especially) the twin conventions of language and literature. Isabella Thorpe's indiscriminate gush, her brother John's inflationary bragging, General Tilney's unctuous and ingratiating politesse, Mrs Allen's empty oscillations, even Henry Tilney's textbook aesthetics—all this adds up to a complex criticism of the way in which reality gets distorted by a mishandling of the most fundamental convention of any society: the convention of language. Austen extends her critique to include whole varieties of current intellectual discourse when she has Catherine apologise to Henry: 'I cannot speak well enough to be unintelligible'. 'Bravo!' says Henry on Austen's behalf, 'an excellent satire on modern language.'[27] So is *Northanger Abbey*. Indeed, there are suggestions in the novel that effective communication can only take place in the absence of language altogether: 'Catherine wished to congratulate him, but knew not what to say, and her eloquence was only in her eyes. From them, however, the eight parts of speech shone out most expressively, and James could combine them with ease.'[28]

From here it is only a small step to satirising the popular literary forms in which the distortions of public speech can often be seen to originate. Self-referring and self-conscious, *Northanger Abbey* attempts to develop and to justify its own, alternative values, its own aesthetic, and its own form, and it does this in a variety of ways—paradoxically, in a *formal* variety of ways. Of all the Austen novels the earliest written and last published, *Northanger Abbey* is the most formally various. Exemplary episodes or set pieces like the one on Catherine's anti-heroism quoted above; formal debates about literary pleasure, literary value, and

---

27 Austen, *Northanger Abbey*, ed. Benedict and Le Faye, 135.
28 Austen, *Northanger Abbey*, ed. Benedict and Le Faye, 122–23.

1 Coleridge, Austen, and the Two Romanticisms

the picturesque; direct references and indirect allusions to a number of texts familiar to the reader of the 1790s; even direct, extra-narrative addresses to the reader[29]—all contribute to Austen's recurrent argument with the corrosive unrealities of Gothic romance and all directly or indirectly argue for the kind of domestic realism that features in the Catherine narrative.

The language of Gothic romance shares with the linguistic abuses of the various characters a mechanical repetitiousness, hyperbole, stylisation, and want of discrimination. So clichéd has the Gothic novel become, even by the 1790s, that, like her character Henry Tilney, Austen is able to turn her hand to the genre with ease, mastering and parodying its style to expose its absurdities.

> The night was stormy; the wind had been rising at intervals the whole afternoon; and by the time the party broke up, it blew and rained violently. Catherine, as she crossed the hall, listened to the tempest with sensations of awe; and, when she heard it rage around a corner of the building and close with sudden fury a distant door, she felt for the first time that she was really in an Abbey ...
>
> Catherine's heart beat quick, but her courage did not fail her. With a cheek flushed with hope, and an eye straining with curiosity, her fingers grasped the handle of a drawer and drew it forth. ... Her quick eyes fell directly on a roll of paper into the further part of the cavity, apparently for concealment, and her feelings at that moment were indescribable. Her heart fluttered, her knees trembled, and her cheeks grew pale ...
>
> The dimness of the light her candle emitted made her turn to it with alarm; but there was no danger of its sudden extinction, it had yet some hours to burn; and that she might not have any greater difficulty in distinguishing the writing than what its ancient date might occasion, she hastily snuffed it. Alas! it was snuffed and extinguished in one. A lamp could not have expired with more awful effect. Catherine, for a few moments, was motionless with horror. It was done completely; not a remnant of light in the wick could give hope

---

29   Austen, *Northanger Abbey*, ed. Benedict and Le Faye, 5–6; 111–12; *passim*; 30–31.

to the rekindling breath. Darkness impenetrable and immoveable filled the room. A violent gust of wind, rising with sudden fury, added fresh horror to the moment. Catherine trembled from head to foot. In the pause which succeeded, a sound like receding footsteps and the closing of a distant door struck on her affrighted ear. Human nature could support no more. A cold sweat stood on her forehead.[30]

As well as the predictable atmospherics of wind and rain, tremulous candles, 'receding footsteps', 'dimness' and 'darkness', and a 'gust of wind'; as well as a heroine typically 'motionless with horror', trembling and in a cold sweat; as well as the conjuring with typically prescriptive Gothic abstracts like 'horror', 'violent', 'awful'; as well as the 'indescribable' (as words fail the novelist)—we run up against a handful of patent absurdities like 'immoveable' darkness. 'Human nature', we are told, 'could support no more'. It might be Isabella Thorpe talking. The romance reader accepts it uncritically, but the truth is human nature can support a good deal more, and in Catherine's case has and will. 'The Romance', writes Clara Reeve, 'in lofty and elevated language, describes what has never happened nor is likely to'.[31] Literary satire like this enables Austen to bring realism and romance into confrontation, a confrontation that is at times dramatic, but never melodramatic; at times painful, but never tragic; at times ironic, but never nihilistic; at times laughable, but never absurd—for 'melodrama' and 'nihilism', 'the absurd' and even 'the tragic' are themselves exaggerations offensive to a certain kind of common-sense understanding.

It is not just Gothic romance that Austen counters here with a lecture on the dangers of the imagination, however; it is also the Romantic poets, whose investment in the imagination, as we saw, is one of the few things that unequivocally unite them (however equivocal the faculty itself may seem to them at times). Catherine's ignorance may endear her to Henry Tilney's vanity, but, to her author, ignorance

---

30 Austen, *Northanger Abbey*, ed. Benedict and Le Faye, 171-74.
31 Clara Reeve, *The Progress of Romance, through Times, Countries, and Manners; with Remarks on the Good and Bad Effects of It, on Them Respectively; in a Course of Evening Conversations*, in 2 vols (Colchester: W. Keymer, 1785), 1:111.

can be as dangerous as affectation, and just as much a distortion. At times this ignorance of Catherine's is comic, as with her excited anticipation that 'something very shocking indeed, will soon come out in London',[32] but this comic confusion of literature and life looks forward to the more serious confusion that takes place later, at the Abbey, when her imagination conjures a vision of General Tilney as a wife-murderer. Catherine's natural credulity makes her prey to the excesses of Gothic romance, and Henry is right to remind her of the exigencies of reality:

> 'If I understand you rightly, you had formed a surmise of such horror as I have hardly words to—Dear Miss Morland, consider the dreadful nature of the suspicions you have entertained. What have you been judging from? Remember the country and the age in which we live. Remember that we are English, that we are Christians. Consult your own understanding, your own sense of the probable, your own observation of what is passing around you—Does our education prepare us for such atrocities? Do our laws connive at them? Could they be perpetrated without being known, in a country like this, where social and literary intercourse is on such a footing; where every man is surrounded by a neighbourhood of voluntary spies, and where roads and newspapers lay every thing open? Dearest Miss Morland, what ideas have you been admitting?'[33]

'The visions of romance were over', begins the next chapter. Catherine has to wake up to the fact that she is the heroine of a domestic novel set in the 1790s, and not the heroine of a Gothic romance set in a superstitious past.

Romantic realism

Or does she? Just how satisfactory is the differentiation between the romantic and the real in *Northanger Abbey*? Austen's dismissing the

---

32 Austen, *Northanger Abbey*, ed. Benedict and Le Faye, 113.
33 Austen, *Northanger Abbey*, ed. Benedict and Le Faye, 203.

seductions and corruptions of romance is genuine enough (the manipulative hypocrisies of the 'romantic' Isabella are a case in point), but it is not without qualification—not without self-interrogation. Here, as throughout Austen, there is no easy answer, no simple choice between two self-contained alternatives. Rather than being mutually exclusive, romance and realism turn out to be mutually illuminating and mutually modifying. There are, for example, analogies to all the horrors of the Gothic romance in the waking world of Austen's England, with its 'roads and newspapers' and 'voluntary spies'. The abductions and cruelties and incarcerations of the Gothic romance have their counterparts in life that are not just comic or parodic imitations, and are in their own way no less horrifying for being commonplace. Women are rarely locked up in hidden cells in dank Gothic abbeys, but they can be no less prisoners of their social conditioning, of the expectations and proscriptions that a society collaborates to create. There may not be banditti around every corner, but there are family and friends enough to try and rob you blind. The Gothic villain, haunted by past sins and using his arbitrary power to satisfy his lusts, may be a sado-masochistic fantasy, but the patriarchal power exercised by General Tilney—'accustomed on every ordinary occasion to give the law in his family'—over the happiness of his own children, over their fortunes, and over the fate of a woman, such as Catherine, of a lower class, is arbitrary and brutal enough: 'Catherine, at any rate, heard enough to feel, that in suspecting General Tilney of either murdering or shutting up his wife, she had scarcely sinned against his character, or magnified his cruelty.'[34] There is, as it turns out, an element of complacency in Henry Tilney's protesting that none of the sinister events of the Gothic novel would be allowed in his thoroughly modern England, a complacency not shared by his author.

To see that everyday life has trials and pains that correspond to the conventional incidents in Gothic romance is just one way in which Austen revises the relationship between reality and romance. Another is to recognise that, while the domestic, so-called realistic novel may be *about* reality, that is not the same as its being real. Catherine's problem is precisely her inability to distinguish fiction from reality, her inability

---

34   Austen, *Northanger Abbey*, ed. Benedict and Le Faye, 256.

1 Coleridge, Austen, and the Two Romanticisms

to suspend her disbelief (as Coleridge suggests we need to do, and as Henry Tilney does so effectively) and to get involved in a story without losing a sense that a difference obtains. Austen may be arguing that Gothic romance is unrealistic and that the more familiar or realistic novel (like her own and Fanny Burney's and Maria Edgeworth's) is more of a challenge and more of an achievement, but Austen is not suggesting that her novel is more real. More realistic, perhaps, but not more real.

And even here we have to be careful. For while *Northanger Abbey* pleads the case for the realistic novel, it is in fact the least realistic of all of Austen's novels. I have already registered the fact of its formal heterogeneity: its set descriptive pieces and specimen conversations, direct address and interpolated parodies and allusions. More than that, however, there appear to be two quite incompatible if not contradictory things driving the novel: one is the argument about language and literature, the thrust of which is anti-romantic; the other is the narrative of Catherine Morland's entrance into the world, and the thrust of that is romantic—not Gothic romance, perhaps, but romance nonetheless, the stuff of *desire*. We are back with the love story. These two driving or motivating interests are constantly interwoven throughout *Northanger Abbey*; Catherine is both an anti-heroine (as we saw at the opening) and a heroine—atypical perhaps, in being a typical human being, but still a heroine. She is, by turns, an individual and a cipher.

Catherine's youth and rusticated upbringing make her an excellent satiric vehicle for exposing the formalities and pretensions and sophistications and duplicities of metropolitan society—as well as making her an excellent vehicle for indulging vicariously in its pleasurable diversions. This naivety of Catherine's is also central to the romantic plot, for it is a naivety that has as much to do with personality as with age and background, and it is this (whether we approve or not) that makes her so attractive to Henry Tilney. Catherine has a capacity for wonder and admiration, not least regarding Henry himself, that complements and to some extent redeems his patronising knowingness. Indeed, Austen's romance is realistic enough to make it plain that the hero's feelings for the heroine are inspired as much by his own vanity as by Catherine's openness and bright disposition. My point, however, is that Catherine is obliged to be both culpably ignorant *and* endearingly ingenuous, both gullible *and* clear-eyed, physically undistinguished *and*, at the same time, somehow beautiful, or becoming so: an ugly duckling turned swan; Cinderella transformed by the unlikely godmother, Mrs Allen. Catherine turns out to be not nearly so far removed as we are led to believe from that impossibly blue-eyed, quintessentially feminine, exquisitely beautiful, endearingly vulnerable heroine that her author disavows in the opening passage.

Catherine, in other words, functions on a variety of levels in Austen's plot to educate her readers, while she herself undergoes an education in a plot all her own. It is a tribute to Austen that she manages to get away with both, or perhaps I should say with *all* the Catherines in the novel—and all the Henrys, for that matter, for as so often with Austen's heroes there is much about Henry that threatens to alienate the reader. However, if it is a tribute to Austen that she can orchestrate the formally and thematically various elements of the novel yet retain our interest in the main plot, it is also a tribute to the irrepressible romanticism in us, her readers. Indeed, so irrepressible is the reader's romanticism, that our imaginative and emotional investment in Catherine's story can survive the disruptive literary games, the digressive argumentativeness, and the fictional self-consciousness of the book—all of which reflect ironically upon Catherine's own romantic plot and threaten to undermine it. Take the final flourish, for example, as the novel draws to a close:

> The anxiety, which in this state of their attachment must be the portion of Henry and Catherine, and of all who loved either, as to its final event, can hardly extend, I fear, to the bosom of my reader, who will see in the tell-tale compression of the pages before them, that we are all hastening together to perfect felicity.[35]

Austen is aware that, even without being allowed to confuse this fiction with reality, her readers will, like Henry, take their pleasure where they can find it, and steal off to the Hermitage-walk to finish the novel regardless.

The pleasures and pains of aesthetic experience do not come because we confuse reality with works of art, as Austen's favourite, Dr Johnson, pointed out in his *Preface to Shakespeare*, 'but because they

---

35 Austen, *Northanger Abbey*, ed. Benedict and Le Faye, 259.

1 Coleridge, Austen, and the Two Romanticisms

bring realities to mind'.[36] But it is more than that. In a discussion of Austen's early novels, Rachel Brownstein suggests that a certain worldliness in Austen 'speaks to the portions of our brains that suspect romantic fiction—portions Jane Austen has cultivated'.[37] But the very act of recognising a strong reality principle acknowledges that there are portions of our brains that hunger after one or other form of the ideal, of the two romanticisms. It may be that Austen's appeal is precisely to our need for both—to our need for a clear-sighted view of our own and of human limitation, on the one hand, and to our need for the romantic dream as an expression of irrepressible desire on the other. What Austen calls 'the common feelings of common life'[38] need to find a literary form at once faithful and flexible enough to express without falsifying not just what we mostly are, but also what we most desire.

---

36 Samuel Johnson, *Selected Writings*, ed. Patrick Cruttwell (Harmondsworth: Penguin, 1968), 276.
37 Rachel M. Brownstein, '*Northanger Abbey, Sense and Sensibility, Pride and Prejudice*', in *The Cambridge Companion to Jane Austen*, ed. Edward Copeland and Juliet McMaster (Cambridge: Cambridge University Press, 1997), 32–57 (33).
38 Austen, *Northanger Abbey*, ed. Benedict and Le Faye, 11.

2
Wordsworth and the Language of Nature

In his *Memoirs of William Wordsworth*, published in 1851 a year after Wordsworth's death, the poet's nephew, Christopher, remarked on the extent to which Wordsworth's radical politics had informed the theory of language expounded in the Preface to *Lyrical Ballads* (1800). The clue to Wordsworth's '*poetical* theory, in some of its questionable details', he wrote,

> may be found in his *political* principles; these had been democratical, and still, though in some degree modified, they were of a republican character. At this period he entertained little reverence for ancient institutions, as such; and he felt little sympathy with the higher classes of society.[1]

It takes no great subtlety to see the analogy between the false distinctions created by eighteenth-century poetic diction on the one hand and, on the other, the 'titles', 'stars, ribbands, and garters, and other badges of fictitious superiority' that Wordsworth stigmatises in his unpublished *Letter to the Bishop of Llandaff*. The arbitrary monarch of the same *Letter*, whose 'own passions and caprice' become 'the sole guides

---

1 Christopher Wordsworth, *Memoirs of William Wordsworth, Poet-Laureate, D.C.L.*, 2 vols (London: Edward Moxon, 1851), 1:125.

of his conduct', is first cousin to the wilful poet described in the Preface as rendering the reader 'utterly at [his] mercy' by employing 'poetic diction, arbitrary and subject to infinite caprices'.[2]

The language of eighteenth-century poetry and the authority of the aristocracy were both examples of 'Hereditary distinctions and privileged orders' which the young Wordsworth thought 'must necessarily counteract the progress of human improvement'.[3] The educated gentlemen to whom the literary elite appealed, and who shared their coterie language, might constitute the reading public that would pay for 'books of half a guinea price, hot-pressed, and printed upon superfine paper', but this was a social and economic distinction for Wordsworth, and therefore an arbitrary and irrelevant one.[4] In *The Prelude* of 1805–1806, Wordsworth recalls discovering

> How books mislead us—looking for their fame
> To judgments of the wealthy few, who see
> By artificial lights—how they debase
> The many for the pleasure of those few,
> … flattering their own self-conceit
> With pictures that arbitrarily set forth
> The differences, the outside marks by which
> Society has parted man from man,
> Neglectful of the universal heart.
>   (XII, 207–10, 215–19)[5]

As the best practical exemplar of a language purified of class association, Wordsworth chose the language of 'low and rustic life'. The

---

2 *The Prose Works of William Wordsworth*, ed. W. J. B. Owen and Jane Worthington Smyser, 3 vols (Oxford: Clarendon, 1974), 1:44, 40, 144.
3 As he wrote to William Matthews, [8] June [1794], *The Letters of William and Dorothy Wordsworth*, ed. Ernest de Selincourt, Volume 1, rev. by Chester L. Shaver (Oxford: Oxford University Press, 1967), 1:123. (Hereafter *Wordsworth Letters*.)
4 Letter to John Wilson, [June 7, 1802], *Wordsworth Letters*, 1:355.
5 Unless otherwise noted, I am using *The Poems of William Wordsworth: Collected Readings from the Cornell Wordsworth*, ed. Jared Curtis, 3 vols (Penrith: Humanities-Ebooks, 2009) for all quotations from Wordsworth's poetry.

2 Wordsworth and the Language of Nature

egalitarianism and 'unluxuriant' manners of rustics, 'connected with permanent objects of nature', ensured that their language was not decadent in Wordsworth's terms—not urban, not effeminate, not elitist: 'from their rank in society and the sameness and narrow circle of their intercourse, being less under the action of social vanity they convey their feelings and notions in simple and unelaborated expressions'.[6] Wordsworth's 'turn to nature', as Scott Hess observes, is 'also a turn to a particular form of social organization'.[7] In his tendentious choice of 'low and rustic life' lay the source of the 'long continued controversy concerning the true nature of poetic diction' to which Coleridge would address himself in the *Biographia Literaria*.[8] Contemporary readers could not have been insensible to the challenge in the word 'low'; 'words used commonly upon low and trivial occasions' (to quote Dr Johnson) were precisely those shunned and censured by the Augustan critics.[9] Nor could they have been insensible to Wordsworth's dubbing this 'the real language of men'. They were being told that their own life and language were an elaborate fiction.

Philosophical language

If this rustic language is a political and social challenge, however, it is also an approach to a language of more pristine integrity. An understanding of this begins at the possible source, in David Hartley's *Observations on Man*, of the phrase 'philosophical language', which Wordsworth uses to distinguish the language of the rustic:

---

6 See *The Prelude* (1805), VIII, 205–210; Wordsworth's letter to Coleridge of 27 February [1799]—*Wordsworth Letters*, 1:255, and the Preface to *Lyrical Ballads*, *The Prose Works of William Wordsworth*, 1:124.

7 Scott Hess, *William Wordsworth and the Ecology of Authorship: The Roots of Environmentalism in Nineteenth-Century Culture* (Charlottesville: University of Virginia Press, 2012), 3.

8 *Biographia Literaria*, The Collected Works of Samuel Taylor Coleridge, 7, ed. James Engell and W. Jackson Bate, 2 vols (Princeton, N. J.: Princeton University Press, 1983), 1:5.

9 The quotation is from Samuel Johnson, 'Life of Cowley', *Lives of the English Poets*, ed. George Birkbeck Hill, 3 vols (Oxford: Clarendon, 1905), 1:59.

If we suppose Mankind possessed of such a Language, as that they could at Pleasure denote all their Conceptions adequately, i.e., without any Deficiency, Superfluity, or Equivocation; if, moreover, this Language depended upon a few Principles assumed, not arbitrarily, but because they were the shortest and best possible ... this Language might be termed a philosophical one.[10]

Essential to all Hartley's theorising is a belief in the return of an earthly paradise and, because he was an optimist, the related supposition that all mental associations contain a preponderance of pleasure that is driving mankind towards this millennium. 'Association', Hartley argued, 'has a Tendency to reduce the State of those who have eaten of the Tree of the Knowledge of Good and Evil, back again to a paradisiacal one'. Which is where the 'philosophical language' comes in. Having been the language of Eden—'it is no improbable Supposition', writes Hartley, 'that the Language given by God to *Adam* and *Eve*, before the Fall, was of this Kind'—a philosophical language would signal the advent of the final paradise: 'Was human Life perfect, our Happiness in it would be properly represented by that accurate Knowledge of Things which a truly philosophical Language would give us'. In the meantime, however, until this language can be attained, 'where the Writer endeavours to express himself with Plainness, Sincerity, and Precision', and the Reader 'pays a due Regard to him, as his Teacher', then 'the ill Effects of the Confusion of Tongues become evanescent'.[11]

The 'Confusion of Tongues': a second fall, in the words of George Steiner, 'in some regards as desolate as the first'.[12] In conflating the story of Eden with that of the Tower of Babel, Hartley implicitly identifies the two myths. Behind or beyond this corruption of language lay the *Ur-Sprache* or primal language, perfectly referential, perfectly expressive—to quote Steiner again:

---

10 *Observations on Man, His Frame, His Duty, and His Expectations*, 2 vols. (London: Samuel Richardson, 1749), 1:315. For other analogues, see Olivia Smith, *The Politics of Language 1791–1819* (Oxford: Clarendon, 1986), 213–26.
11 Hartley, *Observations on Man*, 1:83; 1:316; 1:320; 1:317–8. Compare *The Prose Works of William Wordsworth*, 1:124.
12 George Steiner, *After Babel: Aspects of Language and Translation* (Oxford: Oxford University Press, 1975), 59.

This Adamic vernacular not only enabled all men to understand one another, to communicate with perfect ease. It bodied forth, to a greater or lesser degree, the original Logos, the act of immediate calling into being whereby God had literally 'spoken the world' ...

Being of direct divine etymology, moreover, the *Ur-Sprache* had a congruence with reality such as no tongue has had after Babel, or the dismemberment of the great, enfolding serpent of the world as it is recounted in the mythology of the Carib Indians. Words and objects dovetailed perfectly.[13]

No thinker, occult or orthodox, but had a theory about this ideal language—and, what is more suggestive, a name for it. Leibniz called it the *characteristica universalis*. Bishop Wilkins anticipated Hartley in his *Essay towards a Real Character and a Philosophical Language* (1668). More interesting for our purposes, Jacob Boehme called it 'the language of nature' and believed it to be hypostasised in humbler languages like his own '*mother tongue*'.[14] (Boehme thought Latin and Hebrew had monopolised and corrupted scholarly attention.) As the eighteenth century wore on, true expression was becoming more and more a primitive affair.

Wordsworth chose the language of rustic life for similar reasons. It approximated to, and represented, this paradisal ideal in which all 'Conceptions' are denoted 'adequately', in which word and object come together in a way that differed radically from the licentious poetry of the previous century. What annoyed Wordsworth was the perversity with which his eighteenth-century predecessors had refused to call a spade a spade—translating it, though periphrasis, into a tool of the flat and metal kind. Fastidiousness masquerading as a sense of decorum had resulted in the Augustan belief that, as Dr Johnson observed in Thomas Gray, their language was 'more poetical as it was more remote from common use'.[15] At its worst, eighteenth-century poetry shunned

---

13 Steiner, *After Babel*, 58.
14 The 'language of nature' is integral to Boehme's work, and occurs throughout. For a typical comment on the '*mother tongue*', see *The Aurora*, trans. John Sparrow [1656] (repr. London: John Watkins, 1914), 173 [ch. 8, § 126].
15 Johnson, *Lives of the English Poets*, ed. Hill, 3:435.

common usage so scrupulously that it created an entire poetic world that was a paraphrase or translation of reality, with little obligation towards the original. Words took precedence over things in the struggle to create an elegant, *literary* language that claimed attention for its own sake. Indeed, the narcissistic poet studied himself in the mirror of his own language, while the world around him was ignored. The same Wordsworth who wrote the long autobiographical 'poem on his own mind', *The Prelude*, also believed

> The man whose eye
> Is ever on himself doth look on one,
> The least of Nature's works.
> ('Lines Left upon a Seat in a Yew Tree', ll. 55–57)

And so, attributing poetic diction to poetic vanity, he set about introducing into poetry a plainer language.

The Puritan spirit of the argument is no less apparent than the republican. The sophistication (both senses) of Augustan verse is metaphorically associated with Babylon, 'the great whore that sitteth upon many waters: With whom the kings of the earth have committed fornication' (Revelation 17:1–2). Besides hierarchy, the unjustified mystery and lavish waste that contemporary nonconformist critics like the young Coleridge discovered in the Churches of Rome and England were both characteristic of poetic diction. But most relevant was the charge of idolatry. 'Thou shalt not make unto thee any graven image' (Exodus 20:4)—shalt not, according to Puritan ideology, erect any barrier between yourself and your God. The medium distracts by claiming attention for its own sake. The idolatrous opacity that the Puritan found in the trappings and symbols of the established churches, Wordsworth and Coleridge found in the distractions of poetic diction.

Coleridge was as aware of the psychological and ethical ramifications of the action and reaction of language and the human mind as he was of the religious significance of this inversion of values:

> When the material forms or intellectual ideas which should be employed to [rep]resent the internal state of feeling, are made to claim attention for their own sake, then commences Lip-worship,

or superstition, or disputatiousness, in religion; a passion for gaudy ornament & violent stimulants in morals; & in our literature bombast and vicious refinements.[16]

The etymological and mystical association of Babylon with Babel is crucial. Insofar as fallen languages substituted words for things, for the young Wordsworth and Coleridge the language of eighteenth-century poetry had fallen further than most.

To go back to Hartley: the development of language towards the sublime coincidence of word and object, or word and idea, was analogous to the development of human perfection:

> since our imperfect Languages improve, purify, and correct themselves perpetually by themselves, and by other Means, so that we may hope at last to obtain a Language, which shall be an adequate Representation of Ideas, and a pure Chanel of Conveyance for Truth alone, Analogy seems to suggest, that the Mixture of Pleasures and Pains, which we now experience, will gradually tend to a Collection of pure Pleasures only.

Not only did it prophesy and would it reflect perfection, in other words, but it would also actively foster perfection: 'the Use of Words', writes Hartley, 'is the principal Means by which we make intellectual and moral Improvements'. Having a language adequate to the expression of what we apprehend and understand, a faithful language that was also adequately understood by a hearer, would be like having new senses, encouraging and sharing new perceptions.[17]

Ur-Sprache

It is this idea of a primal language or *Ur-Sprache*, and the related idea that such a language could become the agent of millenarian progress,

---

16 Letter to William Wilberforce of January 1801, *Collected Letters of Samuel Taylor Coleridge*, ed. Earl Leslie Griggs, 6 vols (Oxford: Oxford University Press, 1956–1971), 2:666. (Hereafter cited as *Coleridge Letters*.)
17 Hartley, *Observations on Man*, 1:320–321, 287, 320.

that lies behind the Preface to *Lyrical Ballads*. Not only is the language of rustics held up as exemplary, but in the hands of right-minded poets a language modelled on it could aid in the rectification of man's relationship with nature—in the recovery, in other words, of Wordsworth's paradise, to which, as to Milton's far happier paradise within, all humanity has immediate access:

> Paradise and groves
> Elysian, fortunate islands, fields like those of old
> In the deep ocean—wherefore should they be
> A History, or but a dream when minds
> Once wedded to the outward frame of things
> In love, find these the growth of common day?
> (*Home at Grasmere*, ll. 996–1001)

Just as the perfect language in Hartley's system was the inevitable result and analogue of paradise, so the Preface treats rustic language as the spontaneous effusion of men whose passions 'are incorporated with the beautiful and permanent forms of nature'.[18] They speak as they feel because they feel as they should.

The identification of poetry with feeling, however, is only one of a series of identifications implicit and explicit in Wordsworth's early poetry and theory. The language of rustics remains an approximation, an imitation. Wordsworth's idea of a natural language is a transcendent language that aspires to the forms of nature themselves, and not just to the passions with which those forms are intertwined. His language, at least in theory, aspires to *present* (rather than to *represent*) these natural forms to the reader without any interference from the artistic medium, as we have seen. It is an attempt to articulate

> things that hold
> An inarticulate language
> (*The Ruined Cottage* MS.B, [46], ll. 2–3)[19]

---

18 *The Prose Works of William Wordsworth*, 1:124.
19 William Wordsworth, *The Ruined Cottage and The Pedlar*, ed. James Butler (Ithaca: Cornell University Press, 1979), 261.

to 'transliterate' or 'transubstantiate' the language of nature into the language of poetry. Though admittedly a clumsy word, a term like *transubstantiation* is required to distinguish the miraculous expressiveness Wordsworth has in mind from the arbitrary *translation* of reality into poetic language of which so much eighteenth-century poetry was guilty.

> The earth
> And common face of Nature spake to me
> Rememberable things
> *(The Prelude* [1798–99], 1:418–20)

Time and again one is reminded of the appropriateness of calling Wordsworth's ideal language a 'language of nature', because time and again the forms he would embody in his language are identified as just that: Nature's language. 'Nature', writes Geoffrey Hartman, 'often has an appeal (passively or actively asserted) as strong as speech, without being speech'.[20]

The language of nature

The idea behind Wordsworth's identification of nature and poetry is the orthodox one of the 'book of nature' (*liber naturæ*), or of nature as a 'book of created things' (*liber creaturarum*), summed up by Coleridge in his lectures of 1795: 'We see our God everywhere—the Universe in the most literal Sense is his written Language'.[21] In his 'Frost at Midnight', Coleridge implicitly contrasts the fallen language of man—the abstruser musings' (l. 6) of the adult Coleridge, and the 'swimming book' (l. 38) of the child Coleridge—with

---

20 Geoffrey Hartman, 'Wordsworth and Metapsychology', in *Wordsworth's Poetic Theory: Knowledge, Language, Experience*, ed. Alexander Regier and Stefan H. Uhlig (Basingstoke: Macmillan, 2010), 195–211 (197).
21 *Lectures 1795 on Politics and Religion*, ed. Lewis Patton and Peter Mann, The Collected Works of Samuel Taylor Coleridge, 1 (Princeton, N. J.: Princeton University Press, 1971), 339.

The lovely shapes and sounds intelligible
Of that eternal language, which thy God
Utters, who from eternity doth teach
Himself in all, and all things in himself.

(ll. 59–63)[22]

In the 'Semi-atheist' Wordsworth, however, this traditional trope is stripped of its theological meaning and given a sensual immediacy and concreteness.[23] Wordsworth talks familiarly—*conversationally*—of 'this mighty sum / Of things for ever speaking'; of 'the voice of Nature in the obscure wind', and, in *The Prelude*, of 'those shapes sublime / Wherewith I had been conversant'; of 'sounds that are / The ghostly language of the ancient earth'; of the 'strange utterance' of 'the loud dry wind'. Even the 'face of every neighbour' that he met 'was as a volume' to him.[24] More directly, in 'Lines written a few miles above Tintern Abbey', he discovers

> In nature and *the language of the sense*
> The anchor of my purest thoughts, the nurse,
> The guide, the guardian of my heart, and soul
> Of all my moral being.
>
> (ll. 108–1; my italics)

The list of allusions to nature's language in Wordsworth's poetry could be extended indefinitely. The characteristic Wordsworthian blend of experiential immediacy with philosophical import, of the sensual with the supersensual, is perhaps best exemplified by the following passage from *The Pedlar*:

---

22 All quotations from Coleridge's poetry are from *Poetical Works I* (Reading Text), The Collected Works of Samuel Taylor Coleridge, 16, ed. J. C. C. Mays, in 2 parts (Princeton, N. J.: Princeton University Press, 2001).
23 Coleridge referred to Wordsworth as a 'Semi-atheist' in a letter to John Thelwall of 13 May 1796, *Coleridge Letters*, 1:216.
24 See 'Expostulation and Reply', ll. 25–6; *The Ruined Cottage*, l. 78; *The Prelude* (1805–1806), III, ll. 102–3; *The Prelude* (1798–1799), Part 2, ll. 357–8; Part 1, l. 64; *The Prelude* (1805–1806), IV, ll. 58–59.

2 Wordsworth and the Language of Nature

> The clouds were touch'd,
> And in their silent faces did he read
> Unutterable love. Sound needed none,
> Nor any voice of joy: his spirit drank
> The spectacle. Sensation, soul, and form
> All melted into him
>
> (*The Pedlar* MS E, ll. 194–99)

The idea of the *liber creaturarum* itself, the quasi-religious 'touch'd', the paradox of reading the unutterable, the sensual verb 'drank' to describe spiritual apprehension—all contribute to the peculiar power of this passage, itself an attempt to convey the 'unutterable'. It is into this final unity of 'Sensation, soul, and form' that Wordsworth hoped language, too, would 'melt'. In a fragment from the *Peter Bell* manuscript, written in 1798 but not published until 1819, Wordsworth makes quite explicit the identification of poetry and transcendent form—and, with that, the potentially *formative* powers of a truly natural poetic language—when he refers to

> that considerate and laborious work,
> That patience which, admitting no neglect,
> [?By] slow creation doth impart to speach
> Outline and substance, even till it has given
> A function kindred to organic power—
> The vital spirit of a perfect form.[25]

The 'outline' of this language would shape the mind of the reader in a way identical to that of the 'mountain's outline' on the mind of the Pedlar, which with 'its steady form'

---

[25] Reprinted as fragment (b) in the Norton Critical Edition of *The Prelude*, ed. Jonathan Wordsworth, M. H. Abrams, and Stephen Gill (New York: W. W. Norton, 1979), 495.

> Gave simple grandeur, & its presence shaped
> The measure & the prospect of his soul
> To majesty, such virtue had the forms
> Perennial of the ancient hills; nor less
> *The changeful language of their countenance*
> Gave movement to his thoughts & multitude
> With order & relation
> *(The Ruined Cottage*, add. to MS.D, [56v–57r]; my italics)[26]

In consonance with nature, then—'that is', with 'eternal nature'—the poet 'ought to a certain degree to rectify men's feelings', as Wordsworth wrote to John Wilson, 'to render their feelings more sane pure and permanent'.[27] The value of the affective, then, is deeply contingent on its connection with the natural world, and what better way to rectify the feelings than for the poet to have his language dissolve before 'the speaking face of earth and heaven', to have the poem become, in its influence on the feelings and habits, one of those 'things that teach as Nature teaches'?[28] That the language of 'low and rustic life' was believed to share this 'power like one of Nature's'[29] is apparent from a passage Wordsworth sent to Thomas Poole in April 1801 for insertion into his copy of *Michael* (though never included in any printed text). It describes the fireside conversation of Michael's exemplary family as

> cloth'd in images
> Lively and beautiful, in rural forms
> That made their conversation fresh and fair
> As is a landscape[30]

This, to borrow a phrase from *The Excursion*, is 'the poetry of common speech'.[31]

---

26 *The Ruined Cottage and The Pedlar*, ed. Butler, 372.
27 *Wordsworth Letters*, 1:355.
28 *The Prelude* (1805–1806),V, ll. 12, 231.
29 *The Prelude* (1805–1806), XII, l. 312.
30 *Wordsworth Letters*, 1:324.
31 *The Excursion*, V, l. 392.

Music

A later, rhetorical question in Wordsworth's *Home at Grasmere* (1800–1806)—a question 'that leads to the centre of his being as man and as poet', to quote Stephen Gill[32]—equates this language, appropriately, with one specific natural phenomenon, a stream:

> Is there not
> An art, a music, and a stream of words
> That shall be life, the acknowledged voice of life?
> Shall speak of what is done among the fields,
> Done truly there, or felt, of solid good
> And real evil, yet be sweet withal,
> More grateful, more harmonious than the breath,
> The idle breath of sweetest pipe attuned
> To pastoral fancies? Is there such a stream,
> Pure and unsullied, flowing from the heart
> With motions of true dignity and grace,
> Or must we seek these things where man is not?
> (ll. 620–31)

The analogy of the stream, with its common metaphorical association with music, captures the yearning after a perfectly expressive metalanguage that will resist analysis and escape the relativities of history and convention—a form of language, to adapt the notorious lines of Archibald MacLeish's 'Ars Poetica', that 'should not mean, but be'.[33] This digression in *Home at Grasmere* is Wordsworth's finest expression of the finest expression theoretically available to the poet: a paradisal language that he hopes will present to the reader the love of a woman for her dead husband, a scene from low and rustic life appropriately enough, echoing what in 'Lines written a few miles above Tintern Abbey' he calls 'the still, sad *music* of humanity' (l. 93, my emphasis). Though the yearning

---

32 Stephen Gill, *Wordsworth's Revisitings* (Oxford: Oxford University Press, 2011), 1.
33 'Ars Poetica', ll. 23–4, *Collected Poems of Archibald MacLeish 1917–1952* (New York: Houghton Mifflin, 1952).

in *Home at Grasmere* for 'an art, a music, and a stream of words' capable of constituting and expressing life itself is bound to fail—'these things', this language, must be sought 'where man is not'—Wordsworth seems reconciled to the alternative of silence:

> Be this
> A task above my skill; the silent mind
> Has its own treasures, and I think of these,
> Love what I see, and honour humankind.
>
> (ll. 642–45)

The aspiration to the condition of music looks back and forward at the same time: back to the Neoplatonists and even further to Pythagorean beliefs about the purity and transcendence of music—more recently, the seventeenth-century mathematician, astronomer, and astrologer, Johannes Kepler, had correlated the angular velocities of the planets and musical intervals and identified them as the primal language—forward to the aesthetic struggle of the *symboliste* movement to identify notes or strains with states of emotion and the soul. Or to Coleridge, for that matter: 'O that I had the Language of Music / the power of infinitely varying the expression, & individualizing it even as it is /—My heart plays an incessant music / for which I need an outward Interpreter /—words halt over & over again'.[34] It is surprising how often nature is actually identified with music in crucial passages in Wordsworth's poetry. No better example could be found than the opening of the 1798–1799 *Prelude*:

> Was it for this
> That one, the fairest of all rivers, loved
> To blend his murmurs with my Nurse's song,
> And from his alder shades, and rocky falls,
> And from his fords and shallows, sent a voice

---

34 *The Notebooks of Samuel Taylor Coleridge*, ed. Kathleen Coburn et al (Princeton, N. J.: Princeton University Press, 1957–2002), vol. 2, note 2035 (compare Vol. 2, note 2998).

> That flowed along my dreams? For this didst thou
> O Derwent, travelling over the green plains
> Near my 'sweet birth-place', didst thou beauteous stream
> Make ceaseless music through the night and day,
> Which with its steady cadence tempering
> Our human waywardness, composed my thoughts
> To more than infant softness, giving me,
> Among the fretful dwellings of mankind,
> A knowledge, a dim earnest of the calm
> Which Nature breathes among the fields and groves?

The movement or modulation from nature and the forms of nature into music in Wordsworth's poetry seems almost instinctive. In the 'Lines written a few miles above Tintern Abbey', for example, the poet looks forward to a time when the mind of Dorothy

> Shall be a mansion for all lovely forms,
> Thy memory be as a dwelling-place
> For all sweet sounds and harmonies
>
> (ll. 139–42)

The movement is only emphasised if we regard the famous line on the 'still, sad music of humanity' in its context, where the subtle transition from sight to hearing reflects the general refinement of the poet's sensibility and the corresponding movement in the poem from the natural to the supernatural. When in the 1805 *Prelude* the poet addresses Nature directly, the identification and aspiration are unmistakable:

> Oh! that I had a music and a voice
> Harmonious as your own, that I might tell
> What ye have done for me.
>
> (XI, ll. 20–22)

Language and self-consciousness

The formal perfection of this ideal language and its superiority to the 'idle breath' of the pastoral pipe meant that it must transcend literature in the conventional, eighteenth-century sense. Wordsworth's suspicion extended beyond what he saw as the factitious language of eighteenth-century poetry, however, to include *all* human language. Exactly why he should have lost confidence in the mutual fit of language and reality and resigned himself to the alternative of silence is bound up with his early belief in the superiority of nature to all human, which is to say *artificial*, forms. The linguistic ability—the power to create and utilise language—by which traditional humanist philosophy had defined and celebrated humanity was inseparable from human self-consciousness. 'The best part of human language, properly so called, is derived from reflection on the acts of the mind itself', writes Coleridge in the *Biographia Literaria*.[35] But self-consciousness remained at best a dubious attribute for Wordsworth, whose contribution to English poetry ironically has been nothing other than an evolutionary and unifying self-consciousness. While it liberated, self-consciousness also alienated man, and (as Geoffrey Hartman has observed) is often felt in Wordsworth 'as a breach or betrayal of Nature'.[36] And the fall into self-consciousness is for Wordsworth a fall into human language.

In the poem 'We Are Seven', accordingly, an implicit association of self-consciousness with death is registered by the inability of human language to express the child's vision of atemporal community. In 'Anecdote for Fathers' to articulate is to lie, a linguistic and characteristically human distortion forced from the child by the myopic adult consciousness. Language and literature are also seen as failing to come to terms with the experience of Wordsworth's privileged Idiot Boy in the poem of the same name, where he represents another type of innocence or 'infancy'. (Our word 'infant' comes from the Latin *infans* or 'without speech'.) The various and verbose speculations of Betty and the narrator on Johnny's experience are revealed to be comically

---

35 *Biographia Literaria*, ed. Engell and Bate, 2:54.
36 Geoffrey Hartman, *Wordsworth's Poetry 1787–1814* (New Haven, Conn.: Yale University Press, 1964), 132.

inappropriate, breaking down over the simple fact of his un(self-)consciousness: 'Of moon and stars he takes no heed' (l. 354). It is worth noting that the verbal interchanges between the adult characters are at best clumsy (Betty and Susan, narrator to reader) and at worst misconstruction (Betty and the doctor, narrator to reader). Johnny, on the other hand, absorbed in nature, has no need for language:

> The silence of her Idiot Boy,
> What hopes it sends to Betty's heart!
>
> (ll. 92–93)

'The silent mind', after all, 'has its own treasures'. Johnny's one early utterance—'burr, burr, burr'—is expressive enough; when he answers with this, and 'with his head, and with his hand', 'Betty well could understand' (ll. 62–63; 66). But when, like 'little Edward' of the 'Anecdote for Fathers', Johnny is *forced* to articulate, the result is a confusion of tongues, underlining the inappropriateness of language:

> The cocks did crow to-whoo, to-whoo
> And the sun did shine so cold.
>
> (ll. 450–51)

'This linguistic incapacity', however (to quote Thomas H. Ford), 'is also a proximity to the materiality of language and an access to pleasure in sound unmediated by meaning'. And these 'onomatopoeic', 'non-signifying attributes of language' identified by Ford point to the most eloquent form of 'sound unmediated by meaning'[37]—or, to express it as a paradox, the most meaningful form of sound unmediated by meaning—which is, of course, music.

'The Idiot Boy', the wordiest of all the *Lyrical Ballads* and arguably the volume's most self-conscious literary experiment, turns out to be Wordsworth's most sustained attack on language generally and, more

---

37 Thomas H. Ford, 'The Romantic Political Economy of Reading: Or, Why Wordsworth Thought Adam Smith Was the Worst Critic Ever', *English Literary History*, 80:2 (Summer 2013), 575–95 (590, 593).

specifically, on certain literary uses of language, working against both heroic and sensationalist traditions through a parody of the Gothic ballad of the night ride. Like the 'meddling intellect' in 'The Tables Turned', language 'Mis-shapes the beauteous forms of things' (l. 27). Setting the theme for many of the *Lyrical Ballads*, 'The Tables Turned' contrasts another, characteristically human confusion of tongues—'Books! 'tis a dull and endless strife' (l. 9)—with the harmonious breath and music of the *liber naturæ*.

Nowhere is the radical incompatibility between the language of man and the language of nature more apparent than when Wordsworth confronts the enviable realm of silence and slow time inhabited by those liminal figures in his mythology known as his 'solitaries':

> the silence and the calm
> Of mute insensate things.
> ('Three Years She Grew', ll. 17–18)

Witness the poet's experience—his apprehension—of the Leech-gatherer in Stanza XVI of 'Resolution and Independence', in which the old man's speech is again likened to a stream:

> The old man still stood talking by my side;
> But now his voice to me was like a stream
> Scarce heard; nor word from word could I divide
> And the whole body of the Man did seem
> Like one whom I had met with in a dream;
> Or like a man from some far region sent,
> To give me human strength, by apt admonishment.
> (ll. 106–112)

The poet's failure to attend to the Leech-gatherer's speech will later become the object of a gently self-mocking irony. His having 'scarce heard' that speech is more impersonally suggestive, however. It is a stanza in which the languages of man and nature converge. As the old man's speech becomes subservient to his 'whole body', what he *says* is incorporated into the higher language of what he *is*. It is the poet's, and thence the reader's, total experience of the old man that is important, not what he had to say, but the quality of the voice, the firmness of the mind, and their articulate relationship with the ancient body. They 'moveth all together' if they move at all.

In the earlier version of the poem, the old man is apprehended precisely as an intractable reality. 'Presented in the most naked simplicity possible', as Wordsworth put it in a letter to Mary and Sara Hutchinson, the Leech-gatherer simply 'was'.[38] Common to both animate and inanimate alike, hard and simple *being* prompts the further dehumanisation of the Leech-gatherer, as he is elaborately, almost ritualistically, likened to 'a huge stone' (l. 57). What we witness is the gradual metamorphosis of the Leech-gatherer into one of the beautiful and permanent forms of nature, gathered up into nature's (and therefore, wishfully, into poetry's) formative language—in this case, into the specifically disciplinary language of 'apt admonishment'. His very existence chastises the poet.

It was perhaps with a feeling that the Leech-gatherer's actual words were incongruous with his role as part of this higher language that Sara Hutchinson complained of his speech as 'tedious'. In his stung reply to this letter, Wordsworth seems unaware that it is precisely because of the claims he is making for the total experience that speech and the suggestion of self-consciousness on the part of the Leech-gatherer seem strangely trivialising.[39] It is the same with Michael in the poem of the same name. Michael is more impressive when, silent, his life and sentiments are rendered in the third person. In his inarticulate grief at the loss of his son, Luke, he is—like the silent symbol of the Leech-gatherer stalking the poet's memory—a more moving and effective, more *expressive* figure. It is the same with the discharged soldier, the damaged solitary who would eventually find his way into Wordsworth's *Prelude*. Discovered like the Leech-gatherer enveloped in silence, his later 'Groans scarcely audible' are akin to the voice of the Leech-gatherer 'Scarce heard'. When forced to speak, the discharged soldier is 'Concise in answer'. Again, however, it is conversation better

---

38   See the letter to Mary and Sara Hutchinson of 14 June [1802], *Wordsworth Letters*, 1:366.
39   *Wordsworth Letters*, 1:367.

reported than repeated, and Wordsworth implicitly recognises the irrelevance of speech to the spectral figure of the soldier by making the two—the speaker and his speech—out of consonance:

> in all he said
> There was a strange half-absence, and a tone
> Of weakness and indifference, as of one
> Remembering the importance of his theme
> But feeling it no longer.[40]

These solitary figures are Wordsworth's 'silent monitors'.[41] It is more than isolation or aloofness that preserves their silence, it is their role as 'things that hold / An inarticulate language'. The Idiot Boy, Johnny, exemplifies this. His one speech is literally inarticulate, out of joint. With a language of nature corresponding to the powers of nature as Wordsworth's ideal, it is little wonder that his major challenge to the contemporary sensibility should have been an inarticulate 'natural' ('A person having a low learning ability or intellectual capacity; a person born with impaired intelligence', according to the *Oxford English Dictionary*). But while, *as* a person, Johnny is inarticulate, *in* his person he is most articulate. 'Man can embody truth but he cannot know it', wrote Yeats.[42] This is certainly the case with the characters in Wordsworth's poetry absorbed in nature and silence. Edward Bostetter has characterised 'the transformation' of the discharged soldier as one 'from individual into abstraction',[43] but this only confuses his inanimation with that of an allegorical figure. Not only did abstractions abound in the poetry against which Wordsworth fought, but Wordsworth's monitorial figures—aloof, indifferent, self-absent—have the non-humanity of nature, not of abstract thought. They are designed to teach in the way Wordsworth believed nature taught, not in man's way.

---

40 *The Prelude* (1805–1806), IV, 432, 473, 474–78.
41 See 'The Old Cumberland Beggar', l. 123.
42 To Lady Elizabeth Pelham, 4 January 1939, *The Letters of W. B. Yeats*, ed. Allan Wade (London: Harte Davis, 1954), 922.
43 E. E. Bostetter, *The Romantic Ventriloquists: Wordsworth, Coleridge, Keats, Shelley, Byron*, rev. ed. (Seattle: University of Washington Press, 1975), 60.

2 Wordsworth and the Language of Nature

There are, to conclude, two 'natural' languages outlined in the Preface to *Lyrical Ballads* and in Wordsworth's early poetry. The first, a transparent language that endeavoured to represent without distortion, became equated with the more direct and unpretentious language of prose. It is symbolic only in the simplest sense of the word: composed of signs designed automatically to invoke the object or idea for which they stand and to become, in Coleridge's (pejorative) phrase, the 'smooth market-coin of intercourse'.[44] This language, for Wordsworth, was authorised by the common-sense demand that a spade be called a spade. The other natural language in the Preface is the exalted idea (ideal) behind this. It transcends art altogether by *being* rather than *representing* nature—eternal nature, of course, not accidental or perishable nature. As with the being or 'Surpassing life' in the *Prelude*, which 'is, / And hath the name of, God',[45] the name and the entity become one and indivisible. Implicit in many of the earlier metaphors of nature's language, it is the identification to which, in the *Home at Grasmere* fragment quoted above, we saw Wordsworth momentarily aspire:

> Is there not
> An art, a music, and a stream of words
> That shall be life, the acknowledged voice of life?

Both languages are ways of mediating between mind and nature without interference from any media, and are essentially anti-literary in their struggle to dispense with the artificial, as well as (ironically for Wordsworth) the subjective element in art. 'Symbolism', as J. F. Danby observes, 'is not Wordsworth's concern. Poetry for Wordsworth should purpose truth to life because it is life that is symbolic'.[46] This is the theory, at least. In practice Wordsworth rarely allows the language of nature to speak without mediation or interference. 'There is, in fact, in Mr. Wordsworth's mind', as Hazlitt remarked, 'a repugnance to admit

---

44 *Biographia Literaria*, 2:122.
45 *The Prelude* (1805–1806), VI, ll. 155–57.
46 John F. Danby, *The Simple Wordsworth: Studies in the Poems 1797–1807* (London: Routledge & Kegan Paul, 1960), 29.

any thing that tells for itself, without the interpretation of the poet.'[47] Partly out of egotism, as Hazlitt concluded, and partly out of a persistent fear that his audience would misinterpret, Wordsworth dramatised and privileged his own deeply felt reading of the book of nature.

But this is only half of it. Not surprisingly, Wordsworth's faith in the possibility of a natural language was contingent upon his faith in nature itself and his faith in nature, never unqualified, proved equivocal and ultimately inadequate. It was the subjective or imaginative element in art that occupied Wordsworth at the turn of the century and the imagination, as Coleridge would argue in the *Biographia*, had a radically artificial and superior idiom. The characteristically Wordsworthian tension between the claims of nature and the claims of the human imagination is almost ludicrously apparent in the 1802 additions to the Preface to *Lyrical Ballads* which manage, on the one hand, to exalt the poet himself above all other people, and on the other to humble, not to say humiliate the poet's art before 'emanations of reality and truth'.[48] The 'internal tensions, inconsistencies, discontinuous argument' and 'confused sense of purpose' that Thomas Pfau remarks in the Preface were carried over into the poetry.[49] If Wordsworth became convinced that the mind was 'lord and master', he also retained a genuine humility before nature throughout his career, and with it the suspicion that 'all symbolism harbours the curse of mediacy', and 'is bound to obscure what it seeks to reveal'.[50] When in the fifth book of *The Prelude* he describes 'the great Nature that exists in works / Of mighty poets', he balances these two priorities precariously:

---

47 In the second part of his review of 'The Character of Mr. Wordsworth's New Poem' in *The Examiner* (28 August 1814), in *William Wordsworth: The Critical Heritage*, Vol. 1, 1793–1820, ed. Robert Woof (London and New York: Routledge, 2001), 372.
48 *The Prose Works of William Wordsworth*, 1:139.
49 Thomas Pfau, '"Elementary Feelings" and "Distorted Language": The Pragmatics of Culture in Wordsworth's Preface to *Lyrical Ballads*', *New Literary History*, 24:1 (Winter 1993), 125–46 (125).
50 I am borrowing Ernst Cassirer's definition of 'naive realism' in his *Language and Myth*, trans. by Suzanne K. Langer (New York: Dover, 1953), 7.

2 Wordsworth and the Language of Nature

> Visionary power
> Attends upon the motions of the winds
> Embodied in the mystery of words;
> There darkness makes abode, and all the host
> Of shadowy things do work their changes there
> As in a mansion like their proper home.
> Even forms and substances are circumfused
> By that transparent veil with light divine,
> And through the turnings intricate of verse
> Present themselves as objects recognised
> In flashes, with a glory scarce their own.[51]

The veil—note—remains transparent, and even while the natural objects rendered or represented by poetry do not recognise their own glory, it is indeed theirs. The 'turnings intricate of verse' must remain *underwritten* by nature itself.

---

51 *The Prelude* (1805–1806), V, ll. 619–629.

3
Crossing Over: Samuel Taylor Coleridge and the Conversation Poems

It was to his poem 'The Nightingale' that Coleridge gave the subtitle ('A Conversation Poem') that would eventually be adapted by George McLean Harper to stand for a whole group or genre within Coleridge's collected works. The exact constitution of the 'conversation poems' is disputable—Ewan Jones rightly calls it 'a conventional label rather than a rigorously defined genre'.[1] For our purposes the group would include:

> 'To a Friend [together with an unfinished Poem]'
> 'Reflections on Having Left a Place of Retirement'
> 'The Eolian Harp'
> 'This Lime-Tree Bower My Prison'
> 'Frost at Midnight'
> 'The Nightingale'
> 'Fears in Solitude'
> 'To William Wordsworth'

---

1   Ewan Jones, '"Less Gross than Bodily": Materiality in Coleridge's Conversation Poem Sequence', *Review of English Studies*, 64:259 (April 2012), 267–88 (268). Jones defends the coherence of the sequence, however, while others doubt it. J. C. C. Mays, for example, finds Coleridge's 1817 title, 'Meditative Poems in Blank Verse', 'less misleading than the category of Conversation poems that has now passed into general currency', *Coleridge's Experimental Poetics* (New York: Palgrave Macmillan, 2013), 76–77, 218, note 34.

When Harper first identified the conversation poems in an essay published in 1925, he wrote of them in a casual, anecdotal way that is bound to strike today's academic literary critic as amateurish and belletristic.[2] Harper begins by introducing a person—'a young poet whom I love'—and a problem: what exactly should he write about Coleridge? With an embarrassing particularity of personal reference, he describes the unnamed poet as having 'just left my house and driven away in the soft darkness of a spring night, to the remote cottage in the Delaware valley where he meditates a not thankless Muse'.[3]

There are, however, two very good reasons why Harper's essay should not be dismissed as oblique and self-indulgent, though it seems both at the beginning. The first is that the essay is an act of homage, its style and structure implicitly evaluating the style and structure of the conversation poems themselves by imitating them. Both the essay and the poems record the apparently casual rhythm of the responsive and reflective mind, expanding and contracting, yet both are organised in a far from casual way. Both are 'so natural and real, and yet so dignified, and harmonious', as Coleridge excitedly declared of the poetry of William Lisle Bowles,[4] and both use an immediate personal experience to dramatise a philosophical or abstract proposition.

Which brings us to the second important contribution of Harper's essay. It recognises, implicitly and explicitly, the importance of love and friendship to the conversation poems, not in any abstract sense—the years following the French Revolution had witnessed a superfluity of pious abstractions from all sides of the political divide—but particular loves and particular friendships. Like Harper's essay, the conversation poems involve a loved one, or loved ones, and a problem; indeed for

---

2 Kelvin Everest in *Coleridge's Secret Ministry: The Context of the Conversation Poems 1795-1798* (Brighton: Harvester, 1979), 186. Harper's essay, republished in his *Spirit of Delight* (1928), is readily available in *English Romantic Poets: Modern Essays in Criticism*, ed. M. H. Abrams (Oxford, London, NY: Oxford University Press, 1960), 144-57.
3 *English Romantic Poets*, 144.
4 In his *Biographia Literaria*, The Collected Works of Samuel Taylor Coleridge, 7, ed. James Engell and W. Jackson Bate, 2 vols (Princeton, N. J.: Princeton University Press, 1983), 1:17.

3 Crossing Over: Samuel Taylor Coleridge and the Conversation Poems

Coleridge, as for Harper, it is the act of love itself that helps to bring about a solution to that problem.[5]

This last point is crucial. The conversation poems are born out of new and intense affections and a sense of coming home. The short poem in which Coleridge announced his departure from the politico-prophetic mode of *Religious Musings*—specifically, from its mental and verbal bombast—is addressed and entitled, significantly, 'To a Friend' (Charles Lamb, as it happens). 'To a Friend, together with an Unfinished Poem' was designed to accompany the incomplete *Religious Musings* and first appeared in a letter to Robert Southey dated 29 December 1794:[6]

> Thus far my scanty brain hath built the rhyme
> Elaborate and swelling:
>
> (ll. 1–2)[7]

It was not as if the more ambitious 'rhyme' were not all about love—indeed, all the beliefs that inform the conversation poems are present in *Religious Musings*. 'Yet', writes Coleridge, 'the heart / Not owns it' (ll. 2–3), choosing instead to identify with the suffering of a particular friend, and to share and compare specific sorrows:

---

5   For good general discussion of the subject, style, and structure of the conversation poems, see, besides Harper's essay, Richard Harter Fogle, 'Coleridge's Conversation Poems', *Tulane Studies in English*, 5 (1955), 103–10 (reprinted in his *The Permanent Pleasure*, Athens, Georgia, 1974, 17–26); Albert Gerard, 'The Discordant Harp: The Structure of Coleridge's Conversation Poems', in his *English Romantic Poetry: Ethos, Structure, and Symbol in Coleridge, Wordsworth, Shelley, and Keats* (Berkeley and Los Angeles: University of California Press, 1968), 20–39; and M. H. Abrams, 'Structure and Style in the Greater Romantic Lyric', in Frederick W. Hilles and Harold Bloom (eds.), *From Sensibility to Romanticism: Essays Presented to Frederick A. Pottle* (London, Oxford, and New York: Oxford University Press 1965), 527–60.
6   *Collected Letters of Samuel Taylor Coleridge*, ed. Earl Leslie Griggs, 6 vols (Oxford: Oxford University Press, 1956–71) [cited throughout as *Coleridge Letters*], 1:147–48.
7   All quotations from Coleridge's poetry are from *Poetical Works*, The Collected Works of Samuel Taylor Coleridge, 16, ed. J. C. C. Mays (Princeton N. J.: Princeton University Press, 2001).

> In fancy (well I know)
> From business wand'ring far and local cares,
> Thou creepest round a dear-lov'd Sister's bed
> With noiseless step, and watchest the faint look,
> Soothing each pang with fond solicitude,
> And tenderest tones medicinal of love.
> I too a SISTER had, an only Sister—
> She lov'd me dearly, and I doted on her!
> (ll. 6–13)

The retreat in 'To a Friend' from the philanthropic generalisations of *Religious Musings* should not be interpreted as a retreat from the eighteenth-century ideal of 'Universal Benevolence', but as an experiment in which the poet endeavours to realise that ideal more fully, to rediscover the universal in the particular. Renouncing the strained rhapsodies of *Religious Musings*, the poet's identification with his friend in this short, deliberately casual poem enables him to feel again the presence of God and brotherly love that he invokes with more ostentation than conviction throughout the *Musings*:

> He knows (the SPIRIT that in secret sees,
> Of whose omniscient and all-spreading Love
> Aught to *implore* were impotence of mind)
> That my mute thoughts are sad before his throne,
> Prepar'd, when he his healing ray vouchsafes,
> To pour forth thanksgiving with lifted heart,
> And praise Him Gracious with a BROTHER'S Joy!
> (ll. 26–32)

The regenerative act of sympathetic love represented in and by 'To a Friend' is the first of many in Coleridge's poetry. 'Philanthropy (and indeed every other Virtue) is a thing of *Concretion*', he wrote to Southey in July 1794, with his mind on the chilling rationalism of William Godwin: 'Some home-born Feeling is the *centre* of the Ball, that, rolling on thro' Life collects and assimilates every congenial Affection.'[8] What the

---

8   *Coleridge Letters*, 1:86.

3 Crossing Over: Samuel Taylor Coleridge and the Conversation Poems

controversial political lecturer and utopian projector who had cried out for universal brotherhood from the lectern and the pulpit discovers in the conversation poems is that charity—which is to say, love—begins at home, and that the intimate, familiar act of love, far from trivialising his poetry by making it narrowly personal and solipsistic, only widened its emotional and intellectual range.

When Coleridge rejects the 'elaborate and swelling' rhetoric of *Religious Musings* in 'To a Friend, together with an Unfinished Poem' he is also rejecting a way of relating to man, to nature, and to God. For the early Coleridge, as for the young Wordsworth, an overwrought poetic diction or expression—in their own poetry, as well as in others'—was not just a lapse of taste, it was also a moral lapse, an act of profound insincerity, setting up an opaque medium between the poet and the reader, on the one hand, and nature and God, on the other. Adapting the confessional ease and informality of Bowles's sonnets and what Coleridge called the 'divine Chit chat' of William Cowper's blank verse, Coleridge developed the supple, informal blank-verse style of the conversation poems, a style capable of modulating from casual anecdote or passing description into an unself-conscious lyric sublimity.[9] The colloquial style and confessional tone of the poems, like their new imagery and naturalistic detail, are symbolic of the poet's altered consciousness and essential to their values of intimacy and 'home-born Feeling'.

Each of the conversation poems, in its different way, has a story to tell that dramatises the transformative power of love. Indeed, no less than a nineteenth-century novel, each poem has a narrative, characters, and a setting—with the narrative of each turning on a regenerative act of sympathetic love for an intimate: a lover, friend, or child. This act of love is an initiating step in the dissolution of the self, the caging and confining ego which is the problem to be overcome in these poems, as it had been the problem of mankind generally in *Religious Musings*:

> Toy-bewitch'd,
> Made blind by lusts, disherited of soul,
> No common center Man, no common sire

---

9   *Coleridge Letters*, 1:279.

> Knoweth! A sordid solitary thing,
> Mid countless brethren with a lonely heart
> Thro' courts and cities the smooth Savage roams
> Feeling himself, his own low Self the whole.
>   (ll. 146–52)

An abstract recognition that the 'most holy name' of God is 'Love' enables the individual to fly 'from his small particular orbit'

> With blest outstarting! From HIMSELF he flies,
> Stands in the Sun, and with no partial gaze
> Views all creation; and he loves it all,
> And blesses it, and calls it very good!
>   (ll. 110–13)

In the conversation poems, on the other hand, the reconciliation with creation is enacted rather than (as here) trumpeted. An initiating, unself-conscious act of love—similar to the Ancient Mariner's blessing the watersnakes 'unaware'—enables the poet to find within the framework of individual poems, if only as a momentary object of desire, the unity with nature and God that he seeks.

The form of the conversation poem that Harper celebrated and imitated derives, as I said, from the casual rhythm of the poet's mind as it observes, experiences, muses, relates—sharing incidents and ideas, consistently or intermittently, with a loved one, while at the same time striving to make an intimate out of us, the readers. But though casual, seemingly accidental in their movement, each of the conversation poems is organised in ways that turn out to be far from casual, implicitly and explicitly using an immediate personal experience to dramatise issues of vital philosophical—or what Coleridge would have called 'metaphysical'—importance. In the best of the conversation poems, the seemingly accidental (associative) movement of the narrative and musing masks a sophisticated structural complexity. Later in his life, Coleridge would recognise that he had developed an original and influential genre:

3 Crossing Over: Samuel Taylor Coleridge and the Conversation Poems

> Let me be excused, if it should seem to others too mere a trifle to justify my noticing it—but I have some claim to the thanks of no small numbers of readers of poetry in having first introduced this species of short blank verse poems—of which Southey, Lamb, Wordsworth, and others have since produced so many exquisite specimens.[10]

'The Eolian Harp'

At the opening of 'The Eolian Harp: Composed at Clevedon, in Somersetshire' the unity with nature, achieved through the mediation of the named lover, Sara, is a *fait accompli* and, as with all the conversation poems, the compatibility of mind and nature is symbolised by the loving detail of the description:

> My pensive Sara! thy soft cheek reclined
> Thus on mine arm, most soothing sweet it is
> To sit beside our cot, our cot o'ergrown
> With white-flowered Jasmin, and the broad-leaved Myrtle,
> (Meet emblems they of Innocence and Love!)
> And watch the clouds, that late were rich with light,
> Slow saddening round, and mark the star of eve
> Serenely brilliant (such should wisdom be)
> Shine opposite! How exquisite the scents
> Snatched from yon bean-field! and the world so hush'd!
> The stilly murmur of the distant Sea
> Tells us of silence.
>
> (ll. 1–12)

'The attentiveness to the material world is such', to quote Ewan Jones, 'that paraphrases of its significance are reduced to two bursts of parenthesis'.[11] The poem then traces the wanderings of the poet's mind,

---

10 Coleridge's marginalia in a friend's copy of his *Sybilline Leaves* (1817), as quoted in *Poetical Works*, 1: 232.
11 Jones, '"Less Gross than Bodily": Materiality in Coleridge's Conversation Poem Sequence', 271-2.

instigated and informed by the interaction of the wind and the harp: the thoughts and 'phantasies', 'uncalled and undetained', that 'traverse' his

> indolent and passive brain
> As wild and various as the random gales
> That swell and flutter on this subject lute!
>
> (ll.41-43)

First it is erotic fantasy, with the provocative 'upbraiding' of the harp looking forward to the more serious sexual upbraiding of Sara's eye at the end of the poem. This dissolves into a folkloric fantasy and, if we ignore for the time being lines 26 to 33 that finally found their way into the poem in 1828 after an appearance in the *errata* of *Sibylline Leaves* (1817), the poem then moves with the drifting consciousness of the poet back to a specific time and place:

> on the midway slope
> Of yonder hill I stretch my legs at noon.
>
> (ll. 34-35)

Finally we have the famous pantheistic speculation for which the speaker is reproved:

> And what if all of animated nature
> Be but organic Harps diversely fram'd,
> That tremble into thought, as o'er them sweeps
> Plastic and vast, one intellectual breeze,
> At once the Soul of each, and God of all?
>
> (ll. 44-48)

The last sixteen lines of the poem represent a retreat to an orthodox Christian attitude which has frustrated criticism.[12] Indeed, the addition of lines 26 to 33—

---

12 Cp. M. H. Abrams: 'a timid and ineptly managed retreat to religious orthodoxy from the bold speculation of the middle of the poem', *The Correspondent Breeze: Essays on English Romanticism* (New York: W. W. Norton, 1984), 159.

3 Crossing Over: Samuel Taylor Coleridge and the Conversation Poems

> O! the one Life within us and abroad,
> Which meets all motion and becomes its soul,
> A light in sound, a sound-like power in light,
> Rhythm in all thought, and joyance everywhere—
> Methinks, it should have been impossible
> Not to love all things in a world so filled;
> Where the breeze warbles, and the mute still air
> Is Music slumbering on her instrument.

—suggests that they frustrated Coleridge himself, who would 'continuously revise the poem into something like philosophical compliance'.[13] As they stand, the lines manage to invalidate the dramatic conclusion of the poem by affirming the very pantheism the poet renounces at the close of the first version.[14]

Faced with a dilemma of Coleridge's own creation, criticism has chosen to stress the pantheism of the poem and treat the closing lines as an aberration for which the narrow-minded Sara is responsible. A knowledge of his and Sara Coleridge's disastrous marriage and our overriding interest in the poet's fragmented philosophical speculations have led us to emphasise what we imagine the poet *would like* to have said, had Sara not been there to reprove him. This, however, is to overlook the ambivalence Coleridge expressed throughout his career towards his own metaphysical speculation. Coleridge the thinker could be profoundly anti-intellectual. If this ambivalence is not recognised, not only is the meaning of 'The Eolian Harp' obscured, but the conversation poems as a group are robbed of their formal justification.

The fantasy and speculation of 'The Eolian Harp' represent not only a narrative development, but also a drifting away—from Sara and back into the self. Though motivated by an original harmony for which they are seeking analogues, the poet's musings are, ironically, both discordant in themselves and divisive. It is no accident that the poet finds himself alone on a hillside, tranquilly musing 'upon tranquillity'. This

---

13 Jones, '"Less Gross than Bodily": Materiality in Coleridge's Conversation Poem Sequence', 271.
14 See Humphry House, *Coleridge*, The Clark Lectures 1951–52 (London: Rupert Hart-Davies, 1953), 76–77.

casual 'flashback' hints at the sundering of the two lovers that occurs in the poem, and with it the sundering of the poet and his God. The ominous 'slow saddening' of the clouds in the opening lines has already suggested that the paradisal unity is tenuous, with the darkening of the day looking forward and back to a state of spiritual darkness ('Wildered and dark', l. 63). This only makes sense if we accept Coleridge's conviction that speculations of the kind he indulges in are 'shapings of the unregenerate mind' that cut him off from Sara, nature, and God, and that the search for intellectual enlightenment leads, paradoxically, to an emotional and spiritual darkness. He finds himself as he was before he achieved the harmony to which domestic peace with Sara had given him access: 'Wildered' or bewildered. It is a crucial word, and bewilderment a familiar state in spiritual autobiography of this kind.

Coleridge's protestations in a letter to his brother, George, that the 'dazzle of Wit' and a fondness for 'subtlety of Argument' had seduced him from the right religious path have been seen as a sign of Coleridge's unconscious conformity to the demands of the stronger, more orthodox personality.[15] (George was an Anglican minister.) But the renunciation of 'the dark & deep perplexities of metaphysic Controversy' is as familiar a feature of Coleridge's private notebooks as it is of his correspondence.[16] At its best, metaphysical speculation is impotent to cope with the emotional demands of privation and suffering:

> My philosophical refinements, & metaphysical Theories lay by me in the hour of anguish, as toys by the bedside of a Child deadly-sick. May God continue his visitations to my soul, bowing it down, till the pride & Laodicean self-confidence of human Reason be utterly done away.[17]

At its worst, it is physically destructive and emotionally crippling. Throughout his life, Coleridge recognised in 'philosophical refinements, & metaphysical Theories' a Circean charm that he came to

---

15   30 March 1794, *Coleridge Letters*, 1:78.
16   *The Notebooks of Samuel Taylor Coleridge*, ed. Kathleen Coburn et al., in 5 vols (London: Routledge & Kegan Paul, 1957–2002), 1, note 27 (c. 1795–96).
17   Letter to Benjamin Flower, [11 December 1796], *Coleridge Letters*, 1:267.

associate, rightly or wrongly, with opium, even speaking of it as an addiction. 'I am so *habituated* to philosophizing', he told Southey in December 1794, 'that I cannot divest myself of it even when my own Wretchedness is the subject'.[18] Like opium, it seemed to offer an initial release, while ultimately leading to disaster. This is the burden of 'Dejection: An Ode':

> not to think of what I needs must feel,
> But to be still and patient, all I can
>   And haply by abstruse research to steal
>   From my own nature all the natural man—
> This was my sole resource, my only plan:
> Till that which suits a part infects the whole,
> And now is almost grown the *habit* of my soul.
> (ll. 87-93, my emphasis)

'Abstruse research', attempting to unravel the 'perplexities of metaphysic Controversy', always had Faustian overtones for Coleridge—'the pride & Laodicean self-confidence of human Reason'—and he was never far away from the conviction that *'Incomprehensibility* is as necessary an attribute of the First Cause as Love, or Power, or Intelligence'.[19] 'The Eolian Harp' is neither the first nor the last time we hear him say that

> never guiltless may I speak of him,
> The Incomprehensible!
> (ll. 58-59)

Distinguishing between two kinds of knowledge in an early note, Coleridge asserts 'the superiority of the knowledge which we have by faith to the knowledge which we have by Natural philosophy'. Precisely where the superiority of faith lies is important to the conversation

---

18 11 December 1794, *Coleridge Letters*, 1:133 (my emphasis).
19 As he wrote in a letter to the Rev. John Edwards, 20 March 1796, *Coleridge Letters*, 1:193.

poems as a group: 'in its dignity, in its moral effects, & lastly in the comforting of sorrow, in the giving of New Joy, & the exaltation of natural pleasures'.[20] Joy would become the powerful, creative emotion that in 'Dejection: An Ode' enabled the poet to see *and* feel how beautiful the world around him was, thus enabling the 'exaltation of natural pleasures'.

Even more important is the statement in one of Coleridge's philosophical lectures that 'in joy all individuality is lost',[21] for it brings us back to the escape from the self that is the aspiration of these poems. In another early note, the same two kinds of knowledge help to distinguish between two kinds of life, the Human and the Divine:

> Human life—in which for the sake of our own Happiness ... & Glory we pursue studies and objects adapted to our intellectual faculties.
> Divine life—when we die to the creatures & to self and become deiform.[22]

The self-centredness of Coleridge's intellectual pursuits is also the theme of Wordsworth's description of his friend at Cambridge and analysis of 'the airy wretchedness / That battened on his youth' in the sixth book of *The Prelude*:

> I have thought
> Of Thee, thy learning, gorgeous eloquence,
> And all the strength and plumage of thy youth,
> Thy subtle speculations, toils abstruse
> Among the Schoolmen, and platonic forms
> Of wild ideal pageantry, shap'd out
> From things well-match'd, or ill, and words for things,

---

20 *The Notebooks of Samuel Taylor Coleridge*, 1, note 6.
21 *The Philosophical Lectures of S. T. Coleridge*, ed. Owen Barfield and Kathleen Coburn (Princeton, N. J.: Princeton University Press, 1949), 179.
22 *The Notebooks of Samuel Taylor Coleridge*, 1, note 256.

3 Crossing Over: Samuel Taylor Coleridge and the Conversation Poems

> The self-created sustenance of a mind
> Debarr'd from Nature's living images,
> Compell'd to be a life unto itself.[23]

Wordsworth, typically, stresses Coleridge's alienation from the natural world, but the disease is the same. Behind the passage lies the metaphor of the spider weaving from its own entrails, used in the Renaissance to satirise the elaborate and dubious speculation of the Schoolmen.

This pattern of paradise lost through metaphysical speculation, and regained through emotional attachment, was one that Coleridge consistently discovered in his own life, the action of 'The Eolian Harp' being but one example. It is with this pattern in mind that the final lines of the poem should be read:

> Well hast thou said and holily dispraised
> These shapings of the unregenerate mind;
> Bubbles that glitter as they rise and break
> On vain Philosophy's aye-babbling spring.
> For never guiltless may I speak of him,
> The Incomprehensible! save when with awe
> I praise him, and with Faith that inly feels;
> Who with his saving mercies healed me,
> A sinful and most miserable Man,
> Wildered and dark, and gave me to possess
> Peace, and this Cot, and thee, heart-honoured Maid!
>   (ll. 54–64)

Coleridge's occasional dread of the seductions of metaphysics may seem unjustified, even evasive, but it was real enough to the poet.

Probably the best known example occurs in the first chapter of the *Biographia Literaria* in a passage which supports my contention

---

23   *The Prelude* (1805–1806), Book VI, ll. 305–14. The text I am using is *The Poems of William Wordsworth: Collected Reading Texts from the Cornell Wordsworth Series*, 3 vols, ed. Jared Curtis (Penrith: Humanities Ebooks, LLP, 2009).

that a suspicion of abstract thought accounts for the very form of the conversation poems:

> At a very premature age, even before my fifteenth year, I had bewildered myself in metaphysicks, and in theological controversy. Nothing else pleased me. ... but from this I was auspiciously withdrawn, partly indeed by an accidental introduction to an amiable family, chiefly however, by the genial influence of a style of poetry, so tender and yet so manly, so natural and real, and yet so dignified, and harmonious, as the sonnets &c. of Mr. Bowles! Well were it for me perhaps, had I never relapsed into the same mental disease.[24]

Ironically, chapters five to thirteen of the *Biographia* will be preoccupied with just such 'metaphysicks' and 'theological controversy', but what concerns us in this passage is the lost and regained paradise and the key word 'bewildered'. The 'amiable family' is the Evans family (Mary Evans had been Coleridge's first love). Because it is a *literary* life that Coleridge is writing, however, the mention of Bowles—indeed the priority given to Bowles's poetry—has far-reaching literary implications. If we go back to 1794 and to Coleridge's analysis of the rescue effected by Bowles's poetry not long after the time he first read it, we find the same story:

> And when the *darker* day of life began,
> And I did roam, a thought-bewilder'd man!
> Thy kindred Lays an healing solace lent
> ('Sonnet: To Bowles', ll. 6–8)

Again, 'Wilder'd and dark', Coleridge finds salvation in the heart; Bowles was 'the first', according to the *Biographia*, who, with Cowper, 'reconciled the heart with the head'.[25] In the blending of thought and feeling in Bowles's poetry, Coleridge found a naturalness and ease which his own rhetorical and philosophical style lacked: 'I cannot

---

24 *Biographia Literaria*, ed. Engell and Bate, 1:15–17.
25 *Biographia Literaria*, ed. Engell and Bate, 1:16.

write without a *body* of *thought*—hence my *Poetry* is crowded and sweats beneath a heavy burthen of Ideas and Imagery! It has seldom Ease'.[26] Coleridge's rescue from too exclusive and self-centred an attention to theological and philosophical issues may seem regrettable in 'The Eolian Harp', but it motivated the conversation poems as a group.

'This Lime-Tree Bower My Prison'

As well as meaning an 'interchange of thoughts and words; familiar discourse and talk', *conversation* means (quoting the OED) 'the act of living or having one's being *in* or *among*', 'the action of consorting with others; living together; commerce, society, intimacy'. Coleridge had found all of this in July 1797 when he gathered around him at Nether Stowey in Somerset a set of intimate friends, new and old. There was Sara Coleridge, his wife, and baby Hartley Coleridge, born in September of the previous year. There was Tom Poole, patron, friend, and father figure whose house (and extensive library) could be reached through the back yard. Into this charmed circle, Coleridge welcomed Wordsworth and his sister Dorothy, with whom he had only recently struck up an intimacy, along with the friend of his London days, Charles Lamb, and John Thelwall, the radical orator and pamphleteer who had been arrested for treason and imprisoned in the Tower of London. This group of intimates was Coleridge's consolation prize for having failed to realise his dream of pantisocratic community on the banks of the Susquehanna in America.[27] Coleridge always claimed that love was 'the vital air of [his] Genius' and now he had it in abundance.[28]

Fittingly, then, 'This Lime-Tree Bower My Prison' is paradigmatic of the Coleridgean conversation poem, and of the way it enacts at the level of language and form the very values it appears to discover in the

---

26   Coleridge to Southey, 11 December 1794, *Coleridge Letters*, 1:137.
27   See Richard Holmes, *Coleridge: Early Visions* (London: Hodder & Stoughton, 1989), 60–99.
28   *Coleridge Letters*, 1:471.

course of its own developmental narrative. It offers the clearest example of all the conversation poems of the redeeming power of love, in which an escape from the self becomes both a poetic technique and a moral and spiritual imperative. The poem begins on a note of petulant self-preoccupation and complaint, with the casual particularity of the poet's imprisonment within the lime-tree bower suggesting his imprisonment within the self:

> Well, they are gone, and here must I remain
> This lime-tree bower my prison! I have lost
> Beauties and feelings, such as would have been
> Most sweet to my remembrance.
>
> (ll. 1-4)

Isolated by a scalded foot and pricked by envy and resentment, the poet in his imagination unwittingly—spontaneously—begins to retrace the journey of his friends, first, down 'the still roaring dell', and then out under 'the wide wide heaven'. By the time the poet feels specifically for, and with, the 'gladness' of his friend—'My gentle-hearted Charles' (l. 28)—all thought of his own discomfort has been lost in sympathy for the 'evil and pain / And strange calamity' from which Charles is imagined to emerge.

Charles's journey has become the poet's own, in more ways than one. The naturalistic detail of the poet's imaginative descent into the purgatorial 'roaring dell' reveals an absorption in the minutiae of the natural world that has replaced his initial absorption in his own vexations, anticipating the spiritual liberation he will undergo:

> The roaring dell, o'erwooded, narrow, deep,
> And only speckled by the mid-day sun;
> Where its slim trunk the ash from rock to rock
> Flings arching like a bridge;—that branchless ash,
> Unsunned and damp, whose few poor yellow leaves
> Ne'er tremble in the gale, yet tremble still,
> Fanned by the water-fall! and there my friends
> Behold the dark green file of long lank weeds,

3 Crossing Over: Samuel Taylor Coleridge and the Conversation Poems

> That all at once (a most fantastic sight!)
> Still nod and drip beneath the dripping edge
> Of the blue clay-stone.
>
> (ll. 10–20)

This loving attention to detail, it will be noted, is all vicarious, all on behalf of Charles. His anticipation of Charles's aesthetic gratification in a rush of sympathetic identification becomes, in turn, the poet's imaginative gift or offering, inspired by the unconscious act of love which is his point of departure from an isolated (incarcerated) self.

There are in fact four journeys alluded to here, some more imaginative than others. There is, firstly, the historical journey undertaken by Charles Lamb, Sara Coleridge, and William and Dorothy Wordsworth. This takes place outside the poem and the poet's imagination. Secondly, there is the poet's imaginative recreation of that journey, undertaken on their behalf. Thirdly, there is Charles's symbolic journey from pain to gladness, from the city (darkness, imprisonment) to nature (freedom and light). And last but not least, there is the poet's own spiritual journey—*via* the journey he imagines for Charles—from self-centred isolation (darkness, imprisonment) to selfless participation in nature and God (freedom and light).

Much of the 'argument' of 'This Lime-Tree Bower My Prison' is carried on by what might otherwise appear merely realistic or incidental imagery, especially by the compound image of the sun and sunlight. Just as the poet begins isolated and cut off, so the 'roaring dell' is 'only speckled by the mid-day sun', while the 'branchless ash'—'*Unsunn'd*', note—hovers in a kind of 'darkness visible'. Once under 'the wide wide heaven', however, the poet wills everything to live 'in yellow light':

> Shine in the slant beams of the sinking orb,
> Ye purple heath-flowers! richlier burn, ye clouds!
> Live in the yellow light, ye distant groves!
> And kindle, thou blue ocean! So my Friend
> Struck with deep joy may stand, as I have stood,
> Silent with swimming sense; yea, gazing round
> On the wide landscape, gaze till all doth seem
> Less gross than bodily; and of such hues

> As veil the Almighty Spirit, when yet he makes
> Spirits perceive his presence.
>
> (ll. 34–43)

'Let there be light', said Coleridge, 'and there was light'. And '*it was good*'.

Not only is the landscape that Coleridge conjures in his imaginative journey transformed by the sunlight, but the very bower which had once been a prison becomes witness to the translucence of God in his creation: 'Pale beneath the blaze / Hung the transparent foliage' (ll. 47–8). This access of sunlight through the 'transparent foliage' spells the dissolution of the imprisoning bower and the release of the prisoner. The prison becomes a bower again as the poet comes home. The poet's act of love for Charles and for the natural world participates in the divine love he can now see sustaining all existence, as the sun sustains the natural world. 'Man knows God only by revelation from God', remarked Coleridge in his notebooks in the same year, 'as we see the sun by his own light'.[29]

In a final, brilliant image, a lone rook—a black, traditionally raucous and ugly bird, symbolising death—is momentarily swallowed up by the sun, gathered into the 'one Life':

> when the last rook
> Beat its straight path along the dusky air
> Homewards, I blest it! deeming its black wing
> (Now a dim speck, now vanishing in light)
> Had cross'd the mighty Orb's dilated glory
> While thou stood'st gazing
>
> (ll. 68–73)

The poet, Charles, and the rook, all with a life of their own, establish covenant or community in this last triangular gesture and become one life. The creaking of the bird's wing, once 'dissonant' like the opening

---

29 *The Notebooks of Samuel Taylor Coleridge*, 1, note 209.

3 Crossing Over: Samuel Taylor Coleridge and the Conversation Poems

mood of the lonely and resentful poet, is now subsumed into a larger harmony: 'No sound is dissonant which tells of Life' (l. 76).

But the significance of the sunlit landscape of 'This Lime-Tree Bower My Prison' does not end here. Implicit in the transformation is an association that Coleridge the literary theorist would make explicitly between the 'plastic', modifying power of the human imagination and the creative and sustaining power of God. The sunlit landscape of 'This Lime-Tree Bower My Prison'—the 'deep radiance' tingeing the walnut tree and 'full on the ancient ivy'; the 'dilated glory' of the setting sun (ll. 51–53, 72)—represents, as well as divine unity, a world transformed by the poet's imagination.

'Frost at Midnight'

Another thing, besides poetry, for which the years 1797–1798 were distinguished in Coleridge's career was autobiography. After the turbulent political years, he was taking stock for the first time, composing himself as he would do again in 1815 when he dictated his *Biographia Literaria* or Literary Life. This time, however, he wrote privately—for himself and for Tom Poole—a long series of letters about his early life growing up in Ottery St Mary in Devonshire and, later, at Christ's Hospital School in London. Having stirred up past memories in this way, it is hardly surprising that some of his poetry should share incidents and images and emotions with the autobiographical letters and attempt to assimilate and imaginatively to recast the past. The result was the finest of his conversation poems, 'Frost at Midnight', and the journey it enacts is another version of the long journey home—to an idea of home that undergoes vital intensification and redefinition in the poem.

'Frost at Midnight' has the same pattern of redemption from self-centred 'solitude' (l. 5) that we see in 'The Eolian Harp' and 'This Lime-Tree Bower My Prison'—only it is less confused than the former and less melodramatic and self-righteous than the latter—and the same reconciliation of apparent informality with tight formal organisation, and of minute natural detail with philosophical significance. The main difference between 'This Lime-Tree Bower My Prison' and 'Frost at

Midnight' is that in 'Frost at Midnight' the redemptive journey undertaken by the poet is through time as well as space.

The poem begins with the landscape in the grip of a frozen calmness that, for the poet, is almost preternatural, Gothic—in the sense of the invasion of the home or *homely* by the uncanny (the *unheimlich* or unhomely). Far from pacifying the poet, as we might expect, the solitude and frozen calmness, punctuated by explosions of sound, only disturbs and agitates him:

> The Frost performs its secret ministry,
> Unhelped by any wind. The owlet's cry
> Came loud—and hark, again! loud as before.
> The inmates of my cottage, all at rest,
> Have left me to this solitude, which suits
> Abstruser musings: save that at my side
> My cradled infant slumbers peacefully.
> 'Tis calm indeed! so calm, that it disturbs
> And vexes meditation with its strange
> And extreme silentness.
>
> (ll. 1–10)

The poet's restlessness betrays the extent to which he is out of phase with the natural world. His child, on the other hand, slumbering 'peacefully', is identified with a universal calm that suggests not death, but hibernation, a slumbering latency. The 'sole unquiet thing' is *not* the film 'which fluttered on the grate' (l. 15), of course, but the poet himself. An 'idling Spirit' (l. 20), 'unquiet', ill at ease, he projects his dissonant mood onto the film. All the while, however, 'The frost performs its secret ministry', a secret that is only revealed—and then obliquely—in the final image or images of the poem.

Then, in one of the subtlest transitions in all the conversation poems, the second verse paragraph moves to memories of the poet's schooldays:

3 Crossing Over: Samuel Taylor Coleridge and the Conversation Poems

> But O! how oft,
> How oft, at school, with most believing mind,
> Presageful, have I gazed upon the bars,
> To watch that fluttering *stranger!* and as oft
> With unclosed lids, already had I dreamt
> Of my sweet birth-place, and the old church-tower,
> Whose bells, the poor man's only music, rang
> From morn to evening, all the hot Fair-day,
> So sweetly, that they stirred and haunted me
> With a wild pleasure, falling on mine ear
> Most like articulate sounds of things to come!
> So gazed I, till the soothing things, I dreamt,
> Lulled me to sleep, and sleep prolonged my dreams!
> And so I brooded all the following morn,
> Awed by the stern preceptor's face, mine eye
> Fixed with mock study on my swimming book:
> Save if the door half opened, and I snatched
> A hasty glance, and still my heart leaped up,
> For still I hoped to see the *stranger's* face,
> Townsman, or aunt, or sister more beloved,
> My play-mate when we both were clothed alike!
> (ll. 23–43)

The connection is obvious enough in one sense: watching the film, the poet recalls the superstition that 'the films were called *strangers* and supposed to portend the arrival of some absent friend' and this, in turn, reminds him of the number of anxious hours he spent as a schoolboy at boarding school in London yearning for the arrival of someone he loved. But the film dancing on the grate not only prompts the recollection, it also expresses in the form of a paradox the imaginative journey from estrangement to love and reconciliation that the poet will undergo. The film, though called a *stranger*, is believed to usher in someone familiar, not a stranger at all but an estranged loved one.

But the recollection of childhood also hints at a complex relationship between the state of the poet now, as expressed in the uncanny stillness of the opening twenty-three lines, and the state of the poet then, as a Christ's Hospital schoolchild. From his isolation as a meditative adult we have moved to his isolation as a child. The memory is both evocative and explanatory, establishing the continuity of human life and personality while at the same time suggesting the way in which (in Wordsworth's fine phrase) 'the child is father to the man'. The anxious, isolated child has fathered or given birth to the poet. The 'orphaned' Coleridge, dispatched and signed over to Christ's Hospital, lives on in the lonely, alienated adult of the poem's opening.

There is, however, still another and for our purposes more vital transition taking place in this movement between the two verse paragraphs. From the slumbering baby (his child Hartley) we have moved to Coleridge the child. We are being prepared for the elaborate *chiasmus* or crossover that will take place in the poem. *Chiasmus—chi* as an X—is a syntactic (and conceptual) reversal used to sharpen the sense and contrast the ideas conveyed, as in John F. Kennedy's famous injunction to the American people: 'ask not what your country can do for you, but what you can do for your country'. Again, 'we don't live to eat but eat to live' and 'when the going gets tough, the tough get going', and so on. The most effective or expressive chiastic figures turn on a more or less surprising inversion of priorities or hierarchies. In 'Frost at Midnight' the *chiasmus* is structural and effects the reversal and substitution of one generation for and by another that is the poem's recognition and the poem's triumph. The poet Coleridge's priority subtly gives way to that of his child, Hartley. 'This is my beloved Son, in whom I am well pleased' (Matthew 3:17)—it spells self-effacement and succession.

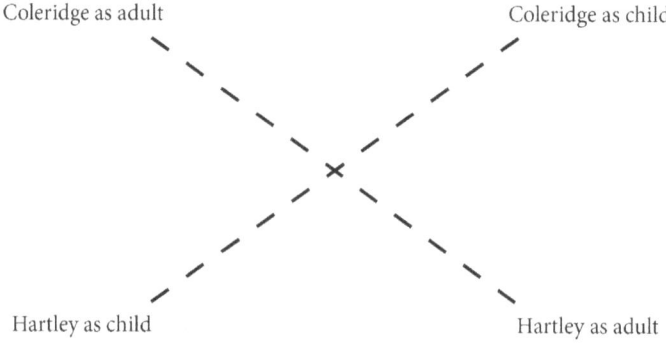

3 Crossing Over: Samuel Taylor Coleridge and the Conversation Poems

Accordingly, the poem returns to the present—to the poet's 'Dear Babe, that sleepest cradled by my side' (l. 44)—and the poet begins the now familiar movement out of the self. A preoccupation with his own isolation, present and past, changes into a promise to his child that he (his child) will not suffer as the poet himself has suffered. 'I was reared', says the poet, deprived of love and Nature:

> In the great city, pent 'mid cloisters dim,
> And saw nought lovely but the sky and stars.
> But *thou*, my babe! shalt wander like the breeze
> By lakes and sandy shores, beneath the crags
> Of ancient mountain, and beneath the clouds,
> Which image in their bulk both lakes and shores
> And mountain crags.
>
> (ll. 51–58)

The reflexivity of lake and sky (the one the 'image' of the other) suggests not only the integrated environment (or ecology) of the countryside but also the more complex reflexivity (the inverted image) of poet and child, subject and object.

Coleridge describes himself as a youth with eyes 'Fixed with mock study on a swimming book' (l. 38), unable in his anxiety to focus on the language of men. His son, Hartley, on the other hand, shall 'see and hear'

> The lovely shapes and sounds intelligible
> Of that eternal language, which thy God
> Utters.
>
> (ll. 58–61)

Through his child, the poet, once homeless and unhomely (*unheimlich*), has rediscovered a home in the world. The personal pronouns say it all. After the reference to 'my babe' in line 54, the first person pronoun disappears altogether, an extraordinary thing in a lyric poem and an index of the success of the poet's self-effacing act of love. (Coleridge carefully removed six anecdotal lines from the end of the first version because 'they destroy the rondo, and return upon itself of the Poem', which 'ought to lie coiled with its tail round its head'.[30]) The best index of all, then, is the beautiful and moving combination of prayer and benediction with which the poem closes:

> Therefore all seasons shall be sweet to thee,
> Whether the summer clothe the general earth
> With greenness, or the redbreast sit and sing
> Betwixt the tufts of snow on the bare branch
> Of mossy apple-tree, while the nigh thatch
> Smokes in the sun-thaw; whether the eave-drops fall
> Heard only in the trances of the blast,
> Or if the secret ministry of frost
> Shall hang them up in silent icicles,
> Quietly shining to the quiet Moon.
>
> (ll. 65–74)

The third line 'has *loud* twice', as Graham Pechey observes, 'the last line of all has *quiet* twice': 'the poem is framed antithetically by these opposites of the ear'.[31] Looking out of and beyond his own isolation in the present and the past and into his child's future, the poet is at last able to see *and* feel the beauty of the world. The frost, like the sunlit landscape of 'This Lime-Tree Bower My Prison', has transformed the landscape, as has Coleridge's imagination, regenerated by love and faith. Coleridge has become part of the landscape. No longer the 'stranger'—the outsider and the 'sole unquiet thing'—he has now been assimilated into Nature, and the contrasting quietude is stressed: '*Quietly* shining to the *quiet* Moon'.

But if the poet has been assimilated into the landscape, so, too, has the landscape been assimilated by the poet. After all, the landscape with which 'Frost at Midnight' closes is not an actual landscape but an imagined or projected landscape—a landscape of desire. As Ewan Jones

---

30 See *Poetical Works*, 1:456n
31 Graham Pechey, '"Frost at Midnight" and the Poetry of Periphrasis', in *The Cambridge Quarterly*, 41:2 (2012), 229–44 (235).

argues, 'the now-archaic subjunctive'—'whether' (l. 66)—'imagines an extended, meticulous world that hovers between possibility and manifestation'.[32] In his vision of his son's future, Coleridge has unified the four seasons and the four elements,[33] present and future, man and child, God and Nature. A fitting end for a long, imaginative journey home.

Coleridge's conversation poems take isolation to be a kind of psycho-spiritual disease (dis-ease, 'unquiet') to be overcome by a mind working in concert with God and nature. They enact and celebrate their own triumph over alienation and loneliness. In a more sceptical, more critical age like our own, conditioned as we are by psychoanalysis and various forms of ideological critique to prefer latent over manifest content, we have become suspicious of the conscious affirmations and willed transcendence of 'This Lime-Tree Bower My Prison' and 'Frost at Midnight'. Not surprisingly, then, it is for us the spiritual and psychological condition of alienation and loneliness that in *The Rime of the Ancient Mariner* Coleridge's poetry expresses most powerfully, most convincingly.

---

[32] Jones, '"Less Gross than Bodily": Materiality in Coleridge's Conversation Poem Sequence', 279.
[33] Pechey, '"Frost at Midnight" and the Poetry of Periphrasis', 241.

4
'The burden of the mystery': William Wordsworth's 'Tintern Abbey'

Wordsworth criticism has yet to come to terms with Keats's observation that the 'Lines written a few miles above Tintern Abbey, On revisiting the banks of the Wye during a tour, July 13, 1798' (hereafter 'Tintern Abbey') proved Wordsworth's 'Genius' to be 'explorative of those dark passages' of human life—an observation made the more challenging by Keats's contingent suggestion that it is precisely in this that 'Wordsworth is deeper than Milton'.[1] There can be little doubt that the observation was, in part at least, a projection of Keats's own sense of direction and poetic responsibility—'Now if we live, and go on thinking', the letter continues, 'we too shall explore them'—but his focusing on the disturbing aspects of 'Tintern Abbey' is itself disturbing, especially when a cursory reading suggests that precisely the opposite is the case, and that the poem sounds a barely qualified note of optimism, even triumph. Certainly, Wordsworth himself would have us believe that 'Tintern Abbey' is a poem of emancipation and enlightenment, discovering and celebrating the harmony—more than that, the pantheistic unity—of man and nature, as his friend Coleridge had done in the conversation poems 'This Lime-Tree Bower My Prison' and 'Frost at

---

1 See Keats's letter to J. H. Reynolds, 3 May 1818, in *The Letters of John Keats 1814–1821*, ed. Hyder Edward Rollins, 2 vols (Cambridge, Mass.: Harvard University Press, 1958), 1:281.

Midnight'.[2] Indeed, on one level or at one stage at least, 'Tintern Abbey' represents an *escape* from the 'dark passages' of life—an escape, literally and metaphorically, from 'lonely rooms ... mid the din / Of towns and cities' (ll. 26-27), in which the poet has felt most acutely 'the burthen of the mystery' and 'the heavy and the weary weight / Of all this unintelligible world' (ll. 39-41).[3] In a therapeutic movement that is, by turns, outwards (escape) and upwards (transcendence), the poet identifies the countryside as at once the cause, the condition, and the symbol of his own salvation. How can it be, then, that a poem which rises to an unprecedented and unparalleled exaltation of nature—

> The anchor of my purest thoughts, the nurse
> The guide, the guardian of my heart, and soul
> Of all my moral being
>
> (ll. 110-12)

—could strike Wordsworth's younger contemporary, Keats, as in any way preoccupied with exploring the 'dark passages' of human life?

'Emotional and ideational changes'

'Written' or 'Composed' in 1798 and published as the last poem in the first edition of *Lyrical Ballads* later that year, 'Tintern Abbey' on first reading stands out in—even outside—the volume that first brought it to public attention, as distinct in its own way as *The Rime of the Ancyent Marinere* with which the *Lyrical Ballads* opened.[4] It has even

---

2 On the similarities between Coleridge's 'Frost at Midnight' and Wordsworth's 'Tintern Abbey', see Mary Jacobus, *Tradition and Experiment in Wordsworth's 'Lyrical Ballads 1798'* (Oxford: Oxford University Press, 1976), 118-25.
3 Unless otherwise noted, I am using *The Poems of William Wordsworth: Collected Readings from the Cornell Wordsworth*, ed. Jared Curtis, 3 vols (Penrith: Humanities-Ebooks, 2009) for all quotations from Wordsworth's poetry.
4 See Robert Mayo, 'The Contemporaneity of the *Lyrical Ballads*' in A. R. Jones and William Tydeman (eds), *Wordsworth: Lyrical Ballads*, Casebook Series (London: Macmillan, 1972), 85-86.

been suggested that Wordsworth's decision to close the volume with the hurriedly composed and only recently completed 'Tintern Abbey' was inspired by a need he felt to offer an antidote or corrective to the sustained and indisputably 'dark passages' of Coleridge's major contribution.[5] The poem's loco-descriptive form; its apparently spontaneous personal voice, modulating from recollection to meditation and from meditation to inspiration and resolution; its quintessentially Wordsworthian blank verse—these are the commonplaces of the critical tradition and in the context of the *Lyrical Ballads* of 1798 are peculiar to 'Tintern Abbey'.[6]

What the poem does have in common with Wordsworth's other contributions to *Lyrical Ballads* is the paradoxical status of being at once highly derivative and highly innovative: derivative, in that the poem is rooted in the eighteenth-century recollective, topographical tradition of Thomson, Warton, Akenside, Cowper, Bowles, Crowe, Rogers, and even Goldsmith;[7] innovative in its fusion of a natural with a mental and remembered landscape, as well as in the audacity or unapologetic reach of its 'impassioned, lofty and sustained diction',[8] identified by Coleridge in his *Biographia Literaria* as commensurate with its 'philosophic' theme:

---

5   See Geoffrey Little, 'Forms of Beauty, Loops of Time—Wordsworth's "Tintern Abbey"', in *Arts* (The Journal of the Sydney University Arts Association), 12 (1984), 60–82 (60).
6   Wordsworth's note to the 1800 edition of *Lyrical Ballads* raises the possibility of 'Tintern Abbey''s being an ode: 'I have written in the hope that in the transitions, and in the impassioned music of the versification, will be found the principal requisites of that species of composition', *William Wordsworth*, The Oxford Authors, ed. Stephen Gill (Oxford: Oxford University Press, 1990), 692.
7   See, for example, Mary Jacobus, *Tradition and Experiment in Wordsworth's Lyrical Ballads (1798)* (Oxford: Oxford University Press, 1976), 104–18. Alan Rawes offers the generic context of the eighteenth-century ode in 'Romantic Form and New Historicism: Wordsworth's "Lines Written a Few Miles above Tintern Abbey"', in his edition, *Romanticism and Form* (Basingstoke: Palgrave Macmillan, 2007), 95–115 (98–109).
8   *Biographia Literaria*, The Collected Works of Samuel Taylor Coleridge, 7, ed. James Engell and W. Jackson Bate, in 2 vols (Princeton, N. J.: Princeton University Press, 1983), 2:8.

> I have felt
> A presence that disturbs me with the joy
> Of elevated thoughts; a sense sublime
> Of something far more deeply interfused,
> Whose dwelling is the light of setting suns,
> And the round ocean, and the living air,
> And the blue sky, and in the mind of man,
> A motion and a spirit, that impels
> All thinking things, all objects of all thought,
> And rolls through all things. Therefore am I still
> A lover of the meadows and the woods,
> And mountains; and of all that we behold
> From this green earth; of all the mighty world
> Of eye and ear, both what they half-create,
> And what perceive.
>
> (ll. 94–108)

Yet it has long been recognised that 'Tintern Abbey' is more (and more subtle) than just a consummate expression, 'hypnotic and incantatory,'[9] of Wordsworth's early and short-lived pantheism (and, consequently, of the influence of Coleridge). What Keats registers in his letter to Reynolds is *not* this celebration of nature and its immanent, unifying spirit, but an anxiety or doubt that remains unresolved, even unmitigated, by the cumulative and powerful conviction of this passage. For Nicholas Roe, 'The poet's voice and vision are troubled, hesitant and conditional in mood.'[10] 'Read as an ode,' writes Alan Rawes, 'Tintern Abbey' reads 'like a poem that sets out to dramatise a tension between an interest in private visionary experience and an ongoing concern with—anxiety about, perhaps—social actualities and that brings these into dialogue and confrontation with each other, allowing each to clash, modify and counter the other'.[11]

---

9   Northrop Frye, *Anatomy of Criticism* (Princeton, N. J.: Princeton University Press, 1957), 327.
10 Nicholas Roe, *The Politics of Nature: William Wordsworth and Some Contemporaries*, second edition (Basingstoke: Palgrave, 2002), 169.
11 Rawes, 'Romantic Form and New Historicism', 102.

4 'The burden of the mystery': William Wordsworth's 'Tintern Abbey'

What Keats registers and respects, I would argue, is Wordsworth's determination to keep faith with the complexity of human experience in and over time—what in his 'Essay, Supplementary to the Preface' of 1815 Wordsworth will call 'transient shocks of conflicting feeling and successive assemblages of contradictory thoughts'.[12] 'Man, anywhere, anytime, betrays in minute emotional and ideational changes', writes Erik Erikson, 'an ever-present conflict manifested in a change of mood from vague anxious depression through what Freud referred to as "a certain in-between" stage to heightened well-being—and back'.[13] 'Tintern Abbey' is not a manifesto, however compelling its expression of 'heightened well-being'—the 'joy / Of elevated thoughts' (ll. 95)—and its 'sense sublime' of active participation in some divine unity (sense, note: intimation, impression, intuition). Instead, the poem represents a struggle to come to terms with identity and relationship; a struggle, of varying and equivocal success, to convert depression into self-possession and loss into power and transcendence. And that struggle—on behalf of himself and his sister, as well as indirectly on behalf of the reader—figures in the poem as a literal and metaphorical journey through time and change: Keats's 'dark passages'.

To overlook time and change in the poem and read it as a unified, spontaneous affirmation is to overlook what is at once the condition and part of the object of the poem's exploration, not to say its informing obsession. From the opening lines, in which the poet reveals the psychological element of time and quietly portends the temporal element of psychological loss and change—

> Five years have passed, five summers
> With the length of five long winters

—to the closing benediction for his sister—

---

12   *The Prose Works of William Wordsworth*, ed. W. J. B. Owen and Jane Worthington Smyser, 3 vols (Oxford: Clarendon, 1974), 3:63.
13   See Erik H. Erikson's paper 'Ego Development and Historical Change: Clinical Notes', in his selected papers entitled *Identity and the Life Cycle*, in *Psychological Issues*, 1:1, monograph I (New York: International Universities Press, 1959), 18–49 (24).

> Nor wilt thou then forget
> That after many wanderings, many years
> Of absence, these steep woods and lofty cliffs,
> And this green pastoral landscape, were to me
> More dear, both for themselves, and for thy sake

—the consciousness of time and its co-ordinate, place (location and dislocation), is pervasive, as are the emotions of loss and regret, triggering reactive surmises and resolutions. What we learn from the poem's exploration is that the 'fall' into selfhood or personal identity in Wordsworth is—as it had been for the theologian and as it would be for the psychoanalyst—a fall from (the sense of) eternity into (a sense of) time, with its inevitable concomitants: separation, decay, and death. But this is to get ahead of myself.

Conflating the different stages of life

The initial result of the poet's struggle with time and its dark implications in 'Tintern Abbey' is a disorientation from which he never quite recovers. To isolate just one example from the extensive physical, psychological, and metaphysical landscape of the poem, we can cite the opening lines of what one recent critic has characterised as the 'remarkably (and deliberately) obscure' fourth verse paragraph (ll. 59–112).[14] The poet confesses to having turned in spirit to the river Wye ever since his first visit when, as a 'wanderer through the woods' (l. 57), he came to resemble the river itself. Having thus paid his respects to the 'sylvan Wye' as redemptive through recollection or *mental* revisiting, he proceeds to record his response to the memories evoked by the actual *physical* revisiting which is the occasion of the poem:

---

14 Sara L. Pearson, 'Allusive Pursuits: The Song of Songs in Wordsworth's "Tintern Abbey"', *Studies in Romanticism*, 53:2 (Summer 2014), 195–216 (195).

4 'The burden of the mystery': William Wordsworth's 'Tintern Abbey'

> And now, with gleams of half-extinguish'd thought,
> With many recognitions dim and faint,
> And somewhat of a sad perplexity,
> The picture of the mind revives again
>
> (ll. 59–62)

What we are dealing with is a mental landscape ('The picture of my mind') *superimposed* upon a present landscape, vision supervening upon vista. 'The operative memories are not distinctive landmarks, but the altogether more instinctive memories of a previous experience of looking', to quote Heather Glen, 'the inarticulate memories of looking that are latent in all perception are being brought to the surface and made conscious'.[15] The consequence is 'a sad perplexity' or—to be accurate where Wordsworth is vague or puzzled—'*somewhat of* a sad perplexity'. 'Sad' could mean 'settled' or 'serious' (OED), which would be entirely in keeping with the poet's mature vision.[16] But why 'perplexity'?

Only the poem can answer that question, as well as the questions of why such perplexity should give way to 'present pleasure' (l. 65) and of how convincingly it does so. One explanation of the 'perplexity' would seem to be that this complex revisiting has invoked the double consciousness to which Wordsworth alludes in *The Prelude*:

> so wide appears
> The vacancy between me and those days
> Which yet have such self presence in my mind
> That sometimes when I think of them I seem
> Two consciousnesses—conscious of myself
> And of some other being.
>
> (*The Prelude* [1805–6], 2:28–33)

---

15 Heather Glen, *Vision and Disenchantment. Blake's 'Songs' and Wordsworth's 'Lyrical Ballads'* (Cambridge: Cambridge University Press, 1983), 252.
16 See OED reference, which cites the expression 'sadder and wiser' from the last stanza of *The Ancient Mariner*.

If so, the 'two consciousnesses' that in 'Tintern Abbey' momentarily perplex the poet remind us that it is not only the world of urban chaos that is 'unintelligible'. While there can be no doubt that some clarity of purpose attends upon the poet's release from the city as prison, we are not dealing with a simple contrast between urban alienation (or self-alienation), on the one hand, and rural reintegration on the other. Indeed, the coveted emancipation only reveals deeper conflicts within the poet himself from this moment onwards, and the discrepancy between the two consciousnesses that has resulted from change and personal development charges the poem with an ambivalence towards time and growth.

This ambivalence leaves its mark on Wordsworth's description of the distinct phases of experience, foremost being the phase of undifferentiated consciousness experienced by the poet on his first visit to the Wye valley. (I am using the psychoanalytic term 'undifferentiated consciousness' loosely to characterise any period in the poet's life when his sense of belonging in, and identification with, nature was exigent and intense, whether or not it overwhelmed his ego.[17]) When 'first I came among these hills', the poet recalls—bounding 'like a roe' over mountains and along rivers, 'wherever nature led'—he was

> more like a man
> Flying from something that he dreads, than one
> Who sought the thing he loved.
>
> (ll. 71–73)

The use of such a negative simile to describe nature's attraction for him confirms a tendency to equivocation, at once grammatical and psychological, in the poem as a whole. How far is the poet *like*, how far is he

---

17 'I was often unable to think of external things as having external existence', Wordsworth noted to Isabella Fenwick, 'and I communed with all I saw as something not apart from but inherent in my own immaterial nature. Many times while going to school have I grasped at a wall or tree to recall myself from this abyss of idealism to the reality', as quoted in Mary Moorman, *William Wordsworth: A Biography*, Vol. 1, *The Early Years 1770–1803* (Oxford: Oxford University Press, 1957), 41–42.

4 'The burden of the mystery': William Wordsworth's 'Tintern Abbey'

unlike, a man in flight? The comparison and allusion here, as Sara Pearson points out, is to the erotic pastoral of the Biblical Song of Songs: 'The voice of my beloved! behold, he cometh leaping upon the mountains, skipping upon the hills. My beloved is like a roe or a young hart' (Song of Solomon 2:8–9). However, unlike the lover in the Song of Songs—seeking 'whom my soul loveth' (3:2)—the young Wordsworth is in flight.[18]

As it happens, by intimating that the poet's participation in the natural world was joyfully self-oblivious and at the same time morally dubious, the image of 'a man' fleeing what he dreads rather than seeking what he loves has a striking, though complex, propriety. Besides capturing the urgency of the poet's breathless self-indulgence, for example, it reiterates the central opposition of the poem between imprisonment—trauma? responsibility? conscience? time itself?—and the freedom or escape offered by nature, while suggesting that such conceptual oppositions were beyond the poet's understanding at the time. On top of this, the passage enacts and anticipates the anticlimactic movement of the poet *in the present* from the city he dreads to a nature whose solace remains equivocal. Embraced without thought and fellow-feeling, nature is only a fool's paradise deriving value not from what it is, but from what it is not.

The realisation on the poet's part that nature has been used as an escape in the past, and may be used as an escape again, can only contribute to his present 'perplexity'. (The latent distrust that he feels towards pantheism also arises from a suspicion that he may be rationalising his escaping from a reality he dreads.) Certainly this is where conflict and ambivalence become most apparent, and where their relevance to Wordsworth's struggle to achieve some understanding in 'all this unintelligible world' (l. 41) is beyond dispute. In spite of his attempts to identify and reconstruct at least three phases of experience, the poet betrays an emotional and conceptual imprecision that results in what is literally a con*fusion* of memories, confirming (among other things) the powerful, often distortive psychological aspect of our experience both in and of time:

---

18 Pearson, 'Allusive Pursuits: The Song of Songs in Wordsworth's "Tintern Abbey"', 202–203. Pearson reads a hidden allusion here to the poet's guilt over having abandoned Annette Vallon and their daughter, Caroline.

> here I stand, not only with the sense
> Of present pleasure, but with pleasing thoughts
> That in this moment there is life and food
> For future years. And so I dare to hope
> Though changed, no doubt, from what I was, when first
> I came among these hills; when like a roe
> I bounded o'er the mountains, by the sides
> Of the deep rivers, and the lonely streams,
> Wherever nature led; more like a man
> Flying from something that he dreads, than one
> Who sought the thing he loved. For nature then
> (The coarser pleasures of my boyish days,
> And their glad animal movements all gone by,)
> To me was all in all.—I cannot paint
> What then I was. The sounding cataract
> Haunted me like a passion: the tall rock,
> The mountain, and the deep and gloomy wood,
> Their colours and their forms, were then to me
> An appetite: a feeling and a love,
> That had no need of a remoter charm,
> By thought supplied, or any interest
> Unborrowed from the eye.
>
> (ll. 64–84)

The recollection of the poet's earlier self, for whom the eye was dictatorial and nature 'all in all', raises the question of that past self's precise relationship with the present self (the speaker of the poem). Mary Jacobus, comparing 'Tintern Abbey' with Coleridge's 'Frost at Midnight', simply refers to the past selves recollected by the two poets as their 'younger selves'.[19] But how much younger? The reader could surely be forgiven for thinking that the contrast between the two consciousnesses that Wordsworth draws here is a contrast between the poet *as a child* and the poet as a twenty-eight-year-old surveying the landscape of his distant past, given that the characterisation of his 'former heart'

---

19 Jacobus, *Tradition and Experiment*, 124.

4 'The burden of the mystery': William Wordsworth's 'Tintern Abbey'

or self in 'Tintern Abbey' bears such a close resemblance in its activity and consciousness to the child of *The Prelude*. Indeed, a passage from the Alfoxden Notebook of 1798 describes revisiting the scene of past ramblings in terms remarkably similar to the opening and other lines of 'Tintern Abbey':

> Yet once again do I behold the forms
> Of these huge mountains, and yet once again,
> Standing beneath these elms, I hear thy voice,
> Beloved Derwent, that peculiar voice
> Heard in the stillness of the evening air,
> Half-heard and half-created.[20]

Yet if Wordsworth has not suddenly invented a visit to the Wye Valley prior to the one 'five years' previously—and both the subtitle of the poem and various, specific references suggest a precision about dating—then in the portrait of 'what then I was' the artist is not a child at all, but a young man of twenty-three years of age.

There *are* discriminations that Wordsworth seems to want to make between the intensity and voracity of his involvement with nature in the summer of 1793 and the 'coarser pleasures' of childhood. But the crucial distinction is worth a closer look:

> ['five years' ago] like a roe
> I bounded o'er the mountains, by the sides
> Of the deep rivers, and the lonely streams,
> Wherever nature led ...
>   For nature then
> (The coarser pleasures of my boyish days
> And their glad animal movements all gone by,)
> To me was all in all.

---

20 See *Lyrical Ballads, and Other Poems, 1797–1800*, The Cornell Wordsworth, ed. James Butler and Karen Green (Ithaca and London: Cornell University Press, 1992), 274.

If in his early twenties the 'coarser pleasures' and 'glad animal movements' of his childhood and youth had in fact 'all gone by', what was he doing bounding over the mountains 'like a roe'? We have only the comparative 'coarser' to enforce whatever distinction Wordsworth may be trying to make. Even here, moreover, his use of the word 'appetite' in line 81 suggests an excess, if not a coarseness, about his experience. The other indication that Wordsworth is describing early manhood, rather than childhood and youth, is the telling simile discussed earlier:

> more like a man
> Flying from something that he dreads, than one
> Who sought the thing he loved.

But the simile allows for the possibility of the poet's having been a child who was *like* a man in flight, without his in fact having been a man. When later (again in line 81) he describes his emotional attachment to nature as 'a love', we have become so tolerant of imprecision that we pass over this flat contradiction without demur.

One reason for this may be that the biographical interest of the passage is precisely in its confusion of the poet as a boy and the poet as a twenty-three-year-old, insofar as it registers a radical regression on the part of the poet in the summer of 1793, during which we happen to know that Wordsworth was disturbed for reasons both ideological (the revolution in France had gone sour and war had been declared between Britain and France) and personal (he had separated from Annette Vallon, his French lover and the mother of his infant daughter). As Jonathan Wordsworth has argued, 'feelings of desertion' in Wordsworth triggered a profound need 'to believe himself part of an integrated whole'; the nature that 'never did betray / The heart that loved her' was in one unambiguous sense 'a substitute for the mother who had done just that'.[21] Deserted by his political heroes and his own moral convictions and alienated from Annette and their child, Wordsworth's impulse would have been to escape a situation that he

---

21   Jonathan Wordsworth, *William Wordsworth: The Borders of Vision* (Oxford: Clarendon, 1982), 79.

4 'The burden of the mystery': William Wordsworth's 'Tintern Abbey'

dreaded rather than vainly to seek the love of which he had been bereft. It is hardly surprising, then, that the regressive young man should be described as *haunted* by passion (l. 78). 'Tintern Abbey' will go on to discover a meaningful though tenuous resolution in the reconstituted family of the poet and his sister, Dorothy (though it is important to register that relationships in the poem are carefully generalised, and that neither Annette nor Dorothy is ever mentioned by name). However consciously, the poet *and* the poem desperately conspire to create a vacuum that only the poet's sister can fill. It is little wonder that, in fulfilling this role, she should be introduced into the poem by an implicit comparison, not with the lover of the Song of Songs, but with the God of the psalms—'For thou art with me, here upon the banks'—as Wordsworth gropes down the 'dark passage' of the valley of the shadow of death.

The absorption of the experience of 1793 into the poet's childhood is taken for granted later when finally the poem shifts to define his altered consciousness. 'That time is past', he insists:

> I have learned
> To look on nature, not as in the hour
> Of thoughtless youth.
>
> (ll. 89–91)

Any attempt to distinguish the 'animal movements' of boyhood from those of his early twenties has been abandoned. Suddenly his twenty-three-year-old self has been assimilated into his 'thoughtless youth', and we are back with the familiar dichotomy of child and man. Nor is there any indication here as to whether this 'hour' refers to an occasional, discrete period of intimacy with nature or to a period of over twenty years. 'So dramatically has the relationship with Coleridge altered his responses', as Lucy Newlyn suggests, 'that the different stages of Wordsworth's development (up till about 1795) become conflated as he looks back'.[22] The parenthetical demarcation of boyhood in lines 74–75, with its recognition that his 'glad' days have 'all gone by', serves

---

22 Lucy Newlyn, *Coleridge, Wordsworth, and the Language of Allusion* (Oxford: Clarendon, 1986), 54.

merely to anticipate the more pronounced sense of loss and regret that comes with the transition or 'dark passage' into a more complete humanity. Whichever way we choose to regard the ecstatic period of the poet's close and unself-conscious involvement with nature, its sacrifice becomes—must become—the price of wisdom.

There are a number of moments in 'Tintern Abbey' when the sense of a lost past borders on the self-pity of eighteenth-century lyrics such as Gray's 'Ode on a Distant Prospect of Eton College', in which the poet's preoccupation with the past produces only the paralysis of sentimental melancholy and a consolatory series of fine epigrammatic phrases. The repeated phrase 'no more' in 'Tintern Abbey' (ll. 85, 148) anticipates the lingering pathos of the same phrase in the 'Immortality Ode' (l. 9), as both poems hover between the pain of loss and a determination amounting to hope. In 'Tintern Abbey', indeed, the poet progresses from a self-preoccupied withdrawal, through altruism, into a pantheistic unity, as the 'dark passages' become universal rites of passage and the maturing humanist poet assumes the responsibility of his calling. And yet, for all their recognition of the inevitability of change and development, the 'recollections of early childhood' in the 'Immortality Ode' and of early manhood in 'Tintern Abbey' are recorded with such sensual immediacy, such power and pathos, as to ensure that an 'elegiac' note survives the stoic resolution and transcendental affirmation respectively.[23] Wordsworth's 'sad perplexity' is more than just 'a fleeting shadow across a poem of steady and shining optimism', to quote John Jones.[24]

---

23 References to 'Tintern Abbey' as 'elegiac' occur in Jonathan Wordsworth's *The Music of Humanity: A Critical Study of Wordsworth's 'Ruined Cottage'* (London: Thomas Nelson & Sons, 1969), 216, and in his *The Borders of Vision*, 235, as well as in Mary Jacobus, *Tradition and Experiment*, 123.
24 John Jones, *The Egotistical Sublime: A History of Wordsworth's Imagination* (London: Chatto & Windus, 1954), 94.

4 'The burden of the mystery': William Wordsworth's 'Tintern Abbey'

Rite de passage

The anthropological concept of *rite de passage* or 'rite of passage', in which the social group ritualises and celebrates an individual member's transition from one stage of development to another, is most often applied to societies that are less developed and more homogeneous than Wordsworth's. Certainly, in some of Wordsworth's poems the destruction of the child to allow the adult to take over is as abrupt and ritualised a form of 'dying into life' as any *rite de passage*—'There Was a Boy', for example. Wordsworth's rituals, however, while symbolic, are generally more personal than social or anthropological and externalise adjustments in the individual's emotional life and consciousness. Yet his preoccupation with radically distinct stages of development and growth—specifically with the transition from child to adult[25]—anticipates this commonplace of nineteenth- and twentieth-century anthropology, just as it anticipates related observations of psychoanalysis. What Wordsworth shares with psychoanalysis is the conviction that these stages of development relate critically to the ego, and to ego-awareness, as the individual seeks realisation through the relationship of the self with the other, and with the self *as* other. And there is in Wordsworth the influential assumption of the formative role childhood experience plays in adult understanding and behaviour:

> My heart leaps up when I behold
> A Rainbow in the sky:
> So was it when my life began;
> So is it now I am a man;
> So be it when I shall grow old,
> Or let me die!
> The Child is Father of the Man;
> And I could wish my days to be
> Bound each to each by natural piety.

---

25   Wordsworth has this in common with 'primitive cultures' which 'usually recognize two main stages of development, childhood and maturity, the border between them often being demarcated by ritual ceremonies'—see John Cleverly and D. C. Phillips, *Visions of Childhood: Influential Models from Locke to Spock* (Sydney, London, Boston: Teachers College Press, 1987), 80.

Concerning 'identity and the life cycle', therefore, it is hardly surprising that the calibration of that cycle in Wordsworth's poetry—especially here in 'Tintern Abbey', in *The Prelude*, and in the 'Immortality Ode'—should resemble that of psychoanalysts like Erik H. Erikson who, after Freud's own *Totem and Taboo*, attempt to assimilate and recast the findings of contemporary anthropologists. Conceiving maturation as a sequence of variously interconnected and necessary phases in the development of a personal 'identity' ('bound each to each'), Erikson betrays a recognisably Wordsworthian preoccupation: 'Ego identity, then, in its subjective aspect, is the awareness of the fact that there is a self-sameness and continuity to the ego's synthesizing methods', a 'self-sameness and continuity in time'.[26] Erikson's model also corresponds significantly to Keats's metaphor of 'human life' as 'a large Mansion of Many Apartments'. The necessary metamorphoses Erikson registers become the 'dark passages' connecting these psychological 'Apartments'.[27]

The analogy should not be pushed too far, however, and certainly not beyond its relevance to 'Tintern Abbey', where it helps to illuminate Wordsworth's idea of development as having distinct yet mutually interdependent stages. For both Keats and Wordsworth, the crucial transition was from an initial stage of human development that Lucien Lévy-Bruhl would later call *participation mystique*: 'a relic of the original non-differentiation of subject and object, and hence of the primordial unconscious state. It is also a characteristic of the mental state of early infancy, and, finally, of the unconscious of the civilized adult'.[28] Wordsworth assumed a stage of full and unself-conscious involvement with nature and Keats talked of 'the infant or thoughtless Chamber in which we remain as long as we do not think'.[29] The passage from this state of undifferentiated consciousness to a thoughtful and, to that extent, alienated stage—Keats's 'Chamber of Maiden Thought'—

---

26 Erikson, *Identity and the Life Cycle*, 23.
27 It was the 'speculation' in which life is compared with a mansion of many apartments that led to Keats's appraisal of 'Tintern Abbey' in the same letter to Reynolds—*Letters of John Keats*, 1:281.
28 As defined by Carl Jung in his *Dictionary of Analytic Psychology* (London: Ark, 1987), 112.
29 *Letters of John Keats*, 1:281.

involved a growing awareness of the difference between self and other, the self-recognition of a divided and divisive personality.

The complexity lies in the transition, yet the emotional reaction—the nostalgia or longing to recapture a 'primordial unconscious state'[30]—is as powerfully felt in Wordsworth's poetry, sometimes more powerfully, than is the desire for personal and poetic growth. In 'Tintern Abbey', Wordsworth appears to find self-oblivion in transcendentalism—'when we are laid asleep in body / And become a living soul'—in 'thoughtless youth', and finally in pantheism itself. For pantheism, in both its primitive and its sophisticated philosophical forms, arguably represents a regression from the burden of self-consciousness as surely as does the mindlessness of a total involvement in nature ('all in all'). To quote Freud:

> Originally the ego includes everything, later it separates off an external world from itself. Our present ego-feeling is, therefore, only a shrunken residue of a much more inclusive—indeed, an all-embracing—feeling which corresponded to a more intimate bond between the ego and the world about it ... the ideational contents appropriate to it would be precisely those of limitlessness and a bond with the universe ... the 'oceanic' feeling.[31]

The parallel between this 'oceanic' feeling and Wordsworth's 'sense sublime / Of something far more deeply interfused' hardly needs a gloss.

Given that the same boundaries that confine the self also define the self, however, pantheism is finally if only implicitly rejected in 'Tintern Abbey' as a form of dehumanisation. The pantheistic passages in the poem are quickly qualified by crucial conditionals. The solution to the poet's unease and self-alienation lies not in 'something far more deeply interfused' but in the complex unity-in-continuity of his relationship with his sister. Through his sister, he is able to overcome his perplexing sense of being two distinct consciousnesses and to discover

---

30 Jonathan Wordsworth is right to associate this fascination with the death-wish—see *The Borders of Vision*, 26.
31 Sigmund Freud, *Civilization, Society, and Religion*, Penguin Freud Library 12 (London: Penguin, 1985), 255.

a 'selfsameness and continuity in time'. The result is a less rapturous version of his love of nature—a version that, as the carefully placed last phrase of the poem indicates, remains vitally contingent upon human relationship:

> Nor wilt thou then forget,
> That after many wanderings, many years
> Of absence, these steep woods and lofty cliffs,
> And this green pastoral landscape, were to me
> More dear, both for themselves, *and for thy sake.*
> (ll. 156–60; my italics)

Belief-in-process

Wordsworth's perplexity and ambivalence remain, however, and 'Tintern Abbey' is riddled with 'elisions, absences, and incomplete comparisons'.[32] If we look closely at his passage from an appetite for nature to a more mature, altruistic attitude, we note the frequency of negative, aspirational, and conditional constructions (marked in italics):

> *That time is past*
> And all its aching joys are now *no more,*
> And all its dizzy raptures. *Not* for this
> Faint I, *nor* mourn *nor* murmur: other gifts
> Have followed, for such *loss, I would believe,*
> Abundant recompence.
> (ll. 84–89)

Working on (and working up) his emotions, Wordsworth exaggerates—even seems to parody—some of his own stylistic habits. Such strenuous negation ('not ... nor ... nor') invariably allows conceptual room for what the poet denies. And in the concentrated ambiguity of

---

32 Pearson, 'Allusive Pursuits: The Song of Songs in Wordsworth's "Tintern Abbey"', 195.

4 'The burden of the mystery': William Wordsworth's 'Tintern Abbey'

the qualifying clause 'I would believe'—an ambiguity of both meaning and purpose—Wordsworth captures 'the emotional and ideational changes' that for Erik Erikson betray an 'ever-present conflict'. If, as William Ulmer suggests, there was 'a revitalized moral optimism' in the Wordsworth of 1797–98, and a 'conviction that human losses are subsumed by "Abundant recompense"', it is heavily qualified.[33] 'I would believe' may be read as resolve or as desire ('I would like to believe')—as anything, in fact, but conviction. In many cases, the poet simply protests too much.

A close reading of 'Tintern Abbey' reveals numerous expressions of hesitation and uncertainty. 'All the verse paragraphs', as Stuart Curran remarks, 'begin with a recognition of shifting ground, either of time or of mental stability'.[34] Qualifiers and disclaimers, wishes and conjectures, and, above all, negatives, abound, qualifying not only the poet's declared convictions and beliefs, but his sensations and responses as well. Witness the following:

(a) These forms of beauty *have not been* to me,
As is a landscape to *a blind* man's eye. (ll. 25–6)

(b)   feelings, too,
Of *unremembered* pleasure; such, *perhaps,*
As may have had no trivial influence
On that best portion of a good man's life;
His little, *nameless, unremembered* acts
Of kindness and of love. *Nor less, I trust,*
To them I *may have* owed another gift,
Of aspect more sublime. (ll. 31–38)

(c)   *If this,*
Be but a vain belief (ll. 51–52)

---

33 William A. Ulmer, 'William Wordsworth and Philosophical Necessity', *Studies in Philology*, 110:1 (Winter 2013), 168–98 (191).
34 Stuart Curran, *Poetic Form and British Romanticism* (Oxford: Oxford University Press, 1986), 77. Alan Rawes summarises this critical recognition in 'Romantic Form and New Historicism', 100.

(d)   so *I dare to hope* (1.66)

(e)   *Nor, perchance,*
If I were not thus taught (ll. 112–13)

(f)   *May* I behold in thee (ll. 121)

(g)   nature *never did betray*
The heart that loved her (ll. 123–24)

(h)   she *can* so inform
The mind (ll. 126–27)

(i)   *Nor perchance,*
If I should be, where I *no more can hear*
Thy voice (ll. 147–49)

Negatives designed to deny the reader's expectations; crucial verbs of uncertain tense and mood; compound conditionals that weaken or undermine the poet's conviction ('may have had', 'may have owed'); conditional clauses framing passages often misread as statements of belief ('If this be but a vain belief', 'If I were not thus taught'); the changing pronoun remarked by Heather Glen[35]—all betray an insecurity that confirms the very anxieties from which a determined poet *would* rescue himself. Far from being a manifesto, 'Tintern Abbey' is belief-in-process, awkward and occasionally even slightly ludicrous in its attempts to avoid (or revoke) too categorical a commitment.

Some indications of the poet's unease with his own beliefs are obvious; others, while less obvious, are equally unsettling—like the presence that '*disturbs*' him with 'the joy / Of elevated thoughts' (ll. 95–96); the vague '*sense* sublime / Of something far more deeply interfused' (ll. 97–98); the pointedly cautious use of the past tense in the closing lines (the poet looks forward to the day his sister recalls that certain aspects of the landscape 'were', and not 'are', more dear to him (l. 159)—whether they will remain dear to him seems an open

---

35   Glen, *Vision and Disenchantment*, 255–56.

question); the subtly equivocal clause that introduces the otherwise magniloquent exaltation of nature quoted earlier:

> well pleased to recognize
> In nature and the language of the sense,
> The anchor of my purest thoughts, the nurse,
> The guide, the guardian of my heart, and soul
> Of all my moral being.
>
> (ll. 108–112)

The cumulative effect of all this is to involve the reader in the doubt that pervades the poem. It would not be perverse to see the often-quoted passage on the transformative power of the human imagination—

> the mighty world
> Of eye and ear, both what they half-create,
> And what perceive
>
> (ll. 103–105)

—as typical of the larger claims made by the poem, all of whose half perceptive, half creative affirmations are shot through with wish-fulfilment. For it is precisely desire and not doctrine that the poem expresses.

Are we then to dismiss the passages of affirmation as rhetorical sleights-of-hand, disingenuous and self-divided? Recent critical theory and practice is so much more receptive to doubt and self-sabotage than it is to a sense of unity and transcendence that it behoves us to be sceptical about its reflex scepticism. In foregrounding the uncertainties of Romanticism, however, and the ironies and vulnerabilities of subjectivity and desire, criticism is indebted to Romanticism itself, no less than it is to Marxism, psychoanalysis, and post-structuralism. Wordsworth, in this case, becomes openly uncomfortable with the long pantheistic *cumulatio* that begins with his sense of 'something far more deeply interfused' and ends with nature as the anchor of his purest thoughts and soul of all his moral being. Responding to praise of his 'nature worship' in January 1815, he dismissed it as an erroneous inference derived from 'a passionate expression uttered *incautiously* in the Poem on the

Wye', and the mistake of 'reading in cold-heartedness and substituting the letter for the spirit'.[36] For the older, more conservative Wordsworth, in other words, the pantheism of the passage had a strictly *dramatic* validity and was not to be confused with the truth claims of either rigorous philosophical discourse or religious faith. 'Thoughts, ideas, or notions, call them what you will', as Shelley wrote, 'differ from each other, not in kind, but in force'.[37]

Far from being an expression of faith, Wordsworth's 'sense sublime / Of something far more deeply interfused' points to what, in a passage in *The Prelude* relevant to this essay, he calls an '*obscure* sense of *possible* sublimity':

> I deem not profitless those fleeting moods
> Of shadowy exultation: not for this,
> That they are kindred to our purer mind
> And intellectual life; but that the soul,
> Remembering how she felt, but what she felt
> Remembering not, retains an obscure sense
> Of possible sublimity, to which,
> With growing faculties she doth aspire.
>   (*The Prelude* [1805–6], 2:331–38)[38]

Obscurity (darkness) and aspiration: so in 'Tintern Abbey', the poet reaches out. The confidence and momentum of the 'rolling' blank verse is undoubtedly a statement in its own right, but a statement of longing, and the metrical conviction only momentarily overcomes the vagueness and the doubt. One thing alone seems clear: the poet's exaltation of

---

36 In a letter to Catherine Clarkson, *The Letters of William and Dorothy Wordsworth*, second edition, Vol. 3, *The Middle Years*, Part 2, 1812–1820, rev. Mary Moorman and Alan G. Hill (Oxford: Oxford University Press, 1970), 188.
37 Percy Bysshe Shelley, 'Speculations on metaphysics', in *Selected Poetry and Prose of Percy Bysshe Shelley*, ed. Carlos Baker (New York: Random House, 1951), 471.
38 On the grammatical and logical ambiguities of Wordsworth's affirmations in 'Tintern Abbey', see William Empson, *Seven Types of Ambiguity*, second edition (London: Chatto & Windus, 1949), 151–54.

4 'The burden of the mystery': William Wordsworth's 'Tintern Abbey'

nature reflects a sense of his 'heightened well-being' in the mood cycle that, according to Erik Erikson, is human life.

Thou art with me

It is time to make the point my argument has been circling around from the beginning, which is that 'Tintern Abbey' does not end with Wordsworth's 'sense sublime/ Of something far more deeply interfused', or with his hymn to nature as the soul of all his moral being. If, as Marjorie Levinson suggests, the 'social world in its actual and compelling character' is 'annihilated by this celebratory representation',[39] it is only momentarily so. The pivotal conditional clause that introduces the closing section of the poem—

> Nor, perchance,
> If I were not thus taught, should I the more
> Suffer my genial spirits to decay:
> For thou art with me.
>
> (ll. 114–17)

—introduces an 'alternative source of consolation should the visionary fail'.[40] It implies that the hymn to his sister, introduced by the line from the twenty-third psalm, will eventually lead us back to an all-supporting, all-consoling nature—and, from there, to an immanent deity informing 'the mighty world / Of eye and ear' and all else besides. The closing lines of *Tintern Abbey*, however, are in no sense a confirmation of nature's guardianship, and the crucial conditional, as so often in the poem, is at best ambiguous and at worst meaningless. There is nothing inherent in the line 'If I were not thus taught' to establish whether it means 'had I not had the privilege of such instruction' *or* 'if I have misunderstood the sense or significance of this experience'.

---

39 Marjorie Levinson, *Wordsworth's Great Poems: Four Essays* (Cambridge: Cambridge University Press, 1986), 47–48.
40 Rawes, 'Romantic Form and New Historicism', 110.

More to the point, however, it opens up new possibilities in the experience of the poem. Instead of simply confirming nature's exalted role, the last section, addressing and invoking the poet's sister, has its own more partial and more human story to tell. If, as Jonathan Bate has written, 'the way in which William Wordsworth sought to enable his readers better to enjoy or to endure life was by teaching them to look and dwell in nature',[41] it was not without qualification and never alone. The major difference between the visionary lines and this last section is that, in the former, the poet remains paradoxically isolated as he preaches the unity of all life, while in the latter he is engaged in genuine relationship:

> For thou art with me here upon the banks
> Of this fair river; thou my dearest Friend,
> My dear, dear Friend; and in thy voice I catch
> The language of my former heart, and read
> My former pleasures in the shooting lights
> Of thy wild eyes. Oh! yet a little while
> May I behold in thee what I was once,
> My dear, dear Sister! And this prayer I make,
> Knowing that Nature never did betray
> The heart that loved her
>
> (ll. 114–24)

As well as functioning metonymically and metaphorically, the figure of his sister also functions literally (including lovingly). Belatedly introducing human relationship into the poem, this final section offers a more authentic account of life as a process and a more honest account of the possibilities and limitations of the mediated vision that is proposed as an alternative to self-transcendence. 'The poem ends', to quote E. D. Hirsch, 'with a sort of cyclic reference':

---

41 Jonathan Bate, *Romantic Ecology: Wordsworth and the Environmental Tradition* (London: Routledge, 2013), 4.

4 'The burden of the mystery': William Wordsworth's 'Tintern Abbey'

In his younger sister, the poet sees a repetition of a stage in the larger cycle of human life. She is what he once was, and fortified by the scene which lies before them, she will become what he is now. The poet's earlier stage exists not only ideally in his memory, but actually in his sister.[42]

The integrity of the poet is thus preserved, both as an individual consciousness and (bearing in mind the threat of dehumanisation posed by pantheism) as an artist dedicated to rendering the 'still, sad music of humanity'. That the question of Wordsworth's integrity should intensify in the concluding lines is only appropriate, given that integrity and sanity (wholeness) is what 'Tintern Abbey' is about. Insofar as the closing benediction is a more tentative, even vexed expression of hope and desire, it is better able to keep faith with the complexity of the poet's experience:

> Therefore let the moon
> Shine on thee in thy solitary walk;
> And let the misty mountain-winds be free
> To blow against thee: and, in after years,
> When these wild ecstasies shall be matured
> Into a sober pleasure; when thy mind
> Shall be a mansion for all lovely forms,
> Thy memory be as a dwelling-place
> For all sweet sounds and harmonies; oh! then,
> If solitude, or fear, or pain, or grief,
> Should be thy portion, with what healing thoughts
> Of tender joy wilt thou remember me,
> And these my exhortations! Nor, perchance—
> If I should be where I no more can hear
> Thy voice, nor catch from thy wild eyes these gleams
> Of past existence—wilt thou then forget
> That on the banks of this delightful stream
> We stood together; and that I, so long

---

42 E. D. Hirsch, Jr, *Wordsworth and Schelling A Typological Study of Romanticism* (New Haven, Conn.: Yale University Press, 1960), 71-72.

> A worshipper of nature, hither came
> Unwearied in that service: rather say
> With warmer love—oh! with far deeper zeal
> Of holier love. Nor wilt thou then forget,
> That after many wanderings, many years
> Of absence, these steep woods and lofty cliffs,
> And this green pastoral landscape, were to me
> More dear, both for themselves and for thy sake!
> (ll. 135-60)

There are two other important functions performed by the sister in the poem that serve to qualify the symmetry she represents. First, time and selfhood being the *conditions* of consciousness and therefore difficult to conceptualise as the *objects* of consciousness, the introduction of his sister allows the poet a perspective on subjectivity that is paradoxically objective. Having gazed 'through a glass darkly', perplexedly, the poet now meets himself face to face, for the sister both is and is not her brother—'re-presenting' him, in other words, both as (like) himself and as another. Her second important function is thus one of actualisation or realisation: while the sister's past, present, and future may repeat stages of the poet's own development, it is the 'sameness *with difference*' (to use Coleridge's phrase) that characterises her imitation of the poet—and this, in spite of the narcissistic poet's desire to reduce her role to a perfect Echo and compel repetition. The cycle is analogous only, and her repetition of his history will be, at best, proximate.

'Joy', writes Nietzsche, 'does not want heirs, or children—joy wants itself, wants eternity, wants recurrence, wants everything eternally the same'.[43] The poet is prompted to shape the perfection of the circle, but cycles are not circles and his sister is not to be seen as a flawed simulacrum of the ideal. On the contrary, the complex combination of the actual and the ideal that she represents makes the figure of the sister, like the landscape itself, an appropriate mediator for an aspiring poet with a stubborn sense of reality. In the poet's benedictory projection,

---

43 As quoted by Norman O. Brown in his *Life Against Death: The Psychoanalytic Meaning of History*, second edition (Middletown, Conn.: Wesleyan University Press, 1985), 108.

4 'The burden of the mystery': William Wordsworth's 'Tintern Abbey'

she combines the current 'sad' self-consciousness of the poet with the coveted state of undifferentiated consciousness of the child the poet once was—combines experience with innocence, in other words—and combines them inextricably, as the love of a sibling combines the love of *both* self *and* other: '*égoïsme à deux*', in Heather Glen's phrase.⁴⁴ Where in 'Frost at Midnight' Coleridge finds continuity with change in the relationship between father and son, Wordsworth in 'Tintern Abbey' finds a condensed version of continuity 'in the blood' and 'along the heart' in the relationship between himself and his sister. All this he captures in a subtle variation on the traditional conceit of the lover gazing on his own reflection in his loved one's eyes. In Wordsworth's version, the poet reads his 'former pleasures in the shooting lights / Of thy wild eyes'.

So much for continuity. The unity the poet discovers—neither crudely incestuous, nor crudely narcissistic—is described in more apocalyptic terms by the German poet Rilke:

> the great renewal of the world will perhaps consist in this, that man and maid freed from all false feeling and aversion, will seek each other not as opposites, but as brother and sister, as neighbours, and will come together as *human beings*.⁴⁵

The closing lines of 'Tintern Abbey' assimilate and contain Wordsworth's solitary vision or 'sense sublime'. The echo of the twenty-third psalm, a Biblical rather than classical pastoral, reconciles green pastures with God, the unity of man and nature of pantheism with the more traditional, vicarial mediation of divine but differential *relationship*. Again, the sister operates as both self (unity) and other (relationship).

---

44   Glen refers to the '*égoïsme à deux*' that forms the central metaphor of these final lines. Where her emphasis falls on the *égoïsme*, however, I would place it on '*deux*'—*Vision and Disenchantment*, 257. On the exploitation of the incest theme, see Richard J. Onorato, *The Character of the Poet: Wordsworth in 'The Prelude'* (Princeton, N. J.: Princeton University Press, 1971), 82.
45   Rainer Maria Rilke, *Letters to a Young Poet*, trans. M. D. Herter (New York: W. W. Norton, 1934), 38.

The poet of 'Tintern Abbey' is not Blake's God-like Bard 'who past, present, and future sees', but a poet in whom the past, present, and future are objects of a struggle for creative fusion and transcendence in a hostile environment of 'evil tongues', 'rash judgments', 'the sneers of selfish men', and 'greetings where no kindness is'. He beholds his past in the present pleasure of return, as well as in the present pain occasioned by the alteration that his experience has effected in the landscape of the Wye valley. And he beholds his past in his sister's present features and fate. His prophetic powers amount to dreams and 'exhortations'—urging his sister to believe—not to divinely inspired foresight. Their credibility, in keeping with the poem's conditionals, is contingent. The primal harmony in which he *would* believe, and would have his sister and his reader believe, is offered as protection against a future orchestrated by chance and unpredictable change, a future that must, in all honesty, encompass 'the still, sad music of humanity', while also being unified by the immanent spirit rolling 'through all things' that once he 'sensed'. Or so he would 'dare to hope'.

That there are no self-authenticating epiphanies in 'Tintern Abbey' is confirmed by the caution Wordsworth exercises, obtrusively and unobtrusively, when qualifying his 'visions' or transcendental meditations. 'For all its avowals of transcendence, permanence, and metaphysical communion', writes Mark Sandy, 'the poetry is repeatedly drawn to demystify its own consolations, revealing a contingent reality of absence, fragmentation, transience, and broken relations'.[46] It is a case rather of will, supplication, yearning—of desire. It is a case, not of inspiration, but of aspiration: 'so I dare to hope'; 'I would believe'; 'I must'; 'may have had'; 'may have owed'; 'perchance'. Using Northrop Frye's functional distinction between the 'episodic' thematic mode as discontinuous and the 'encyclopedic' thematic mode as more extended and continuous,[47] we can say that 'Tintern Abbey' is a record of episodic discontinuities and doubts in search of the continuous and encyclopedic in human experience. Hence the idea of the poem as an exploration of 'dark passages' linking more settled stages or phases of experience and belief.

---

46   Mark Sandy, 'Wordsworth and the Circulations of Grief', *Essays in Criticism*, 62:3 (2012), 248–64 (248).
47   Frye, *Anatomy of Criticism*, 54–55 and ff.

4 'The burden of the mystery': William Wordsworth's 'Tintern Abbey'

What this search suggests—to adapt the famous lines of the sixth book of *The Prelude*—is that 'Our destiny, our nature, and our home' is, if not with 'infinitude' (which must remain a moot point), then at least with 'hope':

> With hope it is, hope than can never die
> Effort, and expectation, and desire,
> And something evermore about to be.
> (*The Prelude* [1805–6], 6:538–42)

In spite of the poet's eloquent advocacy of 'something far more deeply interfused', 'Tintern Abbey' betrays a tentativeness, a self-distrust, even while expressing desire and optimism. The poet aspires rather to a fundamental continuity and community in the integration of past, present and future; of his sister and himself; of man and nature—and to a fundamental continuity and community that can survive the deprivations and dislocations which in the closing section he anticipates with a characteristic honesty. There are no guarantees. When all is said, 'the burthen of the mystery' of human life remains.

Hence Keats's emphasis, which the full context of the passage from the letter to J. H. Reynolds helps to explain. When the individual breathes in what Keats calls the 'Chamber of Maiden Thought':

> among the effects this breathing is the father of is that tremendous one of sharpening one's vision into the heart and nature of Man—of convincing one's nerves that the World is full of Misery and Heartbreak, Pain, Sickness and oppression—whereby This Chamber of Maiden Thought becomes gradually darken'd and at the same time on all sides of it many doors are set open—but all dark—all leading to dark passages. We see not the ballance of good and evil. We are in a Mist—*We* are now in that state—we feel the 'burden of the Mystery'. To this point was Wordsworth come, as far as I can conceive when he wrote 'Tintern Abbey' and it seems to me that his Genius is explorative of those dark Passages.[48]

---

48 *The Letters of John Keats*, 1:281.

5
The Search for Meaning in *The Rime of the Ancient Mariner*

As we saw in the first chapter, the natural credulity of Jane Austen's Catherine Morland leaves her vulnerable to the excesses of Gothic romance. 'Dear Miss Morland, consider the dreadful nature of the suspicions you have entertained', protests Henry Tilney, who is surely right to remind Catherine of the exigencies of reality:

> 'Consult your own understanding, your own sense of the probable, your own observation of what is passing around you—Does our education prepare us for such atrocities? Do our laws connive at them? Could they be perpetrated without being known, in a country like this, where social and literary intercourse is on such a footing ...?'[1]

Catherine has to learn to discriminate between a domestic novel and a Gothic romance. She has to learn to read—which is to say, correctly to interpret. Mistaking the context here—'the country and the age' in which the story unfolds, always a vital determinant—she is constrained to misinterpret the signs (ageing manuscripts, mysterious portraits, locked rooms, ill-tempered patriarchs). Like so many

---

1 Jane Austen, *Northanger Abbey*, The Cambridge Edition of the Works of Jane Austen, ed. Barbara M. Benedict and Deirdre Le Faye (Cambridge: Cambridge University Press, 2006), 203.

heroines in eighteenth-century novels, she has to learn how to read literature *in* life and *about* life, but not *as* life. From the anti-heroic (anti-romantic) set piece with which it opens through its declamatory defence of the novel in Chapter 5 to its speeding self-consciously to a conclusion, *Northanger Abbey* is shot through with metafictional allusions. Genre and fictionality are at once the means and the object of the novel's exploration.

If deconstruction has taught us anything, it has taught us to be alert to the way literature reflects upon its own mode of existence, its own function and survival, and its own interpretation. What is true to some extent of all literature is especially true of Romantic literature, written during a period that was starting to realise and regret the possibilities of a mass culture. 'The human mind is capable of excitement without the application of gross and violent stimulants', writes Wordsworth in his Preface to *Lyrical Ballads*:

> For a multitude of causes unknown to former times are now acting with a combined force to blunt the discriminating powers of the mind, and unfitting it for all voluntary exertion to reduce it to a state of almost savage torpor. The most effective of these causes are the great national events which are daily taking place, and the increasing accumulation of men in cities, where the uniformity of their occupations produces a craving for extraordinary incident which the rapid communication of intelligence hourly gratifies.[2]

And what is true of Romantic literature generally is especially true of Romantic poetry, which time and again makes poetry itself—the mind in the act of creative discrimination and the search for meaning—its subject matter as well as its means. No one is likely to dispute the fact that the main activity of all readers (not just literary critics) is interpretation. But interpretation—seeing and understanding; making sense of things—is also frequently central to works of art themselves. The Romantic poem, certainly, as well as being the object of its reader's interpretative exploration, can be understood as a model for the kind

---

[2] *The Prose Works of William Wordsworth*, ed. W. J. B. Owen and Jane Worthington Smyser, 3 vols (Oxford: Oxford University Press, 1974), 1:128.

5 The Search for Meaning in *The Rime of the Ancient Mariner*

of interpretative activity that goes on in the process of reading and in the critical conversation between readers over time and across space. It would be hard to find a better example of this than Samuel Taylor Coleridge's *The Rime of the Ancient Mariner*.

The strangest story of a cock and a bull that we ever saw

Formally, *The Rime of the Ancient Mariner* is a ballad—a (nominally) third person, narrative poem, its basic stanza an iambic tetrameter/trimeter quatrain of regular rhyme (ABCB), with a strong story line and the mnemonic repetition characteristic of a genre that retains its roots in an oral tradition. In all versions of the poem, as I said in Chapter 1, an original antiquarian impulse is apparent. Its occasional spelling and expression, in imitation of Medieval poetry—'quoth he', 'I wist', 'eftsoons'—identifies the poem as a fashionable anachronism. Coleridge was capitalising on the taste for antiquarianism that had made Thomas Percy's *Reliques of Ancient English Poetry* (1765) a favourite with late eighteenth-century readers. Compare, for example, the anonymous 'The Marriage of Gawaine' from Percy's collection with the first (1798) version of Coleridge's *The Rime of the Ancient Mariner*:

> King Arthur lives in Merry Carleile,
> And seemly is to see;
> And there with him queene Guenever,
> That bride soe bright of blee.
>
> And there with him queene Guenever,
> That bride so bright in bowre:
> And all his barons about him stoode,
> That were both stiffe and stowre.
>
> The king a royale Christmasse kept,
> With mirth and princelye cheare;
> To him repairèd many a knighte,
> That came both farre and neare.

> And when they were to dinner sette,
> And cups went freely round;
> Before them came a faire damselle,
> And knelt upon the ground ...
>
> (ll. 1-16)

The 'faire damselle' who kneels before King Arthur has a woeful tale to tell that demands the immediate attention of the knights and suspends the festivities until such time as 'wrong is turnde to righte'. For his version of the interrupted feast, Coleridge drew exotic images and incidents from a blend of travel literature with fairy and folk tale,[3] as the poem slides effortlessly into the bizarre and threatening world of nightmare, creating an allegory of alienation and isolation of uniquely compelling power.

For *The Rime* is not just a ballad, it is also a *lyrical* ballador, strictly speaking, a lyrical ballad within a ballad. It is 'lyrical' in the sense of being 'musical', highly crafted—a self-consciously *literary* ballad, *The Rime* could serve as a handbook of prosodic and literary devices—but also 'lyrical' in the sense of issuing from and focusing on a responsive consciousness. The tale *within* the tale it tells is a fraught, first person (lyrical) tale that reflects back on the teller (the Mariner) as he struggles to recount and understand his own narrative. The setting and the journey are patently fantastic—a setting and a journey inside the mind and imagination. Coleridge was asking his readers to go somewhere that, like the mariners, they had never been before:

---

[3] Still the most comprehensive and suggestive account of Coleridge's sources remains John Livingstone Lowes, *The Road to Xanadu: A Study in the Ways of the Imagination* (London: Constable, 1927). Since then, commentators have identified other potential sources for different events and phenomena in the poem; Bernard Smith, for example, makes the case for the journals and accounts of Captain James Cook's second voyage to the Pacific in his *Imagining the Pacific: In the Wake of the Cook Voyages* (Melbourne: Melbourne University Press, 1992), 135-71.

5 The Search for Meaning in *The Rime of the Ancient Mariner*

> We were the first that ever burst
> Into that silent sea.
>
> (ll. 105–106)[4]

On this strange journey, Coleridge asks only that the reader suspend his or her expectations of the familiar and trust to the 'human interest' of the tale, as he explained when accounting for the origins of his and Wordsworth's *Lyrical Ballads* in his *Biographia Literaria*:

> The thought suggested itself (to which of us I do not recollect) that a species of poems might be composed of two sorts. In the one, the incidents and agents were to be (in part at least) supernatural—and the excellence aimed at was to consist in the interesting of the affections by the dramatic truth of such emotions as would naturally accompany such situations, supposing them real. And real in this sense they have been to every human being who, from whatever source of delusion, has at any time believed himself under supernatural agency. For the second class, subjects were to be chosen from ordinary life ...
>
> In this idea originated the plan of the *Lyrical Ballads*, in which it was agreed that my endeavours were to be directed to persons and characters supernatural, or at least romantic; yet so far as to transfer from our inward nature a human interest and semblance of truth sufficient to procure for these shadows of imagination that willing suspension of disbelief for the moment, which constitutes poetic faith.[5]

As a way into the poem as an exercise in critical interpretation and (perhaps more to the point) critical humility, let me start by going back to the puzzled response of Coleridge's contemporary, Charles Burney,

---

4   Unless I am referring specifically to the first (1798) edition, all quotations from the poem are from the later, 1834 edition, *Poetical Works*, The Collected Works of Samuel Taylor Coleridge, 16, ed. J. C. C. Mays (Princeton, N. J.: Princeton University Press, 2001).
5   *Biographia Literaria*, The Collected Works of Samuel Taylor Coleridge, 7, ed. James Engell and W. Jackson Bate, 2 vols (Princeton, N. J.: Princeton University Press, 1983), 2:5–6.

which I quoted in the first chapter. Burney was at once bemused and, in spite of himself, impressed:

> The author's first piece, the 'Rime of the ancyent Marinere', in imitation of the *style* as well as the spirit of our elder poets, is the strangest story of a cock and a bull that we ever saw on paper: yet, though it seems a rhapsody of unintelligible wildness and incoherence, (of which we do not perceive the drift, unless the joke lies in depriving the wedding guest of his share of the feast) there are in it poetical touches of an exquisite kind.[6]

What *The Rime* and folk tale and nightmare have in common (besides a strange interiority and the fantastic) is the fact that they all, at some symbolic level, touch upon human anxieties usually censored by the rational mind. The effect of the fantastic, nightmare imagery and fabulous events in *The Rime*, aided and abetted by the romantic *defamiliarisation* of the archaic language—making strange, estranging—and by the primitive ballad form and its sensational immediacy, is to recapture some of the naivety and enigma, as well as the sheer terror, of the folk narrative, with its simple, insistent repetitions and rhyme:

> All in a hot and copper sky,
> The bloody Sun, at noon,
> Right up above the mast did stand,
> No bigger than the Moon.
>
> Day after day, day after day,
> We stuck, nor breath nor motion;
> As idle as a painted ship
> Upon a painted ocean.

---

6   Charles Burney, review of *Lyrical Ballads* in the *Monthly Review* 29 (June 1799), in *Coleridge: The Critical Heritage*, ed. J. R. de J. Jackson (London: Routledge & Kegan Paul, 1970), 55–57 (56).

5 The Search for Meaning in *The Rime of the Ancient Mariner*

> Water, water, everywhere,
> And all the boards did shrink;
> Water, water, everywhere,
> Nor any drop to drink.
>
> The very deep did rot: O Christ!
> That ever this should be!
> Yea, slimy things did crawl with legs
> Upon the slimy sea.
>
> About, about, in reel and rout
> The death-fires danced at night;
> The water, like a witch's oils,
> Burnt green, and blue and white.
>
> And some in dreams assurèd were
> Of the Spirit that plagued us so;
> Nine fathom deep he had followed us
> From the land of mist and snow.
>
> And every tongue, through utter drought,
> Was withered at the root;
> We could not speak, no more than if
> We had been choked with soot.
>
> Ah! well-a-day! what evil looks
> Had I from old and young!
> Instead of the cross, the Albatross
> About my neck was hung.
>
> (ll. 111–42)

If modern academic criticism has found it difficult to determine the exact meaning of the recurrent images in Coleridge's extreme, elemental seascape—sun and moon; heat and cold; movement and stasis (or paralysis); drought and rain; ship and sailor; hermit and pilot; albatross and watersnake; ocean and harbour—we have the dubious comfort of knowing that we share our confusion with Charles Burney and numerous others among Coleridge's original readers.

Although the exact significance of all these images or symbols escapes us, however, it is not difficult to accept that they do indeed signify. And it is the same with the supernatural or demonic elements—the spectre ship; Death and Life-in-Death; the Polar Spirit and his fellow demons; the seraph-band—so figurative, so suggestive of the moral and mental state that Coleridge portrays. For Coleridge, the small-'r' romantic—which is to say, the exotic, the strange, what we would call 'the paranormal'—was always a psychology:

> A lady once asked me if I believed in ghosts and apparitions. I answered with truth and simplicity: *No, madam! I have seen far too many myself.* I have indeed a whole memorandum book filled with records of these phænomena, many of them interesting as facts and data for psychology, and affording some valuable materials for a theory of perception and its dependence on the memory and imagination.[7]

> Indeed, the best service which the Mesmerism or Zoomagnetism has yet done is that it enables us to explain the Oracles and a score of other superstitions without recourse either to downright self-conscious Lying and Imposture on the one side, or to the Devil and his Works on the other—reducing the whole of Dæmonology and Diabolography to Neuropathology.[8]

But the question remains: how exactly are we to read this cock and bull story? How do we navigate its inconsistencies and illogicalities? The virtuoso musical effects of the poem conspire with the stark imagery and bizarre, yet curiously inevitable events (like those of nightmare) to embroil Coleridge's readers in an experience close to their hearts and beyond their understanding. But not, tellingly, beyond their conjecture.

---

7   Coleridge on 'Ghosts and Apparitions' in *The Friend*, in 2 vols, ed. Barbara E. Rooke (Princeton, N. J.: Princeton University Press, 1969), 1:146.
8   From Coleridge's notebooks, as quoted in *Inquiring Spirit: A New Presentation of Coleridge from His Published and Unpublished Prose Writings*, ed. Kathleen Coburn, revised edition (Toronto: University of Toronto Press, 1979), 56–57.

5 The Search for Meaning in *The Rime of the Ancient Mariner*

There are almost as many interpretations of *The Rime* as there have been readers. The visionary, allegorical form of the poem seems, like a dream, to demand interpretation—just as, arguably also like a dream, it frustrates interpretation.

This frustration is only compounded by the fact that we know only too well what happens and what the poem is about (we just do not know what it means). What the poem is about is the impulse to violate, it is about sin or transgression, and about punishment, appeasement, redemption, guilt. What happens is that, unthinkingly, a Mariner kills an albatross that has accompanied his ship under duress and, as a result, all hell breaks loose, leading ultimately to the destruction of all the crew except the Mariner himself. The Mariner is then subject to some exquisite torture until he unthinkingly blesses the slimy watersnakes—and the blessing proves to be the kind of liberating, unself-conscious act of love that occasions redemption and recovery in the conversation poems. Through it, the Mariner finds the reconciliation with nature and God for which he yearns:

> O happy living things! no tongue
> Their beauty might declare:
> A spring of love gushed from my heart,
> And I blessed them unaware:
> Sure my kind saint took pity on me,
> And I blessed them unaware.
>
> The selfsame moment I could pray;
> And from my neck so free
> The Albatross fell off, and sank
> Like lead into the sea.
>
> (ll. 282–91)

It is the very unconsciousness of the Mariner's gesture—its spontaneity—that seems to guarantee its authenticity.

Except that his suffering does not end there:

> The other was a softer voice,
> As soft as honey-dew:
> Quoth he, 'The man hath penance done,
> And penance more will do.'
>
> (ll. 408–409)

Nor, indeed, are we ever allowed to imagine the Mariner has been forgiven for and absolved of his sin—if, indeed, it is a sin; the jury is out on that one, too. Whatever we choose to call it, however, it seems that no amount of confession or expiation will ever relieve the Mariner, other than momentarily, of the burden of what he has done and the burden of what he knows:

> 'O shrieve me, shrieve me, holy man!',
> The hermit crossed his brow.
> 'Say quick,' quoth he, 'I bid thee say—
> What manner of man art thou?'
>
> Forthwith this frame of mine was wrenched
> With a woful agony,
> Which forced me to begin my tale;
> And then it left me free.
>
> Since then, at an uncertain hour,
> That agony returns:
> And till my ghastly tale is told,
> This heart within me burns.
>
> (ll. 574–85)

A prisoner of his own past actions, the Mariner is condemned to 'pass, like night, from land to land' (l. 586) and compelled to repeat his tale to those who, for good or ill, *must* hear it: 'To him my tale I teach' (l. 590).

What it is exactly that the tale teaches, however, remains a mystery, and this in spite of the fact that *The Rime* is one of the most extensively interpreted and famously interpretable poems in the language. Richard Holmes offers an abbreviated critical anthology:

5 The Search for Meaning in *The Rime of the Ancient Mariner*

The ballad has been variously interpreted as a Christian allegory of fall and redemption; a moral study of the origins of Evil; a symbolic account of the *poète maudit* figure; an autobiographical vision of opium addiction; a 'Green parable' of man's destruction of nature and Nature's revenge; and a psychological investigation of post-traumatic stress syndrome with its well established features of obsessive recall and compulsive guilt.[9]

Even the most superficial investigation into the poem's critical history will reveal just how drastically abbreviated Holmes's list is, for all that it can be said to represent the most common readings the poem has occasioned.

As it happens, readers and critics of *The Rime* share this irrepressible desire to understand the significance of the narrative—to make sense of it, as we say—with the unlikely characters that feature in the tale itself: the Mariner, the Wedding Guest, the Hermit, the Pilot's Boy. All, like the reader, have their conjectures. The Mariner, as we saw, is especially busy interpreting his own experience, struggling to identify the meaning and moral significance of the creatures he confronts and the events that overwhelm him. Indeed, it is the Mariner who offers what has become the poem's most common interpretation:

> He prayeth best, who loveth best
> All things both great and small;
> For the dear God who loveth us,
> He made and loveth all.
>
> (ll. 614–17)

But is the Mariner to be trusted? 'What manner of man art thou?', asks the Wedding Guest, insinuating that the Mariner is not human at all, but a demonic spirit, and the Pilot's Boy takes the Mariner to be the devil himself. Whatever else *The Rime of the Ancient Mariner* may be about, then, it is also about interpretation, about the need to reduce the

---

9 Richard Holmes, *Samuel Taylor Coleridge: Selected Poetry* (London: Penguin, 1996), 311.

mysterious and the irrational and the arbitrary in our world, and in our experience, to something manageable and ordered, in a kind of moral mathematics or bookkeeping. The poem dramatises our struggle to use what moral and supernatural constructs are available to us as historical beings to make sense of a universe alternately benign and alienating, and of human actions alternately murderous and altruistic.

The marginal gloss

To assist us in our endeavours, in response to criticism like Charles Burney's and under pressure from his joint author, William Wordsworth, Coleridge provided a marginal gloss. It is interesting to observe the change in the 'Argument' of the poem between its first publication in 1798 and the second edition of *Lyrical Ballads* in 1800, as various textual alterations and a new critical scaffolding conspire to enforce a heavily moral and theological reading of the poem:

> ARGUMENT (1798)
> How a Ship having passed the Line was driven by Storms to the cold Country towards the South Pole; and how from thence she made her course to the tropical Latitude of the Great Pacific Ocean; and of the strange things that befell; and in what manner the Ancyent Marinere came back to his own Country.

> ARGUMENT (1800)
> How a Ship, having first sailed to the Equator, was driven by Storms, to the cold Country towards the South Pole; how the Ancient Mariner cruelly, and in contempt of the laws of hospitality, killed the Sea-bird; and how he was followed by many and strange Judgements; and in what manner he came back to his own Country.

The marginal gloss that we find in all modern editions of the poem, which Coleridge introduced in 1817 and revised six years before his death in 1828, is entirely in keeping with this spirit of pious adjudication:

5 The Search for Meaning in *The Rime of the Ancient Mariner*

> The ancient Mariner inhospitably killeth the pious bird of good omen.
>
> … the Albatross begins to be avenged
>
> His shipmates cry out against the ancient Mariner, for killing the bird of good luck.
>
> But when the fog cleared off, they justify the same, and thus make themselves accomplices in the crime.
>
> The curse is finally expiated.
>
> And ever and anon throughout his future life an agony constraineth him to travel from land to land;
>
> And to teach, by his own example, love and reverence to all things that God made and loveth.

Sometimes the gloss indulges in its own poetry, echoing and extending the imagery and implication of the poem in haunting counterpoint—

> No twilight within the courts of the Sun.

—sometimes in a digressive nostalgia:

> In his loneliness and fixedness he yearneth towards the journeying Moon, and the stars that still sojourn, yet still move onward; and every where the blue sky belongs to them, and is their appointed rest, and their native country and their own natural homes, which they enter unannounced, as lords that are certainly expected and yet there is a silent joy at their arrival.

Far from inspiring confidence, however, Coleridge's glossarist creates as many problems as he solves, and, as with the Mariner, there remains a radical uncertainty as to just how far the glossarist is to be trusted. Most readings of the poem are heavily influenced by the gloss's morally tendentious interpretations, but protests about Coleridge's emendations and additions have sounded periodically throughout the critical history of *The Rime of the Ancient Mariner*, starting with the author himself in his later table talk:

> Mrs Barbauld once told me that she admired the 'Ancient Mariner' very much, but that there were two faults in it,—it was improbable, and had no moral. As for probability, I owned that that might admit some question; but as to the want of a moral, I told her that in my own judgment the poem had too much; and that the only, or chief fault, if I might say so, was the obtrusion of the moral sentiment so openly on the reader as the principle or cause of action in a work of such pure imagination. It ought to have had no more moral than the 'Arabian Nights' tale of the merchant's sitting down to eat dates by the side of a well, and throwing the shells aside, and lo! a genie starts up, and says he *must* kill the aforesaid merchant, because one of the date shells had, it seems, put out the eye of the genie's son.[10]

Some scholars, most notably David Pirie and William Empson, have been openly hostile to what they see as the interpretative manipulations of the 'ageing Coleridge':

> The marginalia turn the speaker into a specimen. Worse, they lie. It is clearly not true, nor ever could be, that 'the curse is finally expiated' and the very real creature that the mariners fed on biscuit-worms cannot become 'a pious bird of good omen' without being ludicrous.[11]

---

10   As quoted in *Samuel Taylor Coleridge*, The Oxford Authors, ed. H. J. Jackson (Oxford: Oxford University Press, 1985), 593–94.
11   *Coleridge's Verse: A Selection*, ed. David Pirie and William Empson (London: Faber & Faber, 1972), 214–15.

5 The Search for Meaning in *The Rime of the Ancient Mariner*

Though at times memorably succinct and often eloquent, the gloss nevertheless remains incommensurate with the experience *of* the text and with the experience *in* the text. The closer we attend to its interpretation of events, the more aware we become of its silences, its reductiveness, its irrelevancies, and its misreadings, over-readings, and under-readings. All of which, incidentally, are endemic to literary interpretation. Empson and Pirie's anger at the glossarist's unjustified arrogation of interpretative authority is one that might be directed at all interpretative criticism, certainly at the kind of criticism that presumes to have settled the issue and to have explained—or explained away—what appears in the text as 'unintelligible wildness and incoherence'.

Empson and Pirie's frustration with the 'ageing Coleridge', however, is itself only an interpretation—yet another interpretation. An alternative way of understanding the gap that opens up between the incidents and sentiments of the poem, on the one hand, and its reductive gloss, on the other, is to see the disjunction itself as a textual and rhetorical device shifting the issue of interpretation into the foreground—as Seamus Perry does:

> the Mariner contemplates hopelessly an identity of church-going communion, and just so his poem (as it were) looks to the would-be paraphrase of the gloss to draw from its private agonies the coherence of a publicly available moral; but the marginal commentary is often obtusely at odds with the poem it is meant to be expounding, as though a dark parody of successful connection, and only compounds the darkness.[12]

Which is why reading *The Rime of the Ancient Mariner*, with or without its gloss, gives us privileged access into the whole issue of what it is we are doing when we engage with a poem—indeed, with any work of art. The question of interpretation is central to the poem itself. In and through its various meta-commentaries, the poem dramatises the search for meaning, even while at the same time soliciting our interpretative interest, our conjecture.

---

12   Seamus Perry, 'Coleridge and the End of Autonomy', in *Samuel Taylor Coleridge and the Sciences of Life*, ed. Nicholas Roe (Oxford: Clarendon, 2001), 246–68 (263).

Let us take the example that Pirie and Empson allude to in their exasperation with the gloss:

At length did cross an Albatross,	Till a great sea-bird, called the
Thorough the fog it came;	Albatross came through the
As if it had been a Christian soul,	snow-fog, and was received
We hailed it in God's name.	with great joy and hospitality.

It ate the food it ne'er had eat,
And round and round it flew.
The ice did split with a thunder-fit;
The helmsman steered us through!

And a good south wind sprung up behind;	And lo! the Albatross proveth
The Albatross did follow,	a bird of good omen, and
And every day, for food or play,	followeth the ship as it
Came to the mariner's hollo!	returned northward through
	fog and floating ice.

In mist or cloud, on mast or shroud,
It perched for vespers nine;
Whiles all the night, through fog-smoke white,
Glimmered the white moon-shine.

'God save thee, ancient Mariner!	
From the fiends, that plague thee thus!—	The ancient Mariner
Why look'st thou so?'—With my cross-bow	inhospitably killeth the
I shot the Albatross.	pious bird of good omen.

PART II

The Sun now rose upon the right:
Out of the sea came he,
Still hid in mist, and on the left
Went down into the sea.

5 The Search for Meaning in *The Rime of the Ancient Mariner*

And the good south wind still blew behind,
But no sweet bird did follow,
Nor any day for food or play
Came to the mariners' hollo!

And I had done an hellish thing,   His ship-mates cry out against
And it would work 'em woe: the ancient Mariner, for killing
For all averred, I had killed the bird   the bird of good luck.
That made the breeze to blow.
Ah wretch! said they, the bird to slay,
That made the breeze to blow!

Nor dim nor red, like God's own head,   But when the fog cleared off,
The glorious Sun uprist: they justify the same, and thus
Then all averred, I had killed the bird   make themselves accomplices
That brought the fog and mist.   in the crime.
'Twas right, said they, such birds to slay,
That bring the fog and mist.

We note throughout this crucial passage a conflicted chorus, not to say chaos, of interpretation. The bird is welcomed '*as if* it had been a Christian soul'—a simile, note, and an index of the way the bird has been *interpreted* rather than of what the bird in fact *is*. The coincidence of the bird's arrival and the splitting of the ice prompts the glossarist to declare it a 'pious bird of good omen', but already we sense the incident is being overlaid by interpretation. The bird's very presence throughout the crew's 'vespers', or evening prayers, makes it a tutelary spirit and devout by association.

Until a change of circumstance—a change in that notoriously unpredictable element in all our lives, the weather—renders the bird's spiritual status equivocal. The credulous crew is bound to associate the renewed beneficence of God, signalled in the change of weather, with the slaughter of the albatross contiguous with it, and to congratulate the Mariner on his ritual sacrifice: 'all *averred*, I had killed the bird / That brought the fog and mist'. *Aver* here means 'to assert as a fact', to 'declare' something to be 'true' (OED). But assertion or declaration, however bold, cannot *make* something true. (A lesson here, incidentally, on how *not* to interpret climate change.) The glossarist himself clings to his reading of the bird as an emissary of God in a moral allegory and spreads the burden of responsibility to implicate the Mariner's shipmates in his 'crime'. In so doing, however, the glossarist unwittingly abandons his reading of events as a simple moral allegory, and the question of the significance of the presence or absence of the bird is quietly passed over. The other arch-interpreter, the Mariner himself, remains undecided throughout the incident: impressionable, *vacillating* along with the crew, reporting his own actions almost entirely through their reading of it.

The phantasms of time and place

Coleridge uses the proliferation of interpretations here and elsewhere partly to intensify the Gothic experience and deepen the mystery of his tale, but also partly to question the nature and presumption of interpretative authority, to hint (and here we get at what we might call the onto-theological point of it all) at the limitation and vulnerability of human reason:

> Every sentence found in a canonical Book, rightly interpreted, contains the *dictum* of an infallible Mind;—but what the right interpretation is,—or whether the very words now extant are corrupt or genuine—must be determined by the industry and understanding of fallible and alas! more or less prejudiced theologians.[13]

---

13 *Confessions of an Inquiring Spirit*, ed. H. N. Coleridge (London: W. Pickering, 1840), 53–54. For Coleridge's interest in the exegetical tradition and 'new approaches to textual criticism which were being most radically pursued in Germany', see Elinor Shaffer, *'Kubla Khan' and the Fall of Jerusalem: The Mythological School of Biblical Criticism and Secular Literature, 1770–1880* (Cambridge: Cambridge University Press, 1975), Chapters 1–3, and Jerome McGann 'The Meaning of the Ancient Mariner', *Critical Inquiry*, 8:1 (Autumn 1981), 35–67 (44).

5 The Search for Meaning in *The Rime of the Ancient Mariner*

So it is dealing with the more or less prejudiced theologian who glosses the Mariner's story. The gloss offers an often stylised reading of an antiquarian narrative by an equally antiquated editor—*not* Coleridge himself, but an at times credulous, always judgemental Coleridgean persona, modelled on Coleridge's reading of sixteenth- and seventeenth-century prose and part of the poem's antiquarian affectation:

> A Spirit had followed them; one of the invisible inhabitants of the planet, neither departed souls nor angels; concerning whom the learned Jew, Josephus, and the Platonic Constantinopolitan, Michael Psellus, may be consulted. They are very numerous, and there is no climate or element without one or more.

As well as being a testament to Coleridge's omnivorous reading, the glossarist's animated universe betrays the superstitions of an utterly alien mentality. '[A] mighty providence subdues the mightiest Minds to the service of the time being', wrote Keats in a letter to J. H. Reynolds, 'whether it be in human Knowledge or Religion'.[14] For Coleridge, too, 'all our notions' were 'husked in the phantasms of Time & Place, that still escape the finest sieve & most searching Winnow of our Reason & Abstraction'.[15] Just as history is the condition of our being, so is it the condition of our seeing and understanding, making *The Rime*, in Jerome McGann's words, 'a special theory of the historical interpretation of texts'.[16] This is the burden of the mock-solemn epigraph from Thomas Burnet, included with the gloss in the 1817 edition of the poem:

> Facile credo, plures esse Naturas invisibiles quam visibiles in rerum universitate. Sed horum omnium familiam quis nobis enarrabit? et gradus et cognationes et discrimina et singulorum munera? Quid agunt? quæ loca habitant? Harum rerum notitiam semper ambivit ingenium humanum, nunquam attigit. Juvat, interea, non diffiteor,

---

14   *The Letters of John Keats 1814–1821*, ed. Hyder Edward Rollins, 2 vols (Cambridge, Mass.: Harvard University Press, 1958), 1:282.
15   *The Notebooks of Samuel Taylor Coleridge*, ed. Kathleen Coburn et al., in 5 vols (London: Routledge and Kegan Paul, 1957–2002), 1, note 334 (c. ?1802).
16   McGann 'The Meaning of the Ancient Mariner', 50.

quandoque in animo, tanquam in Tabulâ, majoris et melioris mundi
imaginem contemplari ne mens assuefacta hodiernæ vitæ minutiis se
contrahat nimis, et tota subsidat in pusillas cogitationes. Sed veritati
interea invigilanum est, modusque servandus, ut certa ab incertis,
diem a nocte, distinguamus.—T. BURNET, *Archæol. Phil.* p. 68

[I can easily believe that there are more invisible creatures in the universe than visible ones. But who will tell us what family each belongs to, what their ranks and relationships are, and what their respective distinguishing characters might be? What do they do? Where do they live? Human wit has always circled around a knowledge of these things without ever attaining it. But I do not doubt that it is beneficial sometimes to contemplate in the mind, as in a picture, the image of a grander and better world; for if the mind grows used to the trivia of daily life, it may dwindle too much and decline altogether into worthless thoughts. Meanwhile, however, we must be on the watch for the truth, keeping a sense of proportion so that we can tell what is certain from what is uncertain and day from night.]

Coleridge is using the Burnet quotation in a complex number of ways. He is using it, in the first instance, as he occasionally uses the gloss: to conjure an historically alien mentality or imagination, one that is credulous, superstitious. Or as he uses the Mariner, whose invocations to Mary and his 'kind saint' suggest an older, pre-Reformation perspective. The Mariner is bound to interpret 'the strange things that befell' him with whatever explanatory systems lie to hand—including, along with what passes as natural philosophy or 'science', prevailing superstitions and theology. And what lies to hand is a primitive array of un-integrated beliefs and values—like transmigration, spectre-barks, and Polar Spirits. In other words, one of the main interpretative gulfs which open up between the different characters in the poem, and between the characters and their readers, is an historical one: a change of taste, of worldview (*Weltanschauung*), and of understanding over time. The antiquarian impulse that survived Coleridge's reluctant modernisation of the poem is still apparent in the final version in the Mariner's (and Burnet's) obviously dated spiritual hierarchies—and, as we saw, in the antiquated gloss.

5 The Search for Meaning in *The Rime of the Ancient Mariner*

At the same time, however, Coleridge also uses the Burnet epigraph to challenge the complacency of the enlightened reader among his contemporaries, for whom the past is nothing more than a tissue of superstitions. 'There are more things in heaven and earth, Horatio', protests Hamlet, 'Than are dreamt of in your philosophy'.[17] That the events of *The Rime of the Ancient Mariner* do not 'make sense'—or, better still, that they do not 'add up'—suggests two things, each of which implies the other. The first is that there is something deeply inadequate about human understanding, about our powers of interpretation. The second is that human life and human action, like God himself for the devout Coleridge, are bound to remain incomprehensible—it is not possible, that is, to get our minds around them, neither is it right that we should. We are back with the conflict between the impulse to know and the need to resign ourselves to the unknowable that fissures Coleridge's 'The Eolian Harp'.

Bernard Smith concludes his examination of Coleridge's use of James Cook's second Pacific voyage as a source and paradigm for the Mariner's journey by emphasising the stark contrast between the two voyages, one 'real', the other 'romantic':

> The most carefully planned and the most scientifically and efficiently conducted expedition ever made up to its time in the realm of reality provided the poet with a world of wonder and a nucleus of recollections from whence emerged in its own good time the most romantic voyage ever undertaken in the realm of the imagination.[18]

And this is Coleridge's point, surely, his 'gloss' on the second scientific revolution, as comprehensive in its own way as Mary Shelley's resilient myth of Victor Frankenstein and his Creature. The rage for scientific knowledge resulted in a riot of interpretative activity that would traverse and itemise the globe (Joseph Banks), and explain the heavens (William Herschel) and the earth (James Hutton). What it all might mean, however, what it can tell us about human purpose and mortality,

---

17 *Hamlet* 1.5.166–7.
18 Bernard Smith, 'Coleridge's *Ancient Mariner* and Cook's Second Voyage', in his *Imagining the Pacific: In the Wake of Cook's Voyages*, 171.

are questions rather begged than answered by this activity. At the explanatory centre of the Mariner's narrative is the throw of dice:

> And is that Woman all her crew?
> Is that a Death? and are there two?
> Is Death that woman's mate?
>
> Her lips were red, *her* looks were free,
> Her locks were yellow as gold:
> Her skin was as white as leprosy,
> The Night-mare Life-in-Death was she,
> Who thicks man's blood with cold.
>
> The naked hulk alongside came,
> And the twain were casting dice;
> "The game is done! I've won! I've won!"
> Quoth she, and whistles thrice.
>
> (ll. 187–98)

The foul rag and bone shop of the heart

Both Cook's and Coleridge's voyages chart the unknown, but in *The Rime* we are left with what cannot be reduced to meaning. However hard we try to understand—to rationalise—the actions of the Mariner, some things remain inexplicable or mysterious: one is human motive (why we do what we do), another the operation of human conscience (how it works, where it comes from). At the time Coleridge and Wordsworth began their intense friendship in June of 1797, both poets were working on tragedies of crime and punishment, guilt and sorrow, fixated on the power of conscience. The character Rivers from Wordsworth's *The Borderers* summed up the incommensurateness of human imagination:

> Action is transitory—a step, a blow,
> The motion of a muscle, this way or that,
> 'Tis done—and in the after-vacancy

5 The Search for Meaning in *The Rime of the Ancient Mariner*

> We wonder at ourselves like men betrayed:
> Suffering is permanent, obscure and dark,
> And hath the nature of infinity.
> (*The Borderers*, 3.5.60–65)

The only certainty about the 'moral' of *The Rime of the Ancient Mariner* is that there is a deeply human compulsion to find a moral in events that ultimately resist moralisation—just as they resist other kinds of explanation and resolution. Through its search for meaning, Coleridge is able to explore the nature of and need for authority—critical, moral, religious. *The Rime of the Ancient Mariner* is about interpretation, but not just in the sense of finding or discovering meaning and value in the face of meaninglessness and arbitrariness. It is also about interpretation in the sense of *making* meaning and value in the face of meaninglessness and arbitrariness.

However we choose to interpret the imagery and action of the poem, one thing remains irrefutable, and that is the Mariner's overwhelming sense of his own guilt and existential isolation:

> Alone, alone, all, all alone,
> Alone on a wide, wide Sea!
> And never a saint took pity on
> My soul in agony.
>
> The many men, so beautiful!
> And they all dead did lie:
> And a thousand, thousand slimy things
> Lived on; and so did I.
> (ll. 232–39)

We are back in what W. B. Yeats, in his poem 'The Circus Animals' Desertion', calls the 'foul rag and bone shop of the heart', back with a Coleridgean isolation at once immediate and personal—not to say psychopathological—and yet at the same time transformed through poetry into something profoundly representative. 'Here is a voice that expresses unrelieved, naked, desperate suffering. It is the voice of a man with no place to go, no one to turn to, least of all providential aid', writes Raimonda Modiano.[19]

> O Wedding-Guest! this soul hath been
> Alone on a wide wide sea:
> So lonely 'twas, that God himself
> Scarce seemed there to be.
>
> (ll. 597–600)

Seamus Perry has pointed out two ways of reading this harrowing stanza: either 'the place was so lonely that God did not seem to be there'—suggestive of a condition of the mind or soul abandoned by all support—or what Perry calls 'a more appalling sense': 'I was so isolated and bereft, that God scarce seemed to exist at all'.[20] There is the further, arguably much larger question of whom or what we are that is begged here: the question of human *being*. And perhaps, after all, that is all there is: human being, not human meaning. The overriding or informing anxiety of *The Rime of the Ancient Mariner*, then, may be an anxiety not just about moral disproportion or the incomprehensibility of human motive, but about an ultimate onto-theological meaninglessness: the vast inanity and inconsequentiality of human being.

In all this existential bleakness, there is one significant consolation, both for Coleridge and for the reader. There is the poetry. Coleridge has succeeded in recapturing from the ballad tradition a dramatic immediacy which, aided by the incantation of its prosody and its prosodic and rhetorical virtuosity, is entrancing in ways that, as all readers have noticed, resemble the Mariner's own. We are dragged along 'like Tom Piper's magic Whistle', as Charles Lamb said, defending the poem against Wordsworth's obtuseness.[21] Listening 'like a three years' child'

---

19   Raimonda Modiano, 'Historicist Readings of "The Ancient Mariner"', in *Samuel Taylor Coleridge and the Sciences of Life*, ed. Nicholas Roe (Oxford: Clarendon, 2001), 271–96 (275).
20   Seamus Perry, 'Coleridge and the End of Autonomy', 250.
21   In a letter to Wordsworth, 30 January 1801, *The Letters of Charles and Mary Anne Lamb*, ed. Edwin W. Marrs, Jr, Vol. 1 (Ithaca and London: Cornell University Press, 1975), 266.

5 The Search for Meaning in *The Rime of the Ancient Mariner*

to the Mariner (l. 15), the Wedding Guest embarks upon what is admittedly an agonising journey, one as far removed experientially and emotionally from the joy and celebration of the wedding feast as the tale is removed from the familiar world. The reader, too, is constrained to hear and to relive the tale. Their consolation is the captivating richness of the Mariner's storytelling—a richness that one recognises not only as 'poetic', but as in some sense representative of the poetic, representative of poetry itself. This magic may make the poetry especially resistant to 'translation' into explanatory paraphrase and moral generalisation, yet this pleasurable magic also insists on the uniqueness of poetry as a way of understanding and articulating and shaping experience.

6
Interpreting the Politics of *Pride and Prejudice*

Progressively more preoccupied with individual sensibility and with the individual as a morally autonomous consciousness, the social phenomenon of the novel reflected changes in political and philosophical thinking that altered the personal and social construction of the self in the eighteenth century. These changes in thinking invariably led writers back to the question of authority: of who should rule over, or overrule, whom; of what entitled or empowered someone—or, more ethically, what qualified someone—to rule at all. Once upon a time the answers, certainly to the first of these questions, had appeared self-evident: nominally, at least, men were to rule over women and parents to overrule their children. In society as a whole, 'land was the most important single passport to social and political consideration', representing 'not merely wealth, but stability and continuity, a fixed interest in the state which conferred the right to govern.'[1] But throughout the eighteenth century the question of authority or 'the right to govern' became progressively more vexed and by the 1790s, the years of Jane Austen's personal maturation and literary apprenticeship and the opening years of the war with the new French republic, the question was not only vexed, but exigent.

---

1 J. V. Beckett, *The Aristocracy in England 1660–1914* (Oxford: Blackwell, 1986), 43.

Jane Austen's changing reputation

I suggested in Chapter 1 that the tension between realism and the romantic is (with the reader's willing complicity) artfully resolved in Jane Austen's fiction, allowing her novels to keep faith with what we are while at the same time pandering to what we most desire. Of this, *Pride and Prejudice* is surely exemplary. A Cinderella romance of extraordinary resilience and popularity, nevertheless it has spawned a multitude of powerful critical readings analysing its social and political awareness. It is no longer possible to discuss Jane Austen's writing independently of the urgent political issues that occupied her more historically minded contemporaries, or to argue (as George Steiner did in 1975) that it was precisely because of her indifference to 'the fierce historical, social crises' which surrounded her that 'the area defined for imaginative penetration could be superbly exploited'.[2] On the contrary, Austen's apparent indifference is now recognised as artistic indirection, and her novels are read as articulate forms of an historical awareness no less acute, and no less earnestly engaged with contemporary political issues, than Edmund Burke's *Reflections on the Revolution in France*, Mary Wollstonecraft's *Vindication of the Rights of Woman*, or William Wordsworth's *Lyrical Ballads*. The titles of critical studies of Jane Austen's novels in recent decades alone challenge the assumption of their decorous atemporality and insularity: *Jane Austen and the War of Ideas*; *Jane Austen and the French Revolution*; *Jane Austen and the State*; *Jane Austen in a Social Context*; *Jane Austen: Women, Politics, and the Novel*; *Jane Austen and Representations of Regency England*; *Jane Austen and the Discourses of Feminism*; *The Politics of Jane Austen*; *The Postcolonial Jane Austen*; *The Historical Austen*; *Jane Austen and the Romantic Poets*—among many, many others.[3] In their concern with

---

[2] George Steiner, 'Eros and Idiom', in *On Difficulty and Other Essays* (Oxford and New York: Oxford University Press, 1978), 95–136 (131).
[3] Marilyn Butler, *Jane Austen and the War of Ideas* (Oxford: Clarendon, 1975); Warren Roberts, *Jane Austen and the French Revolution* (Basingstoke and London: Macmillan, 1979); David Monaghan (ed.), *Jane Austen in a Social Context* (Basingstoke and London: Macmillan, 1981); Mary Evans, *Jane Austen and the State* (London and New York: Tavistock, 1987); Claudia L. Johnson, *Jane Austen: Women, Politics and the Novel* (Chicago and London: University of Chicago Press,

authority in the face of new philosophies that brought all in doubt; in their concern with the relationship between the individual as an autonomous, ethically and emotionally motivated subject, on the one hand, and, on the other, the society or societies to which that individual is somehow contractually related—Austen's fictions have taken their place alongside the dissertations of contemporary ideologues, the articles and pamphlets and open letters of contemporary polemicists, and the dispatches of contemporary politicians.

As literary parodies, her novels show how popular, fictional distortions may reflect and even engender profound ethical and social imbalances of the kind then under debate in more overtly political arenas. As comedies of manners, they are shot through with social and political nuances because for Austen, as for Edmund Burke, manners 'are more important than laws': 'Manners', wrote Burke, 'are what vex or soothe, corrupt or purify, exalt or debase, barbarise or refine us'. Far from being mere conventions (least of all literary ones), manners 'give their whole form and colour to our lives. According to their quality, they add morals, they supply them, or they totally destroy them'.[4] The identification of manners in Austen's novels with morals and with culture—in short, with ideology—charges with significance every character, every utterance, every gesture, every action, every social event. 'A mind lively and at ease', as she comments in *Emma*, 'can see nothing that does not answer'.[5] Far from being seen as cut off and self-contained, the fictional worlds of Jane Austen's novels are now read as symbolic

---

1988); Roger Sales, *Jane Austen and Representations of Regency England* (London: Routledge, 1994); Devony Looser (ed.), *Jane Austen and the Discourses of Feminism* (New York: St Martin's Press, 1995); Edward Neill, *The Politics of Jane Austen* (London: Macmillan, 1999); You Mee Park and Rajeswari Sunder Rajan (eds), *The Postcolonial Jane Austen* (London: Routledge, 2000); William H. Galperin, *The Historical Austen* (Philadelphia: Pennsylvania University Press, 2003); William Deresiewicz, *Jane Austen and the Romantic Poets* (New York: Columbia University Press, 2004).
4   In the first of 'Four Letters on a Regicide Peace', as quoted in Terry Eagleton, *The Ideology of the Aesthetic* (Oxford: Blackwell, 1990), 42.
5   Jane Austen, *Emma*, The Cambridge Edition of the Works of Jane Austen, ed. Richard Cronin and Dorothy Macmillan (Cambridge: Cambridge University Press, 2005), 251.

of English society in a revolutionary age—symbolic in the Coleridgean sense of partaking 'of the Reality which it renders intelligible'.[6]

The divided politics of *Pride and Prejudice*

It is one thing, however, for criticism to acknowledge her high-minded engagement with the urgent questions of authority and its mandate, it is quite another for it to achieve anything like clarity or consensus on what, precisely, Austen's position was on such issues as primogeniture, patronage, the place of women, the slave trade, the distribution of wealth, and parliamentary reform. That the question of authority is at issue in *Pride and Prejudice*, for example, is immediately apparent. It is explored through elaborate patterns of dependence and independence, decision and indecision, control and licence, which constitute the novel's moral design or 'mapping', and is most often raised by its abuse or abrogation. We are witness to Mr Bennet's exercising no control over the destructive inanities of Mrs Bennet, or over the shameless and trivialising behaviour of his shallower daughters (or over his bank account, for that matter); to Sir William Lucas's opting out of bourgeois society in order to indulge in aristocratic fantasies and abandoning his daughters on the marriage market without a creditable dowry, leaving them prey to characters far worse than Mr Collins (or so Charlotte decides); to Bingley's good-natured but whimsical irresolution, leaving him prey to the prejudiced certitude of Mr Darcy; to the Colonel's and Mrs Forster's neglecting their role *in loco parentis*, leaving Lydia prey to Wickham (as well as to her own stupidity); to the Bingley sisters' self-serving representation of the polite world, asserting their authority over good taste and correct behaviour; to Mr Hurst's opting out of responsible, rational existence all together; and so on.

What is less apparent, however, is the origin and precise political nature of this crisis of authority, or what the solution might be. The truth is that there are two ideological or political perspectives in *Pride*

---

6 In *Statesman's Manual*, in his *Lay Sermons*, The Collected Works of Samuel Taylor Coleridge, 6, ed. R. J. White, (Princeton, N. J.: Princeton University Press, 1972), 30.

6 Interpreting the Politics of *Pride and Prejudice*

and Prejudice, and the tension between those two perspectives, as they develop out of the action of the novel, is strategic, rather than merely adventitious. The challenge of the novel lies in its representing *both* sides of what Marilyn Butler identifies in the novels of the 1790s as a 'critical divide':

> between the advocates of a Christian conservatism on the one hand, with their pessimistic view of man's nature, and their belief in external authority; [and] on the other hand, progressives, sentimentalists, revolutionaries, with their optimism about man, and their preference for spontaneous personal impulse against rules imposed from without.[7]

What I propose to explore in this chapter is the divided political allegiance of *Pride and Prejudice* by isolating and examining its two, discrepant perspectives or positions—one progressive, the other conservative—and to ask, among other things, just how persuasive they are individually and whether their political implications are in co-operation or conflict with each other in the novel.[8] More than all of Austen's other novels, *Pride and Prejudice* expresses a yearning after the ideal that is both romantic fantasy and Romantic aspiration, both personal (intellectual and erotic) and socio-historical, blending questions of authority and order with questions of desire.

Novel openings

Of all the characters in the novel, only the Gardiners are consistently responsible and 'gentleman-like' (158), counselling and contributing without ever presuming to take over the affairs or the lives of others. And the Gardiners, significantly, are in trade, bringing to gentility the bourgeois virtues of (among others) expedition, industry, and a genuine

---

7   Butler, *Jane Austen and the War of Ideas*, 164–65.
8   All references to *Pride and Prejudice* included in the text are to the Cambridge Edition of the Works of Jane Austen, ed. Pat Rogers (Cambridge: Cambridge University Press, 2006).

humility. (Like all Jane Austen's figures of ethical authority, the Gardiners—aunt and uncle, word and deed—represent a complex of complementarities.) Their being in trade is significant because *Pride and Prejudice* is an often spirited, occasionally acrimonious attack upon the status quo, participating in 'that tradition in English culture which has consistently, from the seventeenth century, opposed arbitrary aristocratic and patriarchal privilege.'[9] It is in Darcy's unapologetic assumption of control over Bingley's life and destiny, for example, that the pervasive social disease of the abuse of aristocratic authority can be seen most dramatically and most emblematically. 'Why reverence a man because he happens to be born to certain privileges?' asks William Godwin in *Political Justice* (1793). Must we 'renounce our independence, in their presence?' 'In those cases of general justice which are equally within the province of every human understanding', continues Godwin, 'I am a deserter from the requisitions of duty if I do not assiduously exert my faculties, or if I be found to act contrary to the conclusions they would dictate, from deference to the opinions of others'.[10]

The attack on nobility in *Pride and Prejudice* is confined largely, though not exclusively, to the first half of the novel. To begin our tour of the novel's politics by tracing the progressive impulse at work in its actions and sentiments is to preserve Austen's own, carefully calculated priorities. The potential for a radical critique is in fact established at the very opening of the novel by Austen's most famous utterance, on the face of it an ingenious and spirited satire on the inquisitiveness and acquisitiveness of the provincial gentry to which she belonged: 'It is a truth universally acknowledged, that a single man in possession of a good fortune, must be in want of a wife'. Amidst the wealth of implication in this single sentence, three disturbing social strictures formulate themselves—more disturbing than we might expect of a mere flourish of local satire. First, there is the equivocal status of 'truth', here attenuated or debased by its implicit and ironic identification with a dubious, nominally 'universal' consensus. Acknowledgement, however

---

9 Evans, *Jane Austen and the State*, 65.
10 William Godwin, *Enquiry Concerning Political Justice* [1793], ed. Isaac Kramnick (Harmondsworth: Penguin, 1976), 245.

universal, cannot make something true. Accordingly, the verifying universality of the opening sentence shrinks comically to 'a neighbourhood' in the second: 'However little known the feelings or views of such a man may be on his first entering a neighbourhood, this truth is so well fixed in the minds of the surrounding families, that he is considered as the rightful property of some one or other of their daughters'. The novel will go on to suggest just how capricious both public and personal 'truth' can be, with the case of *Darcy v. Wickham* at the Meryton Assizes as exemplary: 'All Meryton seemed striving to blacken the man, who, but three months before, had been almost an angel of light' (325).

The second and third strictures of the opening sentence are legally and linguistically inseparable. They concern the socially constructed 'truth' of the relationship between marriage and money, on the one hand, and the dehumanisation of women into property, on the other. Both are established by a terminology of enormous suggestiveness:

'in possession of' (owning) / 'in possession of' (possessed by)
'a good fortune' (wealth) / 'a good fortune' (luck)
'in want' (need) / 'in want' (desire)
'must' (of necessity) / 'must' (imperative)

Even the strictly hierarchical 'man' and 'wife' from the Anglican Book of Common Prayer is smuggled in. And what the sentence does *not* say—what it surely tempts without attempting —is 'that a single man in want of a good fortune, must be in possession of a wife'. Simply by reversing the adverbial phrases in the relative clause we have the predicaments of Wickham and Colonel Fitzwilliam in a nutshell. Such is the double-edged nature of possession, moreover, that the subtle political and emotional symbiotics captured in these opening lines is soon established, as the 'single man' becomes 'the rightful property' of the daughters of 'the surrounding families'. Seeking to extend his rightful property by marriage, the single man becomes the property of those he would appropriate!

The critique of aristocracy

The satire on the abuses of truth, marriage, and women in these opening lines anticipates the progressivist critique of society in *Pride and Prejudice* that is our first concern. As a critique, certain incidents or episodes are crucial, and the long episode of Elizabeth's visit to the newlywed Collinses at Hunsford is a sensational example. It is during this visit that Darcy discovers that Lady Catherine de Bourgh is not qualified to assume the authority to which her position and wealth automatically entitle her. And when Darcy responds to Lady Catherine's treatment of Elizabeth at Rosings by looking 'a little ashamed at his aunt's ill-breeding' (195), he unwittingly anticipates the barbed accusation of his failing to behave 'in a more gentleman-like manner' (215) that Elizabeth is to level at him not long after. In this, as in his meddling in Bingley and Jane's relationship, Darcy proves himself his Aunt Catherine's nephew. These signal failures in 'that chastity of honour' characteristic of Edmund Burke's 'age of chivalry' mark decisive moments in the novel as an allegorical 'Pride's Progress', a remorseless humiliation of the aristocracy.[11]

Lady Catherine's style of patronage is, after all, an anachronism. Although as a literary character she is immediately identifiable as the dictatorial dowager of the comedy of manners from Congreve to Coward, it is important also to recognise the historically specific impropriety of her behaviour. Patronage, as Lady Catherine exercises it, is rather a patronising intrusion into the private lives—even into the thoughts and feelings—of individuals who have rights (to use an especially loaded word from the period that saw the publication and banning of Thomas Paine's *Rights of Man*) and the relative autonomy to think and choose for themselves. 'Mr. Collins, you must marry. A clergyman like you must marry', she declares (echoing the confusion of necessity with the imperative in the opening sentence): 'Chuse properly, chuse a gentlewoman for *my* sake; and for your *own*, let her be an active, useful sort of person, not brought up high, but able to make a small income go a good way. This is my advice. Find such a woman as

---

11 Edmund Burke, *Reflections on the Revolution in France* [1790], ed. J. D. C. Clark (Stanford: Stanford University Press, 2001), 238.

soon as you can, bring her to Hunsford, and I will visit her' (119). And for the gentlewoman's own sake? Lady Catherine's 'interest', in the old sense—the things that concern her and that come under her aristocratic aegis—is extended comically but tellingly to include matters as trivial as the way in which her serfs grow their vegetables. 'Nothing was beneath this great Lady's attention' (185).

It is hard to resist reading the exaggerated relationship between Lady Catherine and the Rev. Collins, whose Tartuffian blend 'of servility and self-importance' (71) only highlights his impotence and dependence, as a satirical reflection on the relationship between the state and a secularised, pusillanimous Church of England. What we can be certain of, in the comic politics of Austen's allegory of the aristocracy, is that both Mr Collins and Catherine de Bourgh are anachronistic and marginal to a new and commendable spirit, or spiritedness, the main expression or incarnation of which in *Pride and Prejudice* is the character of Elizabeth herself.

Central to the challenge that Elizabeth represents to the status quo is a brazen independence in the face of the intimidations of rank—specifically, in the face of Darcy and of his aunt. In the imposing, baroque context of Rosings, for example, when at last in the company of the woman who has been so self-abasingly and self-importantly heralded by Mr Collins, Elizabeth's composure stands for the defiance of the individual—of individual intelligence and self-possession—in the face of arrogant authoritarianism:

> Elizabeth's courage did not fail her. She had heard nothing of Lady Catherine that spoke her awful from any extraordinary talents or miraculous virtues, and the mere stateliness of money and rank, she thought she could witness without trepidation. (182)

For Elizabeth, 'money and rank' are merely stately, merely gratuitous, and she can witness the merely stately 'without trepidation', just as she has resisted Darcy's 'fortune and consequence' with a comparable intrepidity (87).

Elizabeth is prepared to defer only to talent and virtue, two attributes that, insofar as they ignored or transgressed the artificial boundaries of class, were integral to every program for political reform or revolution. The radical Thomas Holcroft spoke through his eponymous heroine in *Anna St. Ives* (1792):

> It appears evident to my mind, at present, that we ought to consider whether an action be in itself good or bad, just or unjust, and totally disregard both our own prejudices and the prejudices of the world. Were I to pay false homage to wealth and rank, because the world tells me that it is right that I should do so, and to neglect genius and virtue, which my judgment tells me would be an odious wrong, I should find but little satisfaction in the applause of the world, opposed to self-condemnation.[12]

Again, witness Godwin's *Political Justice*: 'the thing really to be desired is the removing as much as possible arbitrary distinctions, and leaving to talents and virtue the field of exertion unimpaired'.[13] In 1808, the Whig *Edinburgh Review* was more uncompromising than either Holcroft or Godwin:

> Now, if any man thinks, that we should not extravagantly rejoice in any conceivable event which must reform the constitution of England,—by reducing the overgrown influence of the crown,—by curbing the pretensions of the privileged orders ...—by raising up the power of real talents and worth, the true nobility of the country,—by exalting the mass of the community, and giving them, under the guidance of that virtual aristocracy, to direct the councils of England ... [he] must have read but few pages of this Journal.[14]

At Rosings, Elizabeth reserves her respect and deference only for the integrity and talents of 'that virtual aristocracy'.

---

12 Thomas Holcroft, *Anna St. Ives*, ed. Peter Faulkner (London: OUP, 1970), 343 (Vol. VI, letter 100).
13 Godwin, *Enquiry Concerning Political Justice*, 184.
14 In a review by Francis Jeffrey and Henry Brougham of Don Pedro Cevallos, *Exposition of the Practices and Machinations which led to the Usurpation of the Crown of Spain, Edinburgh Review*, 13 (October 1808), 215-234 (233-4).

6 Interpreting the Politics of *Pride and Prejudice*

It was the maverick eighteenth-century demagogue John Wilkes's notorious demand for 'a career open to talents' that in the 1760s made the concept and term 'talent' the catchcry of a radical challenge to the pervasive, unapologetic system of patronage and preferment that operated throughout the nation. Lady Catherine, for one, celebrates the power that she derives from the privileges she inherits and confers. Mr Bennet may convert Collins's toadying into broad humour when, at the end of the novel, he recommends that he hastily transfer his allegiance—'the nephew', he reminds Collins, 'has more to give' than his aunt (424)—but the toadying itself was only symptomatic of the institution. His wife Charlotte's passing calculation of the benefits to be gained by the couple from a marriage between Elizabeth and Darcy is too casually hard-edged even to be funny (203).

The politics of marriage

A comparably dark, less comic side to Lady Catherine's anachronism is revealed during her last encounter with Elizabeth at Longbourn, the encounter precipitated by Elizabeth's rumoured engagement to her nephew. Lady Catherine's belated flourish reflects both the crippling nostalgia and the consequent panic of the contemporary ruling class of England in the face of a threatened attenuation of its power. The echo of her shrill insistence upon the priority and authority of her own and her sister's engagement of Darcy with Lady Catherine's daughter, Ann, has a distinctly dying fall:

> 'The engagement between them is of a peculiar kind. From their infancy, they have been intended for each other. It was the favourite wish of *his* mother, as well as of her's. While in their cradles, we planned their union: and now, when the wishes of both sisters would be accomplished, in their marriage, to be prevented by a young woman of inferior birth, of no importance in the world, and wholly unallied to the family! Do you pay no regard to the wishes of his friends? To his tacit engagement to Miss De Bourgh? Are you lost to every feeling of propriety and delicacy?' (393)

It would be difficult to exaggerate the importance of the implicit elegy for a passing order in this and other episodes in the confrontation of Lady Catherine and Elizabeth. That the issue over which the two fall out should be marriage is no coincidence, for marriage was still the single most important power-building exercise in political succession, and in marriage the question of authority—of the individual's right to choose—bears directly upon both heart and holdings, almost exclusively so for most women of the period.

The complicity of author, heroine, and reader established in the exchange between Elizabeth and Lady Catherine suggests Austen's wholehearted approval of the priority of the young couple's rights over an older generation's self-interested preferences, and of the (small 'r') romantic assumption that affection and companionship should be major concerns in the selection of a partner. In line with the growing autonomy of the individual, eighteenth-century England had witnessed a 'marked shift in emphasis' in the motives for marriage 'away from family interest and towards well-tried personal affection.'[15] As life imitated art, the forms and language of romantic love began to influence or constrain the behaviour of all classes of society. 'Without taking into account this powerful, widespread, and impelling passion at the heart of the marriage system, it is impossible to make sense of the other features.'[16] 'Husband and wife are always together and share the same society', remarked the astonished French tourist, the Duc de Rochefoucauld, in 1784, adding that 'the Englishman would rather have the love of the woman he loves than the love of his parents.'[17] Elizabeth is no Marianne Dashwood, but that Elizabeth, too, accepts the shift in priorities is evidenced in her guarded response to her Aunt Gardiner's prudence:

> '... since we see every day that where there is affection, young people are seldom withheld by immediate want of fortune, from entering into engagements with each other, how can I promise to be wiser

---

15 Lawrence Stone, *The Family, Sex and Marriage in England 1500–1800* (Harmondsworth: Penguin, 1979), 183.
16 Alan Macfarlane, *Marriage and Love in England: Modes of Reproduction 1300–1840* (Oxford: Blackwell, 1986), 208.
17 As quoted in Stone, *The Family, Sex and Marriage*, 220.

6 Interpreting the Politics of *Pride and Prejudice*

than so many of my fellow-creatures if I am tempted, or how am I even to know that it would be wisdom to resist?' (164)

Romantic comedy offers such ample precedent for the obstruction of youthful love by superannuated 'interest' that an historically specific, political reading of the scene between Lady Catherine and Elizabeth would seem perverse, were it not for the fact that Lady Catherine's patently anachronistic appeal to tradition and to the authority of her class highlighted contemporary issues of social cohesion and individual rights: 'Are the shades of Pemberley to be thus polluted?' she asks, rhetorically, echoing the histrionic alarmism of the conservative polemicist Edmund Burke (396). The radical novelist Thomas Holcroft had the same political object as Austen in mind when in *Anna St. Ives* he had Anna resist her uncle Lord Fitz-Allen's demand that she marry the villain Coke Clifton:

> I immediately answered—If, sir ... you understand any further intercourse between me and Mr. Clifton, I must not suffer you to continue in such an error. We are and ever must remain separate. Habit and education have made us two such different beings, that it would be the excess of folly to suppose marriage could make us one.
>
> Miss St. Ives—[my uncle collected all his ideas of rank and grandeur] Miss St. Ives, you must do me the honour to consider me as head of the family, and suffer me to remind you of the respect and obedience that are due to that head. The proposal now made you I approve. It is made by a man of family, and I must take the liberty to lay my injunctions upon you to listen to it in a decorous and proper manner.
>
> I answered—I am sorry, sir, that our ideas of propriety are so very opposite. But whether my judgment be right or wrong, I am the person to be married to Mr. Clifton, and not your Lordship.[18]

Like Holcroft, Austen is using a recognisably literary, even archetypal antagonism in an unequivocally political debate—a debate to which all the variously motivated marriages and all the romantic and comic incidents and motifs in *Pride and Prejudice* can be seen to contribute.

---

18 Holcroft, *Anna St. Ives*, 358 (Vol. VI, letter 103).

The politics of human sexuality

I want to go back now to the question raised by Lady Catherine as to who is most entitled or best qualified to marry her nephew, Mr Darcy. While the opening sentence of the novel leads directly to Bingley's arrival at Netherfield, it is with Darcy's 'want of a wife'—again, suggesting both need and desire—that the novel and its politics are more concerned. To find the answer to the question, we need to go back to Rosings, and to the comic strategy of Ann de Bourgh's disqualification. If Lady Catherine's presumption of her daughter's priority is absurdly anachronistic, it is made to seem especially absurd, in a novel in which 'all the characters unabashedly appraise sexual and physical appeal',[19] when we think of Ann herself: 'thin and small' according to Maria Lucas; 'sickly and cross', according to Elizabeth (180). Again, later: 'so thin and so small', 'pale and sickly; her features, though not plain, were insignificant' (183–84). The consensus among the various characters, to which Lady Catherine herself enthusiastically contributes, establishes Ann de Bourgh as 'of a sickly constitution' (75), chronically enervated and even mentally defective, quite apart from being taciturn, haughty, uninformed, and untalented. Her character reflects the satirical Austen at her most savage, recalling Jonathan Swift on the aristocracy in the fourth part of *Gulliver's Travels*: 'a weak diseased Body, a meager Countenance, and sallow Complexion, are the true Marks of *noble Blood*'. Indeed, 'a healthy robust Appearance is so disgraceful in a Man of Quality, that the World concludes his real Father to have been a Groom or a Coachman'.[20]

Swift's construction of interclass breeding as a variety of eugenics, ironically displacing the licensed incest of aristocratic propagation, illuminates Austen's satirical technique in this episode of *Pride and Prejudice*. Like D. H. Lawrence's Sir Clifford Chatterley, the sexually disabled husband of *Lady Chatterley's Lover*—in which Swift's 'groom' or 'coachman' becomes the gamekeeper Mellors—the sickly Ann de

---

19 Jill Heydt-Stevenson, *Austen's Unbecoming Conjunctions: Subversive Laughter, Embodied History* (New York: Palgrave Macmillan, 2005), 70.
20 Jonathan Swift, *Gulliver's Travels*, ed. Paul Turner, World's Classics (Oxford and New York: Oxford University Press, 1976), 261.

Bourgh functions symbolically in the novel as a socio-political allegory. Austen and Lawrence may seem strange bedfellows and Elizabeth an unlikely Mellors, but the fact that the anæmic Ann de Bourgh and the emasculated Sir Clifford should both figure the social and political inanition of a redundant aristocracy confirms the continuity between the two.

Like Mellors, Elizabeth is nothing if not 'healthy' and 'robust', as 'fine, stout, healthy' as the love that she wittily envisages is able to withstand the onslaught of a sonnet (49). Austen goes out of her way to enforce Elizabeth's physical and mental sanity, both at Rosings, where in direct contrast to the 'sickly' Ann's hypothetical proficiency at the piano she performs with gusto and laughs 'heartily', and elsewhere throughout the novel. Swiftian eugenics may not have entered consciously into Darcy's deliberations about marriage, but his attraction to Elizabeth is inspired by a sexuality in which both play and physical robustness feature prominently, even though her 'easy playfulness' is originally found to be in 'mortifying' contrast to the manners 'of the fashionable world' (26). It is Elizabeth who attends to Jane when she is bedridden at Netherfield and Elizabeth who, unlike the luxurious Mr Hurst, prefers 'a plain dish to a ragout' (38). Elizabeth is called upon physically to support the otherwise unfailing Mrs Gardiner in their walks around the extensive Pemberley estate, the full, active appreciation of which demands someone 'healthy' and 'robust' and would be quite beyond the fastidious Caroline Bingley. Indeed, Elizabeth is only rarely 'overcome'— which is to say, only rarely succumbs to what was then seen to be a characteristically feminine reaction to physical or mental distress.

On this point, Jane Austen's 'feminism' endorses an historically recent concept of female beauty, in its turn reflecting a radical reorientation of a woman's relationship with the natural world and, correspondingly, with her own body—witnessed, for example, in the indignant protest of Mary Wollstonecraft:

> Fragile in every sense of the word, [women] are obliged to look up to man for every comfort. In the most trifling danger they cling to their support, with parasitical pertinacity, piteously demanding succour; and their *natural* protector extends his arm, or lifts up his voice, to guard the lovely trembler—from what? Perhaps the frown of an old

cow. ... I am fully persuaded that we should hear none of these infantine airs, if girls were allowed to take sufficient exercise, and not confined in close rooms till their muscles are relaxed, and their powers of digestion destroyed ...

I do not wish them to have power over men; but over themselves.[21]

Wollstonecraft's protest is a salutary reminder of the politics of fresh air in Romantic Britain. The extension to women of the vogue of walking and touring—like Jean Jacques Rousseau, Elizabeth had a 'love of solitary walks' (204)—meant a measure of bodily emancipation, the ideological significance of which is as evident as the ideological significance of Elizabeth's energy and independence:

Elizabeth continued her walk alone, crossing field after field at a quick pace, jumping over stiles and springing over puddles with impatient activity, and finding herself at last in view of the house, with weary ancles, dirty stockings, and a face glowing with the warmth of exercise. (36)

This walk to Netherfield, as Jill Heydt-Stevenson points out, is 'an act of jouissance that heightens her vitality'.[22] Elizabeth is singled out by the novel and by its hero for her 'animal spirits', expressed here in the 'impatient activity' of present participles that might as appropriately be applied to her 'liveliness' of mind and conversation (421): 'crossing', 'jumping', 'springing', 'glowing'. So it is later when she breaks from the unaccommodating order of Netherfield society to run 'gaily off, rejoicing as she rambled about' (58).

An unequivocally sexual energy informs and invigorates Elizabeth's ethical independence, as well as her intrepidity, intellect and wit, and the anarchic sense of the bizarre that she inherits from her father: 'I dearly love a laugh' (62). The same energy would appear implicitly to promise to carry Elizabeth and all that she represents through the

---

21 Mary Wollstonecraft, *A Vindication of the Rights of Woman* [1792], ed. Miriam Kramnick (Harmondsworth: Penguin, 1975), 153-4.
22 Heydt-Stevenson, *Unbecoming Conjunctions*, 72.

political turmoil of the present, of 'such days as these' (41).²³ Which is why she threatens the Bingley sisters:

> Miss Bingley began by abusing her as soon as she was out of the room. Her manners were pronounced to be very bad indeed, a mixture of pride and impertinence; she had no conversation, no stile, no taste, no beauty. Mrs Hurst thought the same and added,
> 'She has nothing, in short, to recommend her, but being an excellent walker. I shall never forget her appearance this morning. She really looked almost wild.'
> 'She did indeed, Louisa. I could hardly keep my countenance. Very nonsensical to come at all! Why must *she* be scampering about the country, because her sister had a cold? Her hair so untidy, so blowsy!'
> 'Yes, and her petticoat; I hope you saw her petticoat, six inches deep in mud ... .'
> '*You* observed it, Mr. Darcy, I am sure,' said Miss Bingley; 'and I am inclined to think that you would not wish to see *your sister* make such an exhibition.'
> 'Certainly not.'
> 'To walk three miles, or four miles, or five miles, or whatever it is, above her ancles in dirt, and alone, quite alone! what could she mean by it? It seems to me to shew an abominable sort of conceited independence, a most country town indifference to decorum.' (38–39)

Solitariness and independence—the sort of independence that consistently challenges decorum and wonders at the wisdom (not to say ethics) of hastily legitimising Lydia and Wickham's doomed relationship, for example (336, 351); an 'impulse of feeling' not always 'guided by reason' that is correctly, if sententiously, identified by her sister Mary (35); pedestrianism and unapologetic provincialism; an indifference to

---

23   When Darcy protests that he 'cannot comprehend the neglect of a family library in such days as these', as Laura G. Mooneyham observes, 'we see that he regards himself as a guardian of his ancestral inheritance and views the present age as particularly threatening', *Romance, Language and Education in Jane Austen's Novels* (London and Basingstoke: Macmillan, 1988), 53.

society's sanctions and conventions ('in her air altogether, there is a self-sufficiency without fashion', 299); a 'wild manner' (46); energy and excess—what these represent is a configuration of values that can be identified as a version of Romantic radicalism. The censures that the Bingley sisters level at Elizabeth extend their own function beyond that of two ugly sisters in a Cinderella story to that of political conservatives, alarmed at Elizabeth's anarchic athleticism and individualism. Even Elizabeth's tan feeds a disgust that is characteristic of a specifically urban refinement as well as a more catholic snobbery. In short, the politics of *Pride and Prejudice* is in large part a complex, sexual politics.[24]

The Bingley sisters' fear is only accentuated by their endeavours metaphorically to belittle (and so contain) Elizabeth's animal energy and its sexual attractiveness. Her 'crossing', 'jumping', and 'springing', it should be noted, are reduced in their account to 'scampering'. On another occasion they describe her eyes as 'shrewish' (299). Darcy, on the other hand, more ingenuous in recognising Elizabeth's sexual attractiveness ('her fine eyes', he notes, 'were brightened by the exercise'), seeks refuge in rigid, social interdictions, forcibly reminding both Bingley and himself that the Bennet sisters' inferior connections 'must very materially lessen their chances of marrying men of any consideration in the world' (40), just as he reminds himself, later, 'that were it not for the inferiority of her connections, he should be in some danger' (57).

Darcy's conservative propriety becomes a victim of his own passion, however, and he must learn through his attraction to Elizabeth that it is 'as ridiculous to attempt to fix the heredityship of human beauty, as of wisdom' (to quote Thomas Paine).[25] No prediction could be less accurate than Mr Collins's concerning Elizabeth's prospects: 'Your portion is unhappily so small that it will in all likelihood undo the effects of your loveliness' (122). The effects of sexual attraction, it

---

24 For Jane Austen on sexuality, though not sexual politics, see Alice Chandler, '"A Pair of Fine Eyes": Jane Austen's Treatment of Sex', *Studies in the Novel*, 7 (Spring 1975), and Daniel Cottom, *The Civilized Imagination: A Study of Ann Radcliffe, Jane Austen, and Sir Walter Scott* (Cambridge: Cambridge University Press, 1985), 71 ff.
25 Thomas Paine, *Rights of Man* [1792], ed. Henry Collins (Harmondsworth: Penguin, 1969), 197.

would appear, are not to be so easily undone. The apparently casual, occasional references to Darcy's 'powerful feeling towards her' (105), to his being 'in her power' (203), to 'the power, which her fancy told her she still possessed' (293), reflect the hierarchical subversion effected by sexual attraction. 'The beautiful expression of [Elizabeth's] dark eyes' (26) becomes the font and focus of an inordinate passion—literally inordinate: out of bounds, or out of his prescribed boundaries. With his proud unease and overcivilised repressions, Darcy has 'never been so bewitched by any woman as he was by her' (57) and construes Elizabeth as a *femme fatale*:

> 'In vain have I struggled. It will not do. My feelings will not be repressed. You must allow me to tell you how much I love and admire you.' ...
> His sense of her inferiority—of its being a degradation—of the family obstacles which judgment had always opposed to inclination, were dwelt on with a warmth which seemed due to the consequence he was wounding ...
> He concluded with representing the strength of that attachment which, in spite of all his endeavours, he had found impossible to conquer. (211)

In an allegory of the ruling class brought literally and metaphorically to its knees, this is a powerfully symbolic moment. Darcy learns that the exclusive and arbitrary propriety of social rank that he invokes to strengthen his resistance is not only impotent, it is also iniquitous, and his own behaviour arrogant. As he later recalls: 'I was properly humbled' (410). Like Elizabeth, the novel is utterly unsympathetic and uncompromising throughout this first proposal, refusing to allow the honesty of Darcy's tortured confession 'of the scruples that had long prevented my forming any serious design' to mitigate the offence given by his insensitivity to her moral and emotional individuality, an insensitivity surely understandable, if not 'natural and just' (215). There are, it seems, no excuses for Darcy's pretensions or, generalising, for such pride and presumption on the part of the ruling class.

And this is only the beginning of Darcy's ritual abasement. To be closeted with George Wickham in Gracechurch Street, for example, where once Darcy would hardly have thought 'a month's ablutions enough to cleanse him of its impurities' (161), and to be haggling with Wickham over the price of buying him off is, for Darcy, a punishment more exquisitely fitted to the crime than anything W. S. Gilbert could invent. A self-confessed spoilt child of the aristocracy—'allowed, encouraged, almost taught ... to think meanly of the rest of the world, to *wish* at least to think meanly of their sense and worth compared with my own'— Darcy ultimately emerges chastened and subdued, and willing to acknowledge rather as his saviour, the woman with the wild, wild eyes he had once seen as *la belle dame sans merci*: 'What do I not owe you! You taught me a lesson, hard indeed at first, but most advantageous. By you, I was properly humbled' (410).

The tables turned

The triumph of progressive individualism over an arrogant ruling class reluctant to forego the unwarranted power it has inherited with its landed estates? On one level, certainly. There are, however, complications. The character in the novel most inclined to politicise Darcy's behaviour is Wickham, for example, and there is a certain danger in adopting the interpretative strategies and specific political inferences of the novel's villain. Political criticism needs to take account of the fact that part of Wickham's 'inducement' was an irrational resentment and 'the hope of revenging himself' (225). There is, however, less oblique evidence to hand of the ultimate inadequacy of reading *Pride and Prejudice* as a radical or reformist text. For one thing, there is the second half of the novel. After the heady episodes at Netherfield and Rosings, the reader is only once again allowed such faith in Elizabeth's iconoclastic wit and energy (when countering Lady Catherine's intervention). Her surprise at Darcy's proposal at Hunsford shifts the focus to her own misinterpretation and self-ignorance, even hypocrisy, for not only has she chosen 'wilfully to misunderstand' his manifest feelings (63)—fully apparent though they are to the reader (25)—but she has consciously or unconsciously solicited and encouraged those feelings with a provocative flirtatiousness from the beginning. Her later apology to Darcy represents the sustained reassessment that her values—and with them the values privileged by the novel—have undergone since the proposal: 'My manners must have been at fault, but not intentionally I assure you. I never meant to deceive you, but my spirits might often lead me wrong' (410). Elizabeth, 'virtual aristocrat', is required to suffer a humiliation—and 'how just a humiliation' (230)—comparable with Darcy's own.

This humiliation and reassessment, along with the genuinely disturbing consequences of actions that at the time had seemed innocuous or merely irresponsible, demand of the reader a radical revision of many incidents that occur earlier in the narrative. 'Follies' that evoke Elizabeth's wit and satiric enthusiasm lose their 'light & bright & sparkling'[26] appearance when Jane's happiness is seriously threatened by 'the folly and indecorum of her own family' (236). More importantly, episodes that the reader has been encouraged to interpret as the triumph of rational individualism and natural candour over the privilege and presumption of rank can now be reinterpreted, in part at least, as exemplifying the threat posed by undisciplined spirits to polite or correct manners. What for Darcy and the reader was 'liveliness of mind' in Elizabeth, she herself now dismisses as 'impertinence. It was very little less' (421)—'impertinence', tellingly, being an epithet used of her by the Bingley sisters (38, 57). After Lydia's elopement, Elizabeth's challenging Lady Catherine over Lydia's and Kitty's 'coming out', for example, is to be radically revised as more confident and forthright than just (187), as is her attitude generally. And along with the respect that Elizabeth discovers for Darcy's judgement comes the belated validity of what had once seemed a repressive formality on his part, a validity that threatens to include even his disapproving comparison of Elizabeth's eruption into the lifeless rituals of Netherfield with the restrained behaviour of his sister Georgiana (39).

The novel's and Elizabeth's conservative renunciation of her wilfulness generally, and of her wilful interpretation of human motive in particular, suggests that it is precisely the reader's complacent identification with Elizabeth's voice and vision, and of Elizabeth's voice

---

26 Jane Austen, of *Pride and Prejudice*, to her sister Cassandra, 4 February 1813, *Jane Austen's Letters*, third edition, ed. Deirdre Le Faye (Oxford: Oxford University Press, 1995; 2003), 203.

and vision with the author's own, that Austen sets out strategically to qualify, if not undermine.[27] *Pride and Prejudice* demands a more extensive and more radical revision of events in retrospect than any other Austen novel. So much so that if we were to 'remember at night all the foolish things that were said in the morning' (53), the delayed revelation of Elizabeth's improprieties might well leave the reader feeling betrayed or resentful at having been duped into enjoying and sharing her wit and gusto in the first place. In spite of these revisionary strategies, however, an ineradicable sense that the novel genuinely endorses Elizabeth's earlier behaviour remains. Nor is this simply a wilful misreading comparable with Elizabeth's own. Austen was a true poet and of the devil's party, with or without knowing it. The reader's allegiance to the more vital Elizabeth can only be renounced at the cost, not just of a large part of the novel's appeal, but also of its coherence.

The view from Pemberley

As it turns out, the strategically discrepant political positions assumed by the novel over the issue of Elizabeth's independence and iconoclasm remain in ironic, arguably destructive tension. Elizabeth and the narrator have become confused—in their wit and irony, obviously, and more tellingly perhaps in the 'strong', sometimes ungenerous language of their censure (5, 78, 96, 153)—too confused, certainly, for so radical a conversion in Elizabeth as takes place when she sees Pemberley for the first time:

> They gradually ascended for half a mile, and then found themselves at the top of a considerable eminence, where the wood ceased, and the eye was instantly caught by Pemberley House, situated on the opposite side of a valley. ... It was a large, handsome, stone building, standing well on rising ground, and backed by a ridge of high woody hills;—and in front, a stream of some natural importance was swelled into greater, but without any artificial appearance. Its banks were neither formal, nor falsely adorned. Elizabeth was delighted. She had

---

27 Butler, *Jane Austen and the War of Ideas*, 124.

never seen a place for which nature had done more, or where natural beauty had been so little counteracted by an awkward taste. They were all of them warm in their admiration; and at that moment she felt, that to be mistress of Pemberley might be something! (271)

In one of the oldest apocalyptic *topoi*, Elizabeth takes up a position atop 'a considerable eminence' from where, like Blake's bard, she 'past, present, and future sees'. Her vision is of the power and continuity represented by the Country House, a power that 'reveals itself in the balance and reconciliation of opposite and discordant qualities', to quote Coleridge, 'of sameness with difference; of the general with the concrete; the idea, with the image; the sense of novelty and freshness with old and familiar objects'; 'and while it blends and harmonizes the natural with the artificial, still subordinates art to nature'.[28] Pemberley functions as a synecdoche of patriarchal order as well as a metonym for Darcy himself: 'a large, handsome, stone building standing well on rising ground' belonging to one who 'drew the attention of the room by his fine, tall, person, handsome features, noble mien' (10). It is, in fact, the second of a sequence of metonyms through which Elizabeth comes to reconcile 'the idea, with the image' of her future husband. (The first is the letter that Darcy wrote after his proposal at Hunsford.)

After her apocalyptic vision of Pemberley, Elizabeth will spend the remainder of the novel endeavouring to rationalise the instantaneous revaluation that inspires her charged self-confession: 'to be mistress of Pemberley might be something!' Perhaps because the political implications are anomalous and the emotional implications awkward, the reader tends to gloss over this first episode at Pemberley. Not only is Elizabeth's cherished independence sacrificed to a more powerful and spontaneous desire, but the desire itself—the desire to appropriate—is profoundly unromantic, romantic love being conventionally indifferent to the self-interest of social and material rewards and constraints.

Elizabeth's next insight into Darcy comes through his furniture:

> The rooms were lofty and handsome, and their furniture suitable to the fortune of their proprietor; but Elizabeth saw with admiration

---

28   Coleridge, *Biographia Literaria*, 2:16–17.

of his taste, that it was neither gaudy nor uselessly fine; with less of splendour, and more real elegance, than the furniture of Rosings. (272)

Again, the impulse to possess is spontaneous, and is underlined by the preponderance of first-person pronouns: "'And of this place,' thought she, "I might have been mistress! With these rooms I might now have been familiarly acquainted! Instead of viewing them as a stranger, I might have rejoiced in them as my own'" (272). As wealth and rank become obscure objects of desire effecting vital transformations, the confident distinction that Elizabeth had made at Rosings between 'virtue and talent' and the 'stateliness of wealth and rank' collapses dramatically. As in Old Testament visions on mountains, where the assumption of divine authority involves a simultaneous submission to God as the highest order, so for Elizabeth 'to be mistress of Pemberley'—to be 'in possession of' Pemberley, like that 'good fortune' of the opening sentence of the novel—is also to be mastered by both Darcy and Pemberley (as Darcy is himself mastered by Pemberley as a squirearchical responsibility). 'He for God only, she for God in him'.[29]

Elizabeth's final insight into Darcy and what he stands for is mediated by his portraits. The first is by Reynolds—by *Mrs* Reynolds, that is, a choice of surname generally recognised as Austen's joke: 'Austen slyly borrows the authority of the real Reynolds for her fictional housekeeper', writes Jane Barchas, 'whose report, or portrait, of the hero must contradict and override the reigning prejudice against him'.[30] Mrs Reynolds' verbal portrait of her master relates Darcy, via his house, to his complex patronage. It is all about relations and relationships: not *family* relations in the narrow sense—Elizabeth is as indifferent to using the Darcy family relations as a form of status as Caroline Bingley was keen to use them to humiliate her—but the relation of Pemberley to its grounds, of art to nature; the relation of landlord to tenant, of brother to sister; ultimately, of course, the relation of man to woman. 'The visibility of power', to quote Marcia Pointon, is 'highly complex

---

29 Milton, *Paradise Lost*, IV, l. 299.
30 Jane Barchas, 'Artistic Names in Austen's Fiction: Cameo Appearances by Prominent Painters', *Persuasions*, 31 (2009), 145–62 (146).

and always relational.[31] Mrs Reynolds' perspective—'I am sure *I* know none so handsome'; 'I do not know who is good enough for him'; 'Some people call him proud; but I am sure I never saw any thing of it' (274–76)—offers an ideal imitation of her master, the infidelities of which can be attributed, ironically, to Mrs Reynolds' faithfulness. She paints not only from a different personal perspective, but also out of a different world from the one Elizabeth knows, a world of hierarchy and patronage that Elizabeth has challenged in the past and (in Lady Catherine) will challenge again. In spite of that challenge, however, in spite of her natural energy and instinctive independence, Elizabeth's perspective is altered by Mrs Reynolds' portrait, as it was by her vision of Pemberley.

The other two portraits are paintings, the one in the gallery further accelerating the revolution in Elizabeth's attitude:

> In the gallery there were many family portraits, but they could have little to fix the attention of a stranger. Elizabeth walked on in quest of the only face whose features would be known to her. At last it arrested her—and she beheld a striking resemblance of Mr. Darcy, with such a smile over the face, as she remembered to have sometimes seen, when he looked at her. She stood several minutes before the picture, and returned to it again before they quitted the gallery. Mrs. Reynolds informed them, that it had been taken in his father's life time.
>
> There was certainly at this moment, in Elizabeth's mind, a more gentle sensation towards the original, than she had ever felt in the height of their acquaintance. (277)

Significantly and ironically, Elizabeth experiences this 'more gentle sensation towards the original' in the *absence* of 'the original'. Is this a reflection on the ingenuity of art, or on its duplicity? Either way, the portrait has always had a complex nature: as art and as possession or commodity, a symbol of mimetic and expressive quest and a symbol of power (most often, like Darcy's library, inherited power): 'As a brother,

---

31   Marcia Pointon, *Hanging the Head: Portraiture and Social Formation in Eighteenth-Century England* (New Haven, Conn: Yale University Press, 1993), 13.

a landlord, a master, she considered how many people's happiness were in his guardianship!—How much pleasure or pain it was in his power to bestow!—How much good or evil must be done by him!' (277). Individuality, in large part, means the fulfilment of responsibilities associated with one's function in society. It also involves Elizabeth's active acquiescence in the patriarchy.

This passage on Darcy's social and familial responsibilities would not be out of place in a 'Jacobin' novel, except that the same 'power' celebrated here by Elizabeth would be stigmatised as oppressive and unwarranted, an encroachment on the very lives that here comprise Elizabeth's awe-struck list. And yet Elizabeth's new-found 'trepidation' is recorded without manifest irony, heavily ironic though it is in the light of her previous confrontations—as heavily ironic as the 'softening' that takes place while she gazes upon the portrait of one whose severity and arrogance has been, literally, 'glossed over': 'as she stood before the canvas, on which he was represented, and fixed his eyes upon herself, she thought of his regard with a deeper sentiment of gratitude than it had ever raised before; she remembered its warmth, and softened its impropriety of expression' (277). The portraitist, Mrs Reynolds, and Elizabeth have all 'softened' their portraits of Darcy, and the narrator's reticence—*Austen*'s reticence—implicitly sanctions Elizabeth's conclusions and Elizabeth's conversion. As a dramatic self-discovery, the episode at Pemberley involves a sudden renunciation of much that Elizabeth has felt and represented. From the beginning, of course, there has been magic in Darcy's 'consequence' for the likes of Charlotte Lucas, and now many of Charlotte's once dubious values are achieving a belated endorsement (102).

Gratitude and esteem

Not only does a renewed respect for Darcy enter the novel via Elizabeth at this point, so too does a new sobriety and restraint. The young woman who knew 'exactly what to think' (96) and 'loved absurdities' (172), and whose habitual tendency was to ironise and, in liveliness of imagination, to misrepresent, becomes the woman who recognises what she does not know and, with that, begins to know what she wants.

Here there is a problem, however. Driven by her vision of patriarchal order and a very unromantic passion to appropriate, 'jealous of his esteem' and thinking 'of his regard with a deeper sentiment of gratitude' (344, 277), Elizabeth embarks upon an agonised search for elusive, possibly non-existent feelings.

The novel is more honest than its heroine on the issue of romantic love, as it turns out, and arguably more honest than its readers. In some places we may even wonder if it is not more honest than its own authorial voice:

> If gratitude and esteem are good foundations of affection, Elizabeth's change of sentiment will be neither improbable nor faulty. But if otherwise, if the regard springing from such sources is unreasonable or unnatural, in comparison of what is so often described as arising on a first interview with its object, and even before two words have been exchanged, nothing can be said in her defence, except that she had given somewhat of a trial to the latter method, in her partiality for Wickham, and that her ill-success might perhaps authorise her to seek the other less interesting mode of attachment. (308)

'Gratitude and esteem', perhaps, but does the author not protest too much? The ironic appeal to experience in this passage is couched in such a way as to appear self-evident, and thus to disarm and even disdain opposition. But the reader's conscious or unconscious assent remains indispensable, and experience may tell us that 'gratitude and esteem' are in fact rather dubious foundations of affection, especially of an affection between two mutually respectful, independent 'rational creature[s] speaking the truth from [their] heart' (to adapt the definition with which a more spirited Elizabeth had challenged Mr Collins's patronising obtuseness [122]). Does the author's satirising the notion that none ever loved 'that loved not at first sight' necessarily validate the 'affection' and 'regard' to which it is (surely falsely) opposed? Is Elizabeth's 'partiality for Wickham'—with whom, by her own confession, she had 'never been much in love' (134)—really a valid counter-example? Can a rational preference for love grounded on 'gratitude and esteem' actually generate that love? (We are reminded of Maryanne Dashwood's exhausted recourse to Colonel Brandon.) For

Mary Wollstonecraft, at least, 'love and esteem are two very different things', with 'esteem' serving only to reinforce 'a degree of imbecility which degrades a rational creature in a way women are not aware of'.[32]

It may even be that Austen at this point is self-consciously renouncing Wollstonecraft's feminist alternative to conduct-book morality. Hard as she tries, however, Elizabeth is unable convincingly to identify in herself the love and the passion she has been implicitly defending throughout the novel, the love and the passion required of her by her radical independence, no less than by romantic comedy. Barbara Hardy argues that it is not Elizabeth's love but her 'self-analysis' that proves inadequate to the occasion: 'the attempts at naming feeling, deny, frustrate, and defeat themselves, but the very persistence of her reasoning shows the strength of feeling'.[33] But what feeling? There are other feelings besides love that compel us to rationalise, the utterance of which are more likely to be repressed: social aspiration, for example, or acquisitiveness. What happened to the social aspiration so dramatically evoked by Pemberley? In Elizabeth's cold conviction that Darcy 'was exactly the man, who, in disposition and talents, would most suit her' (344)—and not the one whom she most desired—one hears a refracted echo of Charlotte Lucas: 'I am convinced that my chance of happiness with him is as fair, as most people can boast on entering the marriage state' (140–41).

Accordingly, from the moment before the portrait when Elizabeth, far from regarding Darcy, focuses Darcy's regard upon herself, she habitually constructs herself as the object of his love and attention, rather than as the subject of her own: 'she longed to know', we are told, 'in what manner he thought of her, and whether, in defiance of everything, she was still dear to him' (280); 'It is impossible that he should still love me' (282); 'Her power [over him] was sinking; every thing *must* sink under such a proof of family weakness' (306); 'How could I ever be foolish enough to expect a renewal of his love' (378); and so on. In the long-awaited moment of their mutual disillusionment and betrothal, Elizabeth achieves the ultimate self-objectification:

---

32 Wollstonecraft, *A Vindication of the Rights of Woman*, 154.
33 Barbara Hardy, *A Reading of Jane Austen* (London: Peter Owen, 1975), 51.

he expressed himself on the occasion as sensibly and as warmly as a man violently in love can be supposed to do. Had Elizabeth been able to encounter his eye, she might have seen how well the expression of heartfelt delight, diffused over his face, became him; but, though she could not look, she could listen, and he told her of feelings, which, in proving of what importance she was to him, made his affection every moment more valuable. (407)

Of what importance Darcy might be *to her* we hear only a confused self-questioning.

'Light, & bright, & sparkling' fade and sober with each new protestation of happiness that Elizabeth makes. And the comparatively few occasions upon which she exercises her wit in the latter half of the novel—her 'spirits soon rising to playfulness again' (421)—can too easily be understood as designed to protect herself from an unacceptable truth. Like the plea for a willed amnesia in response to Jane's reminding her of how much she dislikes Darcy: '*That* is all to be forgot. Perhaps I did not always love him so well as I do now. But in such cases as these, a good memory is unpardonable. This is the last time I shall ever remember it myself' (331). And Elizabeth's dating her love of Darcy from the moment of her 'first seeing his beautiful grounds at Pemberley' (332) is also a joke—except that it's not.

As it happens, the real joke here is the one that Austen addresses to the reader, asking for 'that willing suspension of disbelief that constitutes poetic faith' in the knowledge that only the imaginative collaboration of the reader will allow her to navigate the inconsistencies thrown up by the narrative.[34] There is no magic solution for the self-tamed shrew: 'Elizabeth, agitated and confused, rather *knew* that she was happy, than *felt* herself to be so' (413). If this is designed to elevate a love based upon esteem and understanding above a love based upon

---

34 On the 'deliberately deflationary' endings of Austen's novels, see Daniel Cottom, *The Civilized Imagination*, 94. Robert Garis is more bluntly critical: 'Elizabeth learns to love a man whom she has detested on first acquaintance, doesn't know very well and rarely sees', in 'Learning Experience and Change', *Critical Essays on Jane Austen*, ed. B. C. Southam (London, Boston, Melbourne and Henley: Routledge & Kegan Paul, 1968), 60–82 (72).

feelings, it is curiously self-defeating, serving instead only to render Elizabeth's commitment to Darcy the more doubtful. Elizabeth's feelings of respect and gratitude and Darcy's romantic passion remain categorically distinct and 'the possibility of opportunism in Elizabeth', as Charles McCann has observed, 'can never be dismissed'.[35] We are left with an ironic gulf between the circumstantial and emotional details of the novel and its fairy-tale structure—a gulf that Austen can always rely upon the reader imaginatively to overleap.

Between the two opposing political positions identified by Marilyn Butler at the opening of this chapter—'a Christian conservatism on the one hand', with its 'belief in external authority', and a 'progressive' commitment to individual autonomy—*Pride and Prejudice* aspires to a critically well-documented compromise that takes its dialectical form from its characterisation of Elizabeth Bennet (275, 338).[36] The ruling class is to be purged of its gratuitous pride and self-serving prejudices, and radicalism's 'spontaneous personal impulse' is to be disciplined by assimilation into the prevailing order, in the hope of giving that order new vigour and a more supple propriety—of humanising its face without diminishing its authority. The energy and articulate individualism of Elizabeth is harnessed in a symbolic marriage, one that would enliven but (pre)serve the microcosmic order of a hierarchical society, so that 'the rebellion itself', to quote Judith Lowder Newton, 'works in the interests of tradition'.[37] Accommodation has thus arguably been made to genuine virtue and talent, though it has been made indirectly, by appropriation and mutual submission, rather than by direct political

---

35 Charles J. McCann, 'Setting and Character in *Pride and Prejudice*', in *Jane Austen: Critical Assessments*, ed. Ian Littlewood, in four volumes (Mountfield: Helm Information, 1998), 3:317–25 (323).
36 Butler, *Jane Austen and the War of Ideas*, 164–65. The classic treatment of this tension is Lionel Trilling's dialectic of 'female vivacity' and 'strict male syntax' in his *The Opposing Self* (London: Secker & Warburg, 1955), 222. For a selection of more recent views, see Mary Evans, *Jane Austen and the State*, 24; Claudia L. Johnson, *Jane Austen: Women, Politics and the Novel*, 93; Mooneyham, *Romance, Language and Education in Jane Austen's Novels*, 68; Patricia Meyer Spacks, *The Female Imagination* (New York: Knopf, 1975); 121; Jane Spencer, *The Rise of the Woman Novelist* (Oxford: Blackwell, 1986), 172.
37 Judith Lowder Newton, *Women, Power, Subversion: Social Strategies in British Fiction, 1778–1860* (Athens: University of Georgia Press, 1981), 79.

intervention. And it has been made only after a respect for external authority has been discovered or learned. As with the aspirational romantic narrative in and through which the argument is mediated, it is up to the emotionally invested reader to decide just how persuasive this political compromise is.

7
'Such is modern fame': The Byronic Hero from *Childe Harold* to *Don Juan*

The idea of the hero as one consciously or unconsciously delegated by a culture to do its thinking, feeling, fighting, and suffering for it—to some extent, to do its living for it—is as old as culture itself, and the Romantic hero was only a comparatively recent development of quite traditional notions of courage and honour and fidelity and ingenuity, a development designed to accommodate the new priorities of genius and the imagination, as well as an intensified 'organic sensibility'—the acute sensitivity and responsiveness that made the Romantic hero only too susceptible to 'the slings and arrows of outrageous fortune':

> the good die first,
> And those whose hearts are dry as summer dust
> Burn to the socket.[1]

The Byronic hero is a specialised and intensified version of this Romantic hero, one that proved so fascinating, not to say mesmerising, to the nineteenth-century reading public that it monopolised its

---

1 William Wordsworth, *The Ruined Cottage* (1798), ll.150–52, *The Poems of William Wordsworth: Collected Readings from the Cornell Wordsworth*, ed. Jared Curtis, 3 vols (Penrith: Humanities-Ebooks, 2009).

interest for decades, 'single-handedly invent[ing] the modern paradigm of celebrity', to quote Roderick Beaton,[2] and becoming for most readers and commentators the supreme Romantic paradigm.

Fifteen minutes of fame

In 1812, with the publication of his poem *Childe Harold's Pilgrimage*, Byron famously awoke to find himself famous:[3]

> With false Ambition what had I to do?
> Little with love, and least of all with fame!
> And yet they came unsought and with me grew,
> And made me all which they can make—a Name.
> ('[Epistle to Augusta]', ll. 97–100)[4]

From that date, to quote Gabriele Poole, the 'public view of Byron's heroes was mediated, at every stage, by the public's image of Byron',[5] and Byron's life and poetry would share an immediacy and fascination with other sensational events of the day, stimulating a craving precisely analogous to that for news and opinion, and for the very latest thing in fashion. 'The subject of conversation, of curiosity, of enthusiasm almost, one might say, of the moment, is not Spain or Portugal, Warriors or Patriots, but Lord Byron!', wrote Elizabeth, Duchess of Devonshire:

> going abroad, [he] said that on his return he would answer to any who called on him. He returned ... with a new poem, 'Childe Harold',

---

2 Roderick Beaton, *Byron's War: Romantic Rebellion, Greek Revolution* (Cambridge: Cambridge University Press, 2013), xvi.
3 Thomas Moore, *The Life, Letters, and Journals of Lord Byron* [1830] (London: John Murray, 1860), 159.
4 All quotations of Lord Byron's poetry are from *Byron*, The Oxford Authors, ed. Jerome J. McGann (Oxford: Oxford University Press, 1986).
5 Gabriele Poole, 'The Byronic Hero, Theatricality and Leadership', *The Byron Journal*, 38:1 (2010), 7–18 (7–8).

which he published. This poem is on every table, and himself courted, visited, flattered, and praised whenever he appears. He has a pale, sickly, but handsome countenance, a bad figure, animated and amusing conversation, and, in short, he is really the only topic almost of every conversation—the men jealous of him, the women of each other.[6]

Of all the literature of the period, according to William St Clair, Byron's *Childe Harold* and *The Corsair* are cited most often in personal letters and diaries, while the short poem 'Fare Thee Well', addressed to his wife as he went into exile in 1816, featured most often in the albums in which literate Regency women collected their favourite poetry and sayings (there were 'no less than 57 separate printings of this poem in book or pamphlet form in 1816 and 1817').[7] Not surprisingly, then, Byron's death at the age of thirty-six in 1824 was 'a great loss to the Literature of the Age', to quote the painter Benjamin Robert Haydon:

> He kept it always in excitement, with all the prerogatives of a man of genius—what is he about!—what has he done!—what is he going to do, were always the accompanying questions of those who did not know him privately, and when he was a subject of conversation.[8]

Only Walter Scott was more extensively bought and read than Byron over the period as a whole, but Byron sold more immediately and sensationally, and in larger editions.[9] More to the point for our purposes, however, Scott the man was no part of the interest of his readers—though the actual identity of the anonymous Waverley novelist, referred to at the time as 'the Great Unknown', did keep the reading

---

6 As quoted in *The Two Duchesses: Georgiana, Duchess of Devonshire, and Elizabeth, Duchess of Devonshire*, ed. Aubrey Vere Foster (London: Blackie & Son, 1898), 375–76.
7 William St Clair, 'The Impact of Byron's Writings', in *Byron: Augustan and Romantic*, ed. Andrew Rutherford (London: Macmillan, 1990), 1–25 (10).
8 *The Diary of Benjamin Robert Haydon*, ed. Willard Bissell Pope, in 2 vols (Cambridge, Mass., Harvard University Press, 1960), 2:485 (15 May 1824).
9 For the figures, see William St. Clair, *The Reading Nation in the Romantic Period* (Cambridge: CUP, 2004), 585–90, 632–44.

public guessing and helped to fuel interest in the novels. 'In reading the *Scotch Novels*', however, as William Hazlitt remarked, 'we never think about the author, except from a feeling of curiosity respecting our unknown benefactor: in reading Lord Byron's works, he himself is never absent from our minds'.[10] It is noticeable that Haydon begins by talking about 'Literature', but immediately abandons that to speculate about Byron himself: what he is about, what he has done. Byron's contemporary projection—his *image*, as we are fond of saying, the way he was perceived—was totally different from Scott's, and from 1812 and *Childe Harold* the public perception of Byron became bound up with their reading of the leading characters in his poetry which, as Peter Manning has said, 'furnished the simulacrum of intimacy the new readership craved'.[11]

With the spread of the periodical press during the Romantic period came the spread of interest in *personality* at all levels, of the kind reflected in Haydon's grief at Byron's death. '"Byron"', writes Clara Tuite, 'as life, work, and reception—is the initiating figure, allegory, and apocalyptic event of celebrity as secular divinity'.[12] We still use the noun, 'personality', in the way it came to be used in the early nineteenth century, making us the children of Byron's fascinated and voyeuristic public. The public personality remains to this day a central source of fascination for the culture which creates and receives it, and presumably will remain a source of fascination for as long as ours remains a mass media culture in which the majority live vicariously through a select minority. The Romantics could hardly be said to have invented fame, but the rapid development of media technology throughout the eighteenth and early nineteenth centuries—until finally, only two years after the publication of *Childe Harold*, *The Times* newspaper reached its full production potential with a new steam-operated press that enabled

---

10 William Hazlitt, 'Lord Byron', in *The Spirit of the Age* (1825), *The Selected Writings of William Hazlitt*, 7, ed. Duncan Wu (London: Pickering & Chatto, 1998), 134-42 (136-37).
11 Peter J. Manning, 'Don Juan and the Revolutionary Self', in *Romantic Revisions*, ed. Robert Brinkley and Keith Hanley (Cambridge: Cambridge University Press, 1992), 210-26 (216).
12 Clara Tuite, *Lord Byron and Scandalous Celebrity* (Cambridge: Cambridge University Press, 2015), 1.

it to meet any demand[13]—along with the rapid development of the means of distribution through ever accelerating modes of transportation, meant that an extensive and rapid periodical press was able to give circulation to the kind of low-brow and high-brow gossip stimulated by the life and work of Lord Byron, creating 'a celebrity different in scale from anything that had gone before'.[14]

All of this ensured that the fifteen minutes of fame deplored by Andy Warhol in the 1960s would be substantially the same as the fame deplored by Byron in one of the late cantos of *Don Juan*:

> Such is modern fame.
> 'Tis pity that it takes no further hold
> Than an advertisement, or much the same,
> When ere the ink be dry, the sound grows cold.
>   (*Don Juan*, Canto XIII, st. 51)

The extent and suddenness of fame since the early nineteenth century; the persistence and vividness of the self-image of the 'celebrity' in publicity's many and various, and variously distorting, mirrors, both verbal and graphic (there was a proliferation of visual images of Byron in portraits and prints and busts), has meant that, since Byron, the famous have been constantly confronting reflections or refractions of what they say and contrive to say, and of what they look like and contrive to look like. Scott was the first bestseller, Byron the first pop star.

Byron's fascination for an hysterical readership was not lost on those conservatives for whom his association 'with popular culture, and with free-floating desire', to quote Ghislaine McDayter, 'marked him as one of the most dangerous political forces of the period'.[15] There were precedents in literature's hall of fame, of course, artists famous or infamous in their own period for their work and personalities—among writers, for example, Lord Rochester and Alexander Pope

---

13 See Tom Mole, *Byron's Celebrity Culture: Industrial Culture and the Hermeneutic of Intimacy* (Basingstoke: Palgrave Macmillan, 2007), 39–40.
14 To quote William St Clair, *The Reading Nation in the Romantic Period*, 333.
15 Ghislaine McDayter, *Byromania and the Birth of Celebrity Culture* (New York: State University of New York, 2009), 7.

were notorious in quite different ways in their respective periods, and there were plenty of scurrilous verbal and graphic caricatures of Pope in the pamphlet media of the early eighteenth century. But Byron remains the poet most sensationally well known to the largest possible audience in his own time, which is why one has to seek analogues, not among earlier artists like Pope or figures of public notoriety like the later eighteenth-century demagogue, John Wilkes, but among twentieth- and twenty-first-century film or rock stars.[16] To quote Paul Douglass:

> Awareness of the power of the audience made him more anxious to present himself—in person, in portraits, and in print—as a man of action and not a foppish poet. He had himself painted in various military get-ups, and popularised a rugged open-shirted look. Like the celebrities of two centuries later, he was obsessed with his weight and carefully prepared for public appearances. He practised a special gloomy, smouldering glance he called his 'under-look' that simply devastated his public.
>
> A student of stagecraft, he created characters who paralleled his personality and circumstances so closely it is still impossible to avoid asking, in the words of Peter Cochran, 'Is this then verse, or documentation? Poetry, or journalism? Art, or life?' In embracing this contradiction, Byron speaks to our time.[17]

---

16 See, besides Mole, *Byron's Celebrity Culture*, McDayter, *Byromania and the Birth of Celebrity Culture*, and Tuite, *Lord Byron and Scandalous Celebrity*, George Paston and Peter Quennell, *To Lord Byron: Feminine Profiles based upon Unpublished Letters 1807–1824* (London: John Murray, 1939), Frances Wilson (ed.), *Byromania: Portraits of the Artist in Nineteenth- and Twentieth-Century Culture* (London: Macmillan, 1999), Tom Mole (ed.), *Romanticism and Celebrity Culture 1750–1850* (Cambridge: Cambridge University Press, 2012).
17 Paul Douglass, 'Byron's Life and Biographers', in *The Cambridge Companion to Byron*, ed. Drummond Bone (Cambridge: Cambridge University Press, 2002), 7–26 (12).

7 'Such is modern fame': The Byronic Hero from *Childe Harold* to *Don Juan*

The Byronic hero

What the Byronic hero offered its generation is first sketched in the character of Childe Harold, 'the prototype of those subsequent masked men we call Byronic Heroes', to quote Jerome McGann,[18] on a journey around the Mediterranean indulging in melancholy reflections on life, death, and the world beyond Britain:

> And now Childe Harold was sore sick at heart,
> And from his fellow bacchanals would flee;
> 'Tis said, at times the sullen tear would start,
> But Pride congeal'd the drop within his ee:
> Apart he stalk'd in joyless reverie,
> And from his native land resolv'd to go;
> And visit scorching climes beyond the sea;
> With pleasure drugg'd he almost long'd for woe,
> And e'en for change of scene would seek the shades below.
> ...
>
> Yet oft in his maddest mirthful mood
> Strange pangs would flash along Childe Harold's brow,
> As if the memory of some deadly feud
> Or disappointed passion lurk'd below:
> But this none knew, nor haply car'd to know;
> For his was not that open, artless soul
> That feels relief by bidding sorrow flow,
> Nor sought he friend to counsel or condole,
> Whate'er his grief mote be, which he could not control.
> (*Childe Harold's Pilgrimage*, Canto I, stanzas 6, 8)

More astute contemporary critics, like the editor of the *Edinburgh Review*, Francis Jeffrey, recognised the Byronic hero immediately as a

---

18 Jerome McGann, 'Hero with a Thousand Faces: The Rhetoric of Byronism', in his *Byron and Romanticism*, ed. James Soderholm (Cambridge: Cambridge University Press, 2002), 141–72 (141).

developed version of Milton's Satan—and, one hastens to add, of Satan's progeny in the Gothic villains and the noble outcasts or outlaws of the eighteenth century—modified by features that unmistakably derived from Byron's own physical person, life, and personality:

> the mind of the noble author has been so far tinged by his strong perception of the Satanic personage, that the sentiments and reflections which he delivers in his own name, have all received a shade of the same gloomy misanthropic colouring which invests those of his imaginary hero.[19]

The Byronic hero would be deepened, elaborated, and to some extent complicated in the later narrative romances known as the Turkish Tales—*The Giaour*, *The Corsair*, *The Bride of Abydos*, *Lara*—achieving its pre-eminent, arguably self-parodic expression in Byron's psycho-drama *Manfred*. 'Byron's celebrity career required that each publication should be different', writes Tom Mole, 'while at the same time being connected to the last by a developmental narrative'.[20]

We can identify the Byronic hero by a set of traits which, if they are not to be found in each incarnation, are nonetheless common to the point of being formulaic. There is, for a start, the magnetic physical beauty, with a gloomy, forbidding aspect and attitude (a sneer at the lip) that centres on the windows of the soul, the eyes, tormented but mesmerising. And he is possessed of—and possessed by—powerful, mysterious passions, generally repressed but liable to erupt when triggered by the insensitivity of others or painful personal memories. The 'overnight success' of *Childe Harold's Pilgrimage*, writes Fiona Stafford, betrays a contemporary 'taste for melancholy' and 'a readership hungry for powerful feelings'.[21] 'Hubris, pride, contempt for the "common

---

19 Francis Jeffrey, review of *Childe Harold's Pilgrimage* in the Edinburgh *Review* (1812), reprinted in *Byron: The Critical Heritage*, ed. Andrew Rutherford (London: Routledge & Kegan Paul, 1970), 39. The seminal analysis of the Byronic hero and his literary genetics remains Peter L. Thorslev, *The Byronic Hero: Types and Prototypes* (Minneapolis: University of Minneapolis Press, 1962).
20 Mole, *Byron's Celebrity Career*, 134.
21 Fiona Stafford, *Reading Romantic Poetry* (Malden and Oxford: Wiley-Blackwell, 2012), 17.

crowd", indifference to the opinions of others',[22] the demeanour and profile of the Byronic hero are unmistakably aristocratic—an important point this, to which we will return. The Byronic hero's cultural and literary heritage is preserved in his athleticism and courage. Like Satan and his Gothic progeny, he is a descendant of Hector and Achilles, and of the knights of the Arthurian legend, whose physical agility and courage go with a noble inheritance.

The gloomy aspect of the Byronic hero is the outward and visible sign of a bitter cynicism and world-weariness (in French, *chagrin mondiale*, in German, *Weltschmerz*): 'few earthly things found favour in his sight' (*Childe Harold's Pilgrimage*, Canto 1, st. 16). The Byronic hero's disenchantment is occasioned by past indulgence—he is physically and emotionally exhausted, spent, superannuated; having run 'through Sin's long labyrinth' and lived beyond his years, 'He felt the fullness of satiety' (*Childe Harold's Pilgrimage*, Canto I, st. 4), with the suggestion of a dark crime—betrayal or murder or incest—that is more suggestion than reality.[23]

> There is a power upon me which withholds
> And makes it my fatality to live;
> If it be life to wear within myself
> This barrenness of spirit, and to be
> My own soul's sepulchre, for I have ceased
> To justify my deeds unto myself—
> The last infirmity of evil.
> (*Manfred*, Act I, sc. 2, ll. 23–29)

Though tormented by self-loathing and barely repressed passions, however, Byron's impersonations also contain strategic intimations of a lost altruism and idealism, which, like the passions related to them, are equally liable on occasion to erupt. Byron is always careful to identify

---

22 Poole, 'The Byronic Hero, Theatricality and Leadership', 11.
23 Gabriele Poole finds 'the extent of his crimes is actually fairly limited, especially when contrasted with the behaviour of his antagonists', when she examines these seeming 'crimes' in 'The Byronic Hero, Theatricality and Leadership', 10–12 (12).

beneath the hardened, cynical exterior of his Byronic hero the disappointed idealist, to see in his contempt and cynicism the wreck of a passionate idealism. It is his argument with human life itself—with the fact that, as human beings, we are tempted to dream and to aspire, and thus bound to be betrayed by an intractable reality. The more passionately idealistic we are, as Freud later realised, the more we create the conditions for a melancholy self-loathing. It is the residual idealism behind the moody, isolated Byronic hero that was and is the source of his mixed maternal and erotic attraction. However desperate and cynical, the Byronic hero's behaviour is punctuated by random acts of kindness and of love, sometimes according to the chivalric code under which he continues to live (*noblesse oblige*), sometimes the expression of a more personal, spontaneous, irrepressible goodheartedness.

The result of all this is that the Byronic hero is doomed to perish through his own strength—strength of passion, strength of virtue (again, in the chivalric sense), strength of will—because that strength, turned inwards, eventually destroys him:

> The Mind, that broods o'er guilty woes,
>   Is like the Scorpion girt by fire,
> In circle narrowing as it glows
> The flames around their captive close,
> Till inly search'd by thousand throes,
>   And maddening in her ire,
> One sad and soul relief she knows,
> The sting she nourish'd for her foes,
> Whose venom never yet was vain,
> Gives but one pang, and cures all pain,
> And darts into her desperate brain.—
> So do the dark in soul expire
> Or live like Scorpion girt by fire;
> So writhes the mind Remorse hath riven,
> Unfit for earth, undoom'd for heaven,
> Darkness above, despair beneath,
> Around it flame, within it death!—
>
> (*The Giaour*, ll. 422–38)

7 'Such is modern fame': The Byronic Hero from *Childe Harold* to *Don Juan*

'The heroes find in their ability, indeed compulsion, to remember the pain that devastated them the capacity to still feel', writes Alan Rawes, '[y]et in remembering what devastated him, the hero subjects himself once again to its devastating power'.[24]

Byron repeated the formula again and again over the years 1812 to 1818. Here is the Giaour himself, self-incarcerated in a monastery 'for some dark deed he will not name' and brooding 'within his cell alone':

> Dark and unearthly is the scowl
> That glares beneath his dusky cowl—
> The flash of that dilating eye
> Reveals too much of times gone by—
> Though varying—indistinct its hue,
> Oft will his glance the gazer rue—
> For in it lurks that nameless spell
> Which speaks—itself unspeakable—
> A spirit yet unquelled and high
> That claims and keeps ascendancy,
> And like the bird whose pinions quake—
> But cannot fly the gazing snake—
> Will others quail beneath his look,
> Nor 'scape the glance they scarce can brook. ...
> Not oft to smile descendeth he,
> And when he does 'tis sad to see
> That he but mocks at Misery.
> How that pale lip would curl and quiver! ...
> But sadder still it were to trace
> What once were feelings in that face—
> Time hath not yet the features fixed,
> But brighter traits with evil mixed—
> And there are hues not always faded,
> Which speak a mind not all degraded
> Even by the crimes through which it waded—
> The common crowd but see the gloom

---

24 Alan Rawes, '1816–17: *Childe Harold* III and *Manfred*', in *The Cambridge Companion to Byron*, ed. Bone, 118–32 (118).

Of wayward deeds—and fitting doom—
The close observer can espy
A noble soul, and lineage high.
                    (*The Giaour*, ll. 832–53, 859–69)

Through the catalogue of moody heroes in these exotic Turkish tales, each burdened by an albatross of his own shooting, Byron envisions the human condition as tragically divided and paralysed by irreconcilable impulses. Perhaps the most enduring and certainly the most influential version of the Byronic hero (in terms of its going on to inspire a myriad dramatic adaptations, musical compositions, operas, and paintings) is the eponymous hero of Byron's blank-verse psychodrama, *Manfred*:

ABBOT
This should have been a noble creature: he
Hath all the energy which would have made
A goodly frame of glorious elements,
Had they been wisely mingled; as it is,
It is an awful chaos—lightness and dark,
And mind and dust, and passions and pure thoughts
Mix'd and contending without end or order
                    (*Manfred*, Act III, scene 1, ll. 160–66)

MANFRED
How beautiful is all this visible world,
How glorious in its action and itself!
But we, who name ourselves its sovereigns, we,
Half dust, half deity, alike unfit
To sink or soar, with our mix'd essence make
A conflict of its elements, and breathe
The breath of degradation and of pride,
Contending with low wants and lofty will,
Till our mortality predominates—
And men are what they name not to themselves,
And trust not to each other.
                    (*Manfred*, Act I, scene 2, ll. 37–47)

7 'Such is modern fame': The Byronic Hero from *Childe Harold* to *Don Juan*

Manfred's and Byron's sense of impotence and anticlimax is best understood by tracing it to two distinct and powerful influences on the poet and his poetry. In his characterisation of the human condition ('Half dust, half deity'), Manfred echoes Alexander Pope's Essay on Man:

> Plac'd on this isthmus of a middle state,
> A being darkly wise, and rudely great:
> With too much knowledge for the Sceptic side,
> And too much weakness for the Stoic's pride,
> He hangs between; in doubt to act, or rest,
> In doubt to deem himself a God, or Beast;
> In doubt his Mind or Body to prefer,
> Born but to die, and reas'ning but to err;
> Alike in ignorance, his reason such,
> Whether he thinks too little, or too much:
> Chaos of Thought and Passion, all confus'd;
> Still by himself abus'd, or disabus'd;
> Created half to rise, and half to fall;
> Great lord of all things, yet a prey to all;
> Sole judge of Truth, in endless Error hurl'd:
> The glory, jest, and riddle of the world!
> (*Essay on Man, Epistle 2*, ll. 3–18)[25]

On the other hand, when Byron resorts to the same unproductive and irresolvable dualisms to express, not so much a human and existential predicament as a personal sense of frustration and depression, Byron and his heroes echo the anxious bipolar alternations of Shakespeare's moody Hamlet:

> I have of late, but wherefore I know not, lost all my mirth ... this goodly frame the earth, seems to me a sterile promontory, this most excellent canopy the air, look you, this brave o'erhanging firmament, this majestical roof fretted with golden fire, why it appeareth nothing

---

25 *The Poems of Alexander Pope*, ed. John Butt (London and New York: Routledge, 1963).

to me but a foul and pestilent congregation of vapours. What a piece of work is a man[;] how noble in reason, how infinite in faculties[;] in form and moving, how express and admirable[;] in action, how like an angel[;] in apprehension, how like a god: the beauty of the world, the paragon of animals; and yet to me, what is this quintessence of dust?

(*Hamlet*, 2.2.295ff.)[26]

What we find clearly delineated in Byron's verse are two arguably conflicting impulses, one communal, the other personal. The first is the impulse to characterise the human condition as necessarily ironic, bathetic, and contradictory. 'He hallows in order to desecrate', writes Hazlitt, 'takes a pleasure in defacing images of beauty his own hands have wrought; and raises our hopes and our belief in goodness to Heaven only to dash them to the earth again, and break them in pieces the more effectually from the very height they have fallen'.[27] In this sense, the Byronic poem is an eminently public, declamatory document in which an acute historical self-consciousness discourses on the meaning and value of action and event, offering what Philip Martin calls 'anti-teleological explorations of history, politics and contemporary affairs'.[28] At the same time, however, there is an habitual impulse to a kind of self-dramatisation (or melodramatisation) in which the existential dilemma and the existential agony, far from being endemic to all humankind, are the exclusive privilege of the Byronic hero alone—and, by inference, of Byron himself. Or, if not the existential condition, then the painful recognition. The cynical Byronic persona, like the Romantic hero more generally, is unique precisely in the clarity and insight with which he perceives the ephemerality and insubstantiality of the world and his own insignificance within it. He suffers more because he sees and understands more. 'Sorrow is knowledge' (*Manfred*).

---

26 William Shakespeare, *Hamlet*, ed. Harold Jenkins (London: Methuen, 1982).
27 Hazlitt, 'Lord Byron', 140.
28 Philip W. Martin, 'Heroism and history: *Childe Harold* I and II and the Tales', in *The Cambridge Companion to Byron*, ed. Bone, 77–98 (77).

In this quasi-spiritual elevation, the Byronic hero remains aloof, a larger-than-life figure and part of the broader European cult that we identify as Romantic Prometheanism. Prometheus was the Greek hero who defied Zeus to steal fire on behalf of mankind, for which he was chained to rock and punished eternally. In Howard Mumford Jones's formulation:

> To the romantics it is clear that Prometheus symbolized a will power that included a capacity for infinite endurance, a defiance of deity and therefore of 'priestcraft', a mystical self-justification that might mount to sublime egotism, a hatred of tyranny, and a belief in the brotherhood of man and therefore in equality. But it is equally clear that the theoretical equality of man in this myth is contradicted in a sense by the superiority of the Titan. Man may be, indeed, half divine, and therefore also be half capable of shaping his future. But Prometheus is the incarnation of the aristocratic spirit, a being above those he protects, a leader and a saviour from outside. He has a foresight not found in the common herd.[29]

Byron's acute, though anxious sense of his own nobility only confirms and complicates these two conflicting impulses—the one, centrifugal, moving outwards towards humanity or, politically, towards the people (this is Byron the freedom fighter, the hater of tyrannies and leader of the Greeks in their fight for independence from an oppressive Ottoman empire); the other, centripetal, moving inwards towards the self. 'Lord Byron, who in his politics is a *liberal*', as Hazlitt observed, 'in his genius is haughty and aristocratic'.[30] This characteristically Romantic mixture of sympathetic egalitarianism and arrogant spiritual elitism is perhaps nowhere better symbolised than in the person and career of Napoleon, the 'Conqueror and captive of the earth' and yet another Byronic hero:

---

29 Howard Mumford Jones, *Revolution and Romanticism* (Cambridge, Mass.: Harvard University Press, 1974), 251.
30 Hazlitt, 'Lord Byron', 135–36.

> But quiet to quick bosoms is a hell,
> And *there* hath been thy bane; there is fire
> And motion of the soul which will not dwell
> In its own narrow being, but aspire
> Beyond the fitting medium of desire.
> (*Childe Harold's Pilgrimage*, Canto III, st. 42)

Byron as Byronic hero

Again and again, Byron's poetry encouraged its readers to identify Byron with his heroes, even while Byron himself more or less vigorously protested their status as fictions. 'Celebrity is folded back into literary creation', to quote Tom Mole.[31] The Byron who at twenty-eight gave his age as 100 years in the Hôtel d'Angleterre in Switzerland,[32] who felt that his experience (especially his sexual experience) had exhausted him, professing himself weary of the world and of the humanity whose freedoms he histrionically defended, offered in his Byronic hero a symbol of the world of post-Napoleonic Europe and a surrogate for his own, spent self:

> 'Tis to create, and in creating live
> A being more intense, that we endow
> With form our Fancy, gaining as we give
> The life we imagine, even as I do now.
> What am I? Nothing; but not so thou,
> Soul of my thought! With whom I traverse earth,
> Invisible but gazing, as I glow
> Mix'd with thy spirit, blended with thy birth,
> And feeling still with thee in my crush'd feelings dearth.
> (*Childe Harold's Pilgrimage*, Canto III, st. 6)

---

31 Mole, *Byron's Romantic Celebrity*, 20.
32 Leslie A. Marchand, *Byron: A Portrait* (London: John Murray, 1971), 240.

7 'Such is modern fame': The Byronic Hero from *Childe Harold* to *Don Juan*

It may be, as Bernard Beatty suggests, that 'every sixth-former is a dab hand with personas, projections, masks, doppelgangers, narrators, fictive personalities, and self-fashioning selves',[33] but Byron understood—and understood how to exploit—the masquerade of selfhood from the inside. This well-known stanza,[34] with the psychological (not to say pathological) involutions it reveals and encourages, could stand as a paradigm of 'modern fame'. Even as the author, George Gordon, Lord Byron, confesses a need for his fictional Byronic image in order vicariously to approximate to life, still he persists with the fantasy of the exhausted (post-)hero, soliciting the female reader's interest and sympathy for his state of emotional and sexual impotence. Even as the famous poet confesses to being incommensurate with his own fantastic projection of himself as Childe Harold, he sustains and reinforces the fantasy. 'The necessity to penetrate the hero's facade, to reach the sensitive heart that undeniably throbbed beneath the austere exterior', writes Byron's biographer, Phyllis Grosskurth, 'became the determined purpose of every young woman who copied passages into her commonplace book.'[35]

'Curiously addicted to imitating anything that might impress him as a literary image of himself',[36] Byron shared his readers' fascination with the Byronic. What from a cultural point of view is most interesting (and ironic) about the erotic fascination with the brooding, aristocratic sensation called Byron shown by readers (then and since) is the fact that the social and cultural conditions that nurtured and

---

33 Bernard Beatty, '*Childe Harold's Pilgrimage* I and II in 1812', *The Byron Journal*, 41:2 (2013), 101–14 (111).
34 For recent discussion of this stanza, see Bernard Beatty, '"The Glory and the Nothing of a Name"', *The Byron Journal*, 36 (2008), 91–104, Madeleine Callaghan, '"A Being More Intense": Byronic Poetic Intensity and the Stanza Form', in *Byron's Poetry*, ed. Peter Cochrane (Newcastle-upon-Tyne: Cambridge Scholars, 2012), 163–70, and Michael J. Plygawko, '"The Controlless Core of Human Hearts": Writing the Self in Byron's *Don Juan*', *The Byron Journal*, 42:2 (2014), 123–30.
35 Phyllis Grosskurth, *Byron: The Flawed Angel* (Toronto: Macfarlane, Walter, & Ross, 1997), 155.
36 Ralph Milbanke, Earl of Lovelace, *Astarte: A Fragment of Truth Concerning George Gordon Byron, Sixth Lord Byron, Recorded by his Grandson*, ed. Mary, Countess of Lovelace (London: Christophers, 1921), 5.

indulged the Byronic are in some striking ways opposed to what the Byronic itself represents. Like the fascination with the Gothic generally, the public fascination with Byron is the fascination of a modern, enlightened, commercial world with a more irrational, more overtly passionate, darker, small 'r' romantic world remote from its own experience, which it approaches with an awe that only reinforces the distance between them.

Some, like Hazlitt, see Byron's attitude simply as hypocritical. For more recent critics, like Philip Martin, it is a socio-historical paradox in which the poet's growing contempt for his middle-class audience for *not* being outlaws of their own dark minds and for *not* being (like him) aristocratic only excites that audience more and more[37]—an aristocratic dinosaur among middle-class mammals who take a masochistic pleasure in watching dinosaurs treading on mammals:

> I have not loved the world, nor the world me;
> I have not flattered its rank breath, nor bow'd
> To its idolatries a patient knee,—
> Nor coin'd my cheek to smiles,—nor cried aloud
> In worship of an echo; in the crowd
> They could not deem me one of such; I stood
> Among them, but not of them; in a shroud
> Of thoughts which were not their thoughts, and still could,
> Had I not filed my mind, which thus itself subdued.
> (*Childe Harold's Pilgrimage*, Canto III, st. 113)

Another modern critic, Jerome Christensen, sees Byron's ambivalent relations to his middle-class audience as economic, a case of aristocratic strength caught up in an alien, bourgeois world of commerce and accountability. 'The literary system of Byronism', argues Christensen, exploited 'the residual affective charge that still clung to the paraphernalia of aristocracy in order to reproduce it in commodities that could

---

37 Philip W. Martin, *Byron: A Poet before His Public* (Cambridge: Cambridge University Press, 1982).

7 'Such is modern fame': The Byronic Hero from *Childe Harold* to *Don Juan*

be vended to a reading public avid for glamour.'[38] Whether we read it with Hazlitt or Martin or Christensen, it adds up to the same irony.

The Byronic hero was not as mercenary as Christensen makes it sound, though both Byron and his publisher, John Murray, could be cunning in their exploitation. What Byron's success represents, in fact, is a genuine marriage of complementary compulsions: on the one hand, the compulsion of a flamboyant and exhibitionist personality to write a version of his life into his poetry and, on the other, the compulsion of a public hungry for sensational details of an exotic and erotic kind, and for provocatively pessimistic and misanthropic opinions, especially when leavened by lyricism and a residual romantic idealism that persists in spite of the poetry's overwhelming testimony to the contrary. Such is modern fame.

Don Juan: 'Is it not *life*?'

'As time went by', however, as Gabriele Poole remarks, 'Byron's works began to increasingly show signs of reservations—psychological, political and artistic—about the various early embodiments of the Byronic Hero.'[39] *Don Juan*, the long poem left unfinished by the poet's death at Missolonghi in Greece in 1824, was different, bringing out the mock-heroic elements often close to the surface in Byron's heroic poems.

> I want a hero: an uncommon want,
> When every year and month brings forth a new one.
> (*Don Juan*, Canto I, st. 1)

The works of Lord Byron 'are enough to corrupt the morals of a nation', protested John Angell James in the year after Byron's death: 'If young people would not be cursed by the infidelity and immorality which lurks in its pages, let them beware how they touch his volumes, as

---

38 Jerome Christensen, *Lord Byron's Strength: Romantic Writing and Commercial Humanism* (Baltimore and London: Johns Hopkins University Press, 1993), xvi.
39 Poole, 'The Byronic Hero, Theatricality and Leadership', 16.

much as they would to embrace a beautiful form infected with the plague.'[40] 'Fatal, unutterably fatal has been the influence of Moore and Byron to many thousands of youthful readers', agreed the Rev. W. M. Hetherington nearly two decades later in *A Course of Lectures to Young Men*.[41] Both authors were responding to *Don Juan*, and two important things are revealed by this violent reaction to Byron's last great poem.

The first is that the readership of Byron's poetry had not only increased with *Don Juan*, it had also spread. There were far more readers from among the labouring classes excited by its sexual frankness and anti-authoritarianism, reading it in any one of the proliferation of cheap or pirated versions available.[42] Byron found a much more various readership for his avowedly liberal to libertarian sentiments on all aspects of life and society, but specifically for his aggressive and uncompromising opposition to British and European 'legitimacy'—the Tory ministry in Britain and its Unholy Alliance with reactionary governments abroad.

The second important thing is that it registers the extent of *Don Juan*'s challenge to contemporary ideas and values. Byron had persisted with the poem regardless of what seemed to be a drop, or threatened drop, in his official readership. What saved Byron when enormous pressures were being brought to bear to force him to abandon *Don Juan* altogether, or to accept his publisher's (and others') censorship, was simply a healthy egotism—just as it was egotism that had helped him survive Henry Brougham's savage attack on his *Hours of Idleness* in the *Edinburgh Review* in 1808.[43] Though Byron had always been willing to make some concessions to Murray in his earlier poems, his conviction in this case was strong enough for him to continue writing when he felt he had, at last, found the appropriate form and poetic voice to express his wilfully, wittily perverse, evasive, and contradictory vision of 'the world exactly as it goes'.

---

40   J. A. James, *The Christian Father's Present to His Children* [1825], seventeenth edition (New York: Robert Carter & Bros, 1853), 226.
41   *A Course of Lectures to Young Men: Science, Literature, and Religion: Delivered in Glasgow, by Ministers of Various Denominations* (Glasgow: William Collins, 1842), 342.
42   See William St Clair, *The Reading Nation in the Romantic Period*, 322–36.
43   See William Christie, *The Edinburgh Review in the Literary Culture of Romantic Britain* (London: Pickering & Chatto, 2009), 123–31.

7 'Such is modern fame': The Byronic Hero from *Childe Harold* to *Don Juan*

For this was his professed aim in *Don Juan*: 'To sketch the world exactly as it goes'. What changes with *Don Juan* is not Byron's construction of the human condition itself, which he still conceives as frustrated and futile:

> Well—well, the world must turn upon its axis,
>   And all mankind turn with it, heads or tails,
> And live and die, make love and pay our taxes,
>   And as the veering wind shifts, shift our sails;
> The king commands us, and the doctor quacks us,
>   The priest instructs, and so our life exhales,
> A little breath, love, wine, ambition, fame,
> Fighting, devotion, dust,—perhaps a name.
>   (*Don Juan*, Canto II, st. 4)

Humanity remains for Byron (in the words of Pope quoted earlier) a 'Chaos of Thought and Passion, all confus'd'. Indeed, in the abstract sense, Byron's thinking on all issues (hardly a philosophy) changes very little, if at all, throughout his work. What changes are Byron's priorities, both existential and artistic, and his attitude or attitudes (plural) to the inevitable anticlimax that is the human condition. What changes is the way Byron perceives himself and his own position in relation to 'the world exactly as it goes'. Instead of brooding over the frustration and futility of existence and over the inconsistencies, cruelties, and self-sabotaging tendencies of humanity, as he had in the earlier works, Byron now wallows in it. Humanity becomes a rich and varied field or forum through which he can romp with comic irreverence, exposing the emptiness of its pretensions and the multiplicity of its follies and vices, and both exemplifying and recommending an approach to life that is sceptical and self-sceptical, ironic and self-ironic, mocking and self-mocking. Above all, the attitude struck by the narrator of *Don Juan* is what we could call *knowing*:

> As to 'Don Juan'—confess—confess—you dog—and be candid—that it is the sublime of *that there* sort of writing—it may be bawdy—but is it not good English?—it may be profligate—but is it not *life*, is it not *the thing*?—Could any man have written it—who has not lived

in the world?—and tooled in a post-chaise? in a hackney coach? in a Gondola? against a wall? in a court carriage in a vis a vis?—on a table?—and under it?[44]

What can Byron mean by describing *Don Juan* as a sketch of the world exactly as it goes, and on another occasion as 'real life, either my own or others'? 'I hate things *all fiction*', he once protested, 'There should always be some foundation of fact for the most airy fabric'.[45] As usual, Byron's philistinism is self-consciously polemical or oppositional. What he is rejecting is what *he* would have called the 'romantic' and we have been calling the small-'r' romantic: the exotic and 'insubstantial pageant' of contemporary fantasy, especially utopian fantasy—just as elsewhere he uses common sense or cynicism to reduce Shelleyan aspiration and idealism. It is all part of a concerted attempt to get behind human posturing and self-importance to the reality of self-serving human motive:

> As boy, I thought myself a clever fellow,
>   And wish'd that others held the same opinion;
> They took it up when my days grew more mellow,
>   And other minds acknowledged my dominion:
> Now my sere fancy 'falls into the yellow
>   Leaf', and Imagination droops her pinion,
> And the sad truth which hovers o'er my desk
> Turns what was once romantic to burlesque.
>   (*Don Juan*, Canto IV, st. 3)

The language of *Don Juan*, accordingly, is most often in a colloquial, worldly register, if not quite the aristocratic slang of the Regency—unliterary and anti-literary; unpedantic and anti-pedantic; blunt and clear-eyed, sometimes obscene; a kind of plain speaking fashioned out of the attitude and idiom of the upper-class, metropolitan

---

44 Byron to Douglas Kinnaird, 26 October [1819], *Byron's Letters and Journals*, ed. Leslie Marchand, in 12 vols (Cambridge, Mass.: Harvard University Press, 1973–82), 6:232.
45 Byron to John Murray, 2 April 1817, *Byron's Letters and Journals*, 5:203.

7 'Such is modern fame': The Byronic Hero from *Childe Harold* to *Don Juan*

roué. All of this is typical of satire, plain speaking being the verbal equivalent to its ideal of good sense:

> Were things but only call'd by their right name,
> Caesar himself would be ashamed of Fame.
> *(Don Juan,* Canto XIV, st. 102)

What becomes apparent in the poem, however, is that the turn from the romantic to the burlesque, in order to get at the truth about humanity, was the occasion of resignation and regret for its author, no less than of a satirical, debunking glee. In such episodes as those of the shipwreck and cannibalism in the second canto, and of Juan and Haidée on their island paradise in the third—indeed, in every episode prior to the English cantos—Byron manages to have his fantasy even while mocking and undermining it. The result is that the poem's nominally unflinching realism, like the melancholy pessimism of his Byronic heroes, is charged with the irrepressible yearning of the romantic.

But we will return to that. More important for the moment is the issue of form or genre: the fact that Byron's reality or his version of real life had precious little to do with conventional literary realism. *Don Juan* is patently not an *ottava rima* version of Jane Austen's *Emma*—let alone of a novel by Balzac or Zola. What Byron would claim is that the life that *Don Juan* details is more 'real' than the life of other literature—including the life depicted by the realist or realistic novel—in that it is both more inclusive and less evasive, taking into account human complexity and perversity, for example, sexual motivation and political machination. The incidents of the poem, on the other hand, remain bizarre, improbable, exaggerated, and exotic (in a word, small 'r' romantic). Given that humanity is perverted, unpredictable, grotesque, and hypocritical, this makes *Don Juan* realistic in an altogether different sense from the way we would use the term of a nineteenth-century French novel. 'Realistic', for Byron, means 'disillusioned' in both senses: without illusions about human perfection or perfectibility, in other words, and also, simply, disappointed—existentially so.

As a narrative, *Don Juan* is a challenge to its narrator's whimsical inventiveness, a self-conscious fiction, subject to the narrator/Byron's open and unapologetic manipulation. But in Byron's terms it is precisely this fabulousness—his ability to make things up at will—that allows him to deal more directly with what might seem its opposite, the 'truth':

> But what's this to the purpose? you will say.
>   Gent. Reader, nothing; a mere speculation,
> For which my sole excuse is—'tis my way,
>   Sometimes with and sometimes without occasion
> I write what's uppermost, without delay;
>   This narrative is not meant for narration,
> But a mere airy and fantastic basis,
> To build up common things with common places.
>   (*Don Juan*, Canto XIV, st. 7)

The narrative's manifest *un*realism or lack of realism, in other words, is its way of artistically reconstructing and highlighting the reality of the human condition.

Byronic satire

Though 'too free for these very modest days', still *Don Juan* was 'the most moral of poems', Byron protested to his publisher, John Murray, 'but if people won't discover the moral, that is their fault, not mine'. Far from being the 'eulogy of vice' it was condemned as being, it was 'a satire on the abuses of the present state of society'.[46] (What he did not say was that his correcting 'the abuses of the present state of society' would necessarily involve a radical redefinition of 'vice' and what it meant to be vicious.) Byron's general weapons, accordingly, are those of the satirist: irony, paradox, and bathos or anticlimax, each involving juxtaposition and contrast. The greatness of *Don Juan*'s satirical

---

46 Byron to John Murray, 1 February 1819, *Byron's Letters and Journals*, ed. Marchand, 6:99.

7 'Such is modern fame': The Byronic Hero from *Childe Harold* to *Don Juan*

strength lies in its developed art of disillusionment as I have just defined it, a virtual rhetoric of techniques and arguments designed to reduce the hold of habitual and institutional impositions over the life of both the body and the mind and to free us from the self-sabotaging illusions of human idealism. The fate of 'Platonic love' is typical:

> And then there are such things as love divine,
>   Bright and immaculate, unmix'd and pure,
> Such as the angels think so very fine,
>   And matrons, who would be no less secure,
> Platonic, perfect, 'just such love as mine':
>   Thus Julia said—and thought so, to be sure;
> And so I'd have her think, were I the man
> On whom her reveries celestial ran.
>   (*Don Juan*, Canto I, st. 79)

> Oh Plato! Plato! you have paved the way,
>   With your confounded fantasies, to more
> Immoral conduct by the fancied sway
>   Your system reigns o'er the controlless core
> Of human hearts, than all the long array
>   Of poets and romancers:—You're a bore,
> A charlatan, a coxcomb—and have been,
> At best, no better than a go-between.
>   (*Don Juan*, Canto I, st. 116)

Most often, Byron juxtaposes his incongruities—the significant with the insignificant, the dignified with the undignified, the noble with the ignoble—to produce a comic bathos or subversion, confronting the pretentiousness of moralising, sentimentalising, and idealising with the brute facts of everyday, especially of our bodily or creatural existence—what the Russian critic Mikhail Bakhtin calls 'slum realism'. See, for example, Juan's attempt to read Julia's *billet-doux* or love-letter (the word 'billet-doux' is itself often a euphemism for sexual intrigue) while struggling with seasickness:

'Sooner shall heaven kiss earth'—(here he fell sicker)
    'Oh, Julia! what is every other woe?—
(For God's sake let me have a glass of liquor,
    Pedro, Battista, help me down below).
Julia, my love!—(you rascal, Pedro, quicker)—
    Oh Julia!—(this curst vessel pitches so)—
Beloved Julia, hear me still beseeching!'
(Here he grew inarticulate with reaching.)

He felt that chilling heaviness of heart,
    Or rather stomach, which, alas! attends,
Beyond the best apothecary's art,
    The loss of love, the treachery of friends,
Or death of those we doat on, when a part
    Of us dies with them as each fond hope ends:
No doubt he would have been much more pathetic,
But the sea acted as a strong emetic.
                    (*Don Juan*, Canto II, stanzas 20–21)

Witness the bathos of the assorted, even anarchic, alternation of incongruous responses to the shipwreck, imitative of a drunken chaos induced by fear:

There's nought, no doubt, so much the spirit calms
    As rum and true religion; thus it was,
Some plunder'd, some drank spirits, some sung psalms,
    The high wind made the treble, and as bass
The hoarse harsh waves kept time; fright cured the qualms
    Of all the luckless landsmen's sea-sick maws:
Strange sounds of wailing, blasphemy, devotion,
Clamour'd in chorus to the roaring ocean.
                    (*Don Juan*, Canto II, st. 34)

And, with this, the careful deflation of the lyrical erotic:

7 'Such is modern fame': The Byronic Hero from *Childe Harold* to *Don Juan*

> And she bent o'er him, and he lay beneath,
>   Hush'd as the babe upon its mother's breast,
> Droop'd as the willow when no winds can breathe,
>   Lull'd like the depth of ocean when at rest,
> Fair as the crowning rose of the whole wreath,
>   Soft as the callow cygnet in its nest;
> In short, he was a very pretty fellow,
> Although his woes had turn'd him rather yellow.
>   (*Don Juan*, Canto II, st. 148)

The sequence in which Pedrillo is bled and eaten during the brilliant mix of harrowing and hilarity that is the shipwreck episode can be seen as setting up a prevailing paradigm for social and individual relationships in the world of the entire poem—the world, as Byron would have us believe, 'exactly as it goes'. 'Dog eat dog', we mutter disapprovingly of the ruthless competitiveness of society, so Byron the animal-lover has his humans eat the dog before cannibalism beckons and they begin on each other. Yet within the episode's satiric function as a grotesque paradigm of human relations, and even within a couplet that appears as a parody of the cannibalism implicit in Christian ritual—

> And first a little crucifix he kiss'd,
> And then held out his jugular and wrist.

—Pedrillo still manages to receive his last rites from the poet. 'The blasphemy—Pedrillo enacting his *imitatio Christi*—is lightly carried', argues Jerome McGann, 'barely perceivable and all the more shocking for that deftness'.[47] There is (as always with Byron) a tenuous balance here, one that includes, not just the grotesque and the comic, but also the tender—and, it should be said, along with the tender, the sentimental. Even the hint of heroism in the unlikely Pedrillo is typical. In the seventh and eighth cantos, which contain some of the most devastating anti-war poetry in our language, Byron is determined to retain a sense

---

47 McGann, *Byron and Romanticism*, 292.

of humanity's heroic potential, even in the context of the most brutal, meaningless activity.

Satire is certainly an important part of the shipwreck story, as it is of *Don Juan* as a whole—satire of human pretensions to piety and control, as well as to any kind of cosmic significance: 'an expression not just of irreverence', remarks Fiona Stafford, 'but of profound scepticism'.[48] But also part of *Don Juan* as a whole are romance, the erotic, sentimentalism, comedy of manners, farce or burlesque, adventure, tragedy, and so on. Keeping faith with life means keeping faith with its mixed multiplicity of *genres*. The ludicrous and the tender, the quaint and the horrifying, jostle with each other without any one of them always or necessarily negating any one of the others, all being part of the human comedy or Byron's serious comedy of human imperfection. In this deflationary project, Byron insists—marshalling his authorities—he is not alone:

> They accuse me—me—the present writer of
> The present poem of—I know not what—
> A tendency to underrate and scoff
> At human power and virtue and all that;
> And this they say in language rather rough.
> Good God! I wonder what they would be at!
> I say no more than has been said in Dante's
> Verse and by Solomon and Cervantes,
>
> By Swift, by Machiavel, by Rochefoucault,
> By Fenelon, by Luther, and by Plato,
> By Tillotson and Wesley and Rousseau,
> Who knew this life was not worth a potato
> 'Tis not their fault nor mine if this be so.
> For my part I pretend not to be Cato
> Nor even Diogenes. We live and die,
> But which is best, you know no more than I.

---

48 Stafford, *Reading Romantic Poetry*, 88.

7 'Such is modern fame': The Byronic Hero from *Childe Harold* to *Don Juan*

* * *

> And in this scene of all-confessed inanity,
> By saint, by sage, by preacher, and by poet,
> Must I restrain me through the fear of strife
> From holding up the nothingness of life?
> (*Don Juan*, Canto VII, stanzas 3–4; 6)

Here is the ethical tradition, as Byron breaks it down genetically: Christian pessimism; political expediency; worldliness; predestinism; Platonism and Christian Platonism; Stoicism; Cynicism. (Is it a coincidence that the only one missing is Hedonism?) Is he not saying what all the moralists, especially the Christian moralists, have been saying from the beginning, which is that humankind is inherently and inevitably corrupt and, without reference to something higher, human life is inevitably meaningless?

Byron and his literary precursors

Byron's literary allegiances intersect with these ethical allegiances, and comprise Shakespeare, Swift, Pope, and Fielding most obviously. Further from home, we identify Cervantes, Rabelais, Voltaire, Pulci. But among *Don Juan*'s intertextual relations we can also find, in an oblique way, the epic poets of the classical curriculum and, perhaps most especially, Dante and Milton. Of his contemporaries, of course, Byron spoke slightingly, while making occasional exceptions of William Gifford, Samuel Rogers, Thomas Campbell, Thomas Moore, and Walter Scott. It was to the past that Byron provocatively turned—again, like all satirists. Byron saw himself as self-consciously resisting the tendency of contemporary poetry and parting from the impossibly high moral ground of Wordsworth, the feverish insubstantiality of the idealistic Shelley, not to mention the overwrought sexual sublimations of 'Jack Keats or Ketch or whatever his names are'.[49]

---

49 *Byron's Letters and Journals*, ed. Marchand, 7:217.

Thou shalt believe in Milton, Dryden, Pope;
Thou shalt not set up Wordsworth, Coleridge, Southey;
Because the first is crazed beyond all hope,
The second drunk, the third so quaint and mouthey:
(*Don Juan*, Canto I, st. 205)

Don Juan goes on to establish the extent to which Byron was out of sympathy with most of the poetry we think of as Romantic, including his own earlier verse. His self-conscious alliance with the Augustan satirists Dryden, Swift, Pope, Fielding, Johnson, and Sterne extended beyond sharing their satirical techniques to include the assumptions implicit in their urbane technique about the centrality of a sophisticated, metropolitan society. (The word 'urbane', of course, betrays its commitment to metropolitan society and the narrator of *Don Juan* is nothing if not urbane.)

For all Byron's criticism of Romantic exceptionalism and appeal beyond their idealism to common sense, what distinguishes the narrator of *Don Juan* is his independence and peculiar brand of egotism—a characteristically aristocratic insolence and disdain. But the main difference between Byron and the Augustan satirists he admired and imitated is the alacrity with which the unpredictable Byronic persona celebrates his own inconsistency, priding himself on keeping faith with the unpredictability and inconsistency of existence, and on being honest enough to admit it. 'Byron the aristocratic role-player', to quote Michael O'Neill:

> the dandy on his geographical and spiritual travels, the celebrity figure able to speak of himself as an erstwhile 'Napoleon of the realms of rhyme' (*DJ*, XI, 55), who celebrates yet implies the cost of 'mobility' ... who switches from tone to tone like a daring bareback rider vaulting from horse to horse, who impudently lays an extremely affecting sheet of sorrows on the shelf for fear of seeming rather 'touch'd' himself (*DJ*, IV, 74), who flaunts his uncertainties, mixes up his registers, and is always about to taunt his reader with the question, 'and what know *you* ... ?' (*DJ*, XIV, 3).[50]

---

50 Michael O'Neill, 'The Fixed and the Fluid: Identity in Byron and Shelley', *The Byron Journal*, 38:2 (2008), 105–14 (109).

7 'Such is modern fame': The Byronic Hero from *Childe Harold* to *Don Juan*

Indeed, to adopt a morally or intellectually consistent attitude towards the world, or towards humanity, when the world and its human inhabitants are so utterly *in*consistent, is to betray one's responsibilities as an artist committed to sketching the world exactly as it goes:

> whene'er I have exprest
> Opinions two, which at first sight may look
>   Twin opposites, the second is the best.
> Perhaps I have a third too in a nook
>   Or none at all, which seems a sorry jest.
> But if a writer should be quite consistent,
> How could he possibly show things existent?
>
> If people contradict themselves, can I
>   Help contradicting them and every body,
> Even my veracious self? But that's a lie;
>   I never did so, never will. How should I?
> He who doubts all things nothing can deny.
>   Truth's fountains may be clear, her streams are muddy
> And cut through such canals of contradiction
> That she must often navigate o'er fiction.
>   (*Don Juan*, Canto XV, stanzas 87–88)

Where there is no consistent perspective or position from which the satirist launches his satiric attacks, the attacks themselves remain—like all things in *Don Juan*—contingent, fragmentary, and discontinuous. For all its satiric gusto, in other words, *Don Juan* is not just a satire, just as it is often comic without being a comedy, lyrical without being a lyric, discursive and argumentative without being a discourse or an argument, narrative without being a narration, and epic without being an epic.

This last requires an explanation. *Don Juan* is closest to epic, most often, when mocking it: 'Hail Muse, et cetera' (Canto 3, st. 1). I draw attention to this precisely because it flies in the face of what, in the first canto, the narrator declares (tongue in cheek) his pretensions to be:

> My poem's epic, and is meant to be
>   Divided in twelve books; each book containing,
> With love, and war, a heavy gale at sea,
>   A list of ships, and captains, and kings reigning,
> New characters; the episodes are three:
>   A panorama view of hell's in training,
> After the style of Virgil and of Homer,
> So that my name of Epic's no misnomer.
>
> All these things will be specified in time,
>   With strict regard to Aristotle's rules,
> The *vade mecum* of the true sublime,
>   Which makes so many poets, and some fools;
> Prose poets like blank-verse, I'm fond of rhyme,
>   Good workmen never quarrel with their tools;
> I've got new mythological machinery,
> And very handsome supernatural scenery.
>   (*Don Juan*, Canto I, stanzas 200–201)

Yet everything in this mocking catalogue of correct procedure is, in fact, observed in the poem (if we except the twelve books). *Don Juan* does indeed aspire to an epic comprehensiveness: 'love, war, and a heavy gale at sea', and a lot else besides. Its Miltonic 'panorama view of hell' turns out to be plural, though all its many hells are hells on earth, and its Eden is the island retreat of Juan and Haidée, which, like Eden, is predestined to fall. The comprehensiveness to which epic aspires is manifest in *Don Juan* as miscellaneousness and multiplicity:

> A nondescript and ever varying rhyme,
>   A versified Aurora borealis,
> Which flashes o'er a waste and icy clime
>   (*Don Juan*, Canto VII, st. 2)

Indeed, the very endeavour to keep faith with the complexity and multivalency of existence lies behind *Don Juan*'s betrayal of epic uniformity, leading away from the epic into a generic heterogeneity.

7 'Such is modern fame': The Byronic Hero from *Childe Harold* to *Don Juan*

However, all its miscellaneous and incongruous parts are linked by recurrent themes and motifs: the vanity and hypocrisy of ambition, poetry, and romantic love, for example; the ill-concealed savagery of life as a struggle for self-preservation, radiating from the shipwreck and cannibalism episode as the poem's structuring metaphor; the tyrannies that operate in every area of life, private and public, and cry out for human resistance; humanity's persistent rationalising and romanticising.

Two Byronic heroes

Thus far I have discussed the narrator himself as a Byronic persona and the 'hero' or protagonist of *Don Juan*. But the poem has another, more obvious candidate for the role which is its eponymous hero, the character young Don Juan. No less than the narrator himself, Juan is Byron's alter ego and the hero of the poem's narrative, if not of the poem. He is *l'homme moyen sensuel*, familiar to English readers from Henry Fielding's *Tom Jones*. A naive enthusiast, his spontaneity and ingenuousness throw the narrator's ageing world-weariness and the more sinister worldliness of many of the other characters into relief. Juan is an instinctive or 'natural gentleman', and his being a gentleman or nobleman, while in one sense a parody of the romance tradition and its influence upon the contemporary novel, is in another sense no mere coincidence, any more than it was for the Byronic hero before him.

'Instinctive' here is the operative word. Juan is instinctive and impressionistic rather than rational, certainly not intellectual or what we would unflatteringly call 'academic' in his approach to life. (In this he is contrasted with his bluestocking mother, Donna Inez, like 'the Princess of Parallelograms', Annabella Milbanke.) There can be no doubt that Juan's sexual reputation was a major factor in Byron's choice of hero, but the original Don Juan of myth— heroic-satanic precursor who sold his soul to the devil—has become ironically tame in Byron's tale:

> I meant to have made him a Cavalier Servente in Italy and a cause for a divorce in England—and a Sentimental 'Werther-faced man' in Germany—so as to show the different ridicules of the society in each of those countries—and to have displayed him gradually gaté

and blasé as he grew older—as is natural.—But I had not quite fixed whether to make him end in Hell—or in an unhappy marriage,—not knowing which would be the severest.[51]

If Juan disappoints expectations raised by the name of the legendary lover, this is precisely the point, his essential passivity, especially in the bedroom, being vital to Byron's purposes. Apart from revealing the unrelenting scheming and hypocrisy of women and thus expressing Byron's conviction that the world was a 'gynocracy' and not a patriarchy, Juan's being acted upon, rather than active, makes him a catalyst for action, at the same time as making him symbolic of the essential passivity of the human condition. According to Byron, we are the puppets of our own desires and of circumstances outside our control.

There is no doubt an element of ideal projection in Byron's young and as yet spontaneous, open-minded, and open-hearted hero—an uncorrupted, unfallen Childe Harold—but the contrast with the narrator's Byronic voice is as complete as is the character's active or effective insignificance. Which returns us to the developed, ironic version of the Byronic hero in Byron's narrator as the poem's true hero. Besides liberating both the poet and the reader, the choice of Juan enabled Byron to cultivate in the narrator his most successful character and most successful self-projection—a character who enabled him to live a being, not more intense, but more blasé, more accommodating, and infinitely more entertaining than the moody Byronic heroes of his earlier poems:

> But now at thirty years my hair is gray—
>   (I wonder what it will be like at forty?
> I thought of a peruke the other day)
>   My heart is not much greener; and, in short, I
> Have squander'd my whole summer while 'twas May,
>   And feel no more the spirit to retort; I
> Have spent my life, both interest and principal,
> And deem not, what I deem'd, my soul invincible.
>   (*Don Juan*, Canto I, st. 213)

---

51 Byron to John Murray, 16 February 1821, *Byron's Letters and Journals*, ed. Marchand, 8:78.

7 'Such is modern fame': The Byronic Hero from *Childe Harold* to *Don Juan*

Byron's narrator-hero is largely a product of the verse form itself, insofar as the form is one of apparent artlessness masking self-conscious metrical and rhetorical effects.

> I rattle on exactly as I'd talk
> With any body on a ride or walk
>   (*Don Juan*, Canto XV, st. 19)

The *ottava rima* perfectly suits the paradoxically aimless purposiveness of the narrator's colloquial voice. The casual, digressive complexity and calculated redundancy that Byron achieves in the first six lines of the stanza, combined with the option of concentrated wit offered by the stanza's final couplet, encourages the unhurried verbosity punctuated by sharp insight that is the poem's 'wandering voice'.

> But let me to my story: I must own,
>   If I have any fault, it is digression;
> Leaving my people to proceed alone,
>   While I soliloquize beyond expression;
> But these are my addresses from the throne,
>   Which put off business to the ensuing session:
>   (*Don Juan*, Canto III, st. 96)

The picaresque tale featuring young Don Juan upon which the various incidents are strung is Byron's excuse to bring character, idea, and value into confrontation and to give himself every possible excuse to comment impressionistically and opinionatedly on morals and manners, to abuse (as well as disabuse or *dis*illusion), to peacock over his own talents and achievements, while at the same time or alternately confessing to his own delinquencies and hypocrisies. The aim throughout is to create the sense of an effortless, potentially endless improvisation:

> I don't know that there may be much ability
>   Shown in this sort of desultory rhyme;
> But there's a conversational facility,
>   Which may round off an hour upon a time.

Of this I'm sure at least, there's no servility
   In mine irregularity of chime,
Which rings what's uppermost of new or hoary,
   Just as I feel the 'Improvisatore.'
                              (*Don Juan*, Canto XV, st. 20)

For all the narrator's seeming carelessness, however, the voice and the character associated with it are ultimately ingratiating, even irresistible, as we come to laugh as he laughs, and to adopt his values and self-knowledge even against our will. And so, too, do we weep when he weeps, for though rare, the pathos is never far from the surface and the tears of the clown are compelling:

And if I laugh at any mortal thing,
   'Tis that I may not weep; and if I weep,
'Tis that our nature cannot always bring
   Itself to apathy, for we must steep
Our hearts first in the depths of Lethe's spring
   Ere what we least wish to behold will sleep:
                              (*Don Juan*, Canto IV, st. 4)

Conclusion: on poesis or making

It is a tribute to Byron's astuteness that he knew that in *Don Juan* he had at last found a form and content that were just right for him, and for which he was uniquely qualified: 'It may be bawdy, but is it not good English?—it may be profligate but is it not *life*, is it not *the thing*?—could any man have written it who lives not in the world?' Could any man have written it, Byron is saying, except me? Above and beyond everything else that it is about, *Don Juan* is a poem about its own *poesis* or making, about invention and the making of poetry. Indeed, as I have argued, Byron makes a unifying theme (largely through his narrator) out of the poem's *dis*unity: its inconsistent, digressive, fragmentary, and incomplete making. In *Don Juan*, the activity of discovering or making meaning is often displaced by the activity of making poetry or a poem (*poesis* as making), sometimes of just making rhymes. Ironically, this sheer inventiveness becomes a curiously positive assertion in the face of the nothingness of life discovered by the poem itself and often insisted upon by the narrator. Byron leaves us with the sense that *Don Juan* could go on changing forever while remaining the same—could go on indefinitely, as if the Byronic narrator-hero, like Scheherezade in *A Thousand and One Arabian Nights*, were prolonging his poem to postpone his own death:

> Man's a phenomenon, one knows not what,
>   And wonderful beyond all wondrous measure;
> 'Tis pity though, in this sublime world, that
>   Pleasure's a sin, and sometimes sin's a pleasure;
> Few mortals know what end they would be at,
>   But whether glory, power, or love, or treasure,
> The path is through perplexing ways, and when
> The goal is gain'd, we die, you know—and then
>
> What then?—I do not know, no more do you—
>   And so good night.—Return we to our story:
> 'Twas in November ...
>   (*Don Juan*, Canto I, stanzas 133–34)

If nothing else, it suggests, we have the capacity to imagine, though for Byron the imagination never carried the transformative, redemptive powers that it held for his friend and fellow-traveller, Percy Bysshe Shelley.

8
Amelioration and Madness in Percy Bysshe Shelley's 'Julian and Maddalo'

The subtitle of Shelley's 'Julian and Maddalo' describes it as 'A Conversation'.[1] As well as being a formal characterisation, alluding to the 'gentlemanly' dialogue between the title characters around which the poem is built,[2] this subtitle points to what Shelley in a letter to Leigh Hunt called its 'familiar style of language', chosen 'to express the way in which people talk'.[3] To describe one of *his* conversation poems, Coleridge had used the Horatian phrase *sermoni propriora*, which translates as 'better suited to talk'.[4] Shelley's use of a similar expression in another letter—this time to his publisher, Charles Ollier—reveals what he meant by this stylistic informality: 'Julian and

---

1   All quotations from 'Julian and Maddalo' are from the Norton Critical Edition of *Shelley's Poetry and Prose*, second edition, ed. Donald H. Reiman and Neil Fraistat (New York: W. W. Norton, 2002).
2   See Kelvin Everest, 'Shelley's Doubles: An Approach to *Julian and Maddalo*', in his edition, *Shelley Revalued: Essays from the Gregynog Conference* (Leicester: Leicester University Press, 1983), 63–88 (60, 62, 66, 67).
3   Shelley to Leigh Hunt, 15 August 1819, *The Letters of Percy Bysshe Shelley*, 2 vols, ed. Frederick L. Jones (Oxford: Oxford University Press, 1964), 2:108.
4   Coleridge's used the Horatian tag as an epigraph for 'Reflections on Having Left a Place of Retirement', see *Poetical Works*, The Collected Works of Samuel Taylor Coleridge, 16, ed. J. C. C. Mays (Princeton, N. J.: Princeton University Press, 2001), 1:260–1.

Maddalo' is 'a *sermo pedestris* way of treating human nature', he told Ollier, to be distinguished from the exalted lyrical 'idealism' of a poem like *Prometheus Unbound*.[5] When Coleridge jokingly mistranslated *sermoni propriora* as '*properer for a Sermon*', however, he casually registered his own far from casual intentions.[6] The same may be said of Shelley's.

The first point that needs to be made about 'Julian and Maddalo', then, is that, in spite of Shelley's distinction between the ideal and the pedestrian, the comparative informality of the poem masks an extreme earnestness, a Coleridgean determination to sermonise. Like his persona, Julian, Shelley is 'rather serious' (Preface). The second point that needs to be made is that, at the head of the congregation that Shelley envisaged, sat Byron—it is to Byron that the poem as sermon is primarily addressed.[7]

The significance of Shelley's subtitling the poem 'A Conversation' does not end with its staged dialogue and familiar style, however. Every poem may be said to participate in a number of conversations at the same time. It is in conversation with its readers, for example, though this may be the least of its concerns. Indeed, Shelley suggests as much in his 'Defence of Poetry' when, comparing the poet with a nightingale that sits in the darkness and sings 'to cheer its own solitude',[8] he alludes to what is perhaps the most important conversation of every poem, which is the conversation of the poet with him- or herself. By figuring himself as Julian, for example, Shelley is able critically to interrogate his own political and philosophical position, isolating and exaggerating its inconsistencies and hypocrisies. 'Throughout Shelley's poetry', writes Jeremy Davies, 'the problem with truly passionate idealists is that the alienness of the material world strikes them with shocking and

---

5 *The Letters of Percy Bysshe Shelley*, ed. Jones, 2:196.
6 *Collected Letters of Samuel Taylor Coleridge*, 6 vols, ed. E. L. Griggs (Oxford: Oxford University Press, 1956-71), 2:864.
7 The MS reference to Julian as Sterne's eccentric clergyman Yorick may therefore be one of the more playful self-ironies of the poem. See Timothy Clark, *Embodying Revolution: The Figure of the Poet in Shelley* (Oxford: Oxford University Press, 1989), 197 and thereabouts, for a 'rather serious' reading.
8 Percy Bysshe Shelley, 'A Defence of Poetry', in *Shelley's Poetry and Prose*, ed. Reiman and Fraistat, 509-35 (516).

8 Amelioration and Madness in Percy Bysshe Shelley's 'Julian and Maddalo'

disabling force; Julian is one of Shelley's lessons in the dangers of perfectibilism by which he was always tempted.[9] As a conversation with himself, 'Julian and Maddalo' is arguably the most probing and least forgiving of Shelley's self-anatomisations.

The poet also converses with the dead—a crucial conversation that features in the classical epic and its derivatives as a journey into Hades to interrogate the shades of influential precursors to whose powers and insight the poet desires belated access. 'Julian and Maddalo', for example, is a poem deep in conversation with Plato; with Virgil, especially the Virgil of the *Eclogues*; with Shakespeare, especially the Shakespeare of *The Tempest*; with Dante, especially the Dante of the *Inferno*; and with Milton, especially the Milton of *Paradise Lost*. In keeping with Dante and Milton, the descent from idealism in 'Julian and Maddalo' is less a descent to earth (*pedestris*), than a descent into Hell, and the poem's Maniac might justly cry, with Marlowe's Mephistopheles, 'Why this is hell, nor am I out of it'.[10]

There is another conversation central to the poem, however, a conversation that revisionary theorists of literary influence like Harold Bloom ignore to their cost. This is the conversation with what Coleridge in his *Biographia Literaria* calls 'the productions of contemporary genius'.[11] As I suggested in the first chapter, Shelley's sense of his contemporaries was acute: 'It is impossible to read the compositions of the most celebrated writers of the present day without being startled by the electric life which burns within their words'.[12] The most celebrated writer of Shelley's day and the poet with whom he had most personal contact was, of course, Lord Byron. 'Julian and Maddalo' represents Shelley's most direct contribution to an intense conversation with Byron, and what was at issue was nothing less than Shelley's

---

9 Jeremy Davies, 'The Shelleys and the Art of Suffering', *Journal for Eighteenth-Century Studies*, 34:2 (2011), 267–80 (274).
10 Act I, sc. 3, l. 74 (B-text), Christopher Marlowe, *Doctor Faustus and Other Plays*, World's Classics, ed. David Bevington and Eric Rasmussen (Oxford: Oxford University Press, 1995).
11 *Biographia Literaria*, The Collected Works of Samuel Taylor Coleridge, 7, ed. James Engell and W. Jackson Bate, 2 vols (Princeton, N. J.: Princeton University Press, 1983), 1:12.
12 Shelley, 'A Defence of Poetry', 535.

preoccupation or obsession with the possibility of the amelioration of society and the role poetry might play in achieving it.

To be clear, the conversation I am referring to here is the one between Shelley and Byron, *not* the one between Julian and Maddalo. It is important for us to maintain this crucial distinction. We know from everything Shelley said about the poem that Julian was modelled on Shelley, and Maddalo on Byron, but in spite of Shelley's endeavour to represent in the poem his and Byron's at times radically different attitudes—sometimes divergent, sometimes directly opposed—the two conversations should not be confused. On the one hand, we have the conversation *inside* the poem itself, in which Julian and Maddalo express ideas characteristic of Shelley and Byron respectively. On the other, we have the whole poem, which both contextualises and ironises this fictional dialogue, at the same time contributing to a conversation Shelley is having with Byron *outside* the poem. What I want to offer in the rest of this chapter, then, are thoughts on two quite distinct debates: first, on what Shelley is saying *with* Byron (and with himself and his own dream of human potentiality) *in* the poem 'Julian and Maddalo', and, second, on what Shelley is saying *to* Byron (and to himself) *with* the poem 'Julian and Maddalo'. The first concerns the poem, the second the poets themselves and the metapoem.

Of course, what Shelley is saying to Byron obviously depends heavily on the way in which he chooses to represent himself in the character of Julian and to represent Byron in the character of Maddalo. 'Maddalo is not quite Byron', writes Michael O'Neill, 'but his portraiture reveals, on Shelley's part, a keen awareness of how Byron was about to fictionalise himself in the self-revelations of *Don Juan*'.[13] However, only a distinction of the kind I am making can cope with what Vincent Newey calls 'Shelley's complex personal presence within and behind the poem'. The failure to maintain this distinction, on the other hand, results in the sort of category error to which discussions of Romantic poems, with their disarmingly personal voices, are particularly prone—as we saw with 'Lines written a few miles above Tintern Abbey', for example, and will see again in the more obviously dramatic 'Ode

---

13 Michael O'Neill, 'The Fixed and the Fluid: Identity in Byron and Shelley', *The Byron Journal*, 38:2 (2008), 105–16 (109).

8 Amelioration and Madness in Percy Bysshe Shelley's 'Julian and Maddalo'

on a Grecian Urn'. For while the attitudes represented by young Julian in the poem are often 'made to look severely inadequate', as Newey remarks,[14] the poem itself has a good deal more to offer, especially in the way of human imagination and potentiality.

The debate

The philosophical issue as it is taken up inside the poem—the philosophical issue between Julian and Maddalo, that is—concerns the adequacy of what is often referred to as Julian's *meliorism*, though a term like *voluntarism* might be preferable because the enquiry of 'Julian and Maddalo' focuses on the potential of the individual will, rather than on the more abstract issue of whether or not society is capable of improvement.

> 'We are assured
> Much may be conquered, much may be endured
> Of what degrades and crushes us. We know
> That we have power over ourselves to do
> And suffer—what, we know not till we try'
>
> (ll. 182–86)

To this idealism of Julian's (whatever we choose to label it), the poem opposes Maddalo's intransigent realism:

> 'I think you might
> Make such a system refutation tight
> As far as words go.'
>
> (ll. 193–95)

he counters—and, more succinctly and dismissively: 'You talk Utopia' (l. 179).

---

14 Vincent Newey, 'The Shelleyan Psycho-Drama: "Julian and Maddalo"' in *Essays on Shelley*, ed. Miriam Allott (Liverpool: Liverpool University Press, 1982), 71–104 (98, 74).

Utopia means 'no place'. Words, and the images and ideas or theoretical 'systems' they compose, may be seductive in themselves, Maddalo is saying, but they remain empty ciphers—enchanting, perhaps, but ultimately insubstantial and impotent. And in contrast to words as words, and as the building blocks of dreams and ideals, human life is an altogether more sordid and bathetic affair of unrelenting suffering: 'nasty, brutish, and short', as Thomas Hobbes concluded.[15] This suffering, moreover, far from being alleviated by an idealism like that of Julian's, is only exacerbated, as it is by the inevitable hypocrisy that is the impoverished double or shadow of idealism: 'the madmen who have made men mad / By their contagion' (*Childe Harold's Pilgrimage*, Canto 3, st. 43).[16] To Maddalo, Julian's idealism is just another form of cant—a reflex, uncritical, often self-serving conviction held in defiance of its patent inadequacy, not to say mendacity. Maddalo, too, has had his dreams—like Byron's Manfred:

> I have had those earthly visions
> And noble aspirations in my youth;
> To make my own the mind of other men,
> The enlightener of nations.

'But this is past'. 'My thoughts mistook themselves', Manfred protests. Again, earlier in the same dramatic poem:

> In fantasy, imagination, all
> The affluence of my soul—which one day was
> A Croesus in creation—I plung'd deep,
> But, like an ebbing wave, it dash'd me back
> Into the gulf of my unfathomed thought.

Now, Manfred concludes, 'I dwell in my despair'.[17] So, too, does Shelley's Maddalo.

---

15 *Hobbes's Leviathan: Reprinted from the Edition of 1651*, ed. W. G. Pogson Smith (Oxford: Clarendon, 1909), 99 (Part 1, Chapter 13).
16 Lord Byron, *Childe Harold's Pilgrimage*, Canto III, st. 43.
17 See Byron's *Manfred*, Act 3, scene 1, and Act 2, scene 2.

8 Amelioration and Madness in Percy Bysshe Shelley's 'Julian and Maddalo'

Manfred's using 'imagination' interchangeably with 'fantasy' invokes a long-held pre-Kantian conviction of the imagination's essential untrustworthiness, the belief that the visions of the imagination are seductive *belles dames sans merci*, likely to withdraw at any moment leaving their host, like Keats's knight-at-arms, disillusioned, emasculated, and depressed. 'The dreamer retires to his apartment', writes Dr Johnson, 'and abandons himself to his own fancy; new worlds rise up before him, one image is followed by another'; but '[h]e is at last called back to life by nature, or by custom, and enters peevish into society, because he cannot model it to his own will'.[18] Can we reimagine and change life—modelling it to our own will and charging it with wonder and with love—or do such visionary politics only vex life and poison the spirit, until we recognise too late that 'that way madness lies'? This central Romantic dilemma is what is at issue in the conversation between Julian and Maddalo. For Julian, in the words from *Paradise Lost* which Shelley quotes in his 'Defence of Poetry', 'The mind is its own place' (505).[19] To this, Maddalo replies, 'You talk no place'.

In his poem 'Resolution and Independence', Wordsworth had anxiously articulated a pattern he had observed too frequently in the lives of recent poets—

> We poets in our youth begin in gladness,
> But thereof come in the end despondency and madness

—figuring himself at the opening of the poem as one powerless over his own moods:

> as it sometimes chanceth
> As high as we have mounted in delight
> In our dejection do we sink as low.

---

18 Samuel Johnson, *Rambler*, ed. no. 89 (Tuesday 22 January 1751), The Yale Digital Edition of the Works of Samuel Johnson: http://www.yalejohnson.com/frontend/sda_viewer?n=108298 (accessed 21 February 2015).
19 'A Defence of Poetry', 533. Cp. *Paradise Lost*, Book I, ll. 254–55.

'As it sometimes chanceth': such vulnerability to the flux and reflux of emotion is dramatised by Shelley in an extreme form in 'Julian and Maddalo' in the Maniac, 'a classic exercise in the Romantic iconography of the tortured outcast genius', in the words of Jeremy Davies,[20] and the character whom Maddalo chooses to prove his point that the human will is incapable of triumphing over circumstance. The Maniac himself, it turns out, believes he can transcend his own suffering:

> think not though subdued—and I may well
> Say that I am subdued—that the pale Hell
> Within me would infect the untainted beast
> Of sacred nature with its own unrest;
> As some perverted beings think to find
> In scorn or hate a medicine for the mind
> Which scorn or hate hath wounded—O how vain!
> The dagger heals not but may rend again.
> Believe that I am ever still the same
> In creed as in resolve, and what must tame
> My heart, must leave the understanding free
>
> (ll. 350–60)

'Shelley's Maniac refuses even the desire for revenge', writes Stephen Cheeke, 'a refusal central to the notion of self-sufficiency, or alternatively, "pride", of genius'.[21] In the end, however, the Maniac's disarticulated, logically inconsistent ravings support neither of the disputants, and the pathos generated by his suffering brings the debate to a precipitate and apparently unresolved ending:

> we
> Wept without shame in his society.
> I think I never was impressed so much;
> The man who were not, must have lacked a touch

---

20 Davies, 'The Shelleys and the Art of Suffering', 273.
21 Stephen Cheeke, 'Shelley, Byron and the Maniac Poets', *Keats-Shelley Review*, 12:1 (1998), 131–45 (133).

8 Amelioration and Madness in Percy Bysshe Shelley's 'Julian and Maddalo'

Of human nature ... then we lingered not,
Although our argument was quite forgot

(ll. 515-20)

The fabric of the vision

The collapse of Julian and Maddalo's debate serves to remind the reader that the dialectic set up between their two points of view is only fully significant within the larger dialectic between the debate itself, on the one hand, and the action, setting, and suffering depicted in the poem on the other; the dialectic between ideas and their human context. It is important to note, for example, how the setting aspires beyond its rich, descriptive immediacy to enforce, to counter, and to qualify the philosophical positions of the two disputants, operating 'as an aspect of psychological and ontological events', to quote Newey.[22] Shelley's familiarity with the use of setting in the Platonic dialogues is evident—in July 1818, the year prior to the composition of *Julian and Maddalo*, Shelley was engaged in a translation of Plato's *Symposium*—nor will one find a better instance of the 'Heart and Intellect' of the poet '*combined, intimately* combined & *unified*, with the great appearances in Nature', as Coleridge would have them.[23] I will confine my discussion to the opening lines:

> I rode one evening with Count Maddalo
> Upon the bank of land which breaks the flow
> Of Adria towards Venice:—a bare strand
> Of hillocks, heaped from ever-shifting sand,
> Matted with thistles and amphibious weeds,
> Such as from earth's embrace the salt ooze breeds,
> Is this;—an uninhabitable sea-side
> Which the lone fisher, when his nets are dried,
> Abandons; and no other object breaks

---

22 Newey, 'The Shelleyan Psycho-Drama', 96.
23 See *The Letters of Percy Bysshe Shelley*, ed. Jones, 2:20. For the Coleridge quotation, see *The Collected Letters of Samuel Taylor Coleridge*, ed. Griggs, 2:864.

The waste, but one dwarf tree and some few stakes
Broken and unrepaired.

(ll. 1-11)

The first thing to remark is the lack of firm ground on which the argument itself takes place. Beyond this, Shelley's Waste Land, with its 'ever-shifting sand', suggests the precariousness of both life and sanity, a suggestion underwritten by the phenomenon of the Lido as a penetrable break protecting Venice—at once the most complex and elaborate, as well as the most fragile of man's gestures at civilisation—from swamping by the Adriatic.[24] 'The salt ooze' breeding 'amphibious weeds' associates the scene with an archetypal borderland between life and death—a marginal, indeterminate world witnessing a primeval struggle for form under the threat of oceanic reclamation and dissolution. The Lido is alien, indeed inimical to human habitation, a literal, psychological, and metaphysical Waste Land that prefigures and all but pre-empts the argument of the poem. Its metaphorical identification with the Maniac, for example, is explicit:

> his pale fingers twined
> One with the other, and the ooze and wind
> Rushed through an open casement, and did sway
> His hair, and starred it with a brackish spray

(ll. 274-77)

Possessed by 'love-madness', the unnamed Maniac is as archetypal as the borderland that he is and inhabits, and is associated with the infinitely changeable, oceanic Proteus of classical mythology, described by Shelley's contemporary, the classicist John Lemprière, as 'difficult of access': 'when consulted he refused to give answers, by immediately assuming different shapes'.[25]

---

24 Shelley's letter to Mary is more explicit: the Lido '*defends* Venice [sic] from the Adriatic', *The Letters of Percy Bysshe Shelley*, ed. Jones, 2:36 (my italics).
25 John Lemprière, *A Classical Dictionary*, seventh edition (London: T. Cadell & W. Davies, 1809).

8 Amelioration and Madness in Percy Bysshe Shelley's 'Julian and Maddalo'

And just as the lone fisherman abandons the 'uninhabitable' for the known and familiar—for family and friends, presumably—so Julian at the end of the poem will abandon the 'ever-shifting' landscape of the Maniac's mind for *his* connections in London, thus dramatising the central irony (or hypocrisy) of his position: public humanitarianism and displays of feeling combined with self-preoccupation and private inaction. (Both are measured against the quiet benevolence or *noblesse oblige* of the ostensibly cynical Count Maddalo.) At first, Julian is moved by the Maniac's predicament to psychotherapeutic imaginings:

> I imagined that if day by day
> I watched him, and but seldom went away,
> And studied all the beatings of his heart
> With zeal, as men study some stubborn art
> For their own good, and could by patience find
> An entrance to the caverns of his mind,
> I might reclaim him from his dark estate.
>
> (ll. 568–74)

However:

> this was all
> Accomplished not; such dreams of baseless good
> Oft come and go in crowds or solitude
> And leave no trace.
>
> (ll. 577–80)

'Leave not a rack behind', in other words. Shelley's use of the word 'baseless' (compare the 'ever-shifting' Lido) invokes Shakespeare's *The Tempest*, one of the network of allusions which help both to characterise and contextualise the central debate—along with the various settings, the actors and their behaviour, and the Maniac's suffering. Prospero's vision of human insignificance conspires with the description of both the Lido and Venice to suggest the imminent or ultimate dissolution of such vain imaginings as Venetian civilisation. Compare Julian's description:

> from the funereal bark
> I leaned, and saw the City, and could mark
> How from their many isles, in evening's gleam,
> Its temples and its palaces did seem
> Like fabrics of enchantment piled to Heaven
>
> (ll. 88–92)

with Prospero's lyrical nihilism:

> like the baseless fabric of this vision,
> The cloud-capp'd towers, the gorgeous palaces,
> The solemn temples, the great globe itself,
> Yea, all which it inherit, shall dissolve
> And, like the insubstantial pageant faded,
> Leave not a rack behind
>
> (*The Tempest*, 4:1)

But we have yet to exhaust the significance of the opening scene, for it is also the site of the first of a series of ambiguities that appear to undermine Julian's position in the argument. In this inchoate Waste Land, his optimism and aspiration take wing:

> This ride was my delight.—I love all waste
> And solitary places, where we taste
> The pleasure of believing what we see
> Is boundless, as we wish our souls to be:
> And such was this wide ocean, and this shore
> More barren than its billows;—and yet more
> Than all, with a remembered friend I love
> To ride as then I rode;—for the winds drove
> The living spray along the sunny air
> Into our faces; the blue heavens were bare,
> Stripped of their depths by the awakening North;
> And from the wave, sound like delight broke forth
> Harmonizing with solitudes, and sent
> Into our hearts aërial meriment.
>
> (ll. 14–27)

The reader is caught up in the exhilaration of the moment. 'The sheer physical enjoyment of the ride', writes Fiona Stafford, 'the warmth, the spray and the sounding waves are perfectly captured in couplets, whose regular beat matches the horses hooves, with metrical variations to suggest the surges of speed along the beach'.[26] Only alone, however, and only in a deserted or dehumanised landscape, can Julian taste that pleasure of believing both his vision and his soul to be 'boundless' (l. 17). He remains unaware of the irony, in a state of innocent wonder that makes him acutely vulnerable to the 'still, sad music of humanity' that is to come, when the verse slows and they turn 'Homeward, which makes the spirit tame'. (As it happens, it is an irony that can cut both ways. After all, tenuous though its existence may be, the glory and the dream of Venetian civilisation are built on precisely such unlikely foundations. And human creativity, working with unpromising materials, is the moot point.)

Nor is Julian 'solitary'. Maddalo is present, and friendship is something that Julian values 'more / Than all' (ll. 19–20). By focusing on their sport and conversation, conditioned by freedom and the sun, these lines anticipate the poem's later, analogous contraction or retreat from the cosmic to the human and the intimate, from the barren, uninhabited land of philosophical debate into a private world of friendship and domesticity, as well as into the privacy of *individual* suffering.

Throwing up moral questions in despair

Throughout the poem, the richly observed setting constitutes a multivalent chorus commenting on the argument and the action, becoming as telling in its own way as the biographical context of the fictional characters that Shelley fulsomely portrays. The extensive Preface, with its characterisation of the antagonists, is not simply indulgent, nor is it an invitation to gratuitous 'application' (the traditional practice of identifying the originals of fictional characters). Rather it is Shelley's recognition—better still, perhaps, his concession—that ideas and

---

26   Fiona Stafford, *Reading Romanticism* (Malden and Oxford: Wiley-Blackwell, 2012), 4.

attitudes are things that originate with people, and that people, as Michael O'Neill observes of the poem, 'resist simple definition'.[27] Ideas and attitudes, in other words, are as much an expression or manifestation of life and experience, as they are the rarefied constituents of a theory about them. 'A moral imperative, an aesthetic taste, a scientific discovery, a political stratagem', to quote Peter Gay, 'and all the countless other guises that ideas take', are 'soaked in their particular, immediate, as well as in their general cultural surroundings', at the same time as 'they are also responses to inward pressures, being, at least in part, translations of instinctual needs, defensive maneuvers, anxious anticipations'.[28]

The very composition of the poem in this psycho-biographical form would seem to confirm Maddalo's aphorism that individuals 'learn in suffering what they teach in song' (l. 546) and that reason is subjugated to 'the rent heart' (l. 126)—that the best that human reason can attain, in other words, is the elaborate rationalisation of fear, or anguish, or desire. Exactly what it is that the 'song' of the arbitrating Maniac teaches is ambiguous, his discontinuous ranting being oracular in the strict sense. 'He was difficult of access', as Lemprière notes of Proteus. Several of the Maniac's utterances, for example, support *both* Maddalo's *and* Julian's position:[29]

> What power delights to torture us? I know
> That to myself I do not wholly owe
> What now I suffer, though in part I may
>
> (ll. 320–22)

---

27 'The awareness that human beings resist simple definition makes a major contribution both to the poem's overall achievement and to its occasional opacity and elusiveness'—Michael O'Neill, *The Human Mind's Imaginings: Conflict and Achievement in Shelley's Poetry* (Oxford: Oxford University Press, 1989), 54.
28 Peter Gay, *Freud for Historians* (New York and Oxford: Oxford University Press, 1985), xiii.
29 Ronald Tetreault, *The Poetry of Life: Shelley and Literary Form* (Toronto, Buffalo, and London: University of Toronto Press, 1987), 153.

8 Amelioration and Madness in Percy Bysshe Shelley's 'Julian and Maddalo'

The Maniac's contribution to the issue of the psychogenesis and subjectivity of truth, moreover, is even less clear. While explicitly countering Maddalo's conviction that our ideas are rationalisations of our passions and asserting the immunity of his rational principles from emotional or psychopathological contamination, his speech nevertheless remains vitiated by the scorn that he scorns, and the hate that he hates. With speech comprised of incongruous and contradictory fragments of argument and confession, anecdote and hallucination, the Maniac would appear to be what Ronald Tetreault calls a metaphor 'of uncertainty', rendering his contribution to the debate of limited value. As a phenomenon, however—as a representative sufferer rather than as a philosopher—the Maniac proves powerfully persuasive. His personal nightmare supervenes on the debate itself, and Julian and Maddalo join the Wordsworth of *The Prelude* in throwing up moral questions in despair.

The very intensity of the Maniac's 'love-madness' suggests the fickleness of human relationships and what Newey calls 'an impression of human helplessness'.[30] It also suggests the perversity of all human enterprise, anticipating Freud on the self-sabotaging psyche. Such suffering as the Maniac's can never exhaust its occasion, as the epigraph from Virgil's *Eclogues* reminds us:

> The meadows with fresh streams, the bees with thyme,
> The goats with the green leaves of budding Spring,
> Are saturated not—nor Love with tears.

If, then, the argument in the poem can be resolved at all, Maddalo would appear to get the better of it: 'How vain / Are words' (ll. 472–3). To say that the poem enacts Shelley's discovery 'of the relativist, dramatic, and irreconcilable nature of experience' is not to leave the debate undecided between the two antagonists, as Michael O'Neill suggests, but to read the poem as endorsing Maddalo's position. The 'indeterminacy and frustration' that O'Neill identifies might be a summary version of Maddalo's 'philosophy' of life.[31] Professing

---

30 Newey, 'The Shelleyan Psycho-Drama', 76.

equanimity on the outcome of the debate often unwittingly supports those commentators for whom 'all the evidence' is 'against Julian', who see the poem as an attack 'on the whole idealistic state of mind'.[32] Far from triumphing over experience, the Maniac's impulsive outbursts of hope succeed only in exacerbating his predicament. The 'transcendent worth' that Julian later discovers in Maddalo's daughter—'Like one of Shakespeare's women' (l. 592)—offers none of the consolation that some critics have inferred. In the tragedies, such transcendent worth seems a qualification only for disaster; the fates of Ophelia, Cordelia, and Desdemona, for example, hardly support an argument for the individual's power over circumstance!

And how, other than pessimistically, are we to read the closing lines, as Julian and Maddalo's daughter discuss the subsequent tragic history of the Maniac and his lover?

'.... if thine agèd eyes disdain to wet
Those wrinkled cheeks with youth's remembered tears,
Ask me no more, but let the silent years
Be closed and cered over their memory,
As yon mute marble where their corpses lie.'
I urged and questioned still; she told me how
All happened—but the cold world shall not know.
(ll. 611–17)

Julian's determination that 'the cold world' will not profit from the pathetic details of the Maniac's tragedy moves him finally to withhold evidence. In dismissing the world as 'cold', in other words, Julian ends on a note of distrust in 'the text of every heart' that he mentions in the Preface, rather than of optimism, despairing of 'the immense improvements' that—again, according to the Preface—he once had envisioned.

---

31 O'Neill, *The Human Mind's Imaginings*, 70, 65.
32 See Timothy Clark, *Embodying Revolution: The Figure of the Poet in Shelley* (Oxford: Oxford University Press, 1989), 177, and Christine Gallant, *Shelley's Ambivalence* (London: Macmillan, 1989), 64.

8 Amelioration and Madness in Percy Bysshe Shelley's 'Julian and Maddalo'

We know not till we try

Against this pessimistic, pro-Maddalo reading of life, we can only protest, firstly, that Julian's capitulation is excessive, like so many of his actions and arguments. When he retires from the Maniac's life, disenchanted and depressed, we are reminded of the 'melancholy' of 'the wise' that Byron mentions in his poem 'The Dream': a 'telescope of truth'

> Which strips the distance of its phantasies
> And brings life near to utter nakedness,
> Making the cold reality too real!
> ('The Dream', sect. 7)

Julian's new-found wisdom, like the equivocal wisdom of Keats's unaccommodating philosopher Apollonius in *Lamia*, ends only by begging the question. It could also be argued, secondly, that the friendship and compassion we do glimpse in the poem testify to a sympathetic imagination and the possibilities of love. Certainly, the suffering of the Maniac witnessed by the two friends cries out for the willed philosophical meliorism upon which the poem appears to foreclose.

'Julian and Maddalo' adopts a similar strategy to that of *Prometheus Unbound* in positing an arbiter, prophet, and scapegoat—the Maniac being, in the Romantic sense, an ironic version of Prometheus—only to have the final resolution of the dilemma of the poem devolve upon the individual: 'Each to itself must be the oracle' (*Prometheus Unbound*, Act 2.4.123). Resolution here would thus function in the sense both of solving and of resolve, which combine to suggest a genuinely creative interpretation of event and utterance. After all, to quote Plotinus, 'he is no great man who thinks it a great thing that sticks and stones should fall, and that men, who must die, should die.'[33] On the contrary, 'those who try', argues Julian,

---

33 As quoted in Thomas McFarland, *Romanticism and the Forms of Ruin* (Princeton, N. J.: Princeton University Press, 1981), 5.

> may find
> How strong the chains are which our spirit bind;
> Brittle perchance as straw. ... We are assured
> Much may be conquered, much may be endured
> Of what degrades and crushes us. We know
> That we have power over ourselves to do
> And suffer—what, we know not till we try
> But something nobler than to live and die
>
> (ll. 180–87)

Admittedly, it is at this crucial point in the dialogue that Maddalo dismisses Julian's idealist 'system' as a purely verbal construction. But Julian's meliorism here is not a system, it is an exhortation, with minimal theoretical pretensions and a great deal of emotional investment. Even in the more formal rendition of the Preface, Julian's meliorism looks only to what '*may* yet be' achieved. His disposition is not towards dogmatism, but towards 'speculating how good may be made superior'. Ironically, it is Maddalo who, of the two, is 'hot for certainties' (in George Meredith's phrase[34])—in this case, for certain impotence, certain frustration. It is Maddalo who expresses himself dogmatically in his formal analogues, in his aphorisms or 'saws' (l. 162), and if Shelley's idealism is a vain 'system', as Count Maddalo says, 'Byron's pessimism is a kind of "system" too', as Stephen Cheeke points out: 'vain, programmatic, formulaic, and most importantly .... containing its own contradictions'.[35] Julian's exemplar uses the child, focusing only upon *potential*. As he says, 'we know not till we try'.

On the issue of hope, moreover, Shelley's contemporaries may have recognised in Maddalo's and Julian's compassionate treatment of the Maniac a sign of recent humanitarian progress—confirmation of the 'improvements of which, by the extinction of certain moral superstitions', according to the Preface, 'human society' is indeed 'susceptible'. The treatment of the insane has a melancholy history. Towards the end

---

34 *Modern Love*, sonnet 50, *The Norton Anthology of English Literature*, eighth edition, ed. Stephen Greenblatt and M. H. Abrams, et al (New York: W. W. Norton, 2006), 1442.
35 Cheeke, 'Shelley, Byron and the Maniac Poets', 137.

of the eighteenth century, however, the understanding of mental illness underwent its own revolution, as theories of humours, spiritual possession, rampant blood toxins, and other 'superstitions' passed, or were passing.[36] For our purposes, a more enlightened 'moral therapy' had evolved, with a telling emphasis *'on stimulating the individual's willpower to fight back against the mania or melancholy by drawing out the residual strength of the patient's saner moral self*—an emphasis on putting 'the patient' (in the words of the enlightened practitioner Samuel Tuke) 'as much in the manner of a rational being as the state of his mind will possibly allow'.[37] If there is implicit support here for someone (like Julian) 'passionately attached to those philosophical notions which assert the power of man over his own mind' (Preface), there is also a powerful vindication of 'Julian and Maddalo' as a metapoem.

Shelley on Byron

Such historical awareness is integral to a metapoetic reading of 'Julian and Maddalo', though it is only one of a variety of rhetorical and argumentative strategies that Shelley employs in the poem as a complex but eloquent appeal in his conversation with Byron outside the poem. In the self-critical, even self-abasing, exaggeration of his own shortcomings in Julian, for example, Shelley seeks a licence to proceed with his impersonation of Byron as Count Maddalo, which might otherwise have seemed gratuitous or spiteful.[38] The philosophical pessimism and

---

36   Rupert Christiansen, *Romantic Affinities: Portraits from an Age 1780–1830* (London: Vintage, 1988), 55.
37   Christiansen, *Romantic Affinities*, 54; Samuel Tuke is quoted in Roy Porter, *Mind-Forg'd Manacles: A History of Madness in England from the Restoration to the Regency* (London: Althone, 1987), 224. On changing constructs and therapies in the late eighteenth century, see also Porter's *A Social History of Madness* (London: Penguin, 1987), 1–38, and Michael Donnelly, *Managing the Mind: A Study of Medical Psychology in Early Nineteenth-Century Britain* (London and New York: Tavistock, 1983), 101–105 and Chapter 5.
38   As it was, Byron was disappointed with the 'figure' he cut in the poem—see Medwin's *'Conversations of Lord Byron'*, ed. Ernest J. Lovell, Jr (Princeton, N. J.: Princeton University Press, 1966), 119.

misanthropy that we confront in Maddalo is born of pride and bitter disappointment, a pessimism and misanthropy originating in the tawdry insufficiency and corruption of human life, as well as in Maddalo's conviction that the world is composed of 'dwarfish intellects' incommensurate with 'his own extraordinary mind' (Preface). This is the Byronic hero of *Manfred, Cain, Childe Harold*, and the Turkish Tales: the isolated, lofty, and contemptuous fatalist deriving from Milton's Satan and the Gothic tradition we looked at in the last chapter. Even Shelley's apparent eagerness to complicate this impersonation and establish a paradoxical split between Maddalo's public pessimism and private warmth and generosity is in keeping with the latent sensitivity and *noblesse oblige* of the Byronic hero:

> Yet there was softness too in his regard,
> At times, a heart as not by nature hard,
> But once perceived his spirit seem'd to chide
> Such weakness, as unworthy of its pride.
>
> (*Lara* 1:17)

Pessimism, then, is Maddalo's official philosophy, never more compellingly and persuasively adumbrated than when he uses the madhouse as his emblem of the human condition:

> like that black and dreary bell, the soul
> Hung in a heaven-illumined tower, must toll
> Our thoughts and our desires to meet below
> Round that rent heart and pray—as madmen do
> For what? they know not,—till the night of death
> As sunset that strange vision, severeth
> Our memory from itself, and us from all
> We sought and yet were baffled.
>
> (ll. 123–30)

Again echoing Byron's *Manfred*, Maddalo here conceives personality—in the ancient faculty psychology upon which he relies—as the triumph of the sensitive soul (passion and imagination) over the

8 Amelioration and Madness in Percy Bysshe Shelley's 'Julian and Maddalo'

rational soul (the will and understanding). The candour and altruism of Maddalo mentioned in the Preface, on the other hand, are exemplified, respectively, by his relations with Julian and his sympathetic treatment of the Maniac—sympathetic in the sense of being informed by the understanding that there, but for God or good fortune, go all of us:

> 'he had no claim,
> As the world says'—'None - but the very same
> Which I on all mankind were I as he
> Fallen to such deep reverse ...'
>
> (ll. 262–65)

Indeed, it was Byron's sudden fall into 'such deep reverse' that in part precipitated 'Julian and Maddalo', Shelley's sermonising contribution to their conversation. To appreciate this, we have to go back to Shelley's arrival in Venice in August 1818 to discuss arrangements for Allegra, Byron's daughter by Claire Clairmont. While Shelley was at Naples he wrote at length to Thomas Love Peacock of Byron's Venetian delinquencies. The letter, which has since become infamous, is worth quoting at length:

> I entirely agree with what you say about [the fourth canto] of *Childe Harold*. The spirit in which it is written is, if insane, the most mischievous and wicked insanity that ever was given forth. It is a kind of obstinate and self-willed folly in which he hardens himself. I remonstrated with him in vain on the tone of mind from which such a view of things alone arises. For its real root is very different from its apparent one, and nothing can be less sublime than the true source of these expressions of contempt and desperation. ... L[ord] B[yron] is familiar with the lowest sort of .... women, the people his gondolieri pick up in the streets. He allows fathers and mothers to bargain with him for their daughters. ... He associates with wretches who seem almost to have lost the gait and physiognomy of man, and who do not scruple to avow practices which are not only not named but I believe seldom even conceived in England. He says he disapproves, but he endures. He .... is heartily and deeply discontented with himself,

and contemplating in the distorted mirror of his own thoughts, the nature and the destiny of man, what can he behold but objects of contempt and despair? But that he is a great poet, I think the address to Ocean proves.[39]

Allowances must be made for Shelley's arguably overwrought imagination, but his sense of the horror at the heart of Byron's darkness is genuine. This is the 'craving void' that Byron mentions in a letter to Annabella Milbanke, driving him to 'intemperate but keenly felt pursuits of every description'.[40] In the sexual debauchery he struggles to name and not to name, Shelley had witnessed in Byron a 'thwarted idealism'[41] and a perverse compulsion to destroy himself.

The accuracy of Shelley's account of Byron's behaviour and state of mind is not the issue. What concerns us is 'Julian and Maddalo' as an articulate response to Byron's extreme behaviour and to the new cultural fascination or vogue for the self-punitive melancholy of the Byronic hero. ('Why do you indulge this despondency?', Shelley demanded of Byron after reading his *Manfred*.[42]) Shelley's letter to Peacock takes what would become the psychoanalytic view of compulsive behaviour: 'their fate is for the most part arranged for themselves' (Freud).[43] Indeed, Shelley's objection to the 'kind of obstinate and self-willed folly in which [Byron] hardens himself' would only have reminded Byron of what he already knew—which was that the notion of 'Fate' itself is 'a good excuse for our own will':[44]

---

39 *The Letters of Percy Bysshe Shelley*, 2:57–58.
40 6 September 1813—see *Byron: A Self-Portrait: Letters and Diaries 1798–1824*, ed. Peter Quennell (Oxford and New York: Oxford University Press, 1990), 173.
41 Walter Perrie, 'The Byronic Philosophy' in *Byron: Wrath and Rhyme*, ed. Alan Bold (London: Vision Press, 1983), 142–65 (145). Cp. Leslie A. Marchand on the 'disillusionment' consequent upon Byron's 'premature sexual awakening': 'the melancholy which springs from physical disgust and the failure of the real experience to measure up to the ideal', *Byron: A Portrait* (London: John Murray, 1971), 21.
42 9 July 1817, *The Letters of Percy Bysshe Shelley*, ed. Jones, 1:547.
43 In his essay 'Beyond the Pleasure Principle' (1924), *On Metapsychology: The Theory of Psychoanalysis*, trans. James Strachey, The Pelican Freud Library, 11, ed. Angela Richards (Harmondsworth: Penguin, 1984), 275–338 (292).
44 *Don Juan*, Canto 13, st. 12.

8 Amelioration and Madness in Percy Bysshe Shelley's 'Julian and Maddalo'

> I have sustain'd my share of worldly shocks,
> The fault was mine—nor do I seek to screen
>   My errors with defensive paradox—
> I have been cunning in mine overthrow
> The careful pilot of my proper woe
>   ('[Epistle to Augusta]', ll. 21-24)

If Byron was 'as mad as the winds' as Shelley had originally believed,[45] or 'half-mad' as Byron himself sometimes claimed to be, it was only ever north by north-west and, like Hamlet, he could tell a hawk from a handsaw. It is not against madness but against the flirtation with madness—Shelley's own, no less than Byron's—that the Maniac's psychic agony and paralysis offer a warning. Shelley's indignation at Byron's Venetian profligacy is informed and intensified by a sense of bitter frustration that 'a noble mind is here o'erthrown'—

> O mighty mind, in whose deep stream this age
> Shakes like a reed in the unheeding storm,
> Why doest thou curb not thine own sacred rage?
>   (Shelley, 'To Byron')

—or, as Byron himself complained in the *Epistle to Augusta*, that a noble mind was in the process of throwing itself over. 'His ambition preys upon itself', writes Shelley of Count Maddalo in the Preface: 'a person of the most consummate genius, and capable, if he would direct his energies to such an end, of becoming the redeemer of his degraded country'. It is hardly unreasonable to read in Maddalo's potential redemption of Venice from Austrian oppression a plea to Byron to co-operate in the political and psychological liberation of Britain, and of humanity more generally—to co-operate, that is, in Shelley's own evangelical mission 'to awaken all mankind' and 'to disseminate opinions which he believed conducive to the happiness of

---

45   Shelley to Peacock, 17 July 1816, *The Letters of Percy Bysshe Shelley*, ed. Jones, 1:491.

the human race', as Mary Shelley described it in her note to *Queen Mab*.⁴⁶

Shelley told Mary that when he and Byron had met in August of 1818 Byron's talk had consisted (among other things) 'in histories of his wounded feelings'.⁴⁷ 'Is it not wise to make the best of ill?' he asks through Julian (l. 47). And using passages of the Maniac's deranged monologue as a form of indirect address, Shelley proceeds to articulate his fears for Byron:

> 'Ye few by whom my nature has been weighed
> In friendship, let me not that name degrade
> By placing on your hearts the secret load
> Which crushes mine to dust. ...
> Yet think not though subdued—and I may well
> Say that I am subdued—that the full Hell
> Within me would infect the untainted breast
> Of sacred nature with its own unrest;
> As some perverted beings think to find
> In scorn or hate a medicine for the mind
> Which scorn or hate have wounded—O how vain!
> The dagger heals not but may rend again. ...
> Believe that I am ever still the same
> In creed as in resolve, and what may tame
> My heart, must leave the understanding free
> Or all would sink in this keen agony—
> Nor dream that I would join the vulgar cry,
> Or with my silence sanction tyranny,
> Or seek a moment's shelter from my pain
> In any madness which the world calls gain,
> Ambition or revenge or thoughts as stern
> As those which make me what I am, or turn
> To avarice or misanthropy or lust.
>   (ll. 344–68)

---

46 *The Poetical Works of Percy Bysshe Shelley*, ed. by Mrs. [Mary] Shelley (London: Edward Moxon, 1839), 100.
47 *The Letters of Percy Bysshe Shelley*, ed. Jones, 2:36.

8 Amelioration and Madness in Percy Bysshe Shelley's 'Julian and Maddalo'

The Maniac's resolution is not to succumb to 'avarice or misanthropy or lust' in self-disgust or despair. To adapt Shelley's comments on Byron in the letter to Peacock: however 'heartily and deeply discontented with himself' the Maniac may become, he vows resistance to 'contemplating in the distorted mirror of his own thoughts, the nature and the destiny of man'. For what, then, could he behold 'but objects of contempt and despair'?

Imaginative transformations

Perhaps the most eloquent defence of poetry's revisionary role in social revolution is the quality of the poetry itself, transforming the 'accident of surrounding impressions' into a source of wonder, to quote the 'Defence of Poetry'.[48] And it is here, in his creative exaltation of the natural world, that we can locate Shelley's most oblique, yet most cogent argument in his metapoetic address to Byron (and to the reader).[49] The symbolic and allusive setting that frequently undermines Julian's argumentative position in the debate with Maddalo ironically empowers Shelley's position in the metapoetic debate:

> we stood
> Looking upon the evening and the flood
> Which lay between the city and the shore
> Paved with the image of the sky ... the hoar
> And aery Alps towards the North appeared
> Through mist, an heaven-sustaining bulwark reared
> Between the East and West; and half the sky
> Was roofed with clouds of rich emblazonry
> Dark purple at the zenith, which still grew
> Down the steep west into a wondrous hue
> Brighter than burning gold, even to the rent

---

48 Shelley, 'A Defence of Poetry', 533.
49 Only Vincent Newey has done justice to the rhetorical trope that is the nature and the quality of the poetry itself, see his 'Shelley's Psycho-Drama', 83–84, especially 94.

> Where the swift sun yet paused in his descent
> Among the many folded hills: they were
> Those famous Euganean hills, which bear
> As seen from Lido through the harbour piles
> The likeness of a clump of peaked isles—
> And then—as if the earth and sea had been
> Dissolved into one lake of fire, were seen
> Those mountains towering as from waves of flame
> Around the vaporous sun, from which there came
> The inmost purple spirit of light, and made
> Their very peaks transparent.
>
> (ll. 64–85)

I referred earlier to the successful combination and unification of Shelley's 'Heart and Intellect' with 'the great appearances of Nature', in accordance with an early Coleridgean poetics of the imagination. It is in this sense that (again in Coleridge's words) 'we receive but what we give, / And in our life alone does nature live' ('Dejection: An Ode').

Because for Byron, as Walter Perrie has argued, 'the world of fact seems so intractable to the ideal',[50] many of the assumptions of contemporary Romantic philosophy and poetics—from the apperceptive idealism of Kantian psychology[51] to the idea of language as constitutive as well as referential—he considered just so much cant. Byron's attitude towards the imagination and poetry was, as we saw, one of scepticism and distrust. The sense of 'limitless opportunity' that Byron occasionally and momentarily finds in his fictions is otherwise consistently and trenchantly condemned as a pernicious fantasy. It is precisely because the imagination is able to 'glance from heaven to earth, and earth to heaven' that for Byron it 'hollows out actuality'—to adapt Kierkegaard[52]—and is often allied with insanity.

---

50 To quote Walter Perrie, 'The Byronic Philosophy', 159.
51 For a brief discussion of Kant, see my Epilogue on the Romantic imagination.
52 See Mark Kipperman, *Beyond Enchantment: German Idealism and English Poetry* (Philadelphia: University of Pennsylvania Press, 1986), 81, for a comparison of *Childe Harold* with the philosophy of Kierkegaard.

8 Amelioration and Madness in Percy Bysshe Shelley's 'Julian and Maddalo'

But the poetry with which Shelley idealises his '*sermo pedestris* way of treating human nature' in 'Julian and Maddalo' suggests that what Byron sees as the cant of the creative imagination was not always cant. 'The mind is its own place', argues Shelley in his 'Defence of Poetry', quoting Milton:

> and in itself
> Can make a heaven of hell, a hell of heaven.
> (*Paradise Lost*, Book 1, ll. 254–55)

This is precisely what we witness in 'Julian and Maddalo' and the metapoetic exchange with Byron. Shelley, on the one hand, makes 'a heaven of hell'. His vision of the sunset 'creates anew' a 'common universe'—here, significantly, a universe in which Dante's, Milton's, Childe Harold's, and the mind's hell are all immanent. But the infernal 'lake of fire', the 'vaporous sun' (melancholia), and the echo of Byron's 'whirling gulf of phantasy and flame' (*Childe Harold's Pilgrimage*, Canto 3, st. 7) are all transformed into heaven by a poetic splendour and glory that for Shelley reflect, not the potential wonder of the natural world alone, but also 'the wonder of our being'. Thus are our perceptions feelings, and is our knowledge imagining: we have 'to imagine that which we know'.[53] And the ease with which Julian's tenuous perspective might collapse into its opposite—has collapsed, in the case of the Maniac—rather confirms than contradicts the need for creative vigilance and revision.

Byronic poetry, on the other hand, and the Byron whom Shelley confronted in Venice in August 1818, had made 'a hell of heaven'—a hell out of the 'Paradise of exiles, Italy!' (l. 57). This, according to Shelley, was a tragic waste both for Byron and for humankind, the more especially because, if there was a way out of the Venetian *inferno*, it was, like the way in, 'self-willed'. The controlled imagination could 'make a heaven of hell'—or at least find its meaning or value in the endeavour. The issue of poetry's 'beautiful idealisms of moral excellence' and whether they function to elevate or to embitter our lives is never resolved in 'Julian and Maddalo'. Shelley's scepticism and

---

53 Shelley, 'A Defence of Poetry', 533.

idealism remain embattled, as word and gesture function expressively and sometimes contrarily in the complex contexts created by the poem. 'At its best, though, and Shelley's poetry would be a good example', writes Paul Hamilton:

> Romantic poetry's self-critical dimension is inseparably bound up with the idea of its autonomy. This combination leaves a poetry agonized by the distance from the real world required for its satisfactions to be plausible and by the violations perpetrated when the enjoyment of such untrammelled self-legislation as its own is attempted outside the aesthetic dispensation.[54]

Having expressed his fear of 'despondency and madness', Wordsworth goes on in 'Resolution and Independence' to celebrate human endurance and the human imagination (the poem's vision becomes a solution to the problem the poet confronts). It was, among other things, a metapoem for Coleridge, part of a lifelong conversation between the two poets. 'Julian and Maddalo' is Shelley's comparable metapoem for Byron. It may only aspire to being *sermo pedestris*, but while Shelley's feet were on the ground his thoughts and desires were, as ever, in the 'belfrey tower' (l. 10).

---

54 Paul Hamilton, 'Romanticism and poetic autonomy', in *The Cambridge History of English Romantic Literature*, ed. James Chandler (Cambridge: Cambridge University Press, 2009), 427–50 (445).

9
Mary Shelley's *Frankenstein*: A Critical and Cultural Heritage

> You must excuse a trifling deviation,
> From Mrs. Shelley's marvellous narration
> — from the musical *Frankenstein; or, The Vampire's Victim*
> (1849)

Like Coleridge's Ancient Mariner, who erupts into Mary Shelley's text as occasionally and inevitably as the Monster into Victor Frankenstein's life, *Frankenstein; or, The Modern Prometheus* passes, like night, from land to land with strangely adaptable powers of speech, addressing itself to a critical audience arguably larger and more diverse than that of any other work of literature in English. 'Mary Shelley's *Frankenstein* is famously reinterpretable', writes Marilyn Butler:

> It can be a late version of the Faust myth, or an early version of the modern myth of the mad scientist; the id on the rampage, the proletariat running amok, or what happens when a man tries to have a baby without a woman. Mary Shelley invites speculation, and in the last generation has been rewarded with a great deal of it.[1]

---

1 Marilyn Butler, '*Frankenstein* and Radical Science', in Mary Shelley, *Frankenstein*, Norton Critical Edition, ed. J. Paul Hunter (New York and London:

How far the critical wedding guests have attended to what *Frankenstein* has to say to them, and how far simply and unashamedly bound the novel to their own purposes, is a moot point. Still, the fact that it has been and continues to be read to mean so many different things is what makes the novel especially fascinating and challenging.

I am concerned in this chapter, moreover, only with what we might call the novel's 'critical metamorphoses': the extent and variety of academic critical attention that *Frankenstein* has received. If we were to add to these critical metamorphoses all the adaptations of the novel or its myth in fiction, on radio and the stage, in the cinema, in video games, on the internet, and in retail accessories, then the number of metamorphoses or different versions is quite literally incomprehensible: impossible to get around, to encircle and take in. Mary Shelley's older contemporary, the literary satirist Thomas Mathias, observed that Gothic novels 'propagated their species with unequalled fecundity' and left their 'spawn' in every bookshop, but Mary Shelley's creation has spawned with a Malthusian menace of which Mathias could not even have conceived.[2]

Indeed, *we* cannot conceive of it. Within two or three years of the establishment of the internet, for example, it was quite simply impossible for any one individual to pursue every reference to Frankenstein in his or

---

Norton, 1996), 302-313 (302). A version of this essay appears as the introduction to Butler's edition of Mary Shelley, *Frankenstein; or, The Modern Prometheus: The 1818 Text*, World's Classics (Oxford and New York: Oxford University Press, 1993), ix–lxi. Butler's edition is the one from which I quote throughout this chapter (with page numbers in parentheses after the quotation). Though based on the first, 1818 edition, Butler's edition includes as its appendices Mary Shelley's Introduction to the quite extensively revised Standard Authors edition of her novel that came out in 1831 as well as all the 1831 variants. There is another World's Classics (Oxford University Press) edition of *Frankenstein; or, The Modern Prometheus*, edited by M. K. Joseph in 1969, and this one is based on the longer, 1831 version of the text. The Penguin edition, edited by Maurice Hindle in 1985, opts for the 1831 version, the Everyman, edited by Paddy Lyons in 1992, and the Broadview, edited by D.L. Macdonald and Kathleen Scherf in 1999, for the 1818 (all record variants). For a comparison, see James O'Rourke, 'The 1831 Introduction and Revisions to *Frankenstein*: Mary Shelley Dictates Her Legacy', *Studies in Romanticism*, 38:3 (Fall 1999), 365–85.
2 [Thomas James Mathias], *The Pursuits of Literature* [1794-7], eleventh edition (London: T. Becket, 1801), 422, note [t].

her lifetime and still, today, 'few, if any, electronic resources', according to Andrew Burkett, 'come even close to approximating the scope and scale of projects involving Shelley's *Frankenstein*'.[3] The form these metamorphoses have taken has varied enormously, as has the degree of familiarity with the original story they manifest,[4] but they can all be said to have originated in Mary Shelley's novel of 1818 or its revised edition of 1831.

In literary criticism and literary history, as it happens, this restless interest in the novel has not always been the case. While popularisations and parodies have continued unabated since *Presumption; or, The Fate of Frankenstein* took to the London stage in July 1823,[5] until forty years ago *Frankenstein* drew from literary critics only an occasional, parenthetical reference to its well-meaning ineptitude. *Frankenstein* was cited as 'an interesting example of Romantic myth-making, a work ancillary to such established Promethean masterpieces as Shelley's *Prometheus Unbound* and Byron's *Manfred*', to quote Sandra Gilbert and Susan Gubar, and Mary Shelley herself only acknowledged because of the 'literary/familial relationships' she represented.[6] Gilbert and Gubar may well have had in mind Harold Bloom's influential visionary hierarchy:

---

3 Andrew Burkett, 'Mediating Monstrosity: Media, Information, and Mary Shelley's *Frankenstein*', *Studies in Romanticism*, 51:4 (Winter 2012), 579–605 (580). Burkett cites Stuart Curran's 2009 Romantic Circles Electronic Edition of *Frankenstein* and the 'Multi-User Dimension, Object Oriented' *FrankenMOO* as recent sensational examples.
4 Paul O'Flinn cites a number of examples, ranging from Mrs Gaskell's *Mary Barton* to newspaper articles from the 1970s, all of which indicate 'a level in ideology at which the text itself has ceased to exist but a myth or metaphor torn and twisted from it is being strenuously put to work', in 'Production and Reproduction: The Case of *Frankenstein*', in *Frankenstein: New Casebooks*, ed. Fred Botting (Basingstoke and London: Macmillan, 1995), 21–47 (31).
5 A conspectus of Frankenstein's popular metamorphoses can be found in Donald F. Glut, *The Frankenstein Legend: A Tribute to Mary Shelley and Boris Karloff* (Metuchen N.J.: Scarecrow Press, 1973); Martin Tropp, *Mary Shelley's Monster: The Story of Frankenstein* (Boston: Houghton Mifflin, 1976), 84 ff.; Albert J. Lavelly, 'The Stage and Film Children of *Frankenstein*: A Survey', in *The Endurance of Frankenstein: Essays on Mary Shelley's Novel*, ed. George Levine and U. C. Knoepflmacher (Berkeley, Los Angeles, London: University of California Press, 1979), 243–89.
6 Sandra A. Gilbert and Susan Gubar, *The Madwoman in the Attic: The Woman Writer and the Nineteenth-Century Literary Imagination* (New Haven and London: Yale University Press, 1979), 221–22.

what makes *Frankenstein* an important book, though it is only a strong, flawed novel with frequent clumsiness in its narrative and characterization, is that it contains one of the most vivid versions we have of the Romantic mythology of the self, one that resembles Blake's *Book of Urizen*, Shelley's *Prometheus Unbound* and Byron's *Manfred*, among other works. Because it lacks the sophistication and imaginative complexity of such works, *Frankenstein* affords a unique introduction to the archetypal world of the Romantics.[7]

By saying badly what the canonical male Romantic poets were saying well, *Frankenstein* was thought to function to justify their canonisation and illuminate the otherwise difficult, self-reflexive enterprise of Romanticism. Where Blake and Shelley and Byron wrote of Romanticism from the vexed inside, in other words, Mary Shelley offered what was at best a simplified version from the outside, and at worst 'a passive reflection of some of the wild fantasies which, as it were, hung in the air about her' (Mario Praz).[8] It was an exemplary small-'r' romantic text, in other words, that lacked the imaginative reach and 'complexity' to be fully Romantic, and to realise the implications of its own mythmaking. 'Like almost everything else about her life, *Frankenstein* is an instance of genius observed and admired but not shared', according to Robert Kiely;[9] 'one of those second-rate works written under the influence of more distinguished minds', to quote D. W. Harding.[10]

Thanks largely to some Copernican changes in our critical universe, Mary Shelley's *Frankenstein* now has a reputation commensurate with the looming bulk of its own Monster, having been unofficially canonised by the sheer variety and extent of interpretative activity that

---

7   Harold Bloom, 'Frankenstein; or, The Modern Prometheus', in his *The Ringers in the Tower: Studies in the Romantic Tradition* (Chicago and London: University of Chicago Press, 1971), 119–29 (122).
8   Mario Praz, *The Romantic Agony* [1933], trans. Angus Davidson, second edition (London and New York: Oxford University Press, 1951; 1970), 116.
9   Robert Kiely, *The Romantic Novel in England* (Cambridge, Mass.: Harvard University Press, 1972), 161.
10 D. W. Harding, 'The Character of Literature from Blake to Byron', in *From Blake to Byron*, Pelican Guide to English Literature, Vol. 5, ed. Boris Ford (Harmondsworth: Penguin, 1962), 33–64 (45).

9 Mary Shelley's *Frankenstein*: A Critical and Cultural Heritage

it has inspired over the last thirty or forty years. This chapter offers a critical map of that activity, asking what, in its nature and extent, the sheer variety of different interpretations might have to say about *Frankenstein* itself, as well as about the critical conditions under which Mary Shelley's novel has gone forth and multiplied.

Unnatural and ungodly

I have said that *Frankenstein* has spawned a literally incomprehensible number of different interpretations. For all that, however, and especially among a general public apprised of the myth but innocent of the novel, there remains a remarkable consensus—as Butler herself points out: 'Readers, filmgoers, people who are neither, take the very word Frankenstein to convey an awful warning: don't usurp God's prerogative in the Creation-game, or don't get too clever with technology'.[11] God's prerogative; nature's prerogative; history's prerogative; the prerogative of the conservative, self-correcting principles internal to evolution—the precise providential scheme is less important than its self-licensed priority and the sense of violation offered by experiments like Victor Frankenstein's. The general public's understanding of the Frankenstein myth as a fable of techno-scientific irresponsibility—from the Monster as 'a simulacrum of industrialized reproduction'[12] to nuclear physics and biological cloning[13]—is one of two readings which

---

11 Marilyn Butler, '*Frankenstein* and Radical Science', 302.
12 Jerrold E. Hogle, '*Frankenstein* as Neo-Gothic: From the Ghost of the Counterfeit to the Monster of Abjection', in *Romanticism, History, and the Possibilities of Genre: Re-forming Literature 1789–1837*, ed. Tilottama Rajan and Julia M. Wright (Cambridge: Cambridge University Press, 1998), 177–210 (192).
13 See Theodore Ziolkowski, 'Science, *Frankenstein*, and Myth', *The Sewanee Review*, 89:1 (Winter 1981), 34–56; Maureen Noel McLane, 'Literate Species: Populations, "Humanities", and *Frankenstein*', *English Literary History*, 63:4 (Winter 1996), 959–88; the entry on 'Promise and Peril' at the Frankenstein website compiled by the US National Library of Medicine for its exhibition of October 1997–August 1998, http://www.nlm.nih.gov/; Iwan Rhys Morus, *Frankenstein's Children: Electricity, Exhibition and Experiment in Early Nineteenth-Century London* (Princeton, N. J.: Princeton University Press, 1998); Courtney S. Campbell, 'Biotechnology and the Fear of *Frankenstein*', *Cambridge Quarterly of Healthcare*

scholarly criticism of the novel has been content to share, even to take for granted. 'The Monster', Martin Tropp reminds us, 'has been called the ancestor of "all the shambling horde of modern robots and androids" in science-fiction', while Victor Frankenstein has engendered 'a whole range of demented scientists, from Dr Strangelove to the Saturday morning cartoon madmen whose symptoms include unruly hair, a persistent cackle, and the desire to (dare I say it?) "rule the world!"': 'Mad scientist and monster are figures in a modern myth; they reflect our fears about the future of man in a world of machines'.[14] And in addition to these 'allegories of technoscience', Andrew Burkett has discovered 'an admonition concerning the complexities, if not the discontents, involving the monstrous matrix of our own historical moment's cybernetics and informatics'.[15]

Modern anxieties have driven scholarship back to the past. Since 1980, along with all the other literature of the Romantic period, *Frankenstein* has been resituated and reinterpreted by new and old forms of historicism in a progressively more detailed recreation of the complex and interrelated cultures of the period. This is nowhere more apparent than with the culture of the experimental and theoretical sciences of the eighteenth and early nineteenth centuries. The general scientific background to *Frankenstein* is explored at length in a monograph by Samuel Vasbinder and in Anne Mellor's discussion of the novel as 'A Feminist Critique of Science':

> Mary Shelley based Victor Frankenstein's attempt to create a new species from dead organic matter through the use of chemistry and electricity on the most advanced scientific research of the early nineteenth century. Her vision of the isolated scientist discovering the

---

Ethics, 12 (2003), 342–52; Teresa Heffernan, 'Bovine Anxieties, Virgin Births, and the Secret of Life', *Cultural Critique*, 53 (Winter 2003), 116–33. For background on the second scientific revolution, see Richard Holmes, *The Age of Wonder: The Romantic Generation and the Discovery of the Beauty and Terror of Science* (London: Penguin: 2010).
14 Tropp, *Mary Shelley's Monster*, 2–3, 9.
15 Burkett, 'Mediating Monstrosity: Media, Information, and Mary Shelley's *Frankenstein*', 584.

secret of life is no mere fantasy but a plausible prediction of what science might accomplish.[16]

Moving beyond Mellor's more abstract approach to the history and philosophy of science, however—on the conviction that (to quote Marilyn Butler) 'the academic reading-list needs qualifying or replacing with a form of newspaper and journal-talk which *could* be thought of as current language'[17]—many recent essays have focused more intensively on Mary Shelley's and the novel's relation to the immediate discoveries and controversies of the contemporary scientific world:

> The fluid boundary between death and life—a dominant theme in the bio-medical sciences of this time—was of such importance that Frankenstein imagined that, in time, he might be able to 'renew life where death had apparently devoted the body to corruption'. The belief that the boundary between life and death was reversible was widely held at the time, indeed for most of the eighteenth century there had been sustained interest in suspended animation, techniques for reviving the drowned and the hanged, premature burial—indeed in any aspect of medicine that held out the hope that death could be delayed, avoided, held at bay. Medical writers imagined doctors in a quasi-divine role, shedding new light on nature's processes.[18]

---

16 Samuel Holmes Vasbinder, *Scientific Attitudes in Mary Shelley's Frankenstein* (Ann Abor: UMI Research Press, 1984); Anne Mellor's discussion comprises Chapter 5 of her *Mary Shelley: Her Life, Her Fiction, Her Monsters* (London: Methuen, 1988), 89–114 (107). For *Frankenstein*, electromagnetism, and the science of the Captain Walton plot, see Rudolf Beck, '"The Region of Beauty and Delight": Walton's Polar Fantasies in Mary Shelley's *Frankenstein*', *Keats-Shelley Journal*, 49 (2000), 24–29, and Jessica Richard, '"A Science of My Own Creation": *Frankenstein* and the Improbable Romance of Polar Exploration', *Nineteenth-Century Contexts*, 25:4 (2003), 295–314. Miranda Burgess, in 'Transporting *Frankenstein*: Mary Shelley's Mobile Figures', *European Romantic Review*, 25:3 (2014), 247–65, endeavours to bring the science of the main and the framing plot together.
17 Butler, in the introduction to her World's Classics edition of *Frankenstein*, xvi.
18 Ludmilla Jordonova, 'Melancholy Reflection: Constructing an Identity for Unveilers of Nature', in *Frankenstein, Creation, and Monstrosity*, ed. Stephen Bann (London: Reaktion, 1994), 60–76 (66).

Ludmilla Jordanova, from whom I quote, reads into Victor Frankenstein's aspirations 'the fantasies of (at least some) medical practitioners of the time'—'a new breed of metropolitan medical men'—and their struggle to create 'a *culture* of medical and scientific power' as 'one way of securing power itself'. To highlight the issue of the social pathology of the medical profession and relate it to the critical preoccupation with the 'birth myth' in *Frankenstein* that I will discuss later, Jordanova focuses her discussion on the controversy of 'man midwifery' in the later eighteenth century.[19] Marilyn Butler, on the other hand, traces more narrowly the flux and reflux of 'the vitalist debate' over the years of the novel's intellectual gestation, concentrating on the Shelleys' relationship with one of its more articulate contributors, William Lawrence, and showing how the very language of this often personal and always political debate enters the novel.[20] Since Butler, Richard Sha and Denise Gigante have elaborated even as they adjusted to the early nineteenth-century story of electricity and its relation to life.[21]

The closer scholarship brings us to Regency Britain, especially to the hybrid 'science' of medical practice and its day-to-day, often ad hoc procedures, the more apparent it becomes that any line drawn between the Gothic on the one hand, and the theory and practice of the medical sciences in the age of Burke and Hare on the other, must remain tentative. The title of Tim Marshall's study says it all: *Murdering to Dissect: Grave-Robbing, Frankenstein, and the Anatomy Literature*.[22] The closer we approach such historical phenomena as the 1832 Anatomy Act or the attempts by Giovanni Aldini to resuscitate the corpses of the condemned using an electrical charge, the more history (both as the past itself, and as a narrative of the past) becomes a Gothic genre. And the Gothicisation of history—in this case the teaching and practice

---

19 Jordonova, 'Melancholy Reflection', 67, 73ff.
20 '*Frankenstein* and Radical Science', in *Frankenstein*, Norton Critical Edition, 302-13 *passim*.
21 Richard Sha, 'Volta's Battery, Animal Electricity, and *Frankenstein*', *European Romantic Review*, 23:1 (2012), 21-41, and Denise Gigante, *Life: Organic Form and Romanticism* (New Haven, Conn.: Yale University Press, 2009), 161-65, 190-94.
22 Tim Marshall, *Murdering to Dissect: Grave-Robbing, Frankenstein, and the Anatomy Literature* (Manchester and New York: Manchester University Press, 1995).

of anatomy and surgery—serves simultaneously to familiarise episodes like the following in *Frankenstein*:

> Now I was led to examine the cause and progress of this decay, and forced to spend days and nights in vaults and charnel houses. My attention was fixed upon every object the most insupportable to the delicacy of the human feelings. I saw how the fine form of man was degraded and wasted; I beheld the corruption of death succeed to the blooming cheek of life; I saw how the worm inherited the wonders of the eye and brain. I paused, examining and analysing all the minutiæ of causation, as exemplified in the change from life to death, and death to life, until from the midst of this darkness a sudden light broke in upon me. (34)

So it is with the many other historicist studies that similarly move to contextualise and demystify the text by bringing it back into a more familiar, less sensational relation to the social and political quotidian. The point they make and remake is the point that Mary Shelley herself stressed in her 1831 introduction, that invention 'does not consist in creating out of void': 'the materials must, in the first place, be afforded'.[23] Of the revolutions effected in our understanding of *Frankenstein* over the last thirty years, this move to refigure and to some extent normalise the story within the rich context of Romantic cultural and scientific history may well prove the most lasting.

Though at a cost, it seems to me. Victor Frankenstein may have shared his arrogance and research with a number of Mary Shelley's contemporaries. Just as the 'projectors' in Swift's seemingly fantastic Academy of Lagado were only carrying out experiments that had been performed by members of the Royal Society, so Percy Shelley insisted of *Frankenstein* that 'The event on which this fiction is founded has been supposed, by Dr. Darwin, and some of the physiological writers of Germany, as not of impossible occurrence'.[24] But Mary Shelley's natural

---

23 Mary Shelley, 'Author's Introduction to the Standard Novels Edition (1831)', in *Frankenstein*, ed. Butler, 192–97 (195).
24 Referring to Erasmus Darwin, see Mary Shelley, *Frankenstein*, ed. D. L. Macdonald and Kathleen Scherf (Peterborough: Broadview, 1999), 47.

philosopher and his Creature, like Swift's Laputans, step out of another imaginative realm altogether, and this in spite of all the authentic 'wild boys' and 'savages' that roamed the pages of Enlightenment speculation on psychology and education. Jordanova protests that she is 'not claiming for *Frankenstein* some kind of "documentary" status it does not possess', but in doing so betrays the danger of an historical reconstruction so thoroughgoing that the text disappears into the material conditions that produced it, or the reconstruction itself becomes nothing more than a theoretically sophisticated search for sources and analogues. It is one thing to attend to *Frankenstein*'s running argument with contemporary practices and another to allow it 'to speak to the mysterious fears of our nature, and awaken thrilling horror', as Mary Shelley certainly hoped it would.[25]

Political fable

The other interpretation scholarly critics have been content to share with the general public is of *Frankenstein* as a political fable, a reading that became idiomatic soon after publication and one that dominated nineteenth-century usage.[26] 'Like her father', William Godwin, writes biographer William St Clair, Mary Shelley 'provided a metaphor for the upheavals of the age. The phrase "to create a Frankenstein monster" was to become a nineteenth-century political cliché'.[27] In this, the Monster is seen either as a composite symbol of the lower or labouring classes or, more often, as symbolising an historically specific, especially unruly section of the lower classes turning threateningly on their social superiors. The poet Shelley explained and exonerated revolutionary

---

25 Mary Shelley, 'Author's Introduction to the Standard Novels Edition (1831)', 195.
26 See, for example, Lee Sterrenberg, 'Mary Shelley's Monster: Politics and Psyche in *Frankenstein*', in *The Endurance of Frankenstein*, ed. Levine and Knoepflmacher, 143–71 (166 ff.) and Chris Baldick, *In Frankenstein's Shadow: Myth, Monstrosity, and Nineteenth-Century Writing* (Oxford: Clarendon, 1987), passim.
27 William St Clair, *The Godwins and the Shelleys: The Biography of a Family* (London: Faber & Faber, 1989), 437.

psychology while revealing the allegorical key to this family of readings in a review of *Frankenstein* that remained unpublished in his lifetime:

> nor are the crimes and malevolence of the single Being, though indeed withering and tremendous, the offspring of any unaccountable propensity to evil, but flow irresistibly from certain causes fully adequate to their production. They are the children, as it were, of Necessity and Human Nature. In this the direct moral of the book consists, and it is perhaps the most important and of the most universal application of any moral that can be enforced by example—Treat a person ill, and he will become wicked. Requite affection with scorn; let one being be selected, for whatever cause, as the refuse of his kind—divide him, a social being, from society, and you impose upon him the irresistible obligations—malevolence and selfishness.[28]

For Shelley's and subsequent radical readings, monstrous intimidation follows necessarily from monstrous and dehumanising neglect. 'Oh, Frankenstein', protests the Monster to his maker, 'be not equitable to every other, and trample upon me alone, to whom thy justice, and even thy clemency and affection, is most due. Remember, that I am your creature: I ought to be thy Adam, but I am rather the fallen angel, whom thou drivest from joy for no misdeed' (77-78).

In the bulk of historically specific political readings, *Frankenstein* 'is traversed with the images and effects of the French Revolution'.[29] Lee Sterrenberg, for example, cites intriguing detail like Mary Shelley's choice of Ingolstadt for Victor's research, a place that had been identified in the Abbé Barruel's *Memoirs Illustrating the History of Jacobinism* (1798) and by John Robison in his *Proofs of a Conspiracy* (1797) as the home of a secret society called *Illuminati* and the intellectual nursery of the French Revolution.[30] Chris Baldick, on the other hand, traces

---

28 Percy Bysshe Shelley, 'On *Frankenstein*', in Mary Shelley, *Frankenstein*, Norton Critical Edition, ed. J. Paul Hunter (New York and London: Norton, 1996), 185–86.
29 Fred Botting, '*Frankenstein* and the Language of Monstrosity', *Reviewing Romanticism*, ed. Philip W. Martin and Robin Jarvis (New York: St Martin's Press, 1992), 51.
30 Sterrenberg, 'Mary Shelley's Monster', 156.

the accusation of monstrosity back and forth between anti-Jacobin and Jacobin throughout the revolution controversy of the 1790s. *Frankenstein* is seen to participate in the battle for rhetorical supremacy instigated by 'the monster image' of filial ingratitude 'organizing, understanding, and at the same time preserving the chaotic and confused nature of the revolutionary events' in Edmund Burke's account in his *Reflections on the Revolution in France* (1790).[31] Finally, Marie Roberts discovers an allegorical specificity, not in the historical origins of the novel, but in the political theory it proposes: 'The dialectic between Victor and the monster may be understood in terms of Marx's theory of alienation, part of which concerns mankind's alienation from the product of its labour, seen in the estrangement of the monster from his maker. The creature has the characteristics of both worker and product, having been negated and alienated by capitalist society'.[32]

Whether *Frankenstein* is interpreted as a Rousseauistic myth of innocence corrupted by society or—anachronistically, as in Roberts's case—as a political economic myth of industrial capitalist expansion, socio-political readings are often seamlessly combined with readings of the novel as an allegory of the dangers of techno-scientific production out of control. The historical paradigms here were the machine-breaking Luddite uprisings in Nottinghamshire and the North, 'and the Pentridge uprising of 1817', revolts that according to Paul O'Flinn pressed directly on the Shelley-Byron circle and are figured in the clash between Frankenstein and his Monster. 'The strength in the text', for O'Flinn, is its sense of 'the impact of technological developments on people's lives and the possibility of working-class revolution'.[33] This may be among the things Ann Mellor has in mind when she says that Mary Shelley 'initiated a new literary genre, what we now call science fiction'.[34] The same fear of industrialisation out of control informs the typical science-fiction dystopia of our own century: a sinister scientific technocracy whose success is built upon the marginalisation and attempted dehumanisation

---

31   Baldick, *In Frankenstein's Shadow*, 10–29.
32   Marie Roberts, 'Mary Shelley: Immortality, Gender and the Rosy Cross', in *Reviewing Romanticism*, ed. Martin and Jarvis, 60–68 (62).
33   O'Flinn, 'Production and Reproduction', 24.
34   Mellor, *Mary Shelley: Her Life, Her Fiction, Her Monsters*, 89.

of the mass of the people—in Aldous Huxley's *Brave New World* or George Orwell's *1984*, for example, through to the more recent cyberspace equivalents of Philip K. Dick and William Gibson.

Like readings that exhume the prominent or front-page scientists and medical practitioners of the time, political readings come most commonly from the historicists or historical reconstructionists. In its determination to restore the text to the culture out of which it emerged, historicism resists any tendency to read the text as a universal myth, a tendency it identifies as (irresponsibly) Romantic. Two difficulties with historico-political readings of *Frankenstein* are worth mentioning before we leave them, however—two, besides the one I mentioned earlier of substituting for the text itself the material conditions of its production. The first is one of evidence—not a lack of evidence, but a surfeit of evidence. Moves to read the text back into its specific context can always find ample objects and occasions, given that in *any* period there is more going on than we can ever assimilate and organise retrospectively. In the early nineteenth century this was, if anything, only more urgently and self-consciously the case. The fact that the Shelleys and the Godwins were so actively and argumentatively engaged in Romantic political and print culture makes very little, if anything, that was said and done during the period irrelevant to a genetics of *Frankenstein*. Not only is criticism obliged to offer evidence, then, but it is obliged to offer it in the face of a wealth of potentially relevant material that it has more or less consciously excluded from consideration. But then any act of interpretation is as vulnerable for what it fails to consider as it is for what it chooses as relevant.

There is an interesting moment in Gilbert and Gubar's *The Madwoman in the Attic* in which a parenthetical attempt is made to determine the significance of the choice of 'William' for the name of Victor Frankenstein's murdered brother: his 'name is that of Mary Shelley's father, her half-brother, and her son so that one can hardly decide to which male relative she may have been alluding'.[35] Gilbert and Gubar might have thrown in any number of Mary Shelley's friends, a handful of well-known poets, and a huge percentage of the other males living in a country where 'William' was the most popular Christian

---

35 Gilbert and Gubar, *The Madwoman in the Attic*, 242.

name. While none of this rules out the possibility of an allusion to one or more of the close relatives they mention, it surely serves to discipline the impulse to leap at any echo. Establishing the significance of this kind of choice requires stricter laws of probability than *Frankenstein* is used to evoking from its critics.

The second difficulty with historical readings has to do with ideology—the ideology of the author or the novel, that is, for the critic's is less often in doubt. Where, exactly, does *Frankenstein* stand on the issue of scientific experimentation, having raised it? What is its attitude to developments in the medical profession? What is its position on the justice and significance of the French Revolution, or of the Luddite revolts?—and so on. Rephrased as an issue of critical method, the reservation I am expressing concerns a tendency in socio-political readings of *Frankenstein* brilliantly and confidently to recreate aspects of contemporary political culture and invoke the contentious issues without asking how far the novel endeavours to replicate or resolve them. Or if it does so, to ask how successful it is. Chris Baldick's utterly convincing location of the language of monstrosity within the discourse of revolution and reaction, for example, skirts the issue of whose side Mary Shelley is on in the debate (he is comparatively uninhibited in his characterisation of Godwin's position). So it is with many other historical studies whose scholarship and critical relevance is never in question. This reluctance to prosecute the enquiry may have something to do with the fact that the novel is more conservative than many of its modern academic critics have been willing to admit. On the other hand, it may exemplify the 'uncertainty concerning the status of Mary Shelley as a self-conscious artist' that Pamela Clemit identifies as 'a feature of *Frankenstein* criticism down to the present day'.[36]

---

36 Pamela Clemit, 'Mary Wollstonecraft Shelley', in *Literature of the Romantic Period: A Bibliographical Guide*, ed. Michael O'Neill (Oxford: Clarendon, 1998), 284–97 (289).

Feminist fable

We will return to the question of the variety and validity of interpretations of *Frankenstein* later. In the meantime, it is worth remarking how easily criticism has been able to politicise the Monster's predicament as feminine, in spite of his nominal masculinity. For Gilbert and Gubar, for example, 'the monster's narrative is a philosophical meditation on what it means to be born without a "soul" or history, as well as an explanation of what it feels like to be a "filthy mass that move[s] and talk[s]", a thing, an other, a creature of the second sex'[37]—that sex which is not one, in Luce Irigaray's terms. It is especially his 'unique knowledge of what it is like to be born free of history' that is said to ally the Monster with those whose pasts have been effaced or repressed. 'Forced right from its inception into a posture of marginality', writes Meena Alexander, 'the creature bit by bit is forced to discover itself as a monster: its being for itself determined by the gaze of others. And so begins one of the most painful of Romantic educations, one that only a woman, a slave or a colonised subject could imagine'.[38] But for Gilbert and Gubar the Monster's representation of the marginalised and vilified is not politically specific enough; *Frankenstein* is a woman's novel and feminism has no room for other oppressions: 'Though it has been disguised, buried, or miniaturized', they argue, 'femaleness—the gender definition of mothers and daughters, orphans and beggars, monsters and false creators—is at the heart of this apparently masculine book'.[39] If this is special pleading, it nevertheless remains true that the critical identification and exposition of the feminine preoccupations of this male-dominated text have given rise to some of the best, most various and intriguing critical readings of *Frankenstein* over the last forty years.

The mother of *Frankenstein*'s feminist or women's readings, Ellen Moers, was the first to suggest that '*Frankenstein* is a birth myth, and one that was lodged in the novelist's imagination, I am convinced, by the fact that she was herself a mother'. The obsession with birth in

---

37 Gilbert and Gubar, *The Madwoman in the Attic*, 235.
38 Cp. Meena Alexander, *Women in Romanticism* (Basingstoke and London: Macmillan, 1989), 129.
39 Gilbert and Gubar, *The Madwoman in the Attic*, 232.

the novel is said to derive in large part from Mary Shelley's traumatic experiences of loss in childbirth—first of losing her mother, Mary Wollstonecraft, who died only eleven days after giving birth to Mary, then of losing children of her own—as well as from her more general knowledge of the potential dangers in pregnancy and giving birth faced by women at the time. But it is especially in Victor Frankenstein's abandonment of the Monster, writes Moers, 'where Mary Shelley's book is most interesting, most powerful, and most feminine':

> in the motif of revulsion against newborn life, and the drama of guilt, dread, and flight surrounding birth and its consequences. Most of the novel, roughly two of its three volumes, can be said to deal with the retribution visited upon monster and creator for deficient infant care. *Frankenstein* seems to be distinctly a *woman*'s mythmaking on the subject of birth precisely because its emphasis is not upon what precedes birth, not upon birth itself, but upon what follows birth: the trauma of afterbirth.[40]

Again, as in the various political readings, which are in truth social versions of the same psychodrama, the most articulate in defence of this interpretation is the Monster himself: '"Hateful day when I received life!", I exclaimed in agony. "Cursed creator! Why did you form a monster so hideous that even you turned from me in disgust?"' (105). An often clear-eyed and always eloquent interpreter speaking out of the narrative centre of the novel, the Monster in fact can be said to have pre-empted most of the allegorical readings of the novel: scientific, political, feminist, postcolonial, poststructuralist, ecological. It is not the Monster's understanding that is in question, but the motivation behind that understanding and its rhetorical deployment.

Few critics follow Moers' precise emphases and most try to avoid the naively direct biographical equations she comes up with on occasion, but the confidence with which she turned to women's issues proved liberating for feminist and non-feminist critical discussions of *Frankenstein* alike. Moers' 'birth myth' and Robert Kiely's reading of

---

40   Ellen Moers, 'Female Gothic', in *The Endurance of Frankenstein*, ed. Levine and Knoepflmacher, 77–87 (79, 81).

9 Mary Shelley's *Frankenstein*: A Critical and Cultural Heritage

Frankenstein as 'a parable in which Victor Frankenstein's *hubris* lies not in his usurping the creative power of God, but in his attempt to usurp the power of women' became the central themes upon which feminist criticism worked its variations,[41] and feminism and psychoanalysis established a tacit conspiracy that has required the recognition of all subsequent criticism. In her reading of 'Frankenstein's Circumvention of the Maternal', Margaret Homans evolves the most searching and sustained example of this popular synthesis:

> the novel is about the collision between androcentric and gynocentric theories of creation, a collision that results in the denigration of maternal child bearing through its circumvention by male creation. The novel presents Mary Shelley's response to the expectation, manifested in such poems as *Alastor* or *Paradise Lost*, that women embody yet not embody male fantasies. At the same time, it expresses a woman's knowledge of the irrefutable independence of the body, both her own and those of the children that she produces, from projective male fantasy.[42]

Also tacitly established, along with the conspiracy of feminism and psychoanalysis, was the licence to use *Frankenstein* to say anything that needed to be said.

Again, as the readings of Moers and Homans make plain, Mary Shelley's own life only adds possibilities to an already suggestive text. The best of these readings, however, have been able to use biographical detail to reach beyond into the text itself. Perhaps the one that has managed to turn 'the elaborate, gothic psycho-drama of her family' most provocatively to its literary critical purposes is that of Gilbert and Gubar, who proceed on the explicit assumption that a biographical reading of a novel by a young woman with Mary Shelley's experience and aspirations is also and necessarily a highly, if often awkwardly,

---

41   Kiely, *The Romantic Novel in England*, 164.
42   Margaret Homans, 'Bearing Demons: Frankenstein's Circumvention of the Maternal', in her *Bearing the Word: Language and Female Experience in Nineteenth-Century Women's Writing* (Chicago and London: Chicago University Press, 1986), 100–19 (113–14).

literary reading. Mary Wollstonecraft Godwin Shelley's mind and novel offer 'a fictionalized rendition of the meaning of *Paradise Lost* to women' in which 'the part of Eve is all the parts':

> the monster's uniquely ahistorical birth, his literary anxieties, and the sense his readings (like Mary's) foster that he must have been parented, if at all, by *books*; not only all these traits but also his shuddering sense of deformity, his nauseating size, his namelessness, and his orphaned, motherless isolation link him with Eve and with Eve's double, Sin.[43]

How far *Frankenstein* can be promoted as a feminist myth—as well as being a myth of miscreation written by a woman, that is—depends not just upon the way in which the novel itself is read, but also upon what 'feminism' is taken to mean. As a powerful, if oblique plea for an archetypal division of labour, for example, one that focuses critically on Victor's 'usurpation of the role of mother' in bringing to birth,[44] the story is a deeply conservative one, arguably reacting against strategic attempts by early feminists, including the author's mother, Mary Wollstonecraft, to play down or circumvent the issue of biological determinism. Most readers, critical or otherwise, have noticed how 'women are conspicuously absent from the main action', and how passive and self-effacing those women that do appear are,[45] though Kate Ellis notes that 'the female role as one of constant, self-sacrificing devotion to others' is ironised in the earlier, 1818 text.[46] It really turns on a reading of Elizabeth and how we are to interpret her devotion to domesticity and to Victor. But 'because it does not speak the language

---

43 Gilbert and Gubar, *The Madwoman in the Attic*, 221 and 230, 222–23.
44 U. C. Knoepflmacher, 'Thoughts on the Aggression of Daughters', in *The Endurance of Frankenstein*, ed. Levine and Knoepflmacher, 88–119 (105).
45 Stephen Behrendt, 'Mary Shelley, *Frankenstein*, and the Woman Writer's Fate', in *Romantic Women Writers: Voices and Countervoices*, ed. Paula R. Feldman and Theresa M. Kelley (Hanover, N.H. and London: University Press of New England, 1995), 69–87 (69).
46 Kate Ellis, 'Monsters in the Garden: Mary Shelley and the Bourgeois Family', in *The Endurance of Frankenstein*, ed. Levine and Knoepflmacher, 123–42 (131–32).

of feminist individualism which we have come to hail as the language of high feminism within English literature', to quote Gayatri Spivak, as a text of 'nascent feminism', *Frankenstein* 'remains cryptic'.[47] So for Gilbert and Gubar, 'the tale of the blind rejection of women by a misogynistic/Miltonic patriarchy' is only a 'covert plot' of the novel, and the closest it ever comes to critique is merely to clarify the entrenched prejudices of the Miltonic myth—thus presumably serving to expose them to the more alert and motivated criticism of later commentators.[48]

So it is with a reading of *Frankenstein* that might reasonably be called the orthodox feminist reading, which sees the novel as calling into question 'the egotism that Mary Shelley associates with the artist's monstrous self-assertion', in Mary Poovey's words:

> As long as domestic relations govern an individual's affections, his or her desire will turn outward as love. But when the individual loses or leaves the regulating influence of relationship with others, imaginative energy always threatens to turn back upon itself, 'mark' all external objects as its own and to degenerate into 'gloomy and narrow reflections upon self'.[49]

This is orthodox in the sense of its picking up one of the oldest motifs of Western literary culture in the overreacher, and orthodox also in the sense that it casts the feminine in an existentially conservative, even timorous role of the kind against which, again, Mary Wollstonecraft argued so eloquently in her *Vindication of the Rights of Woman*. Indeed, insofar as (to quote Christopher Small) 'Frankenstein himself is clearly and to some extent must intentionally have been a portrayal of Shelley' in a novel which is a meditation on miscreants,[50] then for proponents

---

47 Gayatri Chakravorty Spivak, 'Three Women's Texts and a Critique of Imperialism', *Frankenstein: New Casebooks*, ed. Botting, 248.
48 Gilbert and Gubar, *The Madwoman in the Attic*, 243, 221.
49 Mary Poovey, '"My Hideous Progeny": The Lady and the Monster', in her *The Proper Lady and the Woman Writer: Ideology as Style in the Works of Mary Wollstonecraft, Mary Shelley, and Jane Austen* (Chicago and London: Chicago University Press, 1984), 114–42 (123).
50 Christopher Small, *Ariel Like a Harpy: Shelley, Mary and Frankenstein* (London: Victor Gollancz, 1972), 101ff.

of this orthodox reading like Mary Poovey, Ann Mellor, and Margaret Homans,[51] the feminist critique of masculine (or masculinist) aspiration *is* a conservative critique. In Percy Shelley, according to Ann Mellor, Mary Shelley perceived 'an intellectual hubris or belief in the supreme importance of abstractions that led him to be insensitive to the feelings of those who did not share his ideas and his enthusiasms'.[52]

There is no unqualified or uncritical intellectual hubris in the poetry of Percy Bysshe Shelley, as it happens, or in that of any other Romantic poet for that matter, which is only to say that *Frankenstein* might more faithfully be seen as taking its place beside 'Julian and Maddalo' (and 'Alastor' and *The Triumph of Life*) as ironic or anticlimactic quest. If, as Paul Cantor argues, Mary Shelley 'turned the creation myth back upon Romanticism' to reveal 'the dark underside to all the visionary dreams of remaking man that fired the imagination of Romantic myth-makers',[53] she had that in common with other Romantic myth-makers, not least her husband, for whom (as I suggested in the first chapter) 'Romantic literature is also at the same time anti-Romantic literature, distrustful of its own assertions about transcendence and imagination'.

Psychoanalysis

Translated into the language of psychoanalysis, the Romantic egotism that Victor Frankenstein had in common with Percy Shelley becomes primal or 'radical narcissism, a debilitating obsession with the self'.[54] For Joseph Kestner, narcissism was not only the distinguishing feature of the hero's psychpathology, it was a structural principle in the text itself: 'the *mise en abyme*, the story within the story'. Discussing the episode of Elizabeth's murder on her and Victor's wedding night, Kestner concludes that

---

51 Homans, *Bearing the Word*, 107.
52 Mellor, *Mary Shelley: Her Life, Her Fiction, Her Monsters*, 73.
53 Paul A. Cantor, *Creature and Creator: Myth-Making in English Romanticism* (Cambridge: Cambridge University Press, 1984), 109.
54 David Musselwhite, *Partings Welded Together: Politics and Desire in the Nineteenth-Century Novel* (London and New York: Methuen, 1987), 49.

Like Echo in the Greek myth, Elizabeth is destroyed by her Narcissus. The whole truth of this episode is that, fearing sexual contact, Frankenstein wanted the woman dead, desiring only to love himself, latently homosexual. The narcissistic Other (the Creature), by strangling Elizabeth, intervenes to prevent the normal separation of 'ego-libido' from 'object-libido' discussed by Freud in 'On Narcissism'. Instead, Frankenstein's libido is a narcissistic auto-erotism. Just as the face of the Creature had appeared when Frankenstein awoke from his dream about Elizabeth and his mother, so now does 'the face of the monster' grin at him through the inn window.[55]

What is interesting here is that Kestner's highly technical case history should amount substantially to the same reading as Mellor's and Poovey's. Indeed, most psychoanalytic approaches to the novel, and all of those that make Victor's the central and mediating psyche, focus on one or more of what in Freud is a network of motifs and symptoms, partially invoked here by Kestner: narcissism, the mirror, impotence, autoeroticism, (latent) homosexuality, and so on.

The other common issue for psychoanalytic readings is that of the mother—Frankenstein's or Mary Shelley's or the Monster's—the more palpable and pressing in that in all cases the mother is either dead or non-existent. Writing in answer to her question 'Is There a Woman in This Text?', Mary Jacobus rounds up the usual suspects: in exchanging 'a woman for a monster', Victor Frankenstein prefers an imagined over an actual being (Romantic egotism), which is also, as Victor says, 'a being like myself' (primal narcissism), one tellingly created right after—and thus in obvious compensation for—the death of the egoistically rejected mother.[56] So for Margaret Homans, *Frankenstein* 'is simultaneously about the death and obviation of the mother and about a son's quest for a substitute object of desire'.[57] (In his film version of *Mary Shelley's Frankenstein*, Kenneth Branagh has Victor bring Elizabeth back to life

---

55 Joseph Kestner, 'Narcissism as Symptom and Structure: The Case of Mary Shelley's *Frankenstein*', in *Frankenstein: New Casebooks*, ed. Botting, 68-80 (76–77).
56 Mary Jacobus, 'Is There a Woman in This Text?', *New Literary History*, 14 (1982–3), 117–141 (131).
57 Homans, *Bearing the Word*, 100.

and dance with her a dance he had shared with his mother as a child.) In one way or another, writes Peter Brooks, 'the radically absent body of the mother more and more appears to be the "problem" that cannot be solved in the novel'.[58]

Two vital pieces of evidence are invariably cited and discussed in this connection. One is the miniature portrait of the dead Caroline Frankenstein belonging to her son (and Victor's brother) William, which is used by the Monster to implicate Justine Moritz in William's murder; the other is Victor Frankenstein's post-natal nightmare, whose powerfully suggestive imagery demands critical interpretation:

> I was disturbed by the wildest dreams. I thought I saw Elizabeth, in the bloom of health, walking in the streets of Ingolstadt. Delighted and surprised, I embraced her; but as I imprinted the first kiss on her lips, they became livid with the hue of death; her features appeared to change, and I thought that I held the corpse of my dead mother in my arms; a shroud enveloped her form, and I saw the grave-worms crawling in the folds of the flannel. I started from my sleep with horror; a cold dew covered my forehead, my teeth chattered, and every limb became convulsed; when, by the dim and yellow light of the moon, as it forced its way though the window-shutters, I beheld the wretch—the miserable monster whom I had created. He held up the curtain of the bed; and his eyes, if eyes they may be called, were fixed on me. (39–40)

Still on absent mothers, and like many other critics noting the maternal associations of 'nature' into which Victor pries and penetrates, Marc Rubenstein focuses his analysis on Mary Shelley and her endeavours, as a guilt-ridden daughter feeling responsible for the death of her mother, to make restitution in a tale which Rubenstein interprets as a self-punitive acting out of her own destruction at the hands of her own child.[59]

---

58   Peter Brooks, 'What Is a Monster? (According to *Frankenstein*)', *Frankenstein: New Casebooks*, ed. Botting, 81–106 (92).
59   Marc A. Rubenstein, '"My Accursèd Origin": The Search for the Mother in *Frankenstein*', *Studies in Romanticism*, 15 (1976), 165–194 (174–5, 177).

When Mary Shelley is not understood to be in quest of her dead mother, with 'deep fears about an imbalance within herself', she is seen as using the novel to disburden herself of a 'muted hostility', first, 'toward her younger half-brother'—who 'unlike herself possessed a mother and, as a male, had received his father's identity and approbation'—and then toward the better known William Godwin, her father. The virtue of these accounts, like the one by U. C. Knoepflmacher from which I am quoting, is the corrective they offer to readings that concentrate almost exclusively on the absent feminine, when males of various complexions dominate the text and Victor Frankenstein has the distinction of being not only a bad mother, but a bad father as well.[60]

Finally, in the interpretative economy of critical psychoanalysis, fathers and sons, creators and creatures, have an uncanny habit of standing in for each other, as discussion of parenthood or origins turns to the mutual reflexiveness of the various characters in the text. For Joseph Kestner, for example, the three-fold narrative framing highlights the similarities among what he calls 'the three protagonists'—Walton, Frankenstein, the Monster—similarities 'which signal their doubleness and otherness, the one the *Doppelgänger* of the next, including their desire to explore, their failure to love, their loneliness, their avid reading, and their egoism'.[61] How far the origins of the Gothic motif of the shadow or *Doppelgänger* can be said to lie in narcissism, or in psychotic projection, and how far psychoanalytic theory is itself a development of the Gothic is a moot point, especially when it is Mary Shelley who is under analysis. If the presence of the double is 'symptomatic', a good many undiagnosed writers of the late eighteenth and early nineteenth centuries must have shared Mary Shelley's pathology, for as Martin Tropp suggests 'such tales were popular at the time'.[62] Still, 'almost every critic of *Frankenstein* has noted that Victor and his Monster are doubles' (George Levine).[63] Here it is Victor

---

60 Knoepflmacher, 'Thoughts on the Aggression of Daughters', 105, 103 and passim.
61 Kestner, 'Narcissism as Symptom and Structure', 72.
62 Tropp, *Mary Shelley's Monster*, 37. 'Double Vision', the third chapter of Tropp's *Mary Shelley's Monster* (34-51), offers a brief compendium of psychoanalytic thinking on the issue.

rather than the Monster who pre-empts: 'I considered the being whom I had cast among mankind, and endowed with the will and power to effect purposes of horror, such as the deed which he had now done, nearly in the light of my own vampire, my own spirit let loose from the grave, and forced to destroy all that was dear to me' (57). Paul Cantor explicates: "The monster becomes Frankenstein's *Doppelgänger*, his double or shadow, acting out the deepest darkest urges of his soul, his aggressive impulses and working to murder one by one everybody close to his creator".[64]

Post-structuralism

The 'doubleness and otherness' that Kestner sees as characteristic of relations between the three main characters, Jerrold E. Hogle concentrates in the Monster himself (itself?), whose very hybridity as a composite of pieces sutured together in a 'workshop of filthy creation' (36) is said to make him representative of an 'otherness' at once more capacious and more disturbing. Deferring to a principle of *abjection* derived from the psychoanalytic theory of Julia Kristeva—the self-defensive casting out of a 'dimly recalled and feared multiplicity'—Hogle reads the multiplicitous Monster as a displacement or scapegoat embodying the threat of an archetypal 'otherness':

> The creature is a 'monster' in that it/he embodies and distances all that a society refuses to name—all the betwixt-and-between, even ambisexual, cross-class, and cross-cultural conditions of life that Western culture 'abjects', as Kristeva would put it—... It/he is 'the *absolutely* Other' ... pointing immediately, as we have just seen, to intermixed and repressed states of being, the divisibility of the body, 'thrown-down' social groups, class struggles, gender-confusions, birth-moments, and death-drives ... as well as to a cacophony of ideological and intertextual differences. All the while, though, he/it both

---

63   George Levine, 'The Ambiguous Heritage of *Frankenstein*', in *The Endurance of Frankenstein*, ed. Levine and Knoepflmacher, 3–30 (14).
64   Cantor, *Creature and Creator: Myth-Making in English Romanticism*, 117.

re-presents each of these alterities and keeps them at a great remove by being quasi-human yet strictly artificial.[65]

'The *absolutely* Other': Frankenstein's Monster has never been busier than he is here, in Hogle's *psychomachia* or battle of the soul. Rarely, moreover, has the Monster borne so ponderous a symbolic burden, for his condition of being 'all of the betwixt-and-between' conditions of life is said (again, after Julia Kristeva) to indicate 'the most primordial form of being half-"inside" and half-"outside"':

> the 'heterogeneous flux' of being partly held inwards and partly pushed outwards by the mother's body at the moment of birth ... *and* the state, at the same time, of emerging *out* of death (pre-natal non-existence) and starting to live *towards* death (the end point of all the 'want' that begins at birth ...). This liminal condition of multiple contradictions, where each supposedly distinct state slides over into its 'other', is the radical heterogeneity.[66]

Like the Monster at its centre, the Frankenstein story can thus be characterised as a 'radical heterogeneity' inclusive enough to contain any and every possible meaning.

From here it is a short step to reading the Monster, not as a mythical figure in itself, but as a *source* of myth: an *Ur*-myth, as it were. Thus the claims that the Monster represents certain aspects of the human psyche, for example, or certain genders or races or social classes, or certain abstract ideas, or even (as with Hogle) a complex of 'alterities'—these claims are subordinated to the sheer fact of the Monster's illimitable suggestiveness. What follows from this suggestiveness are readings of *Frankenstein* as an allegory of making meaning or of symbolising: of metaphoricity, mythopoesis, and making things *like*. Monstrously so, it would seem. For *like* the Monster, myth is made and released into culture, to undergo certain formative and deformative metamorphoses according to that culture's instinctual, ethical, and spiritual needs or anxieties. But not only does this Monster of a

---

65 Hogle, '*Frankenstein* as Neo-Gothic', 186–87.
66 Hogle, '*Frankenstein* as Neo-Gothic', 195.

myth mean what it was intended to mean by its author or culture, it is also liable to get out of control and to assume an independent, even potentially destructive life of its own. For Beth Newman, for example, narrative and narrator in *Frankenstein* are 'emphatically separable', indeed psychologically and ethically disruptive of each other: 'once a narrative has been uttered, it exists as a verbal structure with its own integrity, and can, like myth, think itself in the minds of men (and women). Being infinitely repeatable in new contexts, it has achieved autonomy; it now functions as a text, divested of its originating voice'.[67] Like a Grecian urn, or an 'Ode on a Grecian Urn', for that matter—but if this is true of *Frankenstein*, as it might well be of any work of art, is it what *Frankenstein* is about?

By extending the idea of 'autonomy' from the framed tales within *Frankenstein* to the novel as a whole, Newman not only defends the independence of the Frankenstein myth, she also rather neatly underwrites her own determination to proceed with indifference to anything Mary Shelley might have intended, and to trace within the text an autonomous concern 'with general tendencies in the nature of narrative itself'.[68] According to Newman, *Frankenstein* is an essay in and on narrative. We have shifted from *Frankenstein* as a map or drama of the psyche—whether Mary Shelley's or Victor Frankenstein's—to *Frankenstein* as a map of its own origins and constitution as a literary or mythic 'text'. There is a whole genre of critical approaches to *Frankenstein* in which, with competitive ingenuity, numerous critics have addressed themselves directly to what Gilbert and Gubar call 'the anxious pun on the word *author* so deeply embedded in *Frankenstein*'.[69] In what for convenience we can call poststructuralist readings, *Frankenstein* is revealed to be an allegory, not of Faustian 'epistemophilia' or revolutionary monstrosity or male arrogation of the birth privilege or primal narcissism or 'otherness', but of the primal act or scene of writing, or of literary criticism itself. Popular culture may

---

67 Beth Newman, 'Narratives of Seduction and the Seduction of Narrative: The Frame Structure of *Frankenstein*', *Frankenstein: New Casebooks*, ed. Botting, 166-90 (171-72).
68 Newman, 'Narratives of Seduction and the Seduction of Narrative', 168.
69 Gilbert and Gubar, *The Madwoman in the Attic*, 233.

want its mad scientist, but academic culture, for a while at least, wanted its *écriture*.

So for Fred Botting, 'the text, like the monster, solicits and resists attempts to determine a single line of significance', frustrating

> the desires for authority that are represented in and resisted by the text-monster. Identifying the novel's fixed, singular and final meaning by way of historical and biographical archives, [certain] readings return to the unifying figure of the author as they attempt to authorize their own accounts and arrest the monstrously overdetermined play of significance that operates in and between criticism's 'pre-texts'. Thus they repeat Frankenstein's project. But the monster, this time *Frankenstein*, again eludes capture even as it sustains the pursuit.[70]

The monstrous in *Frankenstein* is both the source and the explanation of the story's uninterpretability, an uninterpretability that nonetheless draws us 'towards an illusory centre' and invites, rather than discourages, our vain attempts to interpret.[71] This elusiveness, according to Botting, prefigures the fate of meaning in the poststructuralist theory of Jacques Derrida and Jacques Lacan, as the text turns into a Derridean nightmare of destabilising *différance*: 'Difference, though constitutive of opposition, also exceeds it. The instability produced by monstrous difference offers no resting place for meaning and thus undermines the role of the literary critic, whose job it is to reveal authoritative meaning'.[72] *Frankenstein*, in short, in common with all other texts, discourses on its own discursive unmeaning.

In a similar attempt to account for the vain pursuit of meaning inside and outside the text, Peter Brooks also invokes Lacan. 'The Monster', writes Brooks, 'attempts to state the object of his desire':

---

70 Botting, '*Frankenstein* and the Language of Monstrosity', 53–54. Cp. Musselwhite, *Partings Welded Together*, 58–59, 65.
71 Fred Botting, *Making monstrous: Frankenstein, criticism, theory* (Manchester and New York: Manchester University Press, 1991), 4.
72 Botting, '*Frankenstein* and the Language of Monstrosity', 55, 56.

> In constructing his narrative appeal, he has contextualised desire, made it, or shown it to be, the very principle of narrative, in its metonymical forward movement. This movement, in Lacanian terms, corresponds to the slippage of the inaccessible signified—the object of unconscious desire—under the signifier in the signifying chain. ...
> Thus it is that the taint of monsterism, as the product of the unarrestable metonymic movement of desire through the narrative signifying chain, may ultimately come to rest with the reader of the text. ... Perhaps it would be most accurate to say that we are left with a residue of desire *for* meaning, which we alone can realise.⁷³

The cynic might want to argue that to say that the reader-interpreter's attention is driven by a desire to know that can never be completely satisfied is a blinding truism, not only about the act of narrating and reading, but also about human apprehension and consciousness more generally. And Brooks is aware of and slightly embarrassed by this: 'One could no doubt say something similar about any narrative text'. What makes the narrative of *Frankenstein* special for Brooks, however, is that, rather than being simply driven by a narrative whose principles it exposes, *Frankenstein* is *about* 'the very principle of narrative'—as it is for Hogle, Newman, and Botting, except that for Brooks it is narrative 'in its metonymical forward movement', dramatising 'the fact and process of its transmission, as "framed tales" always do'. As an explanation of why *Frankenstein* especially should engender such a proliferation of (necessarily inadequate or incommensurate) critical readings, Brooks is at once self-affirming and curiously fatalistic: 'A monster is that which cannot be placed in any of the taxonomic schemes devised by the human mind to understand and to order nature. It exceeds the very basis of classification, language itself: it is an excess of signification, a strange byproduct or leftover of the process of making meaning'.⁷⁴ Because nothing exceeds like excess, the number and reach of critical readings of *Frankenstein* must be monstrous or disproportionate to anything

---

73 Brooks, 'What Is a Monster?', 91, 96.
74 Brooks, 'What Is a Monster?', 100.

signified by the text. As with Hogle, Botting, and Musselwhite, *Frankenstein* must mean beyond its own meaning.

Not only has the Monster been read poststructurally, in other words, it has also been read as a prototype or prophecy of poststructuralism. Indeed, according to Barbara Claire Freeman, there is a special prescience in the anti-Kantian monstrosity of the text that is figured, metonymically, in the creature's ill-fitting skin, 'comparable to the encasement of the sublime in Kantian theory'. By converting the Kantian sublime into the monstrous, Freeman argues, *Frankenstein* anticipates and encourages the explosion of 'theory' into the complacent world of academic philosophy and literature in the late twentieth century. A 'terrorism' carried out 'by the texts of contemporary French theorists, especially Derrida', rages abroad, a Monster of the academy's own making and likely to overpower the academy itself. *Frankenstein* turns out after all this time to have been a creative prophecy of the triumph of Literary Theory:

> Like Frankenstein's Monster, theory devours whatever it encounters, be it a discourse, text, individual, or institution. The terroristic effect of theory, as of monstrosity, resides in its capacity to incorporate and swallow up another entity without leakage or cessation of appetite. Lately, deconstructive theory in particular has infiltrated and then devoured departments of language and literature, becoming the focus of attention, breaking down institutional divisions and domains. What terrorises those who oppose it—and even those who do not—is its totalising power and the rapidity with which it spreads, as if the university's immune system has no defence against it. ... It is as if the future of the so-called Sciences of Man has been, or is in the process of being, monsterised by theory.[75]

By invoking the popular genre of the campus horror film as a satire on the overreaction in the humanities to the advent of Theory, Freeman good-humouredly endorses theory's deconstructive activities, but the

---

75   Barbara Claire Freeman, '*Frankenstein* with Kant: A Theory of Monstrosity or the Monstrosity of Theory', in *Frankenstein: New Casebooks*, ed. Botting, 191–205 (200–201).

comparison also exposes weaknesses in deconstruction of which she appears unconscious. Freeman, for example, unwittingly parodies the utterly indiscriminate tendency of some theories to discover in any number of historically and generically distinct texts precisely the same preoccupation: their own. And still on institutional narcissism, the mock-horror of the campus Monster not only mocks the overreaction against theory, it also mocks the way the academy insists on projecting its own existential anxieties across a culture that, in truth, remains indifferent to and puzzled by them.

Reading the critical profusion

I have looked briefly at *Frankenstein* as a critique of amoral curiosity in the empirical sciences and as a political allegory, and have managed only a few of the many psychoanalytic and poststructuralist readings that have been lavished on the novel. What I hope to have conveyed, however, in spite of the limitations of my survey, is the 'dizzying profusion of meanings' that *Frankenstein* has unleashed.[76] Indeed, so remarkable is this profusion of meanings that, where the profusion itself does not actually enter into the novel's interpretation (as it does in poststructuralist readings), it is invariably alluded to by the critic before she or he launches into the discovery or recovery of yet another meaning. As a measure of just how extensive and various the critical attention devoted to the 'famously reinterpretable' *Frankenstein* has been, I can turn to the criticism itself in order to summarise my own summary and choose from any one of a huge number of comparable summaries—like Paul Sherwin on interpretations of the Monster:

> If, for the orthodox Freudian, he is a type of the unconscious, for the Jungian he is a shadow, for the Lacanian an *objet à*, for one Romantic a Blakean 'spectre', for another a Blakean 'emanation'; he has also been or can be read as Rousseau's natural man, a Wordsworthian child of nature, the isolated Romantic rebel, the misunderstood revolutionary impulse, Mary Shelley's abandoned baby self, her abandoned

---

76 The phrase is Chris Baldick's, *In Frankenstein's Shadow*, 56.

babe, an aberrant signifier, *différance*, or as a hypostasis of godless presumption, the monstrosity of godless nature, analytical reasoning, or alienating labour. Like the Creature's own mythic version of himself, a freakish hybrid of Adam and Satan.[77]

To which we can add: Eve, a nameless woman, alienated labour, the colonised subject, the id, orgone energy, Frankenstein's dark self or double—in short, anything and everything that has been made (anything artificial), or formless, or multiform, or repressed, or oppressed, or just plain monstrous.

How far such mutually indifferent and sometimes even contradictory interpretations of the text should be tolerated and how far they should be contested; whether an attempt should be made to integrate and reconcile them, is unfortunately itself a matter not just of interpretation—recourse to the text, however disciplined and 'disinterested', is unlikely to settle the issue—but also of theoretical conviction. For some, like Fred Botting, '*Frankenstein* is a product of criticism, not a work of literature'.[78] We cannot talk of the critical metamorphoses of *Frankenstein*, in other words, because *Frankenstein* is nothing other than its critical metamorphoses. And yet, insofar as the act of interpretation is seen by Botting as necessarily and narcissistically refiguring the text to suit its own preoccupations and anxieties, surely it shares an arrogance with Victor Frankenstein himself?

In an ingenious reading by Barbara Johnson, *Frankenstein* is identified as a myth of literary self-fashioning or autobiography. Victor's creating the Monster becomes for Johnson the first of two awkward attempts to shape a life according to his own needs and desires, an attempt in which the 'monster can thus be seen as a figure of autobiography as such'. The second attempt is the account of his activities that Victor gives to Walton, which assimilates events that are in themselves figurative to a self-exonerating narrative: '*Frankenstein* can be read as

---

77 Paul Sherwin, '*Frankenstein*: Creation as Catastrophe', in *Mary Shelley's Frankenstein: Modern Critical Interpretations*, ed. Harold Bloom (New York, New Haven, Philadelphia: Chelsea House, 1987), 27–54 (40).
78 Fred Botting, in the introduction to his edition *Frankenstein: New Casebooks*, 1.

the story of autobiography as the attempt to neutralize the monstrosity of autobiography'.[79] As a sophisticated critical tale within a critical tale, adapting psychoanalytic and mythic readings of what happens in *Frankenstein* to generic and narrative theory, Johnson's discussion is exemplary in both senses: at once characteristic and brilliant. So brilliant, indeed so persuasive is her reading, in fact, that it is easy to overlook the self-professed arbitrariness implicit in the constructions 'can thus be seen as' and 'can be read as'. As figures of contemporary critical speech, these constructions are familiar enough and might be said merely to bear witness to Johnson's dismissal of any single, authoritative reading. But does there not inhere in them a residual indifference to the claims of the text, and a residual doubt as to the validity of her own reading? In what circumstances, say, or how faithfully, can Mary Shelley's novel be read in this way? 'From a certain point of view everything bears relationships of analogy, contiguity and similarity to everything else', observes Umberto Eco.[80] If *Frankenstein* means what it 'can be read as', is there not a risk of the meaningful becoming meaningless?

More to the point, however, is the question of how we can turn this excess of critical attention, not into a reading of the text, but into an understanding of the text. One obvious thing about *Frankenstein*, for example, is that however convinced we may be about what the Monster symbolises, say, or about what Victor Frankenstein might represent, we neither expect nor find that everything the two say and do neatly conforms with that figuration. Gilbert and Gubar pause, searchingly, over this elusiveness:

> If Victor Frankenstein can be likened to both Adam and Satan, who or what is he *really*? Here we are obliged to confront both the moral ambiguity and the symbolic slipperiness which are at the heart of all the characterizations in *Frankenstein*. In fact, it is probably these continual and complex reallocations of meaning, among characters whose histories echo and re-echo each other, that have been so

---

79 Barbara Johnson, 'My Monster/My Self', in her *A World of Difference* (Baltimore and London: Johns Hopkins University Press, 1987), 144–54 (146).
80 Umberto Eco et al., *Interpretation and Overinterpretation*, ed. Stephan Collini (Cambridge: Cambridge University Press, 1992), 48.

bewildering to critics. Like figures in a dream, all the people in *Frankenstein* have different bodies and somehow, horribly, the same face, or worse—the same two faces.[81]

Nor is it possible to devise an allegorical reading comprehensive and supple enough to accommodate the existence and actions of the many secondary characters—the Swiss cast of, besides the Frankensteins and Elizabeth, Clerval and Justine; the Ingolstadt professoriat and the Arctic merchant navy; the de Laceys and the exotic Safie; Scottish islanders and Irish magistrates—suggestive as each is, at times, as a type. Can any adequate allegorical reading of the novel be devised that is not highly selective, turning its back on much of the action (let alone the travelogue and scenic set pieces) and the majority of the characters?

An allegorical reading, in short, can take us so far and no further with *Frankenstein* the novel, however adequately it can account for Frankenstein the myth. Even more than *Caleb Williams*, her father's imaginative meditation on 'things as they are' in the 1790s, *Frankenstein* is a miscellany of expressive and analytic modes, and so tempting is the question of its interpretation that the issue of its genre or genres has received proportionately less critical attention than it deserves.[82] A Gothic novel enfolding a variety of disparate narratives that is acutely sensitive to social and political issues and (with the careful excision of one or more of these narratives) can double as an enduring myth and complex moral allegory, *Frankenstein* is also a novel of ideas or 'philosophical novel' in an eighteenth-century mode. There are times when its participation in contemporary intellectual debate is direct—awkwardly so, if we think of Krempe and Waldman on the virtues of modern science echoing the paeans of celebrity chemist, Humphry Davy, and other propagandists for the experimental sciences,[83] or of

---

81 Gilbert and Gubar, *The Madwoman in the Attic*, 229.
82 Pamela Clemit's study of *Frankenstein* in the context precisely of 'the Godwinian novel' explores a formal, *literary* relationship that many take for granted but leave untouched—see her *The Godwinian Novel: The Rational Fictions of Godwin, Brockden Brown, Mary Shelley* (Oxford: Clarendon, 1993).
83 See Laura E. Crouch, 'Davy's *A Discourse, Introductory to a Course of Lectures on Chemistry*: A Possible Scientific Source of Frankenstein', *Keats-Shelley Journal*, 27 (1978), 35–44.

those long episodes in which the Monster regales Victor Frankenstein with his opinions on matters of language, learning, deformity, and parental responsibility. Oblivious to context and psychology, and only minimally dramatic, the novel is content at such times simply to direct the reader to the issues under debate.

The novel's 'complexity', then—a complexity that, as we saw, was denied it by a previous generation of commentators—inheres precisely in its restless, arguably indiscriminate engagement with a wide variety of urgent cultural and intellectual issues. Its willingness to engage with these issues does not mean that *Frankenstein* attempts to adjudicate and resolve them. I have argued throughout these chapters that the Romantic text is more concerned with exploration than with discovery, with passion and aspiration than with reason and affirmation. Acutely sensitive to the 'uncertainties, Mysteries, doubts' surrounding human meaning and human value, the Romantic text enacts the uncertain process of interpretation and *Frankenstein* is no exception. Preoccupied with a vitally creative human imagination in its negotiations with a more or less responsive natural and social world, the Romantics anatomised *desire* in all its creative and destructive consequences, adapting traditional religion and mythology (like the Prometheus myth) to figure an entirely new mental terrain. In all of this, *Frankenstein* the novel and Victor Frankenstein the protagonist are characteristic of their generation, not least in the anti-Romantic thrust of their respective stories and the health warnings they carry about human idealism.

What the novel's engagement with a wide and miscellaneous range of contemporary cultural and intellectual issues does explain is the novel's attraction for criticism and (more recently) the digital humanities: 'The novel is a natural for hypertext', confirms Jack Lynch, 'every page is filled with pointers to other texts, both within the novel itself and beyond Shelley's text to a world of contemporary contexts.'[84] Arguably, moreover, there is simply too much going on for the novel *not* to divide its critics according to their discrete interests and

---

84 Jack Lynch, 'Unexplored Regions: The Pennsylvania Electronic *Frankenstein* as Variorum Edition', in *Literature and Digital Technologies: W. B. Yeats, Virginia Woolf, Mary Shelley, and William Gass*, ed. Karen Schiff (Clemson, S. C.: Clemson University Digital Press, 2003), 51.

methods. Indeed, we might want to go on from here to ask how far the profusion of critical interpretations to which it has given rise testifies to a complex suggestiveness, and how far to the kind of formal defect and intellectual or artistic irresolution that was once a critical commonplace. For Marie Roberts, for example, 'Shelleyan aesthetics, Wollstonecraftian feminism and Godwinian radicalism' combine to produce 'a daughter of the Enlightenment as ideologically hybrid and disparate as the very creature pieced together by Victor Frankenstein', an 'amalgam of conflicting elements destined to propagate both the unexpected and the incongruous'.[85] In an unguarded moment, Fred Botting suggests that the novel ends 'with a confusion of opposites that both attract and repel' and 'cannot resolve the many narrative subject positions that conflict with each other as they contend for sympathy'.[86] Just so, Edith Birkhead, back in 1921, found that 'the involved, complex plot of the novel seemed to pass beyond Mrs. Shelley's control': 'she seems to be overwhelmed by the wealth of her resources'.[87]

Beyond Mrs Shelley's control, note. Birkhead's analogy between the novel and the Monster is as old as Mary Shelley's introduction to the 1831 edition. 'And now, once again', she wrote, 'I bid my hideous progeny go forth and prosper' (197). With almost all critics reflecting on the analogy between the Monster and the novel's form, some have identified her reference to her 'hideous progeny' quite specifically as the uninhibited explosion of interpretative activity that the novel has unleashed. There is in this identification a salutary irony with which I will conclude. Mary Shelley may have bid her hideous progeny go forth, but Victor Frankenstein did not. While the novel's first movement is indeed driven by issues of reproduction, its second movement is driven rather by Victor Frankenstein's *resistance* to reproduction: resistance, literally, to monstrous progeny (again, the Reverend Thomas Malthus hovers). Beyond a dramatic *anagnorisis* or self-revelation, in other words, in which Victor recognises the Monster as his own creation and his own responsibility, the novel's climax and close are precipitated by his

---

85 Roberts, 'Mary Shelley: Immortality, Gender and the Rosy Cross', 60.
86 Botting, '*Frankenstein* and the Language of Monstrosity', 55.
87 Edith Birkhead, *The Tale of Terror: A Study of the Gothic Romance* [1921] (New York: Russell & Russell, 1963), 165.

determination that his experiment in giving life (hardly eugenics) should end there and then, with the one malformed generation. A dream of immaculate conception 'terminates' in the frenzied abortion of the female monster and, with that, the arguably cruel imposition of a law of contraception upon the Monster. Frankenstein's denying *himself* the power and selfish pleasure of the act of generation is of an altogether different moral order from his denying the Monster the comforts of companionship and propagation. It is not an easy decision, nor did Mary Shelley intend it to be. 'The monster's uncreating mate is the book's determining absence', writes Gillian Beer. 'Frankenstein denies to his monster entry into the natural order through mating and generation'.[88] The result is a trail of dead bodies, as the innocent are sacrificed to Victor Frankenstein's belated but ultimately successful attempts to trammel up the consequence.

What this birth control reflects is an anomaly at the very heart of the Frankenstein myth, and thus at the heart of our interpretative procedures. For what if, in spite of criticism's persistent recourse to the myth to justify its own uses of the text, there were in fact no sanction in the story itself for the exponential and indefinite growth of critical and cultural metamorphoses? Both in the popular imagination—when, for example, the name 'Frankenstein' is ascribed to the Monster—and in the sophisticated poststructuralist readings that we sampled, the Monster is invariably used to suggest something out of control. 'The creature turns against him and runs amok', writes Chris Baldick, paraphrasing the mythic action of the book.[89] But *does* he—run amok, that is? Surely the Monster's campaign of deracination remains very much a family affair. Justine and the murdered Clerval, after all, were of the Frankensteins' 'domestic circle' (22), and with his adopted family, the de Laceys, the Monster is content to sate his 'rage of anger' with arson (113). Compared, say, with that monster of modern crime fiction, the serial killer, the Creature's resentment and revenge, while disproportionately violent and manifestly self-gratifying, seem curiously discriminating and, under the spell of his

---

88 Gillian Beer, *Darwin's Plots: Evolutionary Narrative in Darwin, George Eliot and Nineteenth-Century Fiction* (London: Routledge & Kegan Paul, 1985), 110.
89 Baldick, *In Frankenstein's Shadow*, 3.

rhetoric, almost understandable. The reader is surely meant to be torn between sympathy on the one hand and fear and disgust on the other.

That it should remain a family affair is the burden of Victor's pivotal decision to abort the Monster's female counterpart and of his determination, later, to pursue and destroy the Monster himself. And though we are not witness to the Monster's destruction, there is no reason to doubt it. At the end of the novel an experiment that had threatened to explode for various reasons—not least because of Victor Frankenstein's arrogance and neglect—actually implodes. Instead of seeking in the myth of Frankenstein's Monster a curious sanction for its own indiscriminate proliferation, therefore, criticism of Mary Shelley's novel might ask itself whether Victor Frankenstein's difficult and necessarily unsatisfactory decision to abort might not have a sad wisdom to offer.

10
Questing and Questioning in the 'Ode on a Grecian Urn'

In the preface to the 1853 edition of his *Poems*, the Victorian poet and cultural commentator, Matthew Arnold, famously renounced what we would call the Romanticism of his youth. He was explaining to his readers why he had chosen not to republish his *Empedocles on Etna*, one of the poems which had helped establish his reputation as a rising star of his generation:

> I intended to delineate the feelings of one of the last of the Greek religious philosophers, one of the family of Orpheus and Musaeus, having survived his fellows, living on into a time when the habits of Greek thought and feeling had begun fast to change, character to dwindle, the influence of the Sophists to prevail. Into the feelings of a man so situated there entered much that we are accustomed to consider as exclusively modern; how much, the fragments of Empedocles himself which remain to us are sufficient at least to indicate. What those who are familiar only with the great monuments of early Greek genius suppose to be its exclusive characteristics, have disappeared; the calm, the cheerfulness, the disinterested objectivity have disappeared: the dialogue of the mind with itself has commenced; modern problems have presented themselves; we hear already the doubts, we witness the discouragement, of Hamlet and of Faust.[1]

In such situations as that in which Empedocles found himself, explained Arnold, there was 'inevitably something morbid'.[2] Arnold's defensive classicism, self-consciously reacting against Byron and the Romantic poets who were his precursors, has a good deal to tell us about Romantic poetry and its literary heritage, and not just about Arnold's own anxiety of influence. We are being asked to think of the Romantic lyric as a derivation of, and variation on, a Hamlet monologue. 'My heart aches', complains the speaker at the opening of Keats's 'Ode to a Nightingale':

> and a drowsy numbness pains
> My sense, as though of hemlock I had drunk,
> Or emptied some dull opiate to the drains
> One minute past, and Lethe-wards had sunk.
>
> (ll. 1–4)[3]

Now compare the 'numbness' of the melancholic Hamlet, so characteristic of the Byronic hero:

> I have of late, but wherefore I know not, lost all my mirth, forgone all custom of exercises; and indeed it goes so heavily with my disposition that this goodly frame the earth seems to me a sterile promontory ...
> (*Hamlet*, 2.2.295ff.)[4]

Or better still for the purposes of this chapter, compare the lyrical ruminations of the 'Ode on a Nightingale' with the meditation on heartache, sleep, and death of Hamlet's famous suicide soliloquy:

---

1 Matthew Arnold, preface to the first edition of *Poems* (1853), in *Poetry and Criticism of Matthew Arnold*, ed. A. Dwight Culler (Boston: Houghton Mifflin, 1961), 203–14 (203).
2 *Poetry and Criticism of Matthew Arnold*, 204.
3 All quotations from the poetry of Keats are from Jack Stillinger's edition, *Keats* (Cambridge, Mass.: Harvard University Press, 1978).
4 William Shakespeare, *Hamlet*, ed. Harold Jenkins (London: Methuen, 1982).

10 Questing and Questioning in the 'Ode on a Grecian Urn'

> To be, or not to be, that is the question:
> Whether 'tis nobler in the mind to suffer
> The slings and arrows of outrageous fortune,
> Or to take arms against a sea of troubles
> And by opposing end them. To die—to sleep,
> No more; and by a sleep to say we end
> The heart-ache and the thousand natural shocks
> That flesh is heir to.
>
> (*Hamlet*, 3.1.56–63.)

To be or not to be? To act or not to act? Doubting and questioning, Hamlet, notoriously, *vacillates*—meaning 'to swing or sway unsteadily; to be in unstable equilibrium'; 'to vary; to hover doubtfully' (OED). As Matthew Arnold says, 'The dialogue of the mind with itself has commenced'.

I want to look in this chapter at the doubtful hovering of John Keats's 'Ode on a Grecian Urn', like Coleridge's *The Rime of the Ancient Mariner* and so many other Romantic poems vitally concerned with questions of meaning and value and the mind's role in the shaping and valorisation of the world. Both the *Rime* and the 'Grecian Urn' are concerned with experience and understanding; both poems, in different ways, pick up on the Shakespearean precedent and dramatise the doubtful vacillation and questioning that is the act or process of interpretation. In doing so, they anticipate and to some extent pre-empt the reader's own struggle to make sense of the experience they convey.

The vocative gulf

Keats stage manages this large questioning by setting into play different impersonations or dramatic voices offering different interpretations, without attempting to resolve them. In 'Ode on a Grecian Urn', we have a seemingly single-minded (or single-voiced) Romantic lyric that on closer inspection can be seen to be in mysteries and doubts, irritably reaching out after fact and reason in ways that expose that reaching out—the quest for meaning—as frustrated, potentially even futile. In characterising the poem in this way, I am of course adapting one of the most famous passages in Keats's letters:

> I had not a dispute but a disquisition with Dilke, on various subjects; several things dovetailed in my mind, & at once it struck me, what quality went to form a Man of Achievement especially in Literature & which Shakespeare possessed so enormously—I mean Negative *Capability*, that is when man is capable of being in uncertainties, Mysteries, doubts, without any irritable reaching after fact & reason.[5]

Keats's poetry constitutes an elaborate prelude to a poem that would never be written, and not just because he died at the age of twenty-five. As much as any of the Romantics, and any writer before the twentieth century, Keats made poetry out of uncertainty and the making of poetry—out of the question of what he should write, and why he should write. *Eve of St Agnes* and *Lamia* interrogate the human mind's imagining, the *Hyperion* poems dramatise change and succession in poetic taste, and even the famous Odes amount to a synaesthetic movement *towards* a statement of intent (unless you see 'To Autumn' as resolving the issue, as the Victorians did). As with so much Romantic poetry, the concern is with the poetic or creative consciousness itself, and in Keats's case this involves a potentially unending dialogue of the mind with tradition and with itself—or with its *selves*. In Keats, writes Tim Milnes, 'two figures struggle for dominance: on the one hand, a sceptical, idealist, and ultimately negationist Keats, and on the other, a communicative, dialogic, and holistic Keats'.[6] In his poetry he finds ways of dramatising that struggle.

In 'Ode on a Grecian Urn', this is achieved primarily by the use of 'a "speaker" or "dramatic" persona', to quote David Simpson, one 'who is held at a distance from the "poet" whom we conceive to be behind the whole artifact'. The poet, Simpson goes on,

---

5 *The Letters of John Keats 1814–1821*, ed. Hyder Edward Rollins, 2 vols (Cambridge, Mass.: Harvard University Press, 1958), 1:193.
6 Tim Milnes, *The Truth about Romanticism: Pragmatism and Idealism in Keats, Shelley, Coleridge* (Cambridge: Cambridge University Press, 2010), 89.

can be seen to exercise a parodic or ironic overview, placing in a critical light the attempts of the speaker to cull meaning and moral guidance from the silent object before him. As such, the poet would seem to provide that level of heightened self-consciousness and stable positioning which we now tend to call 'metalanguage' or 'meta-commentary'.[7]

It is the speaker of the poem who irritably reaches out after fact and reason, allowing the negatively capable poet to withdraw into creative uncertainty and doubt. This persona or speaker, wilfully misreading or over-reading the urn as the glossarist misreads or over-reads the figures and events of *The Rime of the Ancient Mariner*, says too many things that are irrelevant or self-preoccupied or just plain silly for him to be trusted as an interpretative authority. Quite the contrary, we soon learn to distrust his overly earnest attempts to communicate with an inanimate object—and we should never underestimate Keats's awareness of what we might call the *vocative gulf* exposed by his earnest addresses to indifferent birds, gods, and objects—we suspect his militant idealism and are embarrassed by his manic repetition of the word 'happy' in the third stanza (ll. 21, 23, 25). The speaker is a fiction whom the poet Keats allows only such rope as he needs to hang himself.

What is at issue in the 'Ode on a Grecian Urn' has to do with readers and critical reading. Our attention in the Ode is focused less on the poetry *per se*, in other words, and less on the aesthetic object (the urn), than it is on the interpretative consciousness of the speaker/beholder, on his responses to and relations with that object. And insofar as critical reading or the making of meaning and value also (as with *The Rime of the Ancient Mariner*) invokes questions of human motive and of human being, then the 'Ode on a Grecian Urn' is an essay on the process of *apperception*: the perception or interpretation of either nature or art 'which reflects, as it were, upon itself', to quote the eighteenth-century Scottish common-sense philosopher Thomas Reid: 'by which we are conscious of our own existence, and conscious of our own perceptions'.[8]

---

7 David Simpson, *Irony and Authority in Romantic Poetry* (London and Basingstoke: Macmillan, 1979), 8.
8 Thomas Reid, *An Inquiry into the Human Mind, on the Principles of Common Sense.* (Edinburgh: J. Bell & W. Creech, 1785), 220.

The often fraught language and labile sliding of the 'Ode on a Grecian Urn' highlight problems in how we perceive, and the way we interpret, that make us 'conscious of our existence'.

Authority and meaning

The question of who *authors*, who is responsible for the work of art and has authority over its meaning, is implicit from the very opening of the poem. The urn, we are told, has become 'a foster-child of silence and slow time' (l. 2), a characterisation that subtly invokes the ancient, absent craftsman who actually gave birth to the urn as a work of art, the 'natural' parent of the feminised urn from whom 'silence and slow time' have taken over. The word 'foster' betrays the poem's interest in origins—and, I would suggest, in original intentions, in intentionality and the whole question of meaning in art. After all, it is precisely because the original author is dead that the speaker is driven to interrogate the urn, asking it questions that only its original creator would have been qualified to answer:

> What leaf-fring'd legend haunts about thy shape
> Of deities or mortals, or of both,
> In Tempe or the dales of Arcady?
> What men or gods are these? What maidens loth?
> What mad pursuit? What struggle to escape?
> What pipes and timbrels? What wild ecstasy?
>
> (ll. 5-10)

What does the urn figure forth? asks the speaker of the poem, ludicrously or rhetorically interrogating a dumb object—what can it all mean? These, of course, are exactly the kinds of questions the reader will address to the 'dumb object' that is the poem itself. From this moment on, in the absence of the craftsman/creator, the speaker begins to arrogate to himself interpretative authority, to project meaning onto the stories (*mythoi*) on the urn and to use them as a focus for his own anxieties.

10 Questing and Questioning in the 'Ode on a Grecian Urn'

Questions of interpretative authority and of the provenance and status of the urn or work of art do not have to wait until the second line, however. The opening apostrophe to a 'still unravish'd *bride* of quietness' has already established the urn's contingent or relational existence, as well as its essential openness or vulnerability to appropriation. Exchanged or given away (given over to time) by her father, the sculptor—who thus surrenders his proprietorial rights—the urn as bride lies fallow ('unravish'd') before the interpretative husbandry that will bring to fruition its meaning and value. Beyond this matrimonial exchange, however, lies a paradox peculiar to the work of art. Having been given over to time, what the urn 'say'st' (l. 48)—the 'flowery tale' (l. 4) that is the urn's being-as-meaning—cannot be limited exclusively to any original intention on the part of the sculptor. Coming to life only when it is read or beheld (ravished) in a symbolic marriage, the urn is nevertheless described as 'still unravish'd'—*as yet* 'unravish'd', that is, as well as *immobile* ('still' = 'Without change, interruption, or cessation; continually, constantly; on every occasion, invariably; always' [OED], as well as 'not moving'). Bride and maid, ravished and unravished, mobile and immobile, the meaning of the urn remains impenetrable, like the unbreeding 'maidens' on its brede (ll. 41–2). Later the speaker will experience the full implications of his own early metaphors when he discovers to his frustration that the urn will not yield to his various desires, and, if it can be engaged, cannot be married to his own world. Implicit in the images of the perpetually virgin bride and the 'foster-child' is the idea that, while each generation is responsible for the work of art once it has been fathered by an artist and a culture, none can possess it—any more than the father/artist could possess it, being obliged to relinquish it (through marriage) to society, and (through his own death) to history.

John Keats, as father to the poem 'Ode on a Grecian Urn', is implicitly compared with the dead craftsman, as the 'Ode' is implicitly compared with the urn. 'Words as voiced may at least appear to be backed up by the presence of their speaker', to quote Richard Harland, summarising linguistic theory, 'words as written are quite clearly cut off and orphaned from any such authority'.[9] Fostered out to silence and

---

9 Richard Harland, *Beyond Superstructuralism: The Syntagmatic Side of Language* (London and New York: Routledge, 1993), 8.

slow time, the meaning and value of the urn/poem is contingent on the collaborative response of its readers or beholders. Like those 'Things semireal such as Love, the Clouds &c which', according to Keats, 'require a greeting of the Spirit to make them wholly exist',[10] the poem depends for its existence and longevity upon successive generations of readers, though none of its readers can be said to possess it. Keats's implicit theory of interpretation anticipates that of historicist critics like Jerome McGann:

> Once the poem passes entirely beyond the purposive control of the author, it leaves the pole of its origin and establishes the first phase of its later dialectical life (what we call its critical history). Normally the poem's critical history—the moving pole of its receptive life—dates from the first responses and reviews it receives. These reactions to the poem modify the author's purposes and intentions, sometimes drastically, and they remain part of the processive life of the poem as it passes on to successive readers.
>
> From any contemporary point of view, then, each poem we read has—when read as a work which comes to us from the past—two interlocking histories, one that derives from the author's expressed decisions and purposes, and the other that derives from the critical reactions of the poem's various readers. When we say that every poem is a social event, we mean to call attention to the dialectical relation which plays itself out historically among these various human beings.[11]

Misinterpreting the urn

What this does *not* mean, however, is that these 'successive readers' or beholders can suit themselves, seeing anything they want to see in a work of art or saying with impunity whatever they like. On the

---

10 Keats to Benjamin Bailey, 13 March 1818, *The Letters of John Keats*, ed. Rollins, 242–43.
11 Jerome McGann, 'Keats and the Historical Method in Literary Criticism', *Modern Language Notes*, 94:5 (1979): 988–1032 (993–94).

contrary, interpretation may involve acts of culpable *mis*reading of the kind exemplified by the speaker of the 'Ode on a Grecian Urn' in his wilful interpretative negotiations with the configurations on the urn: his interpretative ravishment of it. In the drama of arrogation or appropriation played out in the poem, the urn passively resists the meditative and affective intensities of the speaker/beholder and passively resists being enlisted into his meaningless debate on the relative merits of art and life. It resists, for example, its own imaginative projection as an otherworldly paradise:

> Ah, happy, happy boughs! that cannot shed
> Your leaves, nor ever bid the spring adieu;
> And, happy melodist, unwearied,
> For ever piping songs for ever new;
> More happy love! more happy, happy love!
> For ever warm and still to be enjoy'd,
> For ever panting, and for ever young;
> All breathing human passion far above.
> (ll. 21–28)

The speaker attributes to what are lifeless figures and artistic fictions utterly inappropriate powers of active self-determination ('Forever wilt thou love', he tells the youth on the urn at line 20), as well as of pleasure and pain ('yet do not grieve', he enjoins him at line 18). This is the kind of febrile nonsense that betrays the vulnerabilities and limitations of the speaking voice in the poem. If we needed no other index to just how unsatisfactory this idea of permanent arousal is, the scenes of supposedly erotic joy ('for ever panting') are soon displaced by scenes of ceremonial sacrifice and desolation:

> Who are these coming to the sacrifice?
> To what green altar, O mysterious priest,
> Lead'st thou that heifer lowing at the skies,
> And all her silken flanks with garlands drest?
> What little town by river or sea shore,
> Or mountain-built with peaceful citadel,

> Is emptied of this folk, this pious morn?
> And, little town, thy streets for evermore
> Will silent be; and not a soul to tell
> Why thou art desolate, can e'er return.
>
> (ll. 31–40)

The urn's monumentalising of evacuation and desolation makes death and loss no less permanent (and no more meaningful) than the youth and pleasure captured in the Priapic poise of the previous scene.

Equally, when the speaker recovers his sense of proportion at the end of this fourth stanza, the very indifference of the urn—its silence, its coldness—resists his more rational attempts in the final stanza to explain it away as an archaeological, aesthetic, and metaphysical curiosity:

> O Attic shape! Fair attitude! With brede
> Of marble men and maidens overwrought,
> With forest branches and the trodden weed;
> Thou, silent form, dost tease us out of thought
> As doth eternity: Cold Pastoral!
>
> (ll. 41–45)

If the urn is infinitely interpretable, it is also radically misinterpretable, interpretability necessarily implying the possibility of more or less accurate, more or less faithful interpretations. The speaker of the poem variously interprets, misinterprets, fails to interpret, and over-interprets the urn-as-art, or urn-as-meaning.

Meaning in and over time

Amidst this variety, the speaker—the beholder of the urn—models the alternatives available to the reader of the poem, which brings us to an important caveat offered by the poem as a study of interpretation. As well as there being similarities between the urn and the Ode, and between the original sculptor and John Keats, there are, as I suggested earlier, similarities that should not be lost on us between the speaker's and our own interpretative activities as readers. Our persistent attempts critically to resolve the enigma of the Ode and of its last two lines, for example, might be transcribed as a series of urgent questions addressed, like those of the speaker, to a 'still unravish'd', always impenetrable poem. For Keats's speaker, while he may inhabit the present continuous tense of literature, is no less a fiction than the fair youths and maidens on the urn with whom he enters into futile negotiation, improperly succumbing to the illusion of their physical presence and momentarily feeling them to be responsive to his sympathy and exhortation.

The simulated *anagnorisis* or discovery by the speaker of the inappropriateness of his own responses is the major strategy in the systematic disillusionment enacted by the poem; the lifeless indifference of the figures on the urn is openly confirmed by the speaker's renunciation and almost petulant withdrawal in the fifth stanza. But the speaker's discovery of the urn's indifference is also a major strategy in the poet's attempt to disillusion his readers—which is to say, to rid them of illusions comparable with those of the speaker. The same readers who recognise the mistakes of the speaker are always in danger of making the same mistakes themselves and allowing the speaker to become an overwrought figure of their own imaginations. The very word *voice* we often use to characterise (give character to) the utterance of a poem is anthropomorphic, for like 'the dead' (to quote Joseph Conrad), poems and their fictions 'can live only with the exact intensity and quality of the life imparted to them by the living'.[12] Just as the 'marble men and maidens' are informed with an illusory vitality by the speaker, the speaker himself is frequently treated by critics as alive and capable of active discrimination. The apparent authenticity of the speaker's voice, or of the speaker *as* a voice, though no less a fiction than the figures on the urn he would animate, has been more or less naively taken for granted—a misreading of the 'Ode on a Grecian Urn' that mirrors the speaker's misreading of the Grecian urn.

'They are very shallow people', wrote Keats to his brother and sister-in-law in the weeks leading up to the composition of the 'Ode on a Grecian Urn', 'who take every thing literal'.[13] The speaker misreads the

---

12   Joseph Conrad, *Under Western Eyes* (Harmondsworth: Penguin, 1957), 253.
13   *The Letters of John Keats*, ed. Rollins, 2:67.

urn by taking the figures, or the figurative, too literally. Keats's comment actually comes immediately prior to his far better known speculation that 'A Man's life of any worth is a continual allegory':

> very few eyes can see the Mystery of his life—a life like the scriptures, figurative—which such people can no more make out than they can the hebrew Bible. Lord Byron cuts a figure—but he is not figurative—Shakespeare led a life of Allegory; his works are the comments on it.[14]

The immediate context for this speculation is a discussion of the hypocritical gap between profession and practice in his friend Benjamin Bailey's behaviour towards women, and of the tendency of the infatuated women in Reynolds' family to take Bailey at his word—to take him literally. (For the 'pagan' or agnostic Keats, it was no doubt significant that Bailey 'used to woo [Marian Reynolds] with the Bible and Jeremy Taylor under his arm'.[15]) The context, in other words, is a discussion of the use of speech as dubious evidence of a person's intentions or motives—gossip concerned with personality and the use of a persona—and it includes reflections on the way in which personal motives inspire misinterpretation. The literary comparison of Byron and Shakespeare into which the discussion modulates is another expression of Keats's preference for 'Negative Capability' over the 'egotistical' mode. Byron's inferiority to Shakespeare is accounted for in Byron's striking (and marketing) an 'attitude', his cutting a figure instead of rendering experience through a number of refractive, exploratory figures (as Byron, in his defence, would go on to do in his *Don Juan*).

Correspondingly, then, the reader who takes the figure of the speaker in the 'Ode on a Grecian Urn' too literally misreads, *misinterprets* the poem—especially the reader who takes him to be John Keats. By exposing the illusory sense of live(li)ness in both the urn and, by implication, the poem, Keats further exposes the illusion of life—the creative illusion of the speaking, hortative, questing *voice*—so characteristic of the Romantic lyric and so potentially seductive of the

---

14 *The Letters of John Keats*, ed. Rollins, 2:67.
15 *The Letters of John Keats*, ed. Rollins, 2:67.

self-cheating Fancy of the reader. Moreover, just as the Ode draws attention to its own status as an imitation or fiction, so it draws attention to its own status as *a cultural product*. This is especially true, again, of the fourth stanza, which stresses—besides origins and ends, conflated in the 'green altar' (l. 32), and the re-presentational limits of art—the mysterious otherness of a culture that aestheticises brutality. 'The whole poem', to quote Martin Aske, 'moves towards a recognition of the irreversible alterity of Greece, the inhumanity and (in)difference of the past'.[16]

In recognising this alterity or alien otherness, the strangeness or estrangement of the past, Keats—like Coleridge in *The Rime of the Ancient Mariner*—betrays a sense of his own and of his poem's comparably 'irreversible' cultural otherness for his future reader, a sense of his own poem as no less a product of contemporary exigencies and meanings than the urn was a product of the alien exigencies and meanings of antiquity. Only so much of the past can be recovered. 'What is then to be inferr'd?', we ask with Keats: 'O many things—It proves there is really a grand march of the intellect—, It proves that a mighty providence subdues the mightiest Minds to the service of the time being, whether it be in human Knowledge or Religion'.[17] Just as Coleridge uses the alienated, antiquated voices of a Medieval Catholic Mariner and a pre-Enlightenment glossarist to suggest the vulnerability of human reason and human interpretation to the perishing temporalities of 'the time being', Keats recognises the impossibility of a transcendent meaning, immune to historical and cultural change.

The paradox of the permanent impermanence of art—a paradox accentuated by the speaker's naive, self-interested misreading of the predicament of the indifferent figures on the urn—resurfaces later in the forty sixth line:

> When old age shall this generation waste ...

---

16 Martin Aske, *Keats and Hellenism: An Essay* (Cambridge: Cambridge University Press, 1985), 119.
17 *The Letters of John Keats*, ed. Rollins, 1:282.

Reading from the speaker's perspective, we identify with a voice in the present anticipating its own death in the future. Reading from our own perspective, on the other hand, we read from that future: 'this generation' has become *that* generation, and what we now call 'this generation' (our own) can expect, after its own 'old age' and 'waste', to become *that* generation to a future generation calling itself 'this generation'—and so on and so on, as each generation struggles unsuccessfully to contain its opposite, or *de*generation. In this final stanza, Keats sets up a potentially infinite progression of (de)generations, each conducting its own interpretative negotiations with the alien artefacts of another time and another place.

Keats wrote a poem (past tense) entitled 'Ode on a Grecian Urn' which draws attention (present tense) to his own absence—to the fact that, though he, John Keats, may have been behind the poem, historically the poem has been left behind by him, and like the sculptor of the urn, he (Keats), in his turn, has been left behind or superseded by the poem. John Keats, after all, is dead. In this one sense at least—though it is an important one—we are better qualified to read the poem than Keats's own contemporaries, because we are in a better position to appreciate the analogy between a dead sculptor and his urn, on the one hand, and a dead poet and his poem, on the other. Keats's being dead carries the poem's convictions from the conditional into reality ('When I have fears that I may cease to be'), and thus gives extra force to the simulated discovery of the poem.

The willing suspension of disbelief

In drawing attention to the speaker's labile shift from identifying with the figures on the urn to a calculating withdrawal, I do not mean to imply that the 'Ode on a Grecian Urn' challenges us to choose between complete delusion (talking to clay figures and congratulating them on their good fortune in being always on the brink of erotic pleasure) and cold detachment. The speaker's is a negative example. His emotional oscillation between identification and disengagement represents an awkward, *literal* imagination caught between two irreconcilable extremes—between seeing the figures on the urn wholly from within, as it were, and seeing them wholly from without. The preferred option, intimated in the Ode, is a combination of imaginative participation and ironic alertness, a controlled surrender to artistic illusion—what Coleridge, with *The Rime of the Ancient Mariner* in mind, called 'the willing suspension of disbelief for the moment, which constitutes poetic faith'.[18] E. H. Gombrich has argued that 'we cannot, strictly speaking, watch ourselves having an illusion',[19] but I wonder. Surely we can and do preserve an instinctive, inobtrusive consciousness of our participation in artistic illusion, without experiencing any of the tension that obliged the speaker in the 'Ode on a Grecian Urn' to choose between delusion and disbelief.

As both an illusory *and* awakening artifact—'Do I wake or sleep?' asks Keats in the 'Ode to a Nightingale' (l. 80), and the answer is *both*—the poem can be a 'friend to man' (l. 48), enlightening and consoling. Betrothed as it is to an alien 'quietness', the urn can never be a 'bride' for any one dying generation to cleave to, but the metaphor of friendship, while ruling out the unity symbolised by family and marriage, still allows for partial identification and rich rewards. Friendship, after all, had a special emotional and quasi-spiritual charge in the Romantic period, figuring at times as the highest form of relationship. The idea of the urn as a 'friend to man' contains another paradox, however: the paradox of befriending an inanimate object, of *cold* friendship. Even while the urn offers enlightenment and consolation ('truth' and 'beauty'), it cannot overcome the isolation of the self or alleviate the anxiety of living under the sentence of death. Without this truth—without the 'reality principle', as Freud called it—there can be no consolation, only escapism of the kind in which the speaker indulges when he yearns for the (false) paradise of permanent arousal.

The 'Ode on a Grecian Urn', like the urn in the Ode, is *only* a work of art, and therefore a beautiful lie. All works of art (like all Cretans) are liars, and for all the energy of its verbal activity and all its argumentative

---

18 Samuel Taylor Coleridge, *Biographia Literaria*, The Collected Works of Samuel Taylor Coleridge, 7, ed. J. Engell and W. Jackson Bate (Princeton, N. J.: Princeton University Press, 1983), 2:6.
19 E. H. Gombrich, *Art and Illusion: A Study in the Psychology of Pictorial Representation*, fifth edition (Oxford: Oxford University Press, 1977), 5.

immediacy, the Ode is no exception. In recent years, Romanticists have rediscovered Keats's discovery of the Romantic lyric as an historical product ('cold pastoral'), rather than a living process; a material artefact, rather than an unmediated transcription of the poet's consciousness spontaneously evolving in and through time. Romantic 'sincerity' is now identified as a rhetorical trope, a strategy (if not a subterfuge). In his influential *Romantic Ideology*, for example, Jerome McGann wrote of the 'play or development of ideas' in the Romantic poem and 'the movement of consciousness in its search for what it does not know that it knows' as a mock-search for what it *pretends* not to know that it knows,[20] in order to preserve the illusion of what Keats called 'the true voice of feeling'.[21] The analogy for this histrionic dialogue of the mind is, of course, drama.

Far from being a weakness for Keats, however, this beautiful illusion is art's strength. Out of the lie of the single-tense, eternal present of art—out of the collaborative illusion of immediacy as generations of readers willingly suspend their disbelief—come intimations of the truth of time and mortality; out of the lie of art's serene immobility, messages of our going hence and coming hither:

> we know how to tell many lies that resemble the truth,
> but we know also how to tell the truth when we wish.
> (Hesiod, *Theogony*, 26–27)[22]

And out of *both* lies, along with an understanding of the existential journey comes much of art's beauty and pleasure. 'The excellence of every Art is its intensity', wrote Keats to his brothers at the end of 1817, 'capable of making all disagreeables evaporate, from their being in close relationship with Beauty & Truth—Examine King Lear & you will find this examplified throughout'.[23]

---

20 Jerome McGann, *The Romantic Ideology: A Critical Investigation* (Chicago: Chicago University Press, 1983), 63.
21 *The Letters of John Keats*, ed. Rollins, 2:167.
22 In *Ancient Literary Criticism: The Principal Texts in New Translations*, ed. D. A. Russell, and M. Winterbottom (Oxford: Oxford University Press, 1983), 3.
23 *The Letters of John Keats*, ed. Rollins, 1:192.

10 Questing and Questioning in the 'Ode on a Grecian Urn'

Impassion'd clay

Because *King Lear* 'examplified' for Keats the indivisibility of beauty and truth, I want by way of conclusion to expand on the expression 'impassion'd clay' from his sonnet 'On Sitting Down to Read *King Lear* Once Again' (l. 6), using it as a kind of metaphysical conceit for what is going on in the 'Ode on a Grecian Urn':

> O golden-tongued Romance with serene lute!
> Fair plumed Syren! Queen of far away!
> Leave melodizing on this wintry day,
> Shut up thine olden pages, and be mute:
> Adieu! for once again the fierce dispute,
> Betwixt damnation and impassion'd clay
> Must I burn through; once more humbly assay
> The bitter-sweet of this Shakespearian fruit.
> Chief Poet! and ye clouds of Albion,
> Begetters of our deep eternal theme,
> When through the old oak forest I am gone,
> Let me not wander in a barren dream,
> But when I am consumed in the fire,
> Give me new Phoenix wings to fly at my desire.

'Impassion'd clay' is exactly what the figures on the urn are—and are not. Passionless *per se*, that is, they are impassioned by the speaker, infused 'with the exact intensity and quality of the life imparted to them by the living' (Conrad). Equally, they can be said to express their maker's passion. The analogy here is the ancient one between poetic and divine creativity, the allusion to the Old Testament account of Creation and the inspiration of Adam—'Adam' meaning 'clay' in Hebrew. (The other myth of 'impassion'd clay', and the one most often recalled in discussions of the 'Ode on a Grecian Urn', is the classical myth of Pygmalion in which a statue is imbued with life.)

If it was Adam/clay whom God brought to life, it was also Adam who, with the Eve of his prophetic dream, 'brought death into the world' (*Paradise Lost*, Book I, l. 3). In its origins, that is, art (imagination) conspires with *both* life *and* death. As a generic artist, the sculptor gives life to the clay figures on the urn, just as God is said to have given life to the clay figure of Adam. The 'cold pastoral' of the urn testifies to the once warm passion of the dead sculptor, just as, in the simulated passion of its speaker, the Ode metaphorically contains the ashes of the once warm passion of John Keats.

The paradox of 'impassioned clay'—of the human and of human values enshrined in an alien, inhuman object—does not stop at the work of art, however. The dramatised discovery that art is not life involves not only an achieved understanding of what art is and is not, what it can and cannot do, but also an understanding of what life is and is not. This comes about through the kind of *apperception* that I mentioned earlier, in which the apprehension of and response to an object (in this case an art object) induces a consciousness of the nature of one's own existence: 'the consciousness of whom [we] are', to adapt Wordsworth's *The Prelude*,

> habitually infused
> Through every image, and through every thought,
> And all impressions
>   (*The Prelude* [1805–6], XIII, 108–111)[24]

In the 'Ode on a Grecian Urn', that apperception recuperates the Biblical myth of human being as 'impassion'd clay' in another ironic reversal, as clay that takes on breath and passion only to relinquish them in death. Is it not, after all, this intimation of human mortality, with its inexplicable shifts from nonbeing into being and back again, that the speaker 'discovers' through his experience of art's lifeless liveliness? Is it not our own death that we read in the uncertain certainty of origins and ends in a 'green altar' (l. 32), and in the ghost town from which

>   not a soul to tell
> Why thou art desolate can e'er return
>   (ll. 39–40)

---

24 Text from *The Poems of William Wordsworth: Collected Readings from the Cornell Wordsworth*, ed. Jared Curtis, 3 vols (Penrith: Humanities-Ebooks, 2009).

—like Hamlet's image of death as an 'undiscovered country from whose bourn / No traveller returns'? Is it not our own mortality that, in the end

> dost teaze us out of thought
> As doth eternity?

All this is a part of what the urn/poem 'say'st' (l. 48), and thus of what we 'on earth' will 'know' (l. 50) if we are open to the analogy between the speaker's and our own respective struggles to interpret Grecian urns.

> 'Beauty is truth, truth beauty,'—that is all
> Ye know on earth, and all ye need to know.

What 'we know on earth' in fact neither is, nor can be, contained by an epigram like 'Beauty is truth, truth beauty' (l. 49). But what the urn says to us directly in the closing lines of the poem is by no means the sum total of what we can learn from it, or of what we can learn from the ode upon it. Indeed, the closing epigram is *oracular* in the strict, 'Grecian' sense. Beyond confirming an unexceptionable preference for an engaged over an escapist art, the vexing final lines of the 'Ode on a Grecian Urn' offer 'knowledge of the dissembling and opaque sort generally associated with oracles':[25] a calculated ambiguity delivering a different message to different supplicants, according to their respective understanding and needs. The onus, in short, was and is upon the reader's interpretation, and 'reading being a moral activity', to quote Andrew Cooper, 'one cannot interpret without taking responsibility'.[26]

---

25   George B. Walsh, *The Varieties of Enchantment: Early Greek Views of the Nature and Function of Poetry* (Chapel Hill: University of North Carolina Press, 1984), 27.
26   Andrew M. Cooper, *Doubt and Identity in Romantic Poetry* (New Haven and London: Yale University Press, 1988), 4.

Epilogue: The Romantic Imagination

> Urania, I shall need
> Thy guidance, or a greater Muse, if such
> Descend to earth or dwell in highest heaven!
> For I must tread on shadowy ground, must sink
> Deep, and, aloft ascending, breathe in worlds
> To which the Heaven of heavens is but a veil.
> All strength, all terror, single or in bands,
> That ever was put forth in personal form—
> Jehovah, with his thunder, and the choir
> Of shouting Angels and the empyreal thrones—
> I pass them unalarmed. Not Chaos, not
> The darkest Pit of lowest Erebus,
> Nor aught of blinder vacancy scooped out
> By help of dreams can breed such fear and awe
> As fall upon me often when we look
> Into our Minds, into the Mind of Man,
> My haunt and the main region of my Song.[1]

---

1 Wordsworth, *Home at Grasmere*, ll. 980–90, *The Poems of William Wordsworth: Collected Reading Texts from the Cornell Wordsworth*, 3 vols, ed. Jared Curtis (Penrith: Humanities-Ebooks, LLP, 2009).

So William Wordsworth in the Prospectus to what was to be his magnum opus, *The Recluse*, from which I quoted in the first chapter. *The Recluse* was to be a massive philosophical poem to which Wordsworth's long, fourteen-book autobiographical poem, *The Prelude*, was to be a mere introduction. In this epilogue, I want, like Wordsworth, to make the mind of man the haunt and the main region of my song, and to look at the revolution represented by one of the ideas central to the cultural movement that the nineteenth century in retrospect—and only in retrospect—would denominate 'Romantic': the imagination. To understand the importance of the imagination to the Romantic poets we need a brief history of philosophy in the eighteenth century. Before I do that, however, let me remind the reader of one of the most famous and most annoying passages in all English-language criticism, the passage in the *Biographia Literaria; or Biographical Sketches of My Literary Life and Opinions*, largely dictated by Samuel Taylor Coleridge in 1815 and published in 1817, in which he famously defined the imagination—or, strictly speaking, the imaginations (plural)—and distinguished it from the lower faculty of 'fancy'.

The project of the *Biographia Literaria* was to marry autobiography with philosophy or 'metaphysics' in order to evolve a comprehensive set of critical principles that would allow Coleridge to discriminate good poetry from bad: '*the application of the rules, deduced from philosophical principles, to poetry and criticism*'. This, in turn, would entitle him to argue the claims of William Wordsworth to canonical status in the face of what Coleridge saw as the poet's shameful neglect at the hands of contemporary reviewers—and, by extension, the contemporary reading public.[2] The *Biographia Literaria* is Coleridge's prose counterpart to Wordsworth's *The Prelude*, begun in 1798 but only published after the poet's death in 1850. Both *The Prelude* and the *Biographia Literaria* are elaborate, autobiographical introductions—*The Prelude* to *The Recluse*, the *Biographia* to Coleridge's 'LOGOSOPHIA', 'the PRODUCTIVE LOGOS human and divine'. Where Wordsworth traces 'the growth of the poet's mind', Coleridge records the growth of his philosopher-critic's mind. Where Wordsworth recreates his discovery of Nature, and

---

2   See William Christie, *The Edinburgh Review in the Literary Culture of Romantic Britain* (London: Pickering & Chatto, 2009), 101–22.

then of his own mental powers, Coleridge recreates *his* discovery of *Wordsworth*'s mental powers, and then of a philosophy and a philosophical language capable of discriminating and characterising mental powers themselves:

> I was in my twenty-fourth year, when I had the happiness of knowing Mr. Wordsworth personally, and while memory lasts, I shall hardly forget the sudden effect produced on my mind, by his recitation of a manuscript poem ... It was not however the freedom from false taste, whether as to common defects, or to those more properly of his own, which made so unusual an impression on my feelings immediately, and subsequently on my judgement. It was the union of deep feeling with profound thought; the fine balance of truth in observing, with the imaginative faculty in modifying the objects observed; and above all the original gift of spreading the tone, the atmosphere, and with it the depth and height of the ideal world around forms incidents, and situations, of which, for the common view, custom had bedimmed all the lustre, had dried up the sparkle and the dewdrops. ....
> This excellence, which in all Mr. Wordsworth's writings is more or less prominent, and which constitutes the character of his mind, I no sooner felt than I sought to understand.[3]

A definition of this 'imaginative faculty', of which Wordsworth is possessed above any other contemporary poet, according to Coleridge, is offered to us in summary at the end of the first volume:

> The IMAGINATION then I consider either as primary, or secondary. The primary IMAGINATION I hold to be the living power and prime agent of all human perception, and as a repetition in the finite mind of the eternal act of creation in the infinite I AM. The secondary [imagination] I consider as an echo of the former, coexisting with the conscious will, yet still as identical with the primary in the kind of its agency, and differing only in degree, and in the mode of

---

3 *Biographia Literaria*, The Collected Works of Samuel Taylor Coleridge, 7, ed. James Engell and W. Jackson Bate (Princeton, N. J.: Princeton University Press, 1983), 1:78–80, 82.

its operation. It dissolves, diffuses, dissipates, in order to re-create; or where this process is rendered impossible, yet still at all events it struggles to idealize and to unify. It is essentially vital, even as all objects *(as* objects) are essentially fixed and dead.

FANCY, on the contrary, has no other counters to play with, but fixities and definites. The fancy is indeed no other than a mode of memory emancipated from the order of time and space; and blended with, and modified by that empirical phenomenon of the will, which we express by the word choice. But equally with the ordinary memory it must receive all its materials ready made from the law of association.[4]

The passage is a signal instance of a preoccupation that was shared by all the writers of the period, perhaps the only preoccupation they had in common, which does not mean they meant the same thing by it exactly or that they valued it always in the same way. Witness William Hazlitt, as in most things a barometer of the age, mediating between two generations of writers:

> The best general notion I can give of poetry is, that it is the natural expression of any object or event, by its vividness exciting an involuntary movement of imagination or passion, and producing, by sympathy, a certain modulation of the voice, or sounds expressing it. ...
>
> Poetry is the language of the imagination and the passions. It relates to whatever gives immediate pleasure or pain to the human mind.[5]

Again, Percy Bysshe Shelley, from his 'Defence of Poetry' (1821):

> Poetry, in a general sense, may be defined to be "the expression of the Imagination"; and poetry is connate with the origin of man.

---

4 *Biographia Literaria*, ed. Engell and Bate, 1:304–305.
5 'Introductory—On Poetry in General', *Lectures on the English Poets*, in *The Selected Writings of William Hazlitt*, Vol. 2, ed. Duncan Wu (London: Pickering & Chatto, 1998), 165–80 (165).

Epilogue: The Romantic Imagination

Man is an instrument over which a series of external and internal impressions are driven, like the alternations of an ever-changing wind over an Aeolian lyre, which move it by their motion to ever-changing melody. But there is a principle within the human being, and perhaps within all sentient beings, which acts otherwise than in the lyre, and produces not melody alone, but harmony, by an internal adjustment of the sounds and motions thus excited to the impression which excite them.[6]

John Keats, who had attended Hazlitt's lectures on the English poets in 1818, was 'certain of nothing but of the holiness of the Heart's affections and the truth of imagination':

What the imagination seizes as Beauty must be truth—whether it existed before or not—for I have the same Idea of all our Passions as of Love they are all in their sublime, creative of essential Beauty. ... The Imagination may be compared to Adam's dream—he awoke and found it truth. I am the more zealous in this affair, because I have never yet been able to perceive how anything can be known for truth by consequitive reasoning ... the simple imaginative Mind may have its rewards in the repeti[ti]on of its own silent Working coming continually on the spirit with a fine suddenness.[7]

What I want to do in this epilogue is simply to recover, in part at least, what it was that Coleridge and Hazlitt and Shelley and Keats meant, and how they got there.

---

6 *Shelley's Poetry and Prose*, second edition, ed. Donald R. Reiman and Neil Fraistat (New York: Norton, 2002), 509–35 (511).
7 In a letter to Benjamin Bailey of 22 November 1822, *The Letters of John Keats 1814–1821*, ed. Hyder Edward Rollins (Cambridge, Mass.: Harvard University Press, 1958), 1:184–85.

The philosophical underpinnings

So let's start, like Coleridge himself, with the founders of British empirical philosophy. Firstly, John Locke in 1695:

> 2. *All ideas come from sensation or reflection.*—Let us then suppose the mind to be, as we say, white paper, devoid of all character, without any ideas; how comes it to be furnished? Whence comes it by that vast store, which the busy and boundless fancy of man has painted on it with an almost endless variety? Whence has it all the materials of reason and knowledge? To this I answer, in one word, From experience: in that all our knowledge is founded, and from that it ultimately derives itself. Our observation, employed either about external sensible objects, or about the internal operations of our minds, perceived and reflected upon by ourselves, is that which supplies our understandings with all the materials of thinking.
>
> 9. *The soul begins to have ideas when it begins to perceive.*—To ask, at what time a man has first any ideas, is to ask when he begins to perceive; having ideas, and perception, being the same thing.[8]

But a number of philosophers were unhappy with the way mental processes were described by the empiricists—unhappy with the idea of objects making physical 'impressions', for example, and leaving us with mental 'images'—as if the physical analogy used to describe the process somehow proved the process itself to be a physical one. Again and again, the model for this kind of mental activity was the new Newtonian physics. 'We contemplate the operations of our minds', warned the common-sense philosopher Thomas Reid, 'only as they appear through the deceitful medium of such analogical notions and expressions'.[9]

---

8 John Locke, *An Essay Concerning Human Understanding*[1790], Book II, chapter I, in *British Empirical Philosophers: Locke, Berkeley, Hume, Reid and J. S. Mill*, ed. A. J. Ayer and Raymond Winch (London: Routledge & Kegan Paul, 1952), 43, 45.
9 Thomas Reid, *Essays on the Intellectual Powers* (Edinburgh: J. Bell, 1785), 206.

In keeping with Locke and other British philosophers, the Scottish philosopher David Hume's epistemology was empiricist, offering a passive, material, and visual model of the transformation of sensual experience into knowledge and understanding. What Hume's philosophy lacked was Locke's conviction, his faith in the verified or self-verifying existence of the world and in the causal relationship that was assumed to obtain between objects in the world. All this, he argued, could be explained as the illusion or false inference of *custom*. Far from taking for granted the existence and connectedness of the world, Hume sought to investigate why we made these assumptions, and what right we had to make them. Unwittingly, however, in doing so—in delving into the way the mind worked in the formation of reasoning and experience, and in explaining the objective world in terms of human subjectivity—Hume encouraged the development of a philosophical idealism or subjectivism that became the basis of a set of ideas that we now loosely identify as 'Romantic'. What Hume discovered was a vital mental activity or faculty that traditionally had been suspected of little other than deceit and equivocation: the imagination.

Imagination and Understanding

In Hume's epistemological enquiries, the imagination was manifest in two major forms. The first is in *understanding*. Hume attributed to the imagination the continuity and coherence of our perceiving and living in the world, as well as the very conviction that there *is* an external reality in which we operate. The imagination acts to co-ordinate our customary and habitual ideas, constituting impressions and so creating our experience in and of the world:

> Bodies often change their position and qualities, and after a little absence or interruption become hardly knowable. But here it is observable, that even in these changes they preserve a *coherence*, and have a kind of dependence on each other, which is the foundation of a kind of reasoning from causation, and produces the opinion of their continu'd existence.

... the opinion of the continu'd existence of a body depends on the coherence and constancy of certain impressions.[10]

But how do 'these qualities give rise to so extraordinary an opinion', asks Hume? Why do we think an object viewed from two or more different angles is the same object, even though the visual impression on each different occasion is quite different? Why do we think the person seen by us when we are young is the same person when we meet them decades later, when the visual impression they make on the mind is radically different from the visual impression they made when we first knew them? It cannot only be the effect of 'repeated perceptions'—or 'custom'—that accounts for this conviction and the continuity and coherence of the world, Hume argues, there must be 'the co-operation of some other principles', principles operating within the mind, or mental principles. And these principles of continuity and coherence Hume attributes to the 'imagination':

> the imagination, when set into any train of thinking, is apt to continue, even when its object fails it, and like a galley put in motion by its oars, carries on its course without any new impulse. ... The same principle makes us easily entertain this opinion of the continued existence of an object. Objects have a certain coherence even as they appear to the senses; but this coherence is much greater and more uniform, if we suppose the objects to have a continu'd existence; and as the mind is once in the train of observing an uniformity among objects, it naturally continues, till it renders the uniformity as compleat as possible. The simple supposition of their continu'd existence ... gives us a notion of a much greater regularity among objects, than what they have when we look no farther than our senses.[11]

The compulsion to identify and relate constitutionally disparate sensual experiences and to conceive of the world as continuous and coherent is for Hume a necessary one—without which 'human nature must perish

---

10 David Hume, *A Treatise of Human Nature* [1739], ed. L. A. Selby-Bigge (Oxford: Clarendon, 1888), 195 (1:ii).
11 *A Treatise of Human Nature*, 198–99 (1:ii).

and go to ruin, he says. Our (unjustified) belief in the very existence of the world is a necessary fiction. But for Hume the existence and the continuity and coherence of the world remain just that—fictions—in the sense that we have no proof. We can explain our convictions but cannot *prove* them.

The 'Copernican' Revolution of Immanuel Kant

Immanuel Kant took up where David Hume left off, accusing the Scottish philosopher of failing to appreciate what was implicit in his theory of imagination—which is that there are *a priori* principles operating in our understanding, principles *prior to* and *constitutive of* experience. In the preface to the second edition of his *Critique of Pure Reason* (1781), Kant describes his transcendental philosophy as a Copernican revolution in metaphysics. The original Copernican revolution—an elaborate pun combining the revolution or cycle of the sun and an intellectual disruption or paradigm shift—in which the heliocentric solar system was established, flew in the face both of inherited belief and (more to the point) of the evidence of people's senses. Surely, common sense tells us that the sun circles us and not vice versa? 'Against an empiricist philosophical tradition associated with John Locke', explains Peter Otto, 'which assumed that perception must conform to the object of perception, Kant proposed that objects (if they are to be perceived) must conform to the conditions imposed on them by the human faculties through which they are known'.[12] 'The illustrious Locke', argued Kant in his *Critique of Pure Reason* (1781),

> meeting with pure concepts of the understanding in experience, deduced them also from experience, and yet proceeded so inconsequently that he attempted with their aid to obtain knowledge which far transcends all limits of experience. David Hume recognized that, in order to be able to do this, it was necessary that these concepts

---

12 Peter Otto, 'Literary Theory', in *An Oxford Companion to the Romantic Age: British Culture 1776–1832*, ed. Iain McCalman (Oxford: Oxford University Press, 1999), 378–85 (379).

should have an *a priori* origin. But since he could not explain how the understanding must think concepts, and since it never occurred to him that the understanding might itself, perhaps, through these concepts, be the author of the experience in which its objects are found, he was constrained to derive them from experience, namely, from a subjective necessity (that is, from custom), which arises from repeated association in experience, and which comes mistakenly to be regarded as objective.[13]

This empirical derivation of our experience of the world from physical impressions emanating from outside the human mind has got it backward, argued Kant, and 'cannot be reconciled with the scientific *a priori* knowledge which we do actually possess':

> since every appearance contains a manifold, and since different perceptions therefore occur in the mind separately and singly, a combination of them, such as they cannot have in sense itself, is demanded. There must therefore exist in us an active faculty for the synthesis of this manifold. To this faculty I give the title, imagination. Its action, when immediately directed upon perceptions, I entitle apprehension. Since imagination has to bring the manifold of intuition into the form of an image, it must previously have taken the impressions up into its activity, that is, have apprehended them.[14]

It is the mind itself that organises what it sees, in other words, a 'synthesis of apprehension' that 'constitutes the transcendental ground of the possibility of all modes of knowledge whatsoever—of those that are pure *a priori* no less than those that are empirical': 'We shall therefore entitle this faculty the transcendental faculty of imagination'.[15] What Kant calls the formal aspects of appearances, as distinct from their material aspects, lie *a priori* within the apprehensive human mind, so that qualities like extension and figure, far from belonging to the physical

---

13 Immanuel Kant's *Critique of Pure Reason* [1781], trans. Norman Kemp Smith, corr. ed. (London and Basingstoke: Macmillan, 1933), 127-28.
14 Immanuel Kant's *Critique of Pure Reason*, 144.
15 Immanuel Kant's *Critique of Pure Reason*, 144, 133.

impression or the object, belong in fact to 'pure intuition'. Indeed, and controversially, 'the *a priori* concepts of space and time are merely creatures of the imagination'.[16] 'Both space and time', as Otto remarks, 'turn out to be necessary conditions for all experience, with their origin in the structure of our sensibility rather than in the external world'.[17]

But imagination for Kant is a busy concept; it accounts for more—and is more significant—than an apprehensive faculty that actively 'creates' (in the sense of informing and organising) what it is that we think we passively see. In his *Critique of Judgment* (1790), Kant goes further to infer from this transcendental activity—'the subjective purposiveness of our mind'—what he calls 'the mind's supersensible vocation', 'a vocation that wholly transcends the domain of nature'.[18] This is implicit in the mind's sense that, in its activity, it transcends the physical world that it inhabits, striving to make the world presented to the senses adequate to its own mental ideas, striving 'toward something that lies beyond the bounds of experience'. These are what Kant calls 'inner intuitions to which no concept can be completely adequate':

> A poet ventures to give sensible expression to rational ideas of invisible beings ... by means of an imagination that emulates the example of reason in reaching [for] a maximum, he ventures to give these sensible expression in a way that goes beyond the limits of experience, namely, with a completeness for which no example can be found in nature. And it is actually in the art of poetry that the power [i.e., faculty] of aesthetic ideas can manifest itself to full extent.[19]

The imaginative activity of the poet thus becomes exemplary of the highest possibility of the human mind. Kant's discovery (as it were) of the 'mind's supersensible vocation' is one that we have seen consistently restaged in a variety of more and less positive ways in the Romantic literature we have looked at in these essays, as different poets struggled

---

16 *Immanuel Kant's Critique of Pure Reason*, 66, 81.
17 Peter Otto, 'Literary Theory', 379.
18 Immanuel Kant, *Critique of Judgment*, trans. Werner S. Pluhar (Indianapolis: Hackett Publishing, 1987), 128 ['Critique of Aesthetic Judgment', Part I, § 29].
19 *Critique of Judgment*, 182-3 ['Critique of Aesthetic Judgment', Part I, § 49].

with the exalting, challenging, and often vexing idealism of the human mind's imaginings. Whether or not they had read or even heard of Kant, Romantic writers were preoccupied with perceiving and knowing, and with the function of the imagination in giving shape and meaning and value to human life.

Witness, for example, the famous episode from the sixth book of Wordsworth's *Prelude* in which the poet's excited anticipation of a consummate moment as he crosses the Swiss Alps turns into confusion and anticlimax when he discovers that he has already done so, without even noticing—certainly without experiencing a sublimity commensurate with his anticipation:

> Imagination! lifting up itself
> Before the eye and progress of my Song
> Like an unfather'd vapour; here that Power,
> In all the might of its endowments, came
> Athwart me; I was lost as in a cloud,
> Halted without a struggle to break through,
> And now recovering to my Soul I say
> I recognize they glory in such strength
> Of usurpation, is such visitings
> Of awful promise, when the light of sense
> Goes out in flashes that have shewn to us
> The invisible world, doth Greatness make abode,
> There harbours whether we be young or old.
> Our destiny, our nature, and our home
> Is with infinitude, and only there;
> With hope it is, hope that can never die,
> Effort, and expectation, and desire,
> And something evermore about to be.[20]

It is Wordsworth's Kantian moment in which he realises to his frustration and exaltation the mind's 'supersensible vocation' and it helps us

---

20   *The Prelude* (1805–1806), Book 6, ll. 525–42.

Epilogue: The Romantic Imagination

makes sense of the difficult discriminations of Coleridge's famous but teasing definition.

> The IMAGINATION then I consider either as primary, or secondary. The primary IMAGINATION I hold to be the living power and prime agent of all human perception, and as a repetition in the finite mind of the eternal act of creation in the infinite I AM. The secondary [imagination] I consider as an echo of the former, coexisting with the conscious will, yet still as identical with the primary in the kind of its agency, and differing only in degree, and in the mode of its operation. It dissolves, diffuses, dissipates, in order to re-create; or where this process is rendered impossible, yet still at all events it struggles to idealize and to unify. It is essentially vital, even as all objects *(as objects)* are essentially fixed and dead.

All human perception is radically—at root—creative activity, with the mind (and the eye as its co-extension) literally shaping and generating what we apprehend. In this sense, we daily collaborate to create the world we inhabit—an activity of ongoing creativity that Coleridge here likens to the ongoing creativity of divine 'bringing into being'. The universe for Coleridge was not one created and abandoned to its own materialist devices (Deism), nor one above and beyond which its Creator sat transcendentally, making occasional incursions into sublunary activities in the shape of retributive scourges and gratuitous miracles. It was a universe under constant purposive and collaborative construction—like the universe that, thanks to the prime agency of the human imagination, we creatively perceive.

Analogous to this is the work of the poet (in the general sense of 'maker', or 'artist'). Our perennially creative perception is both unconscious and unwilled—poetry, on the other hand, is a constant struggle of the 'conscious will', taking the elements delivered by perception and reforming them into unified, harmonious shapes in accordance with our transcendental ideas: 'it struggles to idealize and to unify', to bring to life what comes to us as 'fixed and dead'. The Kantian idea of poetry as an exemplary imaginative activity lies behind the anxious valorisation of artistic activity in the Romantic period, defending itself against the forces of a reductive intellectual materialism, deadening mechanisation, and a mass, commercially driven culture threatening 'to blunt the discriminating powers of the mind'.[21]

Romantic irony

From Kant's idea of the 'supersensible vocation' represented by our transcendental consciousness—from the sense of Nature or the world as somehow incommensurate with the grandeur and reach of the human imagination—it is only a short step to the idea of Romantic irony as it was developed by Friedrich Schlegel to characterise, both ontologically and rhetorically, the attitude of detached scepticism adopted by the highest 'modern' or post-classical art towards its own activity: 'Internally: the mood that surveys everything and rises infinitely above all limitations, even above its own art, virtue, or genius'.[22] According to Schlegel's idea, it was not just nature, but art itself, that failed to match up to the demands made upon it by the human mind. This resulted in what he called 'ironic' works of art, informed by an awareness that their own expressive or representational means were necessarily inadequate or incommensurate with the transcendental idea they strove to comprehend and realise—informed by an awareness of themselves as necessarily 'fictions'. This irony of an exalted beauty created only to fail—and the more beautiful the aspiring creation, the more acute the sense of failure and the deeper the irony—was also recognised as a paradigm of 'the human condition'. (One corollary of this awareness of the limits of human apprehension and creativity is that apprehension and creativity—the artist's and the reader's—become themselves the subject matter of the work of art, as we have seen. Creations that are incommensurate with their own ideas are for critical purposes displaced by creations *about* their own fictiveness and fiction-making.)

---

21 Wordsworth, The Preface to *Lyrical Ballads* (1800), *The Prose Works of William Wordsworth*, ed. W. J. B. Owen and Jane Worthington Smyser, 3 vols (Oxford: Clarendon, 1974), 1:128.
22 Friedrich Schlegel, *Kritische Fragmente* (1797), trans. Peter Firchow, in *German Aesthetic and Literary Criticism: The Romantic Ironists and Goethe*, ed. Kathleen Wheeler (Cambridge: Cambridge University Press, 1984), 40–44 (41).

Epilogue: The Romantic Imagination

While for the German Romantic aestheticians such 'Irony is not merely negative, it is rather through and through positive' (Köpke)[23]—a version of the *felix culpa* or fortunate fall, in fact, that finds creative freedom in failure—the term 'romantic irony' sometimes designates a Byronic pessimism about the self-sabotaging idealism of humanity. Byron was writing on the dark side of the Romantic conviction about the centrality of human imagination to all experience. The concomitant awareness of its own fictiveness betrayed by art thus can become desperate, even nihilistic, and begin to anticipate recent forms of anti-humanist deconstruction. For it is no large step from Kant's theory of transcendental apperception to epistemological relativism and various forms of ideological constructivism in the twentieth century. As Kant writes in his *Prolegomena to Any Future Metaphysics* (1783), our senses never enable us to know things in themselves (*ding an sich*), but only in their appearances (which are representations of the mind). From this we may conclude (he argues) that 'all bodies, together with the space in which they are, must be considered nothing but mere representations in us, and exist nowhere but in our thoughts'. Hence (to quote Otto), 'no link can be established between the creative activity of the mind and the nature of things in themselves',[24] making the responsibility for *seeing* in every sense—for perceiving and meaning—an individual affair.[25]

Imagining what we know

It is this sense of responsibility for the future as a collective imagining that lies behind the anxiety, as well as the excitement, of the Romantic enterprise. 'We want the creative faculty to imagine that which we know', writes Shelley in his 'Defence of Poetry':

---

23 As quoted by Wheeler, *German Aesthetic and Literary Criticism: The Romantic Ironists and Goethe*, 19.
24 Peter Otto, 'Literary Theory', 382.
25 Immanuel Kant, *Prolegomena to Any Future Metaphysics*, trans. Paul Caro, rev. W. Ellington (1977) and James Fieser (1997), Section 13, Remark 2, 288. http://web.mnstate.edu/gracyk/courses/phil%20306/kant_materials/prolegomena4.htm (accessed 4 October 2013).

It is impossible to read the compositions of the most celebrated writers of the present day without being startled with the electric life which burns within their words. They measure the circumference and sound the depths of human nature with a comprehensive and all-penetrating spirit, and they are themselves perhaps the most sincerely astonished at its manifestations; for it is less their spirit than the spirit of the age. Poets are the hierophants of an unapprehended inspiration; the mirrors of the gigantic shadows which futurity casts upon the present; the words which express what they understand not; the trumpets which sing to battle and feel not what they inspire; the influence which is moved not, but moves. Poets are the unacknowledged legislators of the world.[26]

So William Blake conjures the future in and through the creative will:

> Bring me my bow of burning gold!
> Bring me arrows of desire!
> Bring me my sword—O clouds unfold!
> Bring me my chariot of fire!
>
> I will not cease from mental fight
> Nor shall my sword sleep in my hand,
> Till we have built Jerusalem
> In England's green and pleasant land.

For the radical Shelley and radical Blake, the Imagination could be the trumpet of a prophecy, altering the future by altering the metaphorical construction of our collective apprehension. The philosophical corollary of the breakdown of the rigid authoritarianism of the *ancien régime* represented by the French Revolution and transition to the collective and representative negotiations of autonomous individuals (or democracy) was the development of a notion of 'truth' in need of constant re-imagination and re-negotiation. The language of creative thinkers is 'vitally metaphorical', insisted Shelley:

---

26 *Shelley's Poetry and Prose*, ed. Reiman and Fraistat, 530, 535.

it marks the before unapprehended relations of things, and perpetuates their apprehension, until the words which represent them, become through time signs for portions or classes of thoughts instead of pictures of integral thoughts; and then if no new poets should arise to create afresh the associations which have been thus disorganized, language will be dead to all the nobler purposes of human intercourse.[27]

For Shelley and Blake, no less than for a conservative thinker like the older Coleridge, the imagination and its 'mental fight' must be turned against a deadening modernity and the indiscriminate development of an industrial, consumer society. If they were anxious about the solipsism implicit in the idea of the creative imagination, they feared the inanition and loss of that imagination even more.

---

27 *Shelley's Poetry and Prose*, ed. Reiman and Fraistat, 512.

Further Reading

Recommended literary anthologies

Black, Joseph et al. (eds). *The Broadview Anthology of British Literature*, Vol. 4, *The Age of Romanticism*. Toronto: Broadview, 2006.
Bromwich, David (ed.). *Romantic Critical Essays*. Cambridge: Cambridge University Press, 1987.
Butler, Marilyn (ed.). *Burke, Paine, Godwin, and the Revolution Controversy*. Cambridge: Cambridge University Press, 1984.
McGann, Jerome (ed.). *The New Oxford Book of Romantic Period Verse*. Oxford and New York: Oxford University Press, 1994.
Wu, Duncan (ed.). *Romanticism: An Anthology*. Oxford: Wiley-Blackwell, 2012.

Introductory surveys

Chaplin, Sue and Joel Faflak (eds). *The Romanticism Handbook*. London: Continuum, 2011.
Day, Aidan. *Romanticism*. New Critical Idiom Series. London: Routledge, 1996.
Ferber, Michael. *Romanticism: A Very Short History*. Oxford: Oxford University Press, 2010.
Higgins, David and Sharon Ruston (eds). *Teaching Romanticism*. Palgrave Macmillan, 2010.

Ruston, Sharon. *Romanticism*. London: Continuum, 2007.
Stafford, Fiona. *Reading Romantic Poetry*. Chichester: Wiley-Blackwell, 2012.
Stevens, David. *Romanticism*, Cambridge Contexts in Literature. Cambridge: Cambridge University Press, 2004.

Companions and encyclopedias

Burwick, Frederick (Ed.). *The Encyclopedia of Romantic Literature*, in 3 vols. Chichester: Wiley-Blackwell, 2012.
Chandler, James and Maureen N. Mclane (eds). *The Cambridge Companion to British Romantic Poetry*. Cambridge: Cambridge University Press, 2008.
Curran, Stuart (ed.). *The Cambridge Companion to British Romanticism*, second edition. Cambridge: Cambridge University Press, 2010.
Dabundo, Laura (ed.). *Encyclopedia of British Romanticism: Culture in Britain, 1780s–1830s*. New York and London: Garland, 1992.
Duff, David (ed.). *The Oxford Handbook of British Romanticism*. Oxford: Oxford University Press, 2016.
Keymer, Thomas and Jon Mee (eds). *The Cambridge Companion to English Literature, 1740–1830*. Cambridge: Cambridge University Press, 2004.
Klancher, Jon (ed.). *A Concise Companion to the Romantic Age*. Chichester: Wiley-Blackwell, 2009.
McCalman, Iain (ed.). *An Oxford Companion to the Romantic Age: British Culture 1776–1832*. Oxford: Oxford University Press, 1999.
Murray, Christopher (Ed.). *Encyclopedia of the Romantic Era, 1760–1850*, in 2 vols. New York and London: Fitzroy Dearborn, 2004.
Roe, Nicholas (ed.). *Romanticism: An Oxford Guide*. Oxford: Oxford University Press, 2005.
Wu, Duncan (ed.). *A Companion to Romanticism*. Oxford: Blackwell, 1998.

Historical, literary, and intellectual background

Abrams, M. H. *The Mirror and the Lamp: Romantic Theory and the Critical Tradition*. London, Oxford, New York: Oxford University Press, 1953.
Blanning, Tim. *The Romantic Revolution*. London: Weidenfeld & Nicholson, 2010.
Butler, Marilyn. *Romantics, Rebels and Reactionaries: English Literature and Its Background, 1760–1830*. Oxford: Oxford University Press, 1981.
Chandler, James (ed.). *The Cambridge History of English Romantic Literature*. Cambridge: Cambridge University Press, 2009.

Further Reading

Christie, Ian R. *Wars and Revolutions: Britain 1760-1815*, A New History of England, Vol. VII. London: Edward Arnold, 1982.
Everest, Kelvin. *English Romantic Poetry: An Introduction to the Historical Context and the Literary Scene*. Milton Keynes and Philadelphia: Open University Press, 1990.
Gaull, Marilyn. *English Romanticism: The Human Context*. New York: Norton, 1990.
Hobsbawm, E. J. *The Age of Revolution, 1789-1848*. London: Weidenfeld & Nicolson, 1962.
Jack, Ian. *English Literature 1815-1832*. Oxford History of English Literature, Vol. X. Oxford: Clarendon, 1963.
Jarvis, Robin. *The Romantic Period: The Intellectual and Cultural Context of English Literature, 1789-1830*. Harlow: Longman, 2004.
Jones, Howard Mumford. *Revolution and Romanticism*. Cambridge, Mass.: Harvard University Press, 1974.
Kitson, Peter J. 'The Romantic Period, 1780-1832'. In *English Literature in Context*, ed. Paul Poplawski. Cambridge: Cambridge University Press, 2008.
Praz, Mario. *The Romantic Agony*, second edition. Foreword by Frank Kermode. London and New York: Oxford University Press, 1970.
St Clair, William. *The Reading Nation in the Romantic Period*. Cambridge: Cambridge University Press, 2004.
Williams, Raymond. *Culture and Society 1780-1850*. London: Chatto & Windus, 1958.

Anthologies of critical essays

Abrams, M. H. (ed.) *English Romantic Poets: Modern Essays in Criticism*. London, New York, Oxford: Oxford University Press, 1960; 1975.
Beer, John (ed.). *Questioning Romanticism*. Baltimore and London: Johns Hopkins University Press, 1995.
Canuel, Mark. *British Romanticism: Criticism and Debates*. Abingdon, UK, and New York: Routledge, 2015.
Chase, Cynthia (ed.). *Romanticism*. London and New York: Longman, 1993.
Copley, Stephen and John Whale (eds). *Beyond Romanticism: New Approaches to Texts and Contexts 1780-1832* (London and New York: Routledge, 1992).
Ford, Boris (ed.). *The Romantic Age in Britain*. The Cambridge Cultural History, Vol. 6 (Cambridge: Cambridge University Press, 1992).
Frye, Northtrop (ed.). *Romanticism Reconsidered*. Ithaca, N. Y. and London: Cornell University Press, 1963.

Johnstone, Kenneth R. et al. *Romantic Revolutions: Criticism and Theory*. Bloomington and London: Indiana University Press, 1990.
Kroeber, Karl and Gene W. Ruoff (eds). *Romantic Poetry: Recent Revisionary Criticism*. New Brunswick, NJ: Rutgers University Press, 1993.
O'Neill, Michael and Mark Sandy (eds). *Romanticism: Critical Concepts in Literary and Cultural Studies*, in four volumes. Abingdon and New York: Routledge, 2006.
Pirie, David B. (ed.). *The Romantic Period*. The Penguin History of Literature, Vol. 5. Harmondsworth: Penguin, 1994.
Rawes, Alan (ed.). *Romanticism and Form*. Basingstoke: Palgrave Macmillan, 2007.
Roe, Nicholas (ed.). *Romanticism: An Oxford Guide*. Oxford: Oxford University Press, 2005.
Wu, Duncan (ed.). *Romanticism: A Critical Reader*. Oxford: Blackwell, 1994.

General literary studies

Abrams, M. H. *The Correspondent Breeze: Essays in English Romanticism*. New York: Norton, 1984.
Abrams, M. H. *Natural Supernaturalism: Tradition and Revolution in Romantic Literature*. London: Oxford University Press, 1971.
Bloom, Harold. *The Visionary Company: A Reading of English Romantic Poetry*, revised edition. Ithaca, N. Y. and London: Cornell University Press, 1971.
Cantor, Paul A. *Creature and Creator: Myth-Making and English Romanticism*. Cambridge: Cambridge University Press, 1984.
Cooper, Andrew. *Doubt and Identity in Romantic Poetry*. New Haven, Conn.: Yale University Press, 1988.
Cronin, Richard. *The Politics of Romantic Poetry: In Search of the Pure Commonwealth*. New York: St Martin's Press, 2000.
Curran, Stuart. *Poetic Form and British Romanticism*. New York and Oxford: Oxford University Press, 1986.
Duff, David. *Romanticism and the Uses of Genre*. Oxford: Oxford University Press, 2007.
Gérard, Albert S. *English Romantic Poetry*. Berkeley and Los Angeles: University of California Press, 1968.
Gigante, Denise. *Life: Organic Form and Romanticism*. New Haven, Conn.: Yale University Press, 2009.
Kermode, Frank. *Romantic Image*. London: Routledge & Kegan Paul, 1957.
Kroeber, Karl. *Romantic Narrative Art*. Madison: University of Wisconsin Press, 1960.
Levinson, Marjorie et al. *Rethinking Historicism: Critical Readings in Romantic History*. Oxford: Blackwell, 1989.

McGann, Jerome J. *The Romantic Ideology: A Critical Investigation*. Chicago and London: University of Chicago Press, 1983.
McLane, Maureen N. *Balladeering, Minstrelsy, and the Making of British Romantic Poetry*. Cambridge: Cambridge University Press, 2008.
Mellor, Anne K. *Romanticism and Gender*. New York: Routledge, 1993.
Newlyn, Lucy. *Reading, Writing, and Romanticism: The Anxiety of Reception*. Oxford: Oxford University Press, 2000.
O'Neill, Michael. *Romanticism and the Self-Conscious Poem*. Oxford: Clarendon, 1997.
Perkins, David. *The Quest for Permanence*. Cambridge, Mass.: Harvard University Press, 1959.
Simpson, David. *Irony and Authority in Romantic Poetry*. Totowa: Rowman & Littlefield, 1979.
Starr, G. Gabrielle. *Lyric Generations: Poetry and the Novel in the Long Eighteenth Century*. Baltimore: Johns Hopkins University Press, 2004.
Wolfson, Susan. *Formal Changes: The Shaping of Poetry in British Romanticism*. Stanford: Stanford University Press, 1997.

Online resources

Eighteenth-Century Collections Online. http://quod.lib.umich.edu/e/ecco/
Freistat, Neil and Steven E. Jones (gen. eds). *Romantic Circles*. [Internet resources for the study of the later Romantics.] http://www.rc.umd.edu/
Literature Compass. [See the Romantics section for articles on the period.] http://www.literature-compass.com/
Lynch, Jack (ed.). *Literary Resources — Romantic*. [A comprehensive and up-to-date listing of online Romantic resources.] http://andromeda.rutgers.edu/~jlynch/Lit/romantic.html
Nineteenth-Century Collections Online. http://gdc.gale.com/nineteenth-century-collections-online/
Romantic Textualities: Literature and Print Culture, 1780–1840. [A journal, including reports and surveys of Romantic period culture.] http://www.romtext.org.uk/
Romanticism and Victorianism on the Net. [A refereed electronic journal.] http://www.ron.umontreal.ca/
The Literary Encyclopedia. [Brief introductions to thousands of literary texts.] http://www.litencyc.com/php/sworks.php?rec=true&UID=5268
Voice of the Shuttle: Romantics. [Listing of online resources for Romanticism.] http://vos.ucsb.edu/browse.asp?id=2750

Index

Abbreviations

JA	Jane Austen	JK	John Keats
LB	Lord Byron	MS	Mary Shelley
PBS	Percy Bysshe Shelley	STC	Samuel Taylor Coleridge
WW	William Wordsworth		

Page numbers in **bold** denote key discussions.

Abrams, M. H., modern scholar
  on 'The Eolian Harp' 58
  on Romanticism 7
Akenside, Mark, 18th-century poet 79
Aldini, Giovanni, 18th-century Italian physicist 238
Analytical Review, radical Romantic periodical, quoted on *The Rime of the Ancient Mariner* 4
Anna St. Ives, novel by Thomas Holcroft 142, 145
Aristotle, in *Don Juan* 195
Arnold, Matthew, Victorian poet and cultural commentator, on his *Empedocles on Etna* 269–270

Aske, Martin, modern scholar, on 'Ode on a Grecian Urn' 281
Austen, Jane, novelist
  as contemporary commentator 134–137
  and romanticism 3, 12, 14–16
Austen, Jane, works of
  Emma 15, 21–25, 135, 187
  Walter Scott review 16
  Northanger Abbey **13–25**, 107–108
    and the Gothic 18–24
    anti-romanticism 17
    on language 19
  Pride and Prejudice **133–163**
    and human sexuality 146–152

Index

conservative vision 152–162
critique of aristocracy 140–143
divided politics 136–137, 162
opening lines 137–139
politics of marriage 143–145

Baldick, Chris, modern scholar, on *Frankenstein* 241, 244, 266
Banks, Joseph, 18th-century botanist 127
Barchas, Jane, modern scholar, on *Pride and Prejudice* 156
Bate, Jonathan, modern scholar, on WW 100
Beatty, Bernard, modern scholar, on *Childe Harold's Pilgrimage* 181
Beckford, William, 18th-century novelist 2
Beer, Gillian, modern scholar, on *Frankenstein* 266
Beers, Henry, 19th-century American critic 9
Birkhead, Edith, 20th-century scholar, on *Frankenstein* 265
Blackwood's Edinburgh Magazine 11
Blake, William, Romantic poet and artist 6, 155, 234
and *Frankenstein* 260
Book of Urizen 234
his 'God-like Bard' 104, 155
his 'Jerusalem' 16
on nature in WW 6
radical imagination 304
unknown to contemporaries 11
Bloom, Harold, modern scholar, on *Frankenstein* 233–234
Boehme, Jacob, 17th-century German theologian and mystic 31
Bostetter, Edward, modern scholar, on 'The Idiot Boy' 46

Botting, Fred, modern scholar, on *Frankenstein* 257, 265
Brooks, Peter, modern scholar, on *Frankenstein* 257–259
Bowles, William Lisle, 18th-century poet 55
influence on STC 52
Brougham, Henry, *Edinburgh* reviewer 142
on LB's *Hours of Idleness* 184
Brownstein, Rachel, modern scholar, on JA 25
Burke, Edmund, 18th-century political theorist 145
'age of chivalry' 140
on manners 135
on the French Revolution 10
Reflections on the Revolution in France 134, 140, 242
Burkett, Andrew, modern scholar, on MS 233, 236
Burnet, Thomas, 17th-century heterodox Anglican commentator, his *Archeologiae Philosophicae* quoted in *The Rime of the Ancient Mariner* 125
Burney, Charles, 18th-century musicologist, on *The Rime of the Ancient Mariner* 4, 8, 111, 118
Burney, Fanny, 18th-century novelist 4, 23
Butler, Marilyn, modern scholar
on *Frankenstein* 231, 235, 237, 238
on *Pride and Prejudice* 137, 162
Byron, Lord (George Gordon), poet 10, 234; *see also* 'Byronic hero' **165–201**
and 'Satanic school' 11
as audience of 'Julian and Maddalo' 204, 205–208, 221–227
as Childe Harold 181

Byronic pessimism 303
  compared with Walter Scott 167–169
  JK on LB 280
  on 'gynocracy' 198
  on JK 193
  on PBS 193
  on STC 205
  on William Gifford, Samuel Rogers, Thomas Campbell, Thomas Moore, and Walter Scott 193
  on WW 193
  urges publication of STC's 'Kubla Khan' and *Christabel* 3
Byron, Lord (George Gordon), works of
Childe Harold's Pilgrimage
  Childe Harold as prototypical Byronic hero 171–172
  fame on publication 166–170
  quoted 171, 173, 180, 182
Don Juan
  LB comments on nature of satire 188–193
  on poesis or making 200–201
  precursors 193–197
  quoted 169, 183, 185, 186, 188, 189, 190, 192, 194, 195, 196, 199, 200, 201
  two heroes 197–200
  worldliness 183–188
'The Dream' 219
['Epistle to Augusta'] 225
'Fare Thee Well', popularity 167
The Giaour 172
  quoted 174, 175
Manfred 208, 233, 234
  quoted 173
'Byronic hero' **165–201**
  and the Gothic 172, 173, 182
  characteristics of 171–179

  Childe Harold as prototypical Byronic hero 171–172
  compared with Juan 198
  influence of Pope and Shakespeare 177
  LB as Byronic hero 180–183
  LB's popularity 166–170
  Romantic Prometheanism 179

Campbell, Thomas, Scottish Romantic poet 193
Cantor, Paul, modern scholar on *Frankenstein* 250
Cassirer, Ernst, 20th-century scholar, on 'naive realism' 48
Cheeke, Stephen, modern scholar, on 'Julian and Maddalo' 210, 220
Christensen, Jerome, modern scholar, on 'Byronism' as a system 182
Clare, John, 19th-century poet 6
Clemit, Pamela, modern scholar, on *Frankenstein* 244, 263
'Cockney School' (JK, Leigh Hunt, William Hazlitt) 11
Coleridge, George, STC's brother 60
Coleridge, Hartley, STC's son 65
  in STC's poem 'Frost at Midnight' 72
Coleridge, Samuel Taylor, poet 3, 11, 29, 102, 231, 293, 294, 305
  ambivalence towards metaphysical speculation 59–65
  and autobiography 69
  and chiasmus (crossing over) 6, **72–74**
  antiquarianism 5
  in WW's 'Resolution and Independence' 230
  influence on WW 80, 89
  interpretation in *The Rime of the Ancient Mariner* **107–131**

Index

LB on 194
nature in the conversation poems
    55–75
nature in *The Rime of the Ancient
    Mariner* 115, 117
on imagination 291, 300–302
on language 42, 48
on music 40
on poetic diction 32–35, 47
on the symbol 6, 135, 136
on WW
pantisocracy 65
poetics of imagination 228
sermoni propriora 203–204
suspension of disbelief 3–4, 283
Coleridge, Samuel Taylor, works of
    Ancient Mariner see Coleridge,
    Samuel Taylor, works of: *The Rime
    of the Ancient Mariner*
Biographia Literaria 3–4
    and the Preface to *Lyrical Ballads*
    29, 42, 48
    on STC's metaphysical speculation
    64
    on the 'plan' of the *Lyrical Ballads*
    3–4, 111
    on imagination 155, 290–292, 301
    notebooks 60
    quoted 61, 62, 114, 125
    quoted 3, 47, 52, 63
Christabel, as archetypal romantic
    poem 3
conversation poems (as a group) 8,
    77, 115, 203
    list 51
    origins and rationale **52–57**
'Dejection: an Ode'
    quoted 61
    and joy 62
'The Eolian Harp' **57–65** 8

and Sara Coleridge 59
'Fears in Solitude' 51
'Frost at Midnight' 8, **69–75**
    crossing over 72–73
    transformed landscape 74–75
    transitions 70–71
    uncanny opening 69–70
'Kubla Khan'
    as archetypal romantic poem 3
    quoted 14
Lay Sermons (comprising *The States-
    man's Manual* and *A Lay Sermon*),
    quoted 6, 136
Lectures on Politics and Religion,
    quoted 35
Lyrical Ballads 79; *see also Lyrical Bal-
    lads*, joint volume by STC and
    WW
'The Nightingale' 8, 51
'Reflections on Having Left a Place of
    Retirement' 51, 203
Religious Musings 53–56
    quoted 53, 55
The Rime of the Ancient Mariner 75,
    107–131
    antiquarian impulse 5, 109
    as archetypal small 'r' romantic
    poem 3, 110–112
    as capital 'r' Romantic poem 8
    compared with 'Ode on a Grecian
    Urn' 271, 281
    interpretation of 114–118
    its reception 4–5
    moral 129
    on interpretation 118–131
    marginal gloss 118–124
    and the Gothic 124
    phantasms of time and place
    124–128
    meaning and being 129–131

psychology 114
'Sonnet: To Bowles' 64
'This Lime-Tree Bower My Prison' 8, **65–69**
   Charles Lamb 66–69
   context 65
   four journeys 67
   light imagery 68–69
'To a Friend, Together with an Unfinished Poem' 51, 53–55
'To William Wordsworth' 51
Coleridge, Sara[h], STC's wife 65, 67
   addressed in STC's poem 'The Eolian Harp' 57–60
Conrad, Joseph, late 19th-century novelist 279
Cook, James, 18th-century explorer 110, 127
Cooper, Andrew, modern scholar, on Romantic interpretation 287
Cowper, William, 18th-century poet 64, 79
   his 'divine Chit Chat' 55
Critical Review, Romantic periodical 4
Curran, Stuart, modern scholar, on 'Tintern Abbey' 95

Danby, J. F., modern scholar, on WW 47
Dante Alighieri, Italian poet
   and 'Julian and Maddalo' 205
Darwin, Erasmus, 18th-century scientist and poet 239
Davies, Jeremy, modern scholar, on 'Julian and Maddalo' 204, 210
Davy, Sir Humphry, Romantic scientist, in *Frankenstein* 263
de Tocqueville, Alexis, 19th-century French political thinker, on the French Revolution 10

Declaration of Independence (USA) 9
Douglass, Paul, modern scholar, on LB 170
Dryden, John, 17th-century English poet 194

Edinburgh Review, major 19th-century periodical 11, 171, 172, 184; *see also* Brougham, Henry, *Edinburgh* reviewer, Jeffrey, Francis, editor of the *Edinburgh Review*
Ellis, Kate, modern scholar, on *Frankenstein* 248
Empson, William, 20th-century scholar on the gloss in *The Rime of the Ancient Mariner* 120–121
Erikson, Erik, 20th-century psychoanalyst 81, 92, 95
Evans, Mary, STC's first love 64

Ford, Thomas H., modern scholar, on WW 43
Freeman, Barbara Claire, modern scholar, on *Frankenstein* 259–260
French Revolution
   and *Frankenstein* 241–242, 244
   and Romanticism **8–13**, 304
   and the Romantic imagination 9–10
   and WW 88
   Burke, de Tocqueville, and PBS, quoted on 10
Freud, Sigmund, 19th/20th-century father of psychoanalysis 2, 81, 92, 93, 224
Frye, Northrop, modern scholar 104
   on 'Tintern Abbey' 80

Garis, Robert, modern scholar, on *Pride and Prejudice* 161

Index

Gay, Peter, modern scholar, on ideas 216
Gigante, Denise, modern scholar, on *Frankenstein* 238
Gilbert, Sandra, modern scholar, on *Frankenstein* 233, 243, 245, 256, 262
Glen, Heather, modern scholar, on 'Tintern Abbey' 83, 96, 103
Godwin, William, Romantic thinker and novelist and MS's father
and *Frankenstein* 240, 244, 253, 263, 265
Enquiry Concerning Political Justice, quoted 138, 142
his rationalism 54
Goldsmith, Oliver, 18th-century author 79
Gombrich, E. H., modern scholar, on artistic illusion 283
Gothic 2, 19, 44, 70, 107, 182; *see also* Austen, Jane, works of: *Northanger Abbey*, Scott, Walter, Romantic poet and author of the Waverley novels: on JA's novels: Shelley, Mary, works of: *Frankenstein*
Gray, Thomas, 18th-century English poet
Dr Johnson on 31
his 'Ode on a Distant Prospect of Eton College' 90
Grosskurth, Phyllis, modern scholar, on LB 181
Gubar, Susan, modern scholar, on *Frankenstein* 233, 243, 245, 256, 262

Hamilton, Paul, modern scholar, on Romantic self-critique 13, 230
Harding, D. W., 20th-century scholar, on *Frankenstein* 234

Hardy, Barbara, modern scholar, on *Pride and Prejudice* 160
Harland, Richard, modern scholar, quoted 275
Harper, George McLean, 20th-century scholar, on STC's conversation poems 51–53
Hartley, David, 18th-century physician and philosopher
his *Observations on Man* and the Preface to *Lyrical Ballads* 29–31, 33–34
Hartman, Geoffrey, modern scholar, on Wordsworth and nature 35, 42
Haydon, Benjamin Robert, Romantic painter, quoted on LB 167
Hazlitt, William, Romantic essayist, journalist, and literary critic
compares LB and Walter Scott 168
in the 'Cockney School' 11
influence on JK 293
on imagination 292
on LB 178, 182, 183
on LB's politics 179
quoted on WW 47
Herschel, William, 18th-century astronomer 127
Hesiod, Greek poet 284
Hess, Scott, modern scholar, on WW's turn to nature 29
Heydt-Stevenson, Jill, modern scholar, on *Pride and Prejudice* 146, 148
Hirsch, E. D., modern scholar, on 'Tintern Abbey' 100
Hobbes, Thomas, 17th-century philosopher 208
Holcroft, Thomas, playwright and radical novelist
his *Anna St. Ives* quoted 142, 145

317

Holmes, Richard, modern biographer and critic
on different interpretations of *The Rime of the Ancient Mariner* 116–117
Hume, David, 18th-century Scottish sceptical philosopher
on the imagination **295–297**
Hunt, [James] Leigh, poet, essayist, and radical journalist 11
Hutton, James, 18th-century geologist 127

imagination **289–305** 3, 6–8, 13, 48, 128–129, 228, 264
and Romantic irony 302–303
and the Romantic hero 165
for LB 201, 209, 228
imagining what we know 303–305
in the Romantic period 250, 289–293, 299–302
in 'Frost at Midnight' 74
in 'Julian and Maddalo' 207, 227–230
in 'Lines written a few lines above Tintern Abbey' 97
in 'This Lime-Tree Bower My Prison' 69
its dangers in JA 20
literal imagination in 'Ode on a Grecian Urn' 282
philosophical background: Kant 297–302
philosophical background: Locke and Hume 294–297
interpretation
in and of *Frankenstein* 231–267
in 'Ode on a Grecian Urn' 271–282
in Romantic literature 108–109, 111, 117, 264

in *The Rime of the Ancient Mariner* 118–131

James, John Angell, 19th-century English clergyman, quoted on LB 183
Jeffrey, Francis, editor of the *Edinburgh Review* 142
on the Byronic hero 171–172
on Wordsworth and the 'Lake poets' 11
Johnson, (Dr) Samuel, 18th-century lexicographer, writer, and critic 194
on dramatic illusion 24
on 'low' language 29
on poetic diction in Thomas Gray 31
on 'romantick' 3
on the dangers of imagination 209
Jones, Howard Mumford, 20th-century scholar, on Romantic Prometheanism 179
Jordanova, Ludmilla, modern scholar, on *Frankenstein* 237–238
Jones, Ewan, modern scholar, on STC's conversation poems 51, 57, 74
Jung, Carl, 20th-century psychoanalytic theorist 92

Kant, Immanuel, 18th-century German philosopher
his *Critique of Judgment*, quoted 299
his *Critique of Pure Reason*, quoted 297, 298
his *Prolegomena to Any Future Metaphysics*, quoted 303
on the imagination **297–302**
Keats, John, poet 6
and the 'Cockney school' 11
and 'Negative Capability' 272, 280
historicism 125, 278–279
LB on JK's poetry 193

Index

mansions of the mind 92
 on imagination 293
 on WW's 'Lines written a few miles above Tintern Abbey' 77–78, 80–81, 105
Keats, John, works of
 Lamia 219
 'La Belle Dame Sans Merci' 8, 209
 'Ode on a Grecian Urn' **269–287**
  (mis)interpreting the urn 276–278
  cold friendship 282–284
  cultural alienation 280–282
  'greeting of the spirit' 276
  'impassion'd clay' 285–287
  origin and authority 274–276
  time 278–279
  vocative gulf 271–274
 'Ode to a Nightingale', quoted 270
 'On Sitting Down to Read *King Lear* Once Again', quoted 285
Kennedy, John F., US president
 and chiasmus 72
Kestner, Joseph, modern scholar, on *Frankenstein* 250–251, 253, 254
Kiely, Robert, modern scholar, on *Frankenstein* 234, 246
Kierkegaard, Soren, 19th-century Danish philosopher 228

'Lake poets' (WW, STC, Robert Southey) 11
Lamb, Charles, Romantic essayist
 in STC's 'This Lime-Tree Bower My Prison' 65–69
 in STC's 'To a Friend' 53
 on *The Rime of the Ancient Mariner* 130
 STC's friend 57
Lawrence, D. H., 20th-century novelist 146

Lawrence, William, Romantic surgeon, and *Frankenstein* 238
Lemprière, John, 18th-century classicist 212, 216
Levinson, Marjorie, modern scholar, on 'Tintern Abbey' 99
Locke, John, 17th-century English empirical philosopher
 on the imagination 294–295
Lovejoy, Arthur O., 20th-century scholar, on Romanticism 1–2
Lowes, John Livingston, 20th-century scholar, on the sources of *The Rime of the Ancient Mariner* 110
Lyrical Ballads, joint volume by STC and WW
 for the Preface to Lyrical Ballads *see* Wordsworth, William, works of
 STC in the *Biographia* on the 'plan' 3–4, 111

Malthus, Thomas, 18th/19th-century political economist 232, 265
Manning, Peter, modern scholar, on LB 168
Marlowe, Christopher, Elizabethan playwright and poet 205
'The Marriage of Gawaine', anonymous ballad, quoted 109–110
Marshall, Tim, modern scholar, on *Frankenstein* 238
Martin, Philip W., modern scholar, on *Childe Harold* 178, 182–183
Mathias, Thomas, 18th-century satirist and scholar
 on Gothic novels 232
Mays, J. C. C., modern scholar and STC editor, on the title 'conversation poems' 51

McCann, Charles, modern scholar, on
 Pride and Prejudice 162
McDayter, Ghislaine, modern scholar,
 on LB 169
McGann, Jerome, modern scholar
 on *Don Juan* 191
 on interpretation in *The Rime of the
 Ancient Mariner* 125
 on interpretation over time 276
 on LB's 'Childe Harold' 12, 171
 on Medievalism in the first version of
 The Rime of the Ancient Mariner 5
 on the Romantic lyric poem 284
Mellor, Anne, modern scholar, on
 Frankenstein 236–237, 242
Meredith, George, Victorian poet and
 novelist, quoted 220
Milbanke, Ralph, Earl of Lovelace, on
 LB 181
Milnes, Tim, modern scholar, on JK
 272
Milton, John, 17th-century poet, author of *Paradise Lost* 156, 193
 and 'Julian and Maddalo' 205, 229
 his *Paradise Lost* quoted by PBS 229
 his paradise compared in WW 34
 his Satan and the Byronic hero
 171–172, 222
 in *Don Juan* 194, 196
 JK compares with WW 77
 'Miltonic patriarchy' and *Frankenstein*
 249
 quoted on the mind as its own place
 209, 229
Modiano, Raimonda, modern scholar,
 on *The Rime of the Ancient Mariner*
 130
Moers, Ellen, modern scholar, on
 Frankenstein 245–247

Mole, Tom, modern scholar, on LB 172,
 180
Moore, Thomas, Romantic poet 184
 cited 166
 LB on 193
Murray, John, LB's publisher 183

Napoleon (Bonaparte) 9, 12, 180
Romantic paradox 179
 and LB 194
nature in Romantic literature 3, **6–8**,
 12, 13, 55–56, 210, 228, 237, 260,
 273, 299, 301
'Negative Capability' and Romantic literature 271–274, 280
Newey, Vincent, modern scholar, on
 'Julian and Maddalo' 206, 211, 217,
 227
Newlyn, Lucy, modern scholar, on
 'Tintern Abbey' 89
Newton, Judith Lowder, modern
 scholar, on *Pride and Prejudice* 162
Nietzsche, Friedrich, 19th-century
 German philosopher 102
novel, the familiar or realistic (JA)
 as anti-romantic 13, 21, 107–108
 as a social and ethical phenomenon
 133
 its evolution 16
 compared with the conversation poems 55

O'Flinn, Paul, modern scholar, on
 Frankenstein 242
Ollier, Charles, publisher of PBS 203
O'Neill, Michael, modern scholar
 on *Don Juan* 194
 on 'Julian and Maddalo' 206, 216, 217

Index

Paine, Thomas (Tom), 18th/19th-century radical writer, author of *Rights of Man* 140
quoted on hereditary government 150
pantisocracy, STC's planned utopian community 65
Pearson, Sara L., modern scholar, on 'Tintern Abbey' 82, 85, 94
Pechey, Graham, modern scholar, on 'Frost at Midnight' 74
Percy, Thomas, 18th-century antiquarian *see Reliques of Ancient English Poetry*, anthology of early popular ballads collected and edited by Thomas Percy
Perry, Seamus, modern scholar, on *The Rime of the Ancient Mariner* 121
Pfau, Thomas, modern scholar, on the Preface to *Lyrical Ballads* 48
Pirie, David, 20th-century scholar, on the gloss in *The Rime of the Ancient Mariner* 120
Plotinus, 3rd-century neoPlatonic philosopher, quoted 219
Pointon, Marcia, modern scholar, on 18th-century society 156
Poole, Gabriele, modern scholar, on LB 166, 173, 183
Poovey, Mary, modern scholar, on *Frankenstein* 249
Pope, Alexander, 18th-century English poet 194
his *Essay on Man* quoted 177
his fame 169–170
Preface to *Lyrical Ballads see* Wordsworth, William, works of

Quarterly Review, major 19th-century periodical 11

Radcliffe, Ann, 18th-century novelist 2
Rawes, Alan, modern scholar
on 'Tintern Abbey' 80, 99
on *Childe Harold* and *Manfred* 175
Reeve, Clara, 18th-century writer, on Romance 20
Reid, Thomas, 18th-century philosopher 273
Reliques of Ancient English Poetry, anthology of early popular ballads collected and edited by Thomas Percy 109; *see also* 'The Marriage of Gawaine', anonymous ballad, quoted
Reynolds, John Hamilton, poet and friend of JK 77, 80, 92, 105
Rilke, Rainer Maria, 19th/20th-century German poet 103
Roberts, Marie, modern scholar, on *Frankenstein* 242
Roe, Nicholas, modern scholar, on 'Tintern Abbey' 80
Rogers, Samuel, Romantic poet and patron 79
LB on 193
Romanticism and Romantic literature
and the French Revolution 10–11
Dr Johnson's definition 3
on the creative mind 290–305
origins in romance 2–3
self-critique 13–13, 234
the 'dialogue of the mind' 269
the two romanticisms **1–25**
Rousseau, Jean-Jacques, 18th-century thinker and novelist
and *Pride and Prejudice* 148
in *Don Juan* 192
in *Frankenstein* 242, 260

Sandy, Mark, modern scholar, on 'Tintern Abbey' 104

Scott, Walter, Romantic poet and author of the Waverley novels 12
  as romantic poet 2
  his reputation compared with LB 167–169
  LB's approval of 193
  on JA's novels 16–17
Sha, Richard, modern scholar, on *Frankenstein* 238
Shakespeare, William, poet and playwright
  Hamlet, quoted 127, 177–178, 270–271
  and 'Julian and Maddalo' 205, 213
Shelley, Mary, novelist 212, 226
Shelley, Mary, works of
  Frankenstein 13, 127, **231–267**
  and Regency science 236–240
  artistic self-assertion and PBS 249–250
  as feminist myth 245–250
  as political fable 240–244
  authorial hybridity 265
  critique of science 235–236
  'famously reinterpretable' 231
  mixed modes 263
  PBS on 240
  post-structuralism 254–260
  problems with historical readings of 242–243
  psychoanalytic readings 250–254
  reputation in earlier criticism 233–235
  understanding the critical profusion 260–265
Shelley, Percy Bysshe, poet 10, 234, 292
  as depicted in *Frankenstein* 250
  LB on 193
  on imagination 292–293, 303, 304
  on the force of ideas 98
  on the French Revolution 10
  on the plausibility of *Frankenstein* 239
  on the politics of *Frankenstein* 240
  relationship with William Lawrence 238
  'Satanic school' 11
Shelley, Percy Bysshe, works of
  'Defence of Poetry', quoted 292, 292, 303, 304
  quotes Milton 209, 229
  'Julian and Maddalo' **203–230**
    as a conversation 203–207
    on LB 221–227
    poetics of imagination 204
    psycho-biographical context 215–218
    role of imagination 227–230
    the debate on amelioration 207–211
    the setting of the opening scene 211–215
  Prometheus Unbound 204, 219
  'To Byron' 225
Sherwin, Paul, modern scholar, on *Frankenstein* 260
Simpson, David, modern scholar, on 'Ode on a Grecian Urn' 272
Smith, Bernard, modern scholar, on *The Rime of the Ancient Mariner* 110, 127
Southey, Robert, STC's friend and brother-in-law 57
  as a 'Lake poet' 11
  in *Don Juan* 194
  quoted on *The Rime of the Ancient Mariner* 4
  STC's letters to 53, 54, 61, 65

Spivak, Gayatri, modern scholar, on *Frankenstein* 249
St Clair, William, modern scholar
  on LB's celebrity and readership in the 19th century 167, 169, 184
  on *Frankenstein* 240
Stafford, Fiona, modern scholar
  on 'Julian and Maddalo' 215
  on LB's 'overnight success' 172
  on LB's scepticism 192
  on the historical context of Romanticism 9
Steiner, George, modern scholar
  on language 30
  on JA 134
Sterrenberg, Lee, modern scholar, on *Frankenstein* 241
Swift, Jonathan, 18th-century satirist
  his Academy of Lagado 239–240
  in *Don Juan* 192, 193–194
  compared with JA on the aristocracy 146–147

Thomson, James, 18th-century poet 79
Thousand and One Arabian Nights, A 120, 201
Trilling, Lionel, 20th-century scholar, on JA 162
Tropp, Martin, modern scholar, on *Frankenstein* 236
Tuite, Clara, modern scholar, on LB 168

Ulmer, William, modern scholar, on WW 95

Vallon, Annette, lover of WW 88
Vasbinder, Samuel, modern scholar, on *Frankenstein* 236

Virgil, Roman poet, and 'Julian and Maddalo' 205

Warton, Thomas, 18th-century poet 79
Wilkins, Bishop [John], 17th-century divine and scholar
  on language 31
Wollstonecraft, Mary, 18th-century philosopher and mother of MS 134, 246, 248, 265
  A Vindication of the Rights of Women 160
Wordsworth, Christopher, WW's nephew
  quoted on the Preface to *Lyrical Ballads* 27
Wordsworth, Dorothy, WW's sister
  in 'Lines written a few miles above Tintern Abbey' 41, 89, **99–104**
  in 'This Lime-Tree Bower My Prison' 67
  with WW and STC 65
Wordsworth, Jonathan, modern scholar, on WW 88, 90, 93
Wordsworth, William, poet 6
  his solitaries 44
  language and self-consciousness 42–48
  liber naturae 35
  on music 39–41
  on nature 77, 78, 80, **82–105**, 290–291
  'philosophical language' 29–33
  on STC 62–63, 130
  STC's friend 128
  'semi-atheist' 36
  the language of nature **27–49**
Wordsworth, William, works of
  The Borderers, quoted 128–129
  'Elegiac Stanzas Suggested by a Picture of Peele Castle in a Storm' 13

'Expostulation and Reply', quoted 36
'The Idiot Boy' 42–44, 46
Letter to the Bishop of Llandaff 27
'Lines written a few miles above Tintern Abbey' 36, 39, 41, **77–105**, 206
'emotional and ideational changes' 78–82
JK on 77–78, 80–81, 105
rite de passage 91–94
self-critique 13
the role of Dorothy Wordsworth 99–104
the stages of life 82–90
uncertainty and conditionality xiii, 94–105
Lyrical Ballads see Lyrical Ballads, joint volume by STC and WW
Michael 38, 45
'My Heart Leaps Up', quoted 91
'Ode. Intimations of Immortality from Recollections of Early Childhood' 90, 92
The Pedlar, quoted 36–37
Peter Bell, quoted 37

Preface to *Lyrical Ballads* 108
theory of language 29–49
The Prelude 45, 87, 92, 217
compared with STC's *Biographia Literaria* 290
on the imagination 300–301
part of *The Recluse* 290
quoted 35, 36, 40–41, 47, 48–49, 98, 105, 286
quoted on STC 62–63
'Resolution and Independence'
as metapoem for STC 230
on mood change 209
the leech-gatherer's speech 44–45
The Ruined Cottage, quoted 34, 36, 38
and the Romantic hero 165
'The Tables Turned', quoted on language 44
'Three Years She Grew', quoted on silence 44
'We Are Seven', quoted on language and self-consciousness 42

Yeats, W. B., Irish poet 129

www.ingramcontent.com/pod-product-compliance
Lightning Source LLC
Chambersburg PA
CBHW050101170426
43198CB00014B/2418